Books Published for NEICSSR, Shillong

- Reorganisation of North East India Since 1947, *B. Dutta Ray* and *S.P. Agrawal*
- Sociological Constraints to Industrial Development in North-East India, *B.K. Dutta Ray et al*
- Population, Poverty and Environment in North East India, *B. Dutta Ray, et al.*
- Agenda for North East India, *B. Datta Ray (Ed.)*
- Development Priorities in North East India, *Bimal J. Deb (Ed.)*
- Linguistic Situation in North East India, *Mrinal Miri (Ed.)*

Releasing Shortly

- Perspective of Security and Development in North East India.
- Ethnic Issues, Secularism and Conflict Resolution in North East India.

About the Editors

Biloris Lyndem is Professor and Head of the Centre for Distance Education, North Eastern Hill University, Shillong and Coordinator of IGNOU Study Centre, Shillong. Presently she is also the director of the College Development Council, NEHU. Prof. Lyndem has been the Director of State Resource Centre, NEHU since its foundation in 1987, first under the University Grants Commission and subsequently under the Ministry of Human Resource Development, Govt. of India — an organisation that provides academic and resource support to literacy programmes of the states of Meghalaya, Mizoram and Nagaland. In 1999 Prof. Lyndem won the Sardar Vallabhbhai Patel Award for Women Empowerment in recognition of her grassroots level efforts empowering women through literacy. Author of the Tryst with Literacy: A Meghalaya Experience and of several research papers in distance education, mass education and higher education in general, Prof. Lyndem has been on the frontline of higher and mass education in the past three decades.

Utpal Kumar De is a Reader in Economics, North Eastern Hill University, Shillong. Earlier he held the post of Senior Lecturer in Analytical and Applied Economics, Tripura University Agartala, for about seven years. He completed his graduation with honours in Economics and post-graduation in Economics from the University of Burdwan, West Bengal. He also acquired M.Phil and Ph.D from the University of Burdwan. His research interests are mostly in Rural Development and Environmental and Resource Economics. He has attended and presented papers in several national seminars and symposia and also completed a few research projects. A number of his articles have been published in several reputed journals.

EDUCATION IN NORTH EAST INDIA

EDUCATION IN NORTH EAST INDIA

Experience and Challenge

Edited by

BILORIS LYNDEM
UTPAL KUMAR DE

CONCEPT PUBLISHING COMPANY, NEW DELHI-110059

ISBN-13: 978-81-8069-063-1

Edition 2016

Published and Printed by

Concept Since 1974

Concept Publishing Company Pvt. Ltd.
A/15-16, Commercial Block, Mohan Garden
New Delhi-110059 (India)
T: 25351460, 25351794, *F*: 091-11-25357109
E: publishing@conceptpub.com, W: www.conceptpub.com
Editorial Office: H-13, Bali Nagar, New Delhi-110 015, India.

Foreword

North East India Council for Social Science Research held on 17-18 June, 2002 a Seminar on Education in the 21st Century North East India: Issues, Prospect and Challenges.

The 1991 Census revealed that the national literacy rate is 52.2 per cent. It is no mean achievement and we have before us a long way to go to achieve the target of Education for all. The Census Report of 2001 could not bring us much cheers. The country remained more than 30 per cent of the target unfulfilled, behind the time schedule. The literacy rate is now 65.4 per cent.

Assam and Meghalaya have recorded in 2001 lower literacy rate than the All India average while Arunachal Pradesh has now got the dubious distinction of maximum number of illiterate persons in the entire North East India as per the Provisional Census Report for the year 2001. The literacy rate in Arunachal Pradesh stands at 54.74 per cent while that in Assam is 64.28 per cent and my state of Meghalaya is 63.31 per cent as against the All India literacy rate of 65.37 per cent as per the report. Mizoram has topped the literacy rate table in the North East India registering 88.49 per cent followed by Tripura 73.66 per cent, Manipur 68.87 per cent and Nagaland 67.11 per cent.

Moving towards a literate India, will undoubtedly mean achieving the major goal of Education for all. With almost one-third of the population still illiterate, the challenge is indeed great. This must engage attention of all sections of the country particularly those who are responsible for framing the policies and deciding the direction in which modern India must move.

Education is now accepted as a fundamental human right. The Universal Declaration of Human Rights proclaimed by U.N. in 1948 begins with the statement that Everyone has the right to Education. Education shall be free at least in the elementary and fundamental stages. The UN Declaration of the Rights of the Child in 1959 also states that the child is entitled to receive education which shall be free and compulsory at least in the elementary stages. The global efforts in the last few decades towards Education for All through

Karachi Plan 1960, Teheran Conference 1965 and other efforts culminated into a major event in the International Literacy Year World Conference on Education for All in 1990 at Jemtien in Thailand.

We have responded by passing 93rd Amendment of the Constitution Bill in November 2001 to make education free for the children between six and fourteen years of age. The original Constitution of India had made it mandatory for the Indian states to provide the children up to the age of 14 years with the opportunity to get free education. The Government has been gradually withdrawing from the responsibility it was bestowed with by the Constitution of India in matters of lending state support to elementary education system. Education is a continuous process that occurs throughout one's life from birth to death. The task of child development in the country is now left to family initiative and to corporate bodies. The 93rd Amendment Bill also said that the state would decide the manner in which education would be provided. This very provision gives the hints at the deliberate policy of the Government for handing over the responsibility to individual initiative. The policy statement declares that the Government would provide education either through educational institutions or through non-formal education which should be developed as a parallel system of formal education.

A majority of our population is semi-illiterate. Female literacy is worse at 54.6 per cent. The development of women's education has hindered women's progress and by extension has negative impact on overall development. The cost of keeping women illiterate is higher than the cost of educating them. The drop out rates up to middle school level is exceptionally high. A small percentage of rural population in North East India like elsewhere else has access to safe drinking water, electricity, toilets and elementary education. The stagnation of growth rate in agricultural productivity is a key factor responsible for the high incidence of rural poverty and consequently low education level. The country must provide capital support to launch a massive education programme for rural children at school level. This will ensure in future a higher rate of economic growth. This is the lesson of history of contemporary world. The state intervention in the field of mass education programmes in North East India should be vigorous, time bound and result-oriented.

The world today is more competitive than ever. The quality of education must be improved. This is critical to the growth of higher education in North East India. Highest priority has to be given to the quality of higher education by the process of continuous evaluation.

Until independence, higher education was confined to upper strata of society. With Independence, the gates of education and of higher education were made wide open and wind of change blows all over the country. Earlier the education remained confined in the hands of a few. All these have changed today with enormously improved access to education for all sections of our people.

With the democratization of educational opportunities we are to provide for equity and access to higher education. There is a need to evaluate the role of distance education and open education systems as instruments of promoting equity in the field of higher education.

There are a few hundred centres of higher education in North East India. The growing pressure from democratic social factors has led to the opening of many centres. But we are to examine and re-examine the quality of higher education to make it progressive and adoptive to social and economic changes to enable the young persons to face the ever growing competitive changing world. The quality of education cannot be sacrificed under the pressure of quantity. We are to improve the educational infrastructure. There should be provision for continuous examination of the examination system, continuous revision of curriculum keeping in mind the rapid changes and developments in the country. A good deal of work has to be done to improve the quality of higher education and research in North East India.

The seemingly settled way of life is gradually disappearing with the impact of technological advances. In the 21st Century there has been significant advancement in the quality of life due to revolutionary changes of technology. The internet has opened an unbelievable communication facilities. The mobile phones have compressed time and space. The technological advancements in the field of transport and communication have opened windows to the global views for the population isolated by geography in places of North East India. Our system of education at every level must move forward and absorb the best in the world of science, technology and humanities.

We take this opportunity to thank his Excellency Mr. M.M. Jacob, Governor of Meghalaya, who inaugurated the seminar with a key note address. We would like to thank also Professor M.N. Karna and

Professor Biloris Lyndem, Chairman and Director, respectively of State Resource Centre, Shillong and Indian Council of Social Research, New Delhi.

Mr. Ashok Kumar Mittal and Mr. Nitin Mittal took much interest for the early publication of the volume. We thank them for this quality publication.

28 January, 2003

B. DATTA RAY
Secretary
NEICSSR
Shillong-793 003

Contents

List of Contributors

Ali, Zeenat Ara, School for Children in need of Special Education, Shillong.

Athparia, R.P., Anthropological Survey of India, Jagdalpur, Chhatisgarh.

Basu, Rama, Department of Political Science, Victoria Institution College, Kolkata.

Bhagabati, D.Ch., Department of Education, Tihu College, Tihu, Assam.

Bhattacharjee, R.P., North Eastern Regional Institute of Science and Technology, Itanagar.

Bhattacharya, Jadab Chandra, Economic Research Unit, Indian Statistical Institute, Kolkata.

Bhattacharya, N.N., Department of Geography, Gauhati University, Guwahati.

Bhattacharyya, Shyama Das, Scholar, Kolkata.

Borah, Jayasree, Department of Geography, Cotton College Guwahati.

Boruah, Kasturi Borkotoki, Assam Institute of Management, Guwahati.

Chakraborti, Subhendu, Economic Research Unit, Indian Statistical Institute, Kolkata.

Chakraborty Gorky, Department of Economics, Doom Dooma College, Assam.

Chakravarti, Mahadev, Department of History, Tripura University, Tripura.

De, U.K., Department of Economics, North Eastern Hill University, Shillong.

Devi, Ksh. Bimola, Professor of Political Science of Manipur University, Imphal, Manipur.

Devi, Premlata, State Resource Centre, NEHU, Shillong.

Devi, Th. Binarani, Department of Political Science, Women's College, Imphal, Manipur.

Ganguly, J.B., Former Vice Chancellor of Tripura University, Tripura.

George, S.K., State Resource Centre, North Eastern Hill University, Shillong.

Ghosh, Anjali, Psychology Research Unit, Indian Statistical Institute, Kolkata.

Ghosh, Bhola Nath, Sociological Research Unit, Indian Statistical Institute, Kolkata.

Guha, A.S., Regional Centre, IGNOU, Shillong.

Handique, Rajib, Dibrugarh University, Assam.

Hazarika, Padmalochan, Department of Commerce, Gauhati University, Guwahati, Assam.

Henia, A., Department of Education, North Eastern Hill University, Shillong.

Lahiri, T.B., Former Registrar, Visva Bharati, West Bangal.

Laltanpuia, B., State Resource Centre, North Eastern Hill University, Shillong.

Lyndem, Biloris, State Resource Centre, North Eastern Hill University, Shillong.

Maiti, A.K., Sociological Research Unit, Indian Statistical Institute, Kolkata.

Mazumder, Sukhendu, Assam Rifles.

Meetei , Kh. Dhiren, Department of Commerce, Manipur University, Imphal.

Paul, Sumona, Women's College, Shillong.

Prasain, G.P., Department of Commerce, Manipur University, Imphal.

Rai, Hemant, Department of Economics, People's College, Mokokchung, Nagaland.

Reddy, K. Prafulla, Department of Home Science, St. Mary's College, Shillong.

Rita, M., Department of Political Science, Manipur University, Manipur.

Siddharthan, J., Department of Economics, Assam University, Silchar, Assam.

Sikidar, Sujit, Department of Commerce, Gauhati University, Guwahati, Assam.

Singh, J.P., NCERT, New Delhi.

Singh, N. Tejmani, Department of Commerce, Manipur University, Manipur.

Introduction

It needs no explanation, why education is from the point of view of social and economic development so important and urgent. Everybody knows the role of education in building human resource. With equal amount of different tangible resources or assets, two different regions may observe significant divergence in patterns and levels of development, if they differ in quality of human resource and mainly in education. An educated person can observe, perceive and plan in a better way. Thus, even with less resource Kerala could manage to build up better human resource, through proper management, reduction in population growth rate and gender differences and that was mainly due to development in the front of education which makes people more aware of such things. Even with growth of mere literacy rate some states like Nagaland could not control the population growth, because of variation in the quality of education, imparted at different levels. In spite of improvement in the level of education in different fronts the north eastern states of India could not achieve the desired level of progress. This volume is an attempt to explore the status of education and its role in the development of north east India.

The first part of the book contributed by Ganguly, De, Maiti, and Chakraborti, addresses on the present status of education and its change over time. They also explained the changes in educational infrastructure in the region overtime and also explain the level of drop-out and reasons behind it.

Ghosh presents his paper with a special reference to the education of women in North East India and India in general. Lahiri analyses the strategies of educational planning, while Chakraborty and Bhattacharya address to the deficiencies in educational front of North East India . Then different issues on school education is explained in detail by Singh, whereas Ghosh analyses how education can help changing self-efficacy of school children. Some papers are then written with an emphasis in deficiencies of present educational scenario especially of higher education in the country as well as in North East India.

Educational problem and system for different sections like adult, under-privileged and challenged children is also discussed for North East India, and for some north eastern states separately.

Thereafter educational scenario of different levels like school education, higher education and their disparities are considered at state level separately. Towards the end, some papers also devoted to the explanation of role of voluntary agencies, the literacy campaign, critically. Also the role of education in economic development is analysed in some papers like that of Athparia. Finally, a few papers deal with the role of distance education system in spreading education to the masses with some policy analysis.

BILORIS LYNDEM
UTPAL KUMAR DE

1

Planning Educational Development in North East India
An Approach

J.B. GANGULY

There has been significant development of the different socio-economic sectors of the north eastern states since the process of planned development was commenced in the early fifties. Basic social and economic overheads have been built up, though much more expansion of this infrastructure has to be made. State Domestic Products as well as per capita incomes and expenditures have risen considerably even as inter-household, inter-state and inter-sectoral distribution of incomes and expenditures has become more marked. Moreover, the problems of poverty and unemployment have causing miseries and deprivations to large segments of the population in each state.

According to the Planning Commission's estimates 40.04 per cent of rural population and 7.47 per cent of the urban population in the region were below the poverty line in 1999-2000. These estimates are based on the consumption expenditures for thirty days' recalled period. Percentages of total populations of these states who were below poverty line were: Arunachal Pradesh: 33.47 per cent, Assam: 36.09 per cent, Manipur: 28.54 per cent, Meghalaya: 33.87 per cent, Mizoram: 19.47 per cent, Nagaland: 32.67 per cent, and Tripura: 34.44 per cent[1].

One of the root causes of persistent poverty has been the inadequate development of the most basic resource of the region, namely the human resource. According to T.W. Schultz, this resource "consists of the acquired abilities of the people—their education, experience, skills and health. This 'human capital'— not space, energy, cropland, or other fiscal properties of the earth — is decisive in improving the welfare of the poor people throughout the World".[2] Besides, health care services, therefore, development and expansion of literacy and educational facilities, is of most crucial importance for promoting the welfare of this region's people.

These states have achieved good progress in raising the literacy rates of the people.[3] As against the all India literacy rate of 65.38 per cent, it is 54.74 per cent in Arunachal Pradesh, 64.28 per cent in Assam, 68.87 per cent in Manipur, 63.31 per cent in Meghalya, 88.49 per cent in Mizoram, 67.11 per cent in Nagaland and 73.66 per cent in Tripura.

Quite a good number of educational and training institutions have been established in these states. As in September 1996, there were all-told 11 universities, 8 boards of secondary education, 397 arts/science and commerce colleges, 5 engineering colleges, 8 medical colleges including ayurvedic colleges, 4 agricultural colleges, one veterinary college, 29 teacher training colleges, 124 junior colleges (+ two stage), 943 higher secondary schools (12+pattern), 5691 high schools, 10473 middle schools, 42901 primary schools, 4026 pre-primary schools, 16 teacher training schools, 17 polytechnics and 51 technical and industrial schools.[4] Since 1996, a few more specialized educational/technical/ medical institutions and universities have started functioning in the region. Some of these are centrally managed and funded. Seats are also reserved in many important professional and technical institutions in other parts of the country for the students of the north eastern region. Liberal provision of stipends, scholarships and other forms of assistance in cash and/or kind enable the students of all the scheduled tribe and caste communities to prosecute their studies at all levels. Students of general categories also get state support for their education on the basis of means-cum-merit criteria.

Even as there has been considerable expansion of educational and training facilities, the structure of educational and skill formation opportunities has been a lopsided and iniquitous one. Therefore the progress has been across gender distribution of population and rural-urban divides, etc. Effective expansion of educational facilities in the urban areas and at higher levels has been disproportionately greater than that in rural areas and at pre-primary, primary and secondary levels. No wonder, educational attainments of the rural people, particularly those of the remote areas and of women still lag far behind than that of the others. The drop out rates in schools are quite high.

The National Policy on Education envisaged provision of free and compulsory education of satisfactory quality up to the age of 14 years before the beginning of the 21st Century. This goal is yet to be realized by ensuring universal access, universal retention and universal achievement. Each of the north eastern states should earnestly strive to achieve this goal on a top priority basis. The possibility of formulating and executing the Educational Guarantee Scheme as under implementation in Madhya Pradesh may be explored. For the purpose the system of delivery of primary educational facilities to the students in rural and hill areas will need to be decentralized by involving the grassroots level people's organizations, such as the gram panchayats, tribal village councils and the civil society.

Emphasis should be given on the spreading of literacy among women and effective education for girl students. For, unless female literacy rates rises, overall literacy ratio will not rise much. It must also be noted that rises in literacy levels as normally defined to mean the mere ability to read and write will not be adequate in today's Information Age. Training of people for acquiring appropriate modern skills and receiving vocational education will make people economically more productive.

Since there exists certain basic infrastructural deficiencies in the region and therefore, communication facilities for the people of the flood-prone rural areas and remote hill villages are extremely precarious, the possibilities of providing internet communication facilities for the people of these areas need to be explored. Such facilities may also benefit the children who are unable to attend the formal schools at specific hours set down in the school time-table on account of their participation in traditional productive activities for meeting subsistence needs.

An important component of development of human resource is the value-orientation of the people. The basic human values of the dignity of labour, honesty, sincerity, fellow-feeling, respect for human rights, gender equality etc., should be promoted through imparting education to the children and youths. They should also be taught to cultivate social values like community service, egalitarianism, commitment to conservation of natural resources and maintenance of bio-diversity etc. The course curricula must be secular; these should also be so designed as to inculcate scientific temper in the minds of the students.

REFERENCES

1. Planning Commission's estimates as quoted in the leading daily of Tripura, *Dainik Sambad,* Agartala, dated 24th January, 2002.
2. T.W. Schultz (1980), *Investing in People: The Economics of Population Quality,* Indian Edition published by Hindustan Publishing Corporation (India), Delhi, Publisher's Introduction in the Jacket.
3. *Manorama Yearbook* (2002), Malayala Manorama, Indian Panorama, States and Union Territories, pp. 628-702.
4. North Eastern Council (2002), *Basic Statistics of North Eastern Region 2002,* Shillong, Table 126, p. 127.

2

Status of Education in North East India
Some Reflections

UTPAL KUMAR DE

Introduction

Education is an important aspect of human resource development. Imparting of education leads to the improvement in understanding, perception, attitude, and efficiency of working population. Education helps raising the quality of leadership of an individual, who earns the ability to guide the others in his/her group (Ghosh & De, 2002). It also increases awareness among the people and helps controlling population and hence it is called the best contraceptive among other measures of family planning. Above all, education is the primary instrument for the improvement of quality of life of the human being. Education is also self-perpetuating. Once a few members of any family are educated in anyway, the next generation onwards generally has a tendency of achieving higher and higher levels of education with a wider base. Not only that, it has also the quality to benefit the neighbours through its external impact.

Considering the aforesaid facts, several attempts have been made since independence to educate the people in order to build their moral character as well as improvement of efficiency of working population and hence nation building. Looking at the dismal performances of the former policies, special emphasis is given by the Ministry of Human Resource Development in the National Policy on Education (NPE), 1986 and with the introduction of Ninety Third Constitution Amendment Bill, 2001 for ensuring free and compulsory elementary education for children of the age group 6-14 years as a fundamental right. The main objectives of the Sarva Shiksha Abhiyan (SSA) are:

1. All children of age 6-14 years in school/education guarantee centres/bridge course by 2003.
2. All children of age 6-14 years to complete 5 years of primary education by 2007.
3. All children of age 6-14 years to complete 8 years of schooling by 2010.
4. Focus of elementary education of satisfactory quality with emphasis on education for life.
5. Bridge all gender and social category gaps by 2007 at primary stage and at elementary education level by 2010.
6. Universal retention by 2010 (*Economic Survey*, 1998-99).

Several programmes have also been initiated for universalisation of elementary education and especially for disadvantageous section of population. These includes Operation Blackboard (OB), Non-Formal Education (NFE), Teacher Education (TE), Mid-day Meal Scheme, District Primary Education Programme (DPEP), Total Literacy Campaign (TLC) etc. The main objectives were to give free and compulsory education up to Class V and eradication of illiteracy. Priority is given to the women, SCs/STs and Backward classes and educationally backward minorities and arrangement for equal access by all. Now it is the duty of every government to afford universal primary education for all irrespective of gender, caste, creed, and religion. Not only that, the parents are also held responsible for sending their children up to 14 years of age to schools.

Educational Situation at All India Level

Even after strong realisation and several efforts, achievement of cent-percent literacy rate is still far away [NCERT (1994), Sharma (1997)]. Till now around one-third of the total population in India are illiterate (Census of India, 2001). Not only that, gender-wise difference in literacy rate is also of major concern to us. Though there has been a considerable progress in female literacy and their enrolment at primary level, we observe the noticeable differences of progress of literacy and gender-wise variation of it across the states. At national level it is

75.85 per cent for male and 54.16 per cent for female according to the 2001 Census Report. The figures were just 39.5 and 18.7 for male and female respectively in 1971 Census. In the north eastern region, the highest difference in literacy rate is observed in Arunachal Pradesh, which is around 20 per cent and the lowest in Mizoram, about 4.5 per cent in 2001 Census.

In spite of giving special thrust and priority at the policy level by the government, the results show it all to be rhetoric because the goal of reaching elementary education to all has still remain a distant cry. Just if we look at the condition of West Bengal it is observed that, in spite of much propaganda and Total Literacy Campaign along with the on going Integrated Child Development Scheme (ICDS) and announcing some districts, as fully literate most of the disadvantageous people still remain illiterate. Not only that very little effort has been made to continue with the newly literate and many of them have thus become illiterate again. A few people only know how to write their names. It has been found rhetoric irrespective of the formation of the government at the central or state level and the promise given to improve and extend educational facilities as, the amount spent by all the governments has been meagre compared to the requirement for imparting knowledge satisfactorily. Not only that, the problem further deepens due to the improper use of funds and resources meant for the development of education. Very low plan allocation by the national government was observed, which was only around fifty rupees (Rs. 53) in 2000-2001. Major part of plan allocation also goes for payment of salary to teachers and only a smaller part is used for the development of infrastructure. The rest is used for the development of library, creation of laboratory facilities, as well as other purposes. So, it is not very difficult to understand that, only a meagre amount is spent, really, for imparting knowledge. Now the government of India has targeted to spend around six per cent of the GDP on education and half of which is to be devoted to the primary education (*Economic Survey*, 1998-99).

The pre-primary education though does not form a part of general educational ladder; it forms a part of Integrated Child Development Scheme (ICDS). It has been in operation in the form of *Anganwadi, Balwadi, Independent Pre-Primary School* and *Pre-Primary Classes* attached to primary school that we earlier used to call *infant class*. However after the introduction of new ICDS centres in most of the primary schools, pre-primary class has been dropped.

Now if we look at the facilities, especially for primary education we observe that around 94 per cent of rural population have access to primary schools within a distance of one km. 76 per cent of rural habitations and 85 per cent of the rural population are served by upper primary schools with a distance of three kms. But just the presence of schools is not sufficient for the development of school. The basic facilities like school building, laboratory facilities for demonstration and practical, library facility, sanitary system separately for male and female students, playground and above all good devoted teachers are essential for providing knowledge in proper way even at primary level. Now-a-days, many schools of West Bengal are found to be closed because of lack of students (in spite of growing population) and in sufficient number of teachers.

Total enrolment at the primary stage (Grade I-V) in the country increased by 5.91 times from 19.2 million in 1950-51 to about 113.61 million in 1999-2000. Out of this, the relative share of girls' enrolment increased from 28.1 per cent in 1950-51 to 43.6 per cent in 1999-2000. Total enrolment in upper primary level (Grade VI-VIII) increased by 13 times from 3.1 million in 1950-51 to 42.06 million in 1999-2000 (Table 2.1). The share of girls' enrolment to total enrolment from primary to higher secondary level was 25.63 per cent in 1950-51. The figure increased to 41.86 per cent in 1999-2000. Though the girls' enrolment at different level has increased, there still remains a wide divergence between the enrolment of boys and girls in the country. However, the relative share of girls' enrolment at elementary level was much higher as compared to that of the boys than the upper stages of education.

Table 2.1: Sex-wise Enrolment by Stages/Classes since 1950-51

(*in millions*)

Year	*Primary*			*Middle/Upper Primary*			*High/Hr. Secondary/ Pre-Degree*		
	Boys	*Girls*	*Total*	*Boys*	*Girls*	*Total*	*Boys*	*Girls*	*Total*
1950-51	13.8	5.4	19.2	2.6	0.5	3.1	1.3	0.2	1.5
1980-81	45.3	28.5	73.8	13.9	6.8	20.7	7.6	3.4	11.0
1990-91	57.0	40.4	97.4	21.5	12.5	34.0	12.8	6.3	19.1
1999-2000	64.1	49.1	113.6	25.1	16.9	42.0	17.2	10.9	28.1

Table 2.2: Number of Educational Institutions in India

Name of Institutions	*1950-51*	*1960-61*	*1978-79*	*1985-86*	*1999-2000*
University	27	45	125*	150*	297*
Colleges for general education	498	1039	3644	4078	11831
High/Higher Secondary School	7288	17257	46731	66290	
Middle/Senior basic/Junior High School	13596	49663	109431	134074	198000
Primary/Junior basic/Basic Primary Schools (in 000's)	210	330	465	528	642
Schools for special education	52813	67084	387**	–	–
Schools for vocational training and technical education	2339	4145	2918**	–	–

Notes: * includes deemed as University and institutions of national importance, which were included under colleges during the earlier years.

** indicates that the data are related to 1977-78 as those were not available for 1978-79.

Source: Ministry of Education and Culture.

There has been a remarkable increase in the number of educational institutions in the post-independence period keeping in view the increasing requirement of the growing population. Table 2.2 shows the growth of number of different educational institutions in India in different years. Number of universities has grown by 11 times from only 27 in 1950-51 to 1999-2000. During the same period, number of colleges has increased from only 498 to 11831,*i.e.* by around 24 times. Similarly, the number of high schools and middle level schools has increased from 13596 in 1950-51 to 198000 in 1999-2000 (*i.e.*, around 15 times to that of 1950-51). Similar is the case of other institutions like special education, technical education etc. Besides these numerical growths, the institutions are not well equipped with the necessities and there is severe lack of general basic infrastructures like buildings, laboratory, and sports facilities etc., due to resource constraint though we are dreaming of imparting computer education to our children. In many cases we observe to held the classes of primary schools in rural and backward areas in the open field. In addition to that, there is lack of teachers, which also varies across the schools of different regions. Just if we look at Table 2.3 we notice that the number of students per teacher at different school level has been increasing over time and the condition is more serious for the primary schools, which is the beginning stage of educational ladder. The conditions of backward regions are worst than the urban areas. Many schools are found where one teacher has to teach more than eighty students at primary and high school level.

Table 2.3: Teacher-Pupil Ratio in India in Different Years

Year	*Primary*	*Upper Primary*	*High/Higher Secondary*
1950-51	1:24	1:20	1:21
1960-61	1:36	1:31	1:25
1970-71	1:39	1:32	1:25
1980-81	1:38	1:33	1:27
1990-91	1:43	1:37	1:31
1999-2000	1:43	1:38	1:32

Source: Ministry of Education and Culture.

Status of Education in the North East India

Like the states of other regions, the north eastern states also have been able to increase the literacy rate manifold and some north eastern states even performed better than the national average. The performance of Mizoram is the best among all the north eastern states in improving the literacy rate for both the male and female and the gender gap is much lower than the national average and the state stands second in terms of literacy, only behind Kerala.

The male-female literacy difference varies among all the north eastern states significantly. Among all the north eastern states, Arunachal Pradesh lies far behind the other states, in spite of the fact that the literacy rate has increased many times since 1971 (Table 2.4). Literacy rate in Arunachal Pradesh is only 54.74 per cent where as, it is 88.49 per cent in Mizoram according to 2001 Census Report. Male literacy rate varies from 64.07 per cent in Arunachal Pradesh to 90.69 per cent in Mizoram. In case of female literacy, the figure is lowest, *i.e.*44.24 per cent in Arunachal Pradesh and the highest 86.13 per cent in Mizoram. So the inter-state variation in female literacy rate is much more than that of male.

The status of higher education in north east is also not of higher standard compared to the other regions of India. Because of the lack of

Table 2.4: Literacy Rates in the North Eastern States in Different Censuses

State	1971			1981			1991			2001		
	Total	*Male*	*Female*	*Total*	*Male*	*Female*	*Total*	*Male*	*Female*	*Total*	*Male*	*Female*
Arunachal Pradesh	11.3	17.8	0.37	20.8	28.9	11.3	41.59	51.45	20.69	54.74	64.07	44.24
Assam	28.7	37.2	19.3	–	–	–	52.89	61.87	43.03	64.28	71.93	56.03
Manipur	32.9	46.0	19.5	41.4	53.3	29.1	59.89	71.63	47.60	68.87	77.87	59.70
Meghalaya	29.5	34.1	24.6	34.1	37.9	30.1	49.10	53.12	44.85	63.31	66.14	60.41
Mizoram*	53.8	–	–	59.9	64.5	54.9	82.27	85.61	78.60	88.49	90.69	86.13
Nagaland	27.4	35.0	18.7	42.6	50.1	33.9	61.65	67.62	54.75	67.11	71.77	61.92
Tripura	31.0	40.2	21.2	42.1	51.7	32.0	60.44	70.58	49.65	73.66	81.47	65.41
India	29.5	39.5	18.7	36.2	46.9	24.8	52.21	64.13	39.29	65.38	75.85	54.16

* *Basic Statistics of North-Eastern Region,* 1980.

Source: Census of India, various issues.

competitive attitude among the students and educational atmosphere, the rate of improvement of quality is very slow. It is clear from the recent observation of National Assessment and Accreditation Council of different Universities in some Universities of the region are established only to cater to the needs of the local students and in most of the cases very few students from outside the region are admitted, because of the particular education policy. Definitely the preference should be given to the students of backward north east area. But it should be remembered that higher education is not for all and the scope should be given to the intelligent students outside the region to build up a more competitive atmosphere and raising the quality of the students if we are really interested in quality production and not only the quantity. Not only that, these universities and colleges are still dependent on the teachers from outside the region (despite given much priority to the backward communities through reservation policies many of the reserved posts remain vacant due to lack of availability of qualified candidates from those areas), whereas the good quality professionals (who come from outside) have always a tendency to quit the area and take up a job outside the region, if it is available. This is partly due to the limited scope for improvement, avenues, and communication problems and to some extent the security reason. The dismal performance of some institutes may also be attributed to the lack of infrastructure and teachers. For example, some departments of Tripura University and some colleges in Tripura, for a long time run with only one or two permanent teachers and many teaching posts always remain vacant (mainly due to reservation policy) and the classes are mostly held by the part-time teachers, who cannot take much interest as it does not guarantee their job. This policy is also adopted, sometimes to save money as most of the state institutes are suffering from financial problem.

Budget Expenditure on Education in North East India

Like the other states of the country most part of the educational expenditure is borne by the governments of the north eastern states (*Basic Statistics of NorthEastern Region*, various issues). If we look at the north eastern states of India, we find that the state per capita budgeted expenditure has always been higher than the national average. However, the per capita budgeted expenditure varies significantly across the north eastern states. The range was from Rs. 26.8 to

Rs. 100.3 in 1976-77 and increased to from Rs. 411.53 to Rs. 919.85 in 1995-96 (Table 2.5). Percentage of budgeted expenditure on education though increased in all the states over time, still there is significant inter-state variation in percentage of budgeted expenditure. It was lowest in Arunachal Pradesh, 8.2 per cent and highest in Assam 24.0 per cent in 1976-77. The range changed to 15.18 per cent in Nagaland to 30 per cent in Manipur during 1995-96.

Table 2.5 shows that, in terms of per capita budgeted expenditure, Mizoram and Nagaland have been at the top two positions. Whereas Assam and Manipur are at the top two positions, in terms of total budgeted expenditure on education. The indication is that though, Assam is the largest state in the North East India, in terms of area and population, and its budget is thus highest among the north eastern states and hence total budget on education, but its population is comparatively so high that in terms of per capita expenditure it finds the last position among all the north eastern states. It is also observed from the Census Report that Mizoram ranks first in terms of percentage of literacy rate in the north eastern region and stands second at all India level, who spends much more on education per head.

If we consider the distribution of education budget it is also observed that the higher education receives the maximum portion of the budget and the primary education receives very low portion of it. This means that though a very few students reach the top level of education and the number of students at the primary level is the highest and though universalisation of primary education is given the first priority, budget allocation always goes against that principle. It is of course true that per student requirement at the higher education level is very high (for library and laboratory expenditure as well as research and development programmes) compared to that of the primary education. However it is the quality of primary education where the children are not only given the information, but also the knowledge on which their future level of research and contribution to the society depends. So there is much scope to be done at the primary level to groom the children for the improvement of quality of science and technology in future. At that stage children should be given not only the information, they are to be taught in such a way that it will help improving their wisdom so that they can think themselves for creating more new things, invent and innovate for the better quality of life.

Also it is to be noted that the major part of expenditure on scientific research and development activities has been incurred by the Central

Table 2.5: Per capita Budgeted Expenditure and Percentage of Total Budgeted Expenditure on Education in the States of North East India

State	*Per Capita Budgeted Expenditure (Rs.)*					*Percentage of Total Budgeted Expenditure*		
	At Current Prices			*At 1976-77 Prices*				
	1976-77	1985-86	1995-96	1985-86	1995-96	1976-77	1985-86	1995-96
(1)	(2)	(3)	(4)	(5)	(6)	(7)	(8)	(9)
Arunachal Pradesh	48.0 (5)	227.8 (3)	735.37 (3)	112.43	154.15	8.2 (7)	10.0 (7)	15.24 (6)
Assam	26.8 (7)	99.7 (7)	411.53 (7)	49.21	86.26	24.0 (1)	22.6 (2)	27.37 (2)
Manipur	57.2 (8)	217.0 (4)	723.06 (4)	107.11	151.56	17.2 (3)	24.1 (1)	30.00 (1)
Meghalaya	47.7 (6)	143.0 (6)	667.12 (5)	70.58	139.84	15.2 (4)	14.9 (4)	22.68 (3)
Mizoram	97.1 (2)	285.9 (2)	919.85 (1)	141.11	192.82	10.6 (6)	14.6 (5)	17.03 (5)
Nagaland	100.3 (1)	309.5 (1)	830.58 (2)	152.76	174.10	12.5 (5)	12.8 (6)	15.18 (7)
Tripura	54.9 (4)	198.6 (5)	619.14 (6)	98.02	129.78	22.3 (2)	19.3 (3)	21.88 (4)
All-India	30.0	100.4	340.69	49.55	71.41	22.7	20.1	21.48

Notes: (i) Figures in the parentheses represent ranks.
Columns 5 and 6 are calculated by the author himself using the general indices of (ii) prices of different years.

Sources: Selected Educational Statistics (various issues), Ministry of Human Resource Development, Government of India.

government and followed by the state government. Even today though some big multinationals have come forward to invest in the social sector and research activities but most of them are guided by their own profit motive and their total contribution is not significant (India. *Statistical Outline*, Different Editions, Tables on Expenditure on Scientific Research and Development). Moreover, the governments are now overburdened with the salaries of the teachers and staffs and thus are unable to bear the load of research expenditure as, such programmes do not yield much in terms of direct revenue or long-term profit like the other developed countries, where venture capital thus, plays a vital role in shaping the advanced research and development programmes.

Table 2.6 shows the growth of educational institutions in different states of north east India during 1978 to 1996. It is observed that number different level of institutions has increased many times during this period. Earlier students from the north east India were compelled to go to outside the region mainly for their higher studies. But now most of them can avail the opportunity from their own region without spending much money. Thus those who could not avail higher studies earlier because of financial reason and communication problem now find it feasible for them. Therefore, enrolment at different levels has been increased many times. Still after the development of those opportunities and special thrust given to the elementary education along with the extension of stipends to the students, even at university level (that is more than any other region); drop out rate at different levels are much higher in north eastern region. This is clear from the NSS Fifty-second Round Survey. The drop out level is also higher in case of females than the males and it is higher in rural areas than the urban areas. In the country as a whole, it is observed that, out of 1000 students, 344 drop out at the primary level and the over-all drop out is 562 (581 in rural areas and 513 in urban areas). It is more distressing in case of north eastern states. Among the north eastern states, the over-all drop out is the highest in Arunachal Pradesh. Out of 1000 students the drop out rate is 810 in rural areas and 383 in urban areas (average 756). Whereas the drop out rate is minimum in Meghalaya. The figures are 359 and 373 for rural and urban areas respectively. The average is 360. Most of the drop outs occur at the primary level.

Several reasons have been identified for the drop out of children. These are economic as well as non-economic. These non-economic causes are the lack of tradition, interests of children, and their parents, inability to cope with education, unfriendly atmosphere, and futility of

Table 2.6: Number of Educational Institutions in the States of North-Eastern Region

Institution	*Arunachal Pradesh*		*Assam*		*Manipur*		*Maghalaya*		*Mizoram*		*Nagaland*		*Tripura*		*Northern Eastern Region*	
	1978	1996	1978	1996	1978	1996	1978	1996	1978	1996	1978	1996	1978	1996	1978	1996
(1)	(2)	(3)	(4)	(5)	(6)	(7)	(8)	(9)	(10)	(11)	(12)	(13)	(14)	(15)	(16)	(17)
University	–	1	3	5	*	2	1	1	*	1#	*	1	*	1	4	12#
General College	1	6	136	247	21	50	13	28	6	29	7	23	6	14	190	397
Engineering College	–	1	3	3	–	–	–	–	–	–	–	–	1	1	4	5
Medical College	–	–	3	7	1	1	–	–	–	–	–	–	–	–	4	8
Agricultural College	–	–	1	2	1	1	–	–	–	–	1	1	–	–	3	4
Veterinary College	–	–	1	1	–	–	–	–	–	–	–	–	–	–	1	1
Teachers Training College	–	–	8	22	3	2	1	1	1	2	1	1	4	1	18	29

(*Contd.*)

Table 2.6 (*Contd.*)

(1)	(2)	(3)	(4)	(5)	(6)	(7)	(8)	(9)	(10)	(11)	(12)	(13)	(14)	(15)	(16)	(17)
Junior Colleges (+2 Stage)	–	–	9	70	–	22	–	–	–	29	–	3	–	–	9	124
HS School	8	67	112	588	13	52	–	28	–	16	–	4	52	188	185	943
High School	25	90	1694	3757	239	501	172	403	114	330	101	240	102	370	2447	5691
Middle School	109	301	3656	7237	381	555	392	851	239	702	288	416	292	411	5357	10473
Primary School	841	1256	21615	30140	3516	2548	3477	4235	518	1263	1114	1414	1572	2045	32653	42901
Pre-primary School	35	137	262	482	1	1	384	–	–	–	–	–	590	3406	1272	4026
Teachers Training School	–	–	32	1	4	–	9	10	2	1	3	2	–	2	50	16
Polytechnics	–	1	7	9	1	3	1	1	–	1	1	1	1	1	11	17
Technical and Industrial Schools	3	2	25	32	22	6	3	3	1	1	1	3	2	4	57	51

Note: # data relates to 2001, *means Post-Graduate centres of different universities.

Source: *Basic Statistics of North-Eastern Region*, various issues.

education, lack of infrastructure. The economic reasons for drop out of children from the class are the compulsion to work for wage, to look after the younger siblings, financial constraints, and compulsions to attend domestic activities (mainly by the girls) as well as to participate in other economic activities. In all the north eastern states, the primary causes of drop out in rural areas are the lack of educational environment at home so the children cannot take interest as their parents, their lack of merit to cope with the higher studies and their compulsion to participate in different economic activities. Still now parents think their daughters as the liabilities and it would be very difficult and costly to find out their comparable grooms if the daughters are given higher education. Moreover, the daughters in rural areas participate more in domestic activities and, also compelled to look after the younger sister/brother or other children in their family, especially if it a large family. In urban areas also the lack of merit and failure to cope with higher studies, non-interest of the children and their parents as well as lack of proper educational environment are the main reasons for major drop outs according to the findings of the NSS Fifty-two Round Survey. In addition to those, the financial constraints for pursuing higher studies, lack of job opportunities and the compulsion of the children to work as child labour for earning livelihood and to add to their family income, are the other reasons of drop out. Especially the poorer and people of backward communities find their children as the source of income and as there is no guarantee of job even after the completion of general education; they find it beneficial to train their children for works in order to gain in efficiency and ensure their future life.

Table 2.7 shows that most of the teachers at higher secondary schools are trained but the teachers of high schools and middle schools are mostly untrained in most of the north eastern states. Even almost half the teachers at primary schools were not trained during 1978. Percentage of trained teachers is very high in Mizoram and it increased sharply at all level of education during 1978 to 1996. The growth of percentage of trained teachers went in opposite direction at all levels and significantly in Tripura, which is worst than that of any other north eastern state in 1996. Number of students per teacher is higher at primary schools than the other stages. The figures also varies across the states. It is observed from Table 2.7 that in almost all the states student-teacher ratio has increased at higher secondary level (except in Manipur). The ratio has decreased at high school level in Assam,

Table 2.7: Percentage of Trained Teachers and Teacher-Student Ratio in the States of North East India

State	*Higher Secondary Schools*				*High Schools*				*Middle Schools*				*Primary Schools*			
	1978		1996		1978		1996		1978		1996		1978		1996	
	P	*R*	*P*	*R*	*P*	*R*	*P*	*R*	*P*	*R*	*P*	*R*	*P*	*R*	*P*	*R*
Arunachal Pradesh	82	20	67	24	52	19	53	27	57	20	43	26	56	31	46	35
Assam	26	20	30	27	23	24	30	22	33	24	36	24	65	34	68	37
Manipur	75	17	46	15	27	21	32	21	30	19	29	19	51	16	50	18
Meghalaya	–	–	88	14	28	20	36	19	23	17	37	17	48	35	45	38
Mizoram	–	–	–	10	22	20	47	14	33	18	74	11	57	32	78	23
Nagaland	–	–	25	17	28	21	30	30	27	17	29	19	38	21	30	23
Tripura	85	12	53	23	79	28	35	20	63	24	30	23	61	31	32	39

Note: Here *P* indicates percentage of trained teachers and *R* indicates the ratio of student per teacher.

Sources: (1) Selected Educational Statistics, 1978-79, Ministry of Education and Culture.
(2) Selected Educational Statistics, 1996-97, Ministry of Human Resource Development, Government of India.
(3) Basic Statistics of North-Eastern Region (various issues).

Meghalaya, Mizoram and Tripura. At primary schools, it has increased in all states significantly except in Mizoram, where it decreased significantly and helped raising quality of elementary education. Thus we observed that though enrolment has increased by several times over the years, number of teachers has not increased at the same pace in many cases and hence ratio of students to teacher has increased and put adverse effect on proper teaching. So more teachers should be engaged where the number of teachers is such that they are unable to manage to provide proper education to the students even after their good effort.

Conclusion

From the over all discussion it is observed that there has been a significant development in the educational scenario in India as well as in the north eastern states of India. Special thrust has also been given to the universalisation of elementary education and to reach the basic education to all sections of the community. In spite of the several steps taken at the government level a significant portion of our population still remains illiterate even, after 55 years of independence. Not only that, because of several economic and social reasons many of them are unable to proceed for higher education. It is interesting to note that for teaching as well as many of the government office works at different levels in the north eastern region, they are dependent on the experts from outside the region. Just making of the provisions for education numerically and giving stipends to the students are not sufficient to create environment and enthusiasm among the people for education. It needs a great change in political will, attitude, devotion, and commitment of all departments and non-government agencies. Teachers' training programme should be given priority to improve the quality of teaching by acquainting the teachers with the newly developed curriculum and thereby improving their ability to teach the new syllabi. Teachers are also to be well equipped to adopt the updated teaching methods. Not only that, more investment for creating basic infrastructure in which the region is lacking more than the other regions of the country are essential.

As the higher education is too expensive and too burdensome as well as non-profit sector, it along with research and development can be treated with industrial and profit-making sector. Special provision should be made for the meritorious students only at the higher level of education. Otherwise if stipend is given to all, the enrolment will be increased in many cases, only to receive the stipend by the students and they will find it a source of supplementary income. Rather it would be encouraging if more and more job oriented courses are introduced and simultaneously efforts are given to create more avenues (may be through changes in industrial policy) for the educated unemployed youth. The private and multinational corporations may be encouraged to come forward to invest in research and development to raise the level of invention and innovation through technological advancement that will benefit them and the society as well.

REFERENCES

Ghosh, B.N. and De, U.K. (2002), "Leadership and the Performance of Panchayat in Rural Development: An Experience from Tripura", paper presented at the UGC National Seminar on *Transformation in Rural Society* held at Tufanganj Mahavidyalaya, West Bengal on 24-25 September, 2002.

Government of India, *Statistical Abstract* (various issues).

Government of India, *The Census of India* (various issues).

Government of India, *Economic Survey* (various issues).

NSS Fifty-two Round Survey.

Sharma, R. (1997), "Dynamics of Learning Three R's in Madhya Pradesh", *Economic and Political Weekly*, Vol. XXXII, No. 17, April 26.

Shukla *et al.*, (1994), *Attainments of Primary School Children in Various States*, National Council for Education, Training and Research (NCERT), New Delhi.

3

Education in North East Indian States

ASOK KUMAR MAITI & SUBHENDU CHAKRABARTI

Background

Education, the principal component of human capital, contributes to economic development through population control, life expectancy, infant mortality, nutritional status and strengthening of civil institution. Economists who generally cannot agree with each other at least agree on this point that social rates of return on investment in all levels of education exceed the long-term opportunity cost of capital.

In spite of the incorporation of right to education in the body of constitution, universal primary education is still a distant cry, even after five and a half decades of independence. Even now, the total expenditure on education in India is 3.8 per cent of GDP (1998). Compared to this investment in education, various unproductive activities have drawn much bigger investments as well as heavy drainage of foreign exchange reserve.

Even though education was given the high priority among all other activities in the social sector, the estimated per capita expenditure, as per central plan allocation, is around Rs. 53 in one year (*i.e.*, Rs. 5450 crores in 2000-2001). Even there is no guarantee that this amount was fully utilised for the purposes it was meant. Again, social sector experiences the first attack after the raising of question on economising plan expenditure.

After 1947, we have built up a 'great Indian tradition' to high-light some issues at some point of time to take advantage of specific socio-political situations. For example, one can very well remember the emphasis on 20-point economic programmes in 1970s (none of which was at all new) by shelving the community development programme, which included all these programmes and many others. Such tradition is also prevalent in case of education. In the last decade, we heard about total literacy mission as well as different programmes of literacy campaign at the initiative of the government, both of the states as well as of the Centre. While compulsory universal primary education was supposed to be successfully implemented within 10 years from the date of declaration of Indian Republic, the government has recently floated a new programme of "Sarva Shiksha Abhiyan", the goals of which are as follows:

(a) All children of age 6-14 in schools/educational guarantee centres/bridge course by 2003.
(b) All children of age 6-14 to complete 5 years of primary education by 2007.
(c) All children of age 6-14 to complete 8 years of schooling by 2010.
(d) Focus on elementary education of satisfactory quality with emphasis on education for life.
(e) Bridge all gender and social category gaps by 2007 at primary stage and at elementary education level by 2010.
(f) Universal retention by 2010.

The Central Government has launched several schemes to meet the needs of educationally disadvantaged as well as for strengthening social infrastructure for education, namely, Operation Blackboard (OB), District Primary Education Programme (DPEP), Education Guarantee Scheme and Alternative and Innovative Education (EGS & AIE), Mahila Samakhta, Teacher Education (TE), Mid-Day-Meal Scheme, Lok Jumbish, Shikhya Karmi Project (SKP), Jnan Shala, etc. In 2001-2002, steps have been taken in partnership with the states by launching Sarba Shiksa Abhiyan (SSA), which would be decentralized and highest priority would be accorded to community ownership and monitoring. This programme will subsume all existing programmes in due course within its overall framework with district as the unit of programme implementation. Following the Directive Principle of the Constitution, there has been 93rd Amendment of the Constitution (passed on 28 November, 2001 in Lok Sabha), which entitled every citizen a fundamental right to free and compulsory education up to the age of 14 and to make it a fundamental duty of the parents/guardians to provide opportunities to children. But the irony of the fate is that the entire programme is dependent on the aids and loans from abroad, like British Development Authority Fund from DPEP, Mid-Day-Meals and other such programmes from UNICEF etc. By now, we have enough experiences of Operation Blackboard, which achieved a little and spent a lot and there was much disruption in the primary educational system. From 1970s onwards, the governments at Centre and State built up a new culture of blindly implementing some foreign advisory bodies' recommendations without care and caution as recommended by our own Educational Commission appointed after 1947 (*e.g.*, Mudalior Commission, Radhakrishnan Commission etc.).

In West Bengal, during Total Literacy Campaign, all the rural primary schools were virtually closed for months together and the teachers were deployed in spreading literacy. Except declaring some districts as fully literate (though questionable) precious little was done in spreading education among the disadvantaged sections of population, the marginal people. Moreover, the system of follow up proved to be inefficient and there was no serious endeavour to keep in touch with the new literates. In spite of the existence of some arrangement called post literacy mission, the authors have found that the new literates of the campaign period have forgotten everything except drawing his/her signature in only two years' time. Certainly this is not education we crave for. Before discussing the quality and purpose of education in the 21st century let us first examine a few information available about the status of education in India with special reference to the north-eastern states.

Status of North-Eastern States in the Field of Education

The development of our country's vast human resource potential is the essence of social sector's development. Now-a-days human resource development is measured by improved demographic indicators, namely health care services, progress in the field of education and adult literacy level. The approach paper to the Tenth five Year Plan (2002-2007) while outlining a GDP growth rate of 8 per cent per annum, laid down a specific focus on human development through broader enhancement of human well-being as well the quality of life. This include not only the basic food consumption needs but also access to basic social services, especially education, health, drinking water and basic sanitation. The attainment of monitorable targets set out in this regard not only necessitates a substantial allocation of resources for the social sectors but also involves an enhanced role of the government.

Setting up of such targets which involves greater participation of the government in the social sector seemed to be quite contradictory with the new economic policies, which have been being implemented vigorously for more than a decade. In fact, the government at the Centre already began withdrawing investment in social sectors and allowing social services to be privatized. The Planning Commission possibly owes an explanation to such commitment expressed in its approach paper to Tenth Five Year Plan in view of the government's exit policy from social sector. The practice of formulating a so-called plan and avoiding the responsibility of its implementation has already cost the nation very cruelly and brutally.

In the following paragraphs we would try to present the available data from the government sources to ascertain the status of North-Eastern (N-E) states in the field of education.

Table 3.1 shows that by 2001 only Arunachal Pradesh, Assam, and Meghalaya fell behind All India average literacy rate (65.38%). Among the North-Eastern states the highest rate of literacy, at present, is at Mizoram, which is the second highest in India. This pattern is consistent among male and female population separately (literacy for male in India in 2001 was 75.85 per cent and that of female was 54.16%). The lowest rate of literacy among the N-E states in 2001 was found in Arunachal Pradesh (54.74%). The figure was 64.07 per cent for male and 44.24 per cent for female.

Table 3.2 presents position of N-E states in terms of literacy rates over various censuses. In terms of literacy rates the ranking of these states varies from 2nd to 24th position for the total population, 2nd to 25th position in terms of male population and 2nd to 23rd position in terms of female population. In the last 40 years N-E states' status underwent significant changes and previously the range was between 9th and 20th. Of them Assam moved from 9th to 17th (a dismal performance), Manipur from 6th to 13th whereas Tripura and Nagaland went up from 15th to 7th and 20th to 15th respectively. This shows that Tripura and Nagaland's performance is better than any other N-E state.

Table 3.1: Literacy rates in the North-Eastern states by sex and overall over various censuses

Category	*Year*	*Arunachal Pradesh*	*Assam*	*Manipur*	*Megha-laya*	*Mizoram*	*Naga-land*	*Tripura*	*All India*
(1)	(2)	(3)	(4)	(5)	(6)	(7)	(8)	(9)	(10)
Total Population	1961#	47.9*	33.0	36.0	–	–	20.4	24.3	28.3*
	1971	11.3	28.7	32.9	29.5	–	27.4	31.0	29.5
	1981	20.8	–	41.4	34.1	59.9	42.6	42.1	36.2$
	1991	41.59	52.89	59.89	49.10	82.27	61.65	60.44	52.21
	2001	54.74	64.28	68.87	63.31	88.49	67.11	73.66	65.38
Male Population	1961#	53.4*	44.3	53.5	–	–	27.2	35.3	40.4*
	1971	17.8	37.2	46.0	34.1	–	35.0	40.2	39.5
	1981	28.9	–	53.3	37.9	64.5	50.1	51.7	46.9$
	1991	51.45	61.87	71.63	53.12	85.61	67.62	70.58	64.13
	2001	64.07	71.93	77.87	66.14	90.69	71.77	81.47	75.85
Female Population	1961#	24.1*	19.6	18.9	–	–	13.0	12.4	15.3*
	1971	0.37	19.3	19.5	24.6	–	18.7	21.2	18.7
	1981	11.3	–	29.1	30.1	54.9	33.9	32.0	24.8$
	1991	26.69	43.03	47.60	44.85	78.60	54.75	49.65	39.29
	2001	44.24	56.03	59.70	60.41	86.13	61.92	65.41	54.16

Note: * Excludes of that portion of NEFA where all India census schedule was not canvassed.

$ Excludes Assam and the population of those areas which are illegal occupation of Pakistan and China where census could not be taken.

Excludes population in age group 0-4.

Source: Statistical Abstract (various issues), Government of India.

Table 3.3 presents the distribution of students pursuing general education by broad class group. It is apparent from the data that the number of students decreases monotonically as one goes from lower to higher levels. This is however expected in each of the states including 'All India'. Among the N-E states Manipur shows very poor rate of primary education (39.4%) compared to All India average (56.4%). In higher level of education there are 4.1 per cent at All India level with which one of the N-E states can compete. They are in the range between 1 and 3.9 per cent. Now very few of North East India students go for higher level of education and that may be due to economic and/ or geographical reasons. Most students give up their studies after primary level and only a few continue up to secondary level. Students from families having little access to power and to out-side world can only think of higher education.

Table 3.2: Position of North-Eastern States based on Ranking of States for Total Population, Male Population and Female Population according to Literacy rates over various Censuses

Category	*States*	1961	1971	1981	1991	2001
Total Population	Arunachal Pradesh	3	24	24	23	24
	Assam	9	13	–	17	17
	Manipur	6	8	10	11	13
	Meghalaya	–	12	17	18	20
	Mizoram	–	–	3	2	2
	Nagaland	20	14	7	8	15
	Tripura	15	11	9	10	17
Male Population	Arunachal Pradesh	4	24	24	25	25
	Assam	9	14	–	18	19
	Manipur	3	6	7	9	11
	Meghalaya	–	16	21	23	23
	Mizoram	–	–	3	2	2
	Nagaland	21	15	11	13	20
	Tripura	14	11	9	10	8
Female Population	Arunachal Pradesh	3	24	24	21	23
	Assam	9	13	–	17	18
	Manipur	10	12	13	12	14
	Meghalaya	–	7	12	15	12
	Mizoram	–	–	2	2	2
	Nagaland	13	14	6	5	10
	Tripura	14	9	9	10	7

Source: *Statistical Abstract* (various issues), Government of India.

Age specific attendance ratio in general education shows much variation among N-E states. It ranges from 65 to 81 in case of children of 6-10 age group, whereas the ratio varies between 80 and 88 in case of 11-13 age group, 61 to 81 among 14-17 age group and 18 to 44 among 18-24 age group. The figures for corresponding age groups at All India level 69, 72, 50 and 14 respectively. The attendance ratios show that the performance of N-E students in terms of attendance is not at all unsatisfactory compared to All India figures. We are not going into the details of urban-rural break-ups of such performance as the attendance in urban areas is comparatively much better than that of rural areas in all N-E states as well as in India (Table 3.4).

Table 3.3: Per 1000 distribution of students (age 5-24 years) pursuing general education by broad class group

State	*Rural/Urban/ Total*	*Broad class group of education*						
		I-V	*VI-VIII*	*IX-X*	*XI-XII*	*Higher level*	*N.R*	*All*
Arunachal	R	662	202	19	17	4	96	1000
Pradesh	U	463	223	157	80	34	44	1000
	T	620	207	48	30	10	85	1000
Assam	R	547	204	142	63	36	8	1000
	U	398	225	170	104	69	33	1000
	T	532	206	145	67	39	11	1000
Manipur	R	397	252	153	103	27	68	1000
	U	388	245	165	130	46	26	1000
	T	394	250	157	111	32	56	1000
Meghalaya	R	634	257	86	5	4	14	1000
	U	420	253	175	65	62	25	1000
	T	593	256	103	17	15	16	1000
Mizoram	R	563	322	74	—	1	40	1000
	U	421	277	184	88	25	5	1000
	T	505	304	119	36	11	26	1000
Nagaland	R	480	267	175	58	12	9	1000
	U	407	233	190	98	55	17	1000
	T	457	257	179	70	25	11	1000
Tripura	R	614	234	101	29	13	8	1000
	U	474	251	134	82	44	15	1000
	T	597	236	105	36	17	9	1000
All India	R	608	219	101	40	22	10	1000
	U	462	234	129	81	85	9	1000
	T	564	223	109	52	41	10	1000

Source: NSS Fifty-second Round (July 1995-June 1996).

Table 3.4: Age specific attendance ratio by broad age group in General Education

State	*Rural/Urban/Total*	*Broad age group of students*			
		6-10	11-13	14-17	18-24
Arunachal Pradesh	R	61	82	54	18
	U	92	81	82	37
	T	65	82	61	21
Assam	R	72	79	64	23
	U	83	90	76	40
	T	73	80	65	25
Manipur	R	66	86	71	38
	U	78	91	86	64
	T	69	87	74	44
Meghalaya	R	67	93	70	13
	U	88	97	96	57
	T	69	94	74	19
Mizoram	R	60	83	76	6
	U	96	98	78	44
	T	71	88	77	18
Nagaland	R	69	86	83	35
	U	78	84	74	49
	T	71	85	81	40
Tripura	R	81	83	59	20
	U	88	94	85	33
	T	81	84	62	22
All India	R	65	67	45	10
	U	83	85	65	23
	T	69	72	50	14

Source: NSS Fifty-second Round (July 1995-June 1996).

Let us now inquire into the situation of distribution of persons of all age groups by attendance and by level of education in terms of current enrolment. 500 out of 1000 children in India are never enrolled at all. The figures for N-E states are relatively better compared to All India as the non-enrolment ranges between 443 and 298 out of 1000 children. In Arunachal Pradesh per 1000 children 443 are not enrolled, which is the highest among the N-E states and lowest in Manipur (298).

In case of India 299 out of 1000 children continue in post-primary stage whereas in N-E states the figures range between 205 (Arunachal Pradesh) and 399 (Nagaland) (*see* Table 3.5). We cannot claim that the data indicates the non-performance of certain states unless we probe into the actual reasons of non-attendance/non-enrolment.

However, a few testable hypotheses are generated from these secondary data.

(i) That non-enrolment may have positive correlation with low level of living of the families.

(ii) That non-attendance has correlation with annual average days of work available to the parents of the children already enrolled.

Scholars ready to undertake primary investigation into this phenomenon in both rural and urban areas in the N-E states can only explain the situation authentically.

Table 3.6 presents (per thousand) proportion of drop outs and their distribution by level at which they drop out. The All India figure of drop outs is 562 (rural 581 and urban 513), Arunachal Pradesh (rural 810, urban 383, total 756) tops the list of drop outs among the N-E states. The drop outs are lowest in Meghalaya (rural 359, urban 373, total 360). Again, it is interesting to note that the drop outs in Mizoram (ranked 2nd in literacy in India) has also high drop out rates (rural 733, urban 795, total 750). Going by the levels of drop outs (*see* Table 3.6) One can see 304 drop outs at primary level in All India out of 1000 drop outs. The figures for middle, secondary, higher secondary and above are 262, 287, 80 and 33 respectively. Among N-E states the primary level drop out is highest in Arunachal Pradesh (550) and lowest in Mizoram (126). In the middle level drop outs are highest in Meghalaya and Mizoram (388).

Table 3.7 gives the data on the reasons of dropping-out discussed above. Thirteen reasons were identified for such drop outs. These are lack of tradition (01), lack of child's interest (02) and lack of parents' interest (03) are reasons which are not directly economical. Reasons, such as inability (04), unfriendly atmosphere (05) and futility of education (06) are other kinds of reasons which has onus on the system of education. Lack of infrastructural facility (07) should also be the responsibility of the states. All other reasons coded (08) to (19) are in

Table 3.5: Per 1000 distribution of persons (age 5-24 years) by current attendance and current enrolment status

State	*Sector*	*Not attending*					*Attending in*			*Total*
		Not enrolled	*Enrolled*							
			Pre-primary	*Primary*	*Post-primary*	*All**	*Pre-primary*	*Primary*	*Post-primary*	
Arunachal	R	479	–	1	–	498	7	330	165	1000
Pradesh	U	238	–	–	–	238	–	330	432	1000
	T	443	–	1	–	459	6	330	205	1000
Assam	R	444	–	0	–	449	4	253	294	1000
	U	295	1	–	–	298	9	233	460	1000
	T	431	0	0	–	437	5	251	307	1000
Manipur	R	332	5	5	8	352	68	240	339	1000
	U	196	–	–	2	202	45	271	482	1000
	T	298	3	4	6	315	62	248	374	1000
Meghalaya	R	349	–	–	–	349	83	251	317	1000
	U	127	–	–	–	127	45	253	575	1000
	T	318	–	–	–	318	77	252	353	1000
Mizoram	R	467	–	–	9	476	19	235	269	1000
	U	227	–	–	1	228	13	263	496	1000
	T	392	–	–	6	399	17	244	340	1000
Nagaland	R	318	–	0	1	322	38	254	386	1000

(Contd.)

Table 3.5: (*Contd.*)

State	*Sector*	*Not attending*					*Attending in*			*Total*
		Not enrolled	*Enrolled*							
			Pre-primary	*Primary*	*Post-primary*	*All**	*Pre-primary*	*Primary*	*Post-primary*	
Nagaland	R	318	–	0	1	322	38	254	386	1000
	U	278	–	–	5	285	33	253	429	1000
	T	306	–	0	2	312	36	253	399	1000
Tripura	R	417	–	–	0	417	8	340	234	1000
	U	300	–	–	–	301	18	309	372	1000
	T	404	–	–	0	405	9	337	249	1000
All India	R	536	0	1	1	539	12	257	192	1000
	U	387	0	0	1	389	17	250	344	1000
	T	500	0	0	1	502	13	256	229	1000

Source: NSS Fifty-second Round (July 1995-June 1996).

essence economical. The data would show how the educational atmosphere in schools on the one hand and the economical constraints on the other have been responsible for the heavy rate of dropping-out. Lack of tradition did feature a little only in case of Arunachal Pradesh and Tripura. Reasons, such as completion of desired level or admission in the next level did not at all figure. The heaviest toll seemed to be the economic constraints coded (08) to (12). The states level data also show the same pattern as in All India.

Table 3.6: Proportion (per 1000) of drop outs (age 5-24 years) and their per 1000 distribution by level at which drop out

States	*Sector*	*Proportion of drop-out*	*Level at which dropped-out*						
			Primary	*Middle*	*Secondary*	*Higher Secon-dary*	*Above HS*	*N.R.*	*All*
Arunachal Pradesh	R	810	563	240	122	43	14	19	1000
	U	383	361	42	334	263	–	–	1000
	T	756	550	227	135	57	13	18	1000
Assam	R	623	370	231	302	58	22	17	1000
	U	564	225	221	348	99	107	–	1000
	T	619	361	230	305	60	28	16	1000
Manipur	R	575	323	296	303	54	11	12	1000
	U	426	104	274	393	90	112	27	1000
	T	554	299	293	313	58	23	14	1000
Meghalaya	R	359	432	403	142	12	–	10	1000
	U	373	497	233	116	154	–	–	1000
	T	360	438	388	140	25	–	10	1000
Mizoram	R	733	153	442	373	32	–	–	1000
	U	795	59	256	490	175	12	8	1000
	T	750	126	388	407	73	3	2	1000
Nagaland	R	368	295	240	389	53	16	8	1000
	U	594	220	366	339	63	11	–	1000
	T	429	267	287	371	56	14	5	1000
Tripura	R	721	424	243	264	38	–	32	1000
	U	620	288	234	404	74	–	–	1000
	T	711	413	242	276	41	–	29	1000
All India	R	581	332	269	269	71	22	38	1000
	U	513	222	242	339	109	67	22	1000
	T	562	304	262	287	80	33	34	1000

Source: NSS Fifty-second Round (July 1995-June 1996).

Table 3.7: Per 1000 distribution of drop-outs (age 5-24 years) by reasons for dropping-out

States	*Sector*	*Reason for dropping-out**															
		01	02	03	04	05	06	07	08	09	10	11	12	13	14	15	Total
Arunachal Pradesh	R	8	62	118	46	–	24	7	16	84	5	472	19	–	–	123	1000
	U	–	189	–	150	–	–	–	526	135	–	–	–	–	–	–	1000
	T	8	70	111	53	–	23	6	49	87	5	441	18	–	–	115	1000
Assam	R	–	218	253	184	5	11	5	15	106	4	38	68	–	–	67	1000
	U	–	180	93	237	–	–	–	45	92	13	11	263	–	–	67	1000
	T	–	215	243	189	5	10	5	17	105	4	36	80	–	–	67	1000
Manipur	R	1	267	5	419	–	–	5	–	33	–	63	92	–	–	119	1000
	U	–	78	31	109	64	–	–	62	103	43	42	448	–	–	9	1000
	T	1	246	8	384	7	–	5	7	41	5	61	132	–	–	103	1000
Meghalaya	R	–	179	47	314	8	–	–	–	156	–	32	195	–	–	18	1000
	U	–	122	–	89	–	–	–	455	180	–	63	–	–	–	–	1000
	T	–	174	43	295	7	–	–	40	158	–	35	178	–	–	16	1000
Mizoram	R	–	445	13	247	1	–	–	12	160	2	–	77	–	–	24	1000
	U	–	464	9	196	–	22	35	26	109	4	8	92	–	–	29	1000
	T	–	451	12	232	1	7	10	16	145	2	2	81	–	–	25	1000
Nagaland	R	–	189	16	399	2	–	–	46	50	8	74	135	–	–	81	1000
	U	–	161	6	230	–	–	–	7	–	–	–	466	–	–	130	1000
	T	–	179	12	336	1	–	–	31	31	5	47	259	–	–	99	1000

(Contd.)

Table 3.7: (*Contd.*)

States	*Sector*	*Reason for dropping-out**															
		01	02	03	04	05	06	07	08	09	10	11	12	13	14	15	Total
Tripura	R	3	211	127	199	–	–	–	8	125	4	59	123	–	–	138	1000
	U	–	296	27	125	–	–	–	27	88	16	9	119	–	–	224	1000
	T	3	218	124	193	–	–	–	9	122	5	55	123	–	–	145	1000
All India	R	5	253	102	215	5	19	20	41	82	14	46	121	–	–	60	1000
	U	6	220	69	256	4	13	8	69	65	10	43	133	–	–	67	1000
	T	5	244	94	225	4	17	17	48	78	13	46	124	–	–	62	1000

Code
01 = no tradition in the family
02 = child not interested in studies
03 = parents not interested in studies
04 = inability to cope with or failure in studies (n.a.)
05 = unfriendly atmosphere at school (n.a.)
06 = education not considered useful
07 = schooling/higher education facilities not available conveniently

Code
08 = has to work for wage/salary
09 = has to participate in other economic activities
10 = has to look after younger siblings
11 = has to attend to other domestic activities
12 = financial constraints
13 = completed the desired level
14 = awaiting admission to the next level
15 = other (incl. 'n.r.' cases)

Source : NSS Fifty-second Round (July 1995-June 1996).

Since we are working with secondary data so we are unable to have further insight into the reasons of drop out. There are such studies for the states of West Bengal, Tamil Nadu and Kerala, which analyse the reasons of drop out in greater details pointing out the fact that most of the drop outs at pre- and post-primary level were due to irregular availability of employment of the parents, large family size and uncertainty of job opportunity. So one may presume that such reasons may also be relevant in case of N-E states.

Data are available for the reasons why children are never enrolled, which are presented in Table 3.8. The same reasons as in Table 3.7 were attributed for non-enrolment. The reasons are almost similar as in case of drop out. So the crux of the problems might lie in the poverty and unemployment of the people. We do not however ignore the reasons like lack of interest of the parents and children. But we believe that economic condition and level of living of the household are certainly responsible for the lack of interest in education also.

From the above discussion about the reasons for the faltering and halting progress of literacy and education, it is clear that access to education cannot possibly be discussed without reference to the level of living and the employment situation of the households.

Lastly, we would like to present the data on average expenditure per student in the N-E states by broad levels of education (Table 3.9). The per student expenditure in India is Rs. 904 whereas for Assam it is Rs. 594. The expenditure in Arunachal Pradesh is also lower than All India average (Rs. 821). All other N-E states spend more than Indian average, highest among them is Nagaland (Rs. 2087). No State Government is free from urban bias. The government spends at least double per student in urban areas and sometimes it goes up to 5 or 6 times. The absolute figures of expenditure show lower expenditure in primary and middle levels of education. The Government of N-E states should rationalise the allocation on different levels of education so that primary and middle level education is given the highest priority. They should also consider setting up of vocational education centres in each of the states and pave the path of self-employment. While doing so the question of ethnic traditions, languages, and diversity of culture in different areas even within the same state should be kept in mind.

Table 3.8: Proportion (per 1000) of never enrolled persons (age 5-24 years) and their per thousand distribution by reason for non-enrolment

States	*Sector*	*Proportion of never enrolled*	*Reason for non-enrolment**															
			01	02	03	04	05	06	07	08	09	10	11	12	13	14	15	Total
Arunachal	R	380	1	174	114	–	–	4	20	1	39	10	32	125	–	–	479	1000
Pradesh	U	139	–	215	16	–	–	–	–	26	66	–	–	83	–	–	593	1000
	T	344	1	177	108	–	–	4	19	3	41	10	30	122	–	–	486	1000
Assam	R	231	3	140	362	–	–	23	5	5	23	1	9	78	–	–	351	1000
	U	118	–	308	170	–	–	7	–	18	4	–	20	147	–	–	326	1000
	T	221	3	148	353	–	–	23	5	5	22	1	9	81	–	–	349	1000
Manipur	R	142	10	59	108	–	–	22	10	–	42	1	47	65	–	–	637	1000
	U	95	8	141	79	–	–	–	–	–	19	–	104	181	–	–	467	1000
	T	130	10	74	103	–	–	18	8	–	38	0	57	86	–	–	606	1000
Meghalaya	R	167	–	246	119	–	–	2	–	2	204	6	58	76	–	–	286	1000
	U	22	74	–	58	–	–	–	–	–	98	–	–	64	–	–	707	1000
	T	146	2	241	118	–	–	2	–	2	202	6	57	76	–	–	295	1000
Mizoram	R	232	16	44	484	–	–	–	4	–	1	–	–	–	–	–	450	1000
	U	24	–	112	52	–	–	–	–	–	–	–	–	–	–	–	836	1000
	T	167	16	47	464	–	–	–	4	–	1	–	–	–	–	–	468	1000
Nagaland	R	108	–	295	53	–	–	–	–	–	138	18	3	224	–	–	268	1000
	U	95	–	10	–	–	–	–	–	9	32	–	9	331	–	–	609	1000
	T	104	–	218	38	–	–	–	–	2	109	13	5	253	–	–	361	1000

(*Contd.*)

Table 3.8: (*Contd.*)

States	*Sector*	*Proportion of never enrolled*	*Reason for non-enrolment*															
			01	02	03	04	05	06	07	08	09	10	11	12	13	14	15	Total
Tripura	R	169	–	242	176	–	–	–	26	24	55	–	11	104	–	–	362	1000
	U	85	–	111	117	–	–	–	–	61	112	–	–	30	–	–	570	1000
	T	160	–	234	173	–	–	–	25	26	58	–	11	99	–	–	374	1000
All India	R	315	39	173	326	–	–	28	22	14	36	13	27	146	–	–	176	1000
	U	120	38	179	265	–	–	15	4	13	25	12	15	197	–	–	244	1000
	T	268	39	173	318	–	–	27	20	14	35	13	26	151	–	–	184	1000

Code

01 = no tradition in the family
02 = child not interested in studies
03 = parents not interested in studies
04 = inability to cope with or failure in studies (n.a.)
05 = unfriendly atmosphere at school (n.a.)
06 = education not considered useful.
07 = schooling/higher education facilities not available conveniently

Code

08 = has to work for wage/salary
09 = has to participate in other economic activities
10 = has to look after younger siblings
11 = has to attend to other domestic activities
12 = financial constraints
13 = completed the desired level
14 = awaiting admission to the next level
15 = other (incl. 'n.r.' cases)

* Children of age 5 not included in the school going age-group classification.

Source: NSS Fifty-second Round (July 1995-June 1996).

Table 3.9: Average expenditure (Rs.) per student of age 5-24 years pursuing general education by broad level of education

States	*Sector*	*Broad level of education*				
		Primary	*Middle*	*Secondary/Higher Secondary*	*Above Higher Secondary*	*All*
Arunachal Pradesh	R	483	893	1027	973	628
	U	1490	1305	1846	1662	1545
	T	631	977	1498	1455	821
Assam	R	199	415	903	2087	506
	U	886	1207	1655	3066	1380
	T	251	498	998	2261	594
Manipur	R	625	1027	1719	2655	1095
	U	1156	1478	1598	2330	1439
	T	769	1161	1679	2517	1199
Meghalaya	R	753	1126	2304	906	1074
	U	1722	1817	2117	2364	1897
	T	890	1239	2233	2070	1232
Mizoram	R	639	988	1213	4200	861
	U	988	1128	1515	1573	1229
	T	756	1033	1402	1718	1011
Nagaland	R	1210	1659	2720	6092	1802
	U	2385	2710	2993	3665	2728
	T	1556	1932	2816	4480	2087
Tripura	R	456	912	2109	1655	847
	U	847	1914	2804	3186	1713
	T	494	1039	2234	2142	952
All India	R	297	640	1180	2294	570
	U	1149	1529	2219	3304	1686
	T	501	915	1577	2923	904

Source: NSS Fifty-second Round (July 1995-June 1996).

A Few Observations

The need for universal and compulsory primary education was most talked of and least attended to an issue in the last 55 years of our independence. The system of education introduced by the colonial government had many virtues and vices. It was in the interest of the colonial rulers that a section of the people would learn in English and majority of the people should be kept uneducated.

In independent India, the aims of education system were changed and made compulsory. Free primary education for all the persons (above five years) was targeted within 10 years of the declaration of the Republic. The performance of last 55 years reflected in the data above is unsatisfactory.

It was apparent that the governments were not at all serious about pursuing the declared objectives and took education as any other activity like mining and quarrying. The state governments, which were a little serious about education made very good performances right in 1950s (*e.g.* Kerala). Even now some southern states with much less per capita expenditure on education have been performing better than some of the eastern and most of the northern states. We do not think that only greater allocation of resources in education or for that matter in primary education would solve the problem. Fixation of responsibility of different agencies dealing with education, strong commitment to achieve the objectives, efficiency in administering education especially primary education through vernacular and designing appropriate syllabi for vocational training would be prerequisite of our educational programme. The Sarva Shiksha Abhiyan while formulating the objectives should also undertake a strategy so that children belonging to all ethnic groups, speaking in Indian languages and belonging to each of the religions can get the advantage of education. Those, who are experienced in administering literacy among minority groups can easily understand that the above exercise involves a lot of hard work and speaking more precisely a lot of homework.

While we are discussing about the prospects and constraints of education in N-E states we should be especially mindful of the peculiarities and diversities among them. Many dialects, which want recognition as languages should be carefully studied and attempts should be made if those can be put in written form. Such exercise would encourage the minorities who would take interest in education. The oversimplified formula of using English as a medium of instruction would end in chaos. There is no denying of the fact that a miniscule minority of the elites of all groups would earn English literacy and be adopted in the ruling socio-political system. If we seriously mean education for all, we should design a system, which looks beyond the labyrinth fabricated by the present system.

4

Human Resource Development in North-Eastern States

With Special Reference to Women

BHOLA NATH GHOSH

Introduction

India since independence has gained momentum in social development. Planned changes have been incorporated in the society. One of the prime aspects of social development is to raise the level of literacy or in other words educational development. Education has been viewed as lever of individual-cum-social development in India. Under the colonial suppression, the ignorance and illiteracy obscured Indian people. The society was under the yoke of archaic feudalism characterized by oriental despotism. To free the individual from the yoke of colonialism, education with an outlook of social justice may be congenial for individual freedom along with the society. Whether those social changes were harbinger of new ideas or not is a matter of discussion. But none can deny that the contact with European civilization Indian social structure has been affected in many ways. Innovation of personal computer instead of rebuts card-based machine computer of the first generation is a European contribution to our present day civilization. None can deny the importance of western education in India that had a definite impact upon the existing feudal society, characterized by oriental despotism. Educational opportunities came to our experience during the renaissance were equal for both sexes. Women education, in particular, was given due importance and such venture had shaken the pre-colonial Indian society to a great extent.

Importance of Education

Education has significance in every society. In pluralistic societies like India, it is only education that can synthesize and crystallize values based on social justice. It plays a significant role in the economic and social growth of both individual status and also prestige. Today, education is a process of human development and has appeared as formal examination oriented learning.

The goals of education may be defined in many contexts, but the most appropriate would be the goal as envisaged by Gandhiji: "The goal of education is to establish a non-violent and non-exploiting social and economic order." Much reflection and wisdom had gone into this pithy statement, which is as relevant today as it was in his time or even more so. This is the purpose of education in a modern democratic society.

The universal education for both male and female has received due importance in a country like India for development of society and constituent individuals. The advancement in literacy for male has improved and still going up but the growth of literacy for women has not been at par with that of the male. In every Census report, this gender disparity in terms of education has been evident.

Women are treated as weaker sex and they are generally discriminated in every respect including in education. If woman is not being educated, the society cannot forward.

National Educational Policy

Government of India announced the New National Policy on Education in 1985. The concept of this national system of education implies that up to a given level, all students, irrespective of their location or sex, have access to education of comparable quality.

The New National Policy also laid special emphasis on the removal of disparities and to equalize educational opportunities by attending to the specific needs of those, who have been denied equality so far. The removal of women's illiteracy and obstacles inhibiting their access to, and retention in, elementary education, according to the new policy, would receive overriding priority, through provision of special support services, setting of time targets and effective monitoring. Major emphasis would be laid on women's participation in professional education at different levels. Education would also be used as an agent of basic change in the status of women. The new National Educational system would play a positive, interventionist role in the empowerment of women.

This paper intends to inquire into the status of women in education in north-eastern states of India where many different ethnic groups in hills and plains are nourishing diverse languages and cultures. It is observed that though North East India have diverse life pattern, serious educational set-back for women are noticed during few decades. The status of women-education is examined by the educational statistics available from different sources. The situation revealed by women's education-data would throw some light on the inadequacy of the educational systems prevalent in this region.

Methodology

To understand the situation of women education in the North East region, we have only considered the secondary data available from different sources.

Observation and Findings

Table 4.1 shows the comparative figures of literacy rates of male and female in India and the north-eastern States. From this table we find that north-eastern States have differential rate of literacy for both sex. Highest literacy rate has been observed in Mizoram. From the data of seven N-E states, we can also have an idea about the state of literacy in general and literacy of the women in particular. In fact, in Arunachal Pradesh, literacy of women is well below the national average in every year as revealed from the table. But in other states like Manipur, Meghalaya, Mizoram, Nagaland and Tripura, the women's literacy is always much higher than the national average. Nagaland follows Mizoram in terms of literacy. From the data, it shows that in Mizoram and Nagaland, women literacy has increased during 1991-97, and ranked above the other North-Eastern States. Better performance in increasing literacy of women here may be due to many factors and among them prime one would be the prevalent matriarchal society and the impact of Missionaries' developmental activities. So one can argue that in other states of the North East, Arunachal Pradesh the literacy rate of women has not increased as like Mizoram and Nagaland.

Table 4.1: Literacy rate of females in India and the states in North-East

States	1991		1993		1994		1995		1996		1997	
	M	*F*	*M*	*F*	*M*	*F*	*M*	*F*	*M*	*F*	*M*	*F*
India	64	39	68	43	69	44	69	46	70	47	73	50
Assam	62	43	76	58	78	62	81	66	81	65	82	66
Arunachal Pradesh	51	30	40	28	50	35	62	44	56	45	69	48
Manipur	62	48	76	66	78	65	81	67	81	58	82	66
Meghalaya	53	45	78	68	72	61	90	76	84	76	79	74
Mizoram	86	79	94	91	92	88	92	88	87	82	96	95
Nagaland	68	55	89	77	91	77	93	83	87	79	91	77
Tripura	71	50	84	66	84	68	84	61	83	68	79	67

Notes: Data for the year 1995, 1996 and 1997 relate to National Sample Survey Organisation 51st Round (July 1994-June 1995); 52nd round (July 1995-June 1996) and 53rd round (July 1996-December 1997) respectively.

Literacy rate is defined as the population of literate in the population aged 7 years and above.

Source: *Statistical Abstract India*, 2000.

Table 4.2 shows that most of the North-Eastern states except Arunachal Pradesh have higher literacy rate among both the males and females compared to national average. Also in Meghalaya, male literacy is less than the national average of male literate. Interestingly, the female literacy of Meghalaya is considerably high. The female literacy rate in the North East seems to be quite satisfactory and in majority of the cases, it is above the national average. Among the seven states, the female literacy rate is the highest in Mizoram. If we arrange the states rankwise it will be as follows: Mizoram (1st), Nagaland (2nd), Tripura (3rd), Manipur (4th), Meghalaya (5th), Assam (6th) and Arunachal Pradesh (7th). It is significant to note that in all the states of North East, excluding Arunachal Pradesh, the female literacy rate is higher compared to National average. However still there is divergence between male and female literacy rates.

The reasons may be due to the remoteness and lack of any zeal as well as awareness to receive formal education by women. In Meghalaya and Manipur, rituals and tells however indicate that there are evidences of prominence of women in terms of domestic, social and religious functions.

Table 4.2: Male-female ratio of literate population (literacy percentage) of seven states of North East India

States	*Male*	*Female*	*Ranking among N-E states*
Arunachal Pradesh	42.26 per cent	23.03 per cent	7th
Assam	50.62 per cent	35.18 per cent	6th
Manipur	58.24 per cent	39.40 per cent	4th
Meghalaya	41.72 per cent	36.45 per cent	5th
Mizoram	70.36 per cent	64.11 per cent	1st
Nagaland	56.04 per cent	45.52 per cent	2nd
Tripura	58.23 per cent	41.01 per cent	3rd
India (National average)	46.89 per cent	24.82 per cent	

Table 4.3 shows a distribution of women in the Age-group of 15-44 years according to the level of education in 1991. This table is also a document of literacy based on rural and urban differences in the same year. Based on the level of literacy, higher education gets priority in estimating the educational status of a state along with general literacy. In terms of the female literacy rate, the ranking of the states of North East India is as follows: Mizoram (95.3%), Tripura (82.2%), Nagaland (78.8%), Assam (75.4%), Meghalaya (69.4%), Manipur (62.7%) and then, Arunachal Pradesh 60.4 per cent according to 1991 Census Report.

Now we are considering the salient features of urban level of education of those states. As usual, higher education in rural areas is much less than the level of higher education in urban areas. In case of matriculate but below graduate of female literate the ranking of states are as follows: Nagaland (25.5%), Assam (25.2%), Arunachal Pradesh (21.2%), Meghalaya (19.8%), Manipur (18.2%), Tripura (17.2%) and Mizoram (14.1%).

Again, if we consider graduate and above category among the females, the Manipur stands first with 11 per cent and followed by Tripura (10.8%), Meghalaya (10%), Assam (7.9%), Arunachal Pradesh (5.9%), Nagaland (5.1%) and Mizoram having only 3 per cent graduates and above level of education.

If we look into the general literacy rate of women, the Table 4.3 reveals that Mizoram occupies the highest rank in the states but if we consider the higher level like graduation and above Mizoram occupies the lower position than other states like Manipur, Tripura and Assam.

Table 4.3: Distribution of women in the Age-group 15-44 by educational level, 1991

State	*TRU*	*No. of women aged 14-55 years ('000s)*	*Per cent of women aged 15-44 by educational level*						
			Total	*Illiterate*	*Below middle*	*Middle but below Matric*	*Matric but below graduate*	*Graduate and above*	*Literate*
(1)	(2)	(3)	(4)	(5)	(6)	(7)	(8)	(9)	(10)
India	T	181446	100.00	59.9	16.3	10.5	10.4	2.9	
	R	131792	100.00	69.7	15.3	8.4	5.8	0.8	66.0
	U	49704	100.00	34.0	18.8	16.1	22.5	8.7	
Arunachal Pradesh	T	177	100.00	71.0	13.0	8.2	6.1	1.7	7th rank
	R	153	100.00	75.9	12.5	6.7	3.7	1.1	60.4
	U	24	100.00	39.6	15.7	17.5	21.2	5.9	
Assam	T	4882	100.00	57.0	15.1	15.4	10.8	1.7	4th rank
	R	4294	100.00	61.4	14.9	14.0	8.8	0.8	75.4
	U	588	100.00	24.6	17.2	25.1	25.2	7.9	
Meghalaya	T	383	100.00	52.9	24.5	13.7	6.4	2.5	5th rank
	R	305	100.00	61.1	25.3	10.0	3.0	6.6	69.4
	U	78	100.00	20.6	21.5	28.1	19.8	10.0	
Mizoram	T	151	100.00	17.0	44.3	28.0	9.1	1.7	1st rank
	R	77	100.00	28.9	47.2	19.4	4.1	0.4	95.3
	U	75	100.00	4.7	41.4	36.8	14.1	3.0	

(*Contd.*)

Table 4.3: (*Contd.*)

(1)	(2)	(3)	(4)	(5)	(6)	(7)	(8)	(9)	(10)
Nagaland	T	264	100.00	42.1	23.3	22.5	10.4	1.7	3rd rank
	R	220	100.00	46.3	23.9	21.4	7.3	1.0	78.8
	U	45	100.00	21.1	20.3	27.9	25.5	5.1	
Tripura	T	605	100.00	48.4	28.7	14.1	6.0	2.8	2nd rank
	R	499	100.00	54.9	28.7	11.7	3.6	1.1	82.2
	U	106	100.00	17.9	28.8	25.4	17.2	10.8	
Manipur	T	433	100.00	49.9	13.1	19.2	12.6	5.2	6th rank
	R	312	100.00	54.7	13.4	18.4	10.4	3.0	62.7
	U	120	100.00	37.3	12.2	21.3	18.2	11.0	

TRU = Total, Rural, Urban

Source: Census of India 1991, State Profile, 1991, India.

Table 4.4 deals with the drop out phenomenon of women in north-eastern states. Drop out from education occurs due to various reasons and/or multiplicity of factors. In many occasions, the cases of drop out occurs both in rural and urban institutions of learning. The saddest part of our learning is the discontinuity in the process. Indifferent attitudes of the government are by and large responsible. A few researchers very often find out the reasons of drop outs and there is a common trend that learners and the family are to blame for these drop outs. That is partly true and a lot of thinking is associated to check the rate of drop outs. Importance of education is understood by everybody but inequality of access to education has to be given serious thinking. It is not that parents are to be held always responsible. They are discouraging and they have no previous experience of education and so on. We have to ponder and think to pin-point where lies the truth. Half-fed belly, without garments, without shoe to cover the feet is not conducive for education of a child or adult. Seeing in that way, education disappears. Apart from these, many other factors—economic, environmental and slightly social implements—accountable for the discontinuity of education, which ultimately leads to drop out in different levels of education. Emphasis on universal primary education is being talked about but what more after the primary level. Is it sufficient for a country to advance? Skewedness in primary level to middle level and the curve falls down at upper level is the normal pattern of educational graph in India. How these could be changed has to be thought and worked out.

Drop out of female students has been estimated in different states of north east India and presented in Tables 4.4 and 4.5 respectively. Per 1000 drop outs at different levels have been given in Table 4.4. Hence, we give the percentagewise distribution per 1000 female learners. In Arunachal Pradesh female drop out occurs at primary level by 24.5 per cent and at Secondary level it is 75.5 per cent. In Assam, per 1000 drop outs of female at different levels of education in urban area is as follows: Drop out occurs at primary level 14.9 per cent followed by middle level 29.1 per cent and at secondary level 35.6 per cent. In Manipur, 139 female dropped out at primary level, 25 per cent dropped out at middle school level, 36.3 per cent at secondary level and 10.1 per cent at higher secondary level and 10.7 per cent discontinued at above higher secondary level are observed. 3.9 per cent drop out was not reported. In Meghalaya 50.2 per cent females in urban area had dropped out at primary level, 17.4 per cent at middle level, 7.1 per cent at secondary level and 25.3

Table 4.4: Proportion (per 1000) of female dropouts age (5-24 years) and their per 100 distribution by level at which dropped out in Urban areas

State	*Proportion of dropout (5-24 years)*	*Level at which dropout (urban area)*								
		Primary	*Middle*	*Secondary*	*Higher Secondary*	*Above Higher Secondary*	*Not reported*	*All*	*Dropouts estimated*	*Ever enrolled estimated*
(1)	(2)	(3)	(4)	(5)	(6)	(7)	(8)	(9)	(10)	(11)
India										
Arunachal Pradesh	290	245	–	755	–	–	–	1000	5	18
Assam	534	149	291	356	95	109	–	1000	348	651
Manipur	512	139	250	363	101	107	39	1000	44	86
Meghalaya	357	502	174	71	253	–	–	1000	18	52
Mizoram	751	31	294	487	187	–	–	1000	44	59
Nagaland	405	219	–	665	116	–	–	1000	21	53
Tripura	652	369	193	4-7	31	–	–	1000	119	182

Source: Attending on Educational Institution in India : Its Level, Nature and Cost, NSS 52nd round, July 1995-June 1996 NSSO, Department of Statistics, Government of India, October 1998, Page No. A-129.

per cent at higher secondary level. In Mizoram 3.1 per cent dropped out at primary level, 29.4 per cent at middle school level, 48.7 per cent at secondary level and 18.7 per cent at higher secondary level in Mizoram. Nagaland is also not an exception to drop out in school/colleges. 21.9 per cent female drop out was noticed at primary level, 66.5 per cent at secondary level and 11.6 per cent at higher secondary level in Nagaland. In Tripura, 36.9 per cent drop out rate was observed at primary level in case of female, and the rate was 19.3 per cent at middle school level. 40.7 per cent female dropped out at secondary level and only 3.1 per cent female had dropped at higher secondary level in Tripura in 1998.

Table 4.5 presents a data on drop out of female learners in North-Eastern States in their rural areas. On national front we find 36.87 per cent females have dropped out at primary level, followed by 26.38 per cent female drop out at middle school level. Again 24.54 per cent women in rural areas of India have dropped out at Secondary level. 6.11 per cent female drop out at national average occurred at higher secondary level. 1.42 per cent female drop out was noticed in Indian rural areas at above the higher secondary level. A significant part has not been reported and by percentage, it is 4.67 per cent national level.

Now, let us see the happenings in different states of North Eeast. 61.4 per cent female drop out took place at primary level in Arunachal Pradesh. 24.1 per cent drop out happened at middle school level in that state. 8.5 per cent women dropped out at secondary level followed by 2.8 per cent and 2.7 per cent female drop out occurred at Higher Secondary level and above higher secondary level respectively. A nearly 0.4 per cent was not reported whether they dropped out or not. In Assam, 27.3 per cent female drop out was recorded at primary level and 24.5 per cent female drop out held at middle school level, whereas, secondary level registered 36.6 per cent, drop out following 8.4 per cent female drop out at higher secondary level and 1.8 per cent drop out held at above higher secondary level. 1.4 per cent was not reported as dropped out or not.

Manipur had noticed 44.9 per cent women drop out at primary level, 29.5 per cent at middle level followed by 13.8 per cent drop out at secondary level and 8.9 per cent drop out for women in rural areas held at higher secondary level. Here also 2.9 per cent were not reported correctly as dropped out or continuing.

In Meghalaya, 35 per cent female drop out took place at primacy level, while 44.4 per cent had dropped at middle school level. 19.2 per cent females dropped out at secondary level, 1.5 per cent females were not reported at all.

Table 4.5: Proportion (per 1000) of female dropouts (age 5-24 years) and their per 100 distribution by level at which dropped out in Rural areas

State	*Proportion of dropout (5-24 years)*	*Level at which dropout (urban area)*								
		Primary	*Middle*	*Secondary*	*Higher Secondary*	*Above Higher Secondary*	*Not reported*	*All*	*Dropouts estimated*	*Ever enrolled estimated*
(1)	(2)	(3)	(4)	(5)	(6)	(7)	(8)	(9)	(10)	(11)
India	140211	51706	36986	34409	8566	1986	6557	140211	–	–
Arunachal Pradesh	831	614	241	85	28	27	04	1000	78	93
Assam	562	273	245	366	84	18	14	1000	4211	7493
Manipur	521	449	295	138	89	–	29	1000	216	415
Meghalaya	296	350	444	192	–	–	15	1000	112	379
Mizoram	713	129	448	378	44	–	–	1000	121	170
Nagaland	386	304	229	414	43	10	–	1000	112	291
Tripura	694	386	263	298	12	–	45	1000	974	1403

Source: Attending on Educational Institution in India : Its Level, Nature and Cost, NSSO 52nd round, July 1995-June 1996, Department of Statistics, Government of India, October 1998, Page No. A-126.

Mizoram registered 12.9 per cent female drop out at primary level, 44.8 per cent female drop out at middle school level and 37.8 per cent and 44 per cent female dropped out at secondary and higher secondary level respectively.

Nagaland also bears the phase of drop out of female literates at different levels. Data show, 30.4 per cent female already dropped out at primary level. 22.9 per cent female drop out held at middle school level and 41.4 per cent drop out female literates took place at the secondary level followed by 4.3 per cent and 1.0 per cent female drop out at higher secondary and above higher secondary level.

Finally, Tripura registered a considerable number of females drop out at primary level. The figure was 38.2 per cent. 26.3 per cent female learners at middle school level dropped out in between, 29.8 per cent female learners at secondary level of education dropped out and followed by 1.2 per cent at higher secondary. 4.5 per cent female could not be reported properly as whether dropped out or not.

So, this is the picture of drop out scenario in rural north-east among the females.

In Table 4.6 reasons for drop out has been given to understand role of different social and economic factors. States of north-east is no exception to the general low level of educational motivation among the females. All together 13 answers to the reasons of drop out of women have been found out. We have numbered them serially from 01 to 13. In Table 4.6 we find frequencies of non-enrolment occurs mostly for 'Child not interested in studies' (02), 'Parents not interested in studies' and (03) inability to cope with or failure in studies (04). These are applicable for almost all states. Percentagewise, we see, 0.7 per cent children are not interested in studies in Arunachal Pradesh, 18.6 per cent children are in Assam, 7.7 per cent children are in Manipur, 23 per cent children have similar attitude in Meghalaya, 28.8 per cent have such attitude in Mizoram and Nagaland and Tripura have 12.6 per cent and 12 per cent respectively. 17.2 per cent parents in Arunachal Pradesh are not interested in studies. 24.7 per cent in Assam expressed similar view. In 0.8 per cent cases in Manipur parents are held responsible for that. In Mizoram it is 1.4 per cent and in Tripura 16.5 per cent. Inability to cope with or failure in studies accounts for 23 per cent in Assam, 38.3 per cent in Manipur, 49.4 per cent in Meghalaya, 36.4 per cent in Mizoram and 48.2 per cent in Nagaland as well as 17.5 per cent have no ability to cope with or failure in studies in Tripura.

Table 4.6: Per 1000 distribution of drop out (age 5-24 years) of female. Try reasons for dropping out in rural areas

States	*Reasons for dropping out#*													
	01	02	03	04	05	06	07	08	09	10	11	12	13	Total
(1)	(2)	(3)	(4)	(5)	(6)	(7)	(8)	(9)	(10)	(11)	(12)	(13)	(14)	(15)
Arunachal Pradesh	04	07	172	–	–	05	–	–	129	11	493	21	157	1000
Assam	–	186	247	230	12	05	–	00	16	01	86	80	113	1000
Manipur	03	77	08	383	–	–	12	–	78	–	148	119	172	1000
Meghalaya	–	230	–	494	–	–	–	–	66	–	13	142	27	1000
Mizoram	–	288	14	364	02	–	–	–	215	–	–	48	48	1000
Nagaland	–	126	–	482	02	–	–	19	32	–	119	90	130	1000
Tripura	07	120	165	175	–	–	–	04	46	09	96	120	251	1000

\# 01 = No tradition in family.
02 = Child not interested in studies.
03 = Parents not interested in studies.
04 = Inability to cope with or failure in studies.
05 = Unfriendly atmosphere at school.
06 = Education not consider useful.
07 = Schooling/higher education facilities not convenient.
08 = Has to work for wage/salary.
09 = Has to participate in other economic activities.
10 = Has to look after younger siblings.
11 = Has to attained other domestic activities.
12 = Financial constraints.
13 = Others.

Another major reason for dropout is non-participation in other economic activities by female. The figure in Arunachal Pradesh is 12.9 per cent. For the same reason, drop out occurs among the women in Assam by 1.6 per cent, in Manipur 7.8 per cent, 6.6 per cent, in Meghalaya, 21.5 per cent in Mizoram, 3.2 per cent in Nagaland and 4.6 per cent women drop out for the said reason in Tripura.

49.3 per cent women drop out due to attendance to domestic work in Arunachal Pradesh and 8.6 per cent in Assam was observed for same reason. In Manipur it was 14.8 per cent, in Nagaland, 11.9 per cent and in Tripura 0.9 per cent women drop out for such reason in school or educational institute.

Financial constraints lead to drop out of women in almost all states. The percentages of dropped out women for such constraints are as follows: Arunachal Pradesh – 2.1 per cent, Assam – 8.0 per cent, Manipur – 11.9 per cent, Meghalaya – 14.2 per cent, Mizoram – 4.8 per cent, Nagaland – 9.0 per cent and Tripura – 12.0 per cent. In addition to that a larger number of women drop out for other reasons, in these seven states was observed. We are not going into the detail of it. As others comprise multiplicity of factors combined other than those 12 reasons.

Drop out occurs in urban areas as well. Women in urban area of north-eastern states drops out of school due to various reasons. We have similarly identified, 13 reasons of drop out of women in different states of north-east India. Almost all reasons were found valid for female drop out (Table 4.7). 16.0 per cent children in Arunachal Pradesh are not interested in studies. The figure was 27.1 per cent in Assam. Children not interested in Manipur is 9.2 per cent. In Meghalaya it is 20.0 per cent, Mizoram – 39.2 per cent and in Tripura – 27.3 per cent respectively. Parents are also not interested and such parents are – 2.2 per cent in Assam, 4.4 per cent in Manipur, 12.6 per cent in Tripura. Inability to cope with or failure in studies is another reason for which, 24.5 per cent female drop out in Arunachal Pradesh, 39.9 per cent in Assam, 2.9 per cent female drop out in Manipur, 8.5 per cent in Meghalaya, 19.8 per cent female drop out in Mizoram, 36 per cent in Nagaland and 28.2 per cent female drop out in Tripura for the same reason were observed. Another reason, which is more responsible for such drop out is that woman has to work for wage or salary. Hence, they could not afford to education and dropped out. Figures for such women statewise are – 59.5 per cent in Arunachal Pradesh, 0.2 per cent in Assam, 8.8 per cent in Manipur, 39.9 per cent in Meghalaya,

2.2 per cent in Mizoram and 2.3 per cent in Tripura, in urban area as they have to work for wage or salary. 6.1 per cent female drop out for looking after their younger children in Manipur, 0.9 per cent women drop out in Mizoram for such reason and 0.6 per cent women drop out for such reason in Tripura was recorded. Drop outs for domestic activities affects 2.2 per cent women in Assam, 6 per cent in Manipur and 10.4 per cent in Meghalaya, 1.8 per cent in Mizoram and 1.4 per cent in Tripura.

In addition to that another prime reason is financial constraints, for which many female drop out from studies. Let us see the percentages of such women statewise. In Assam it was 15.6 per cent, in Manipur – 42.4 per cent women dropped out for financial constraints, 14.5 per cent women in Mizoram and 31.8 per cent in Nagaland and 7.9 per cent women faces financial constraints in Tripura. These are major valid reasons for which female drop outs occurs in different states of north-east. As usual, for other reasons also drop out held for women. Other reasons account for dropout of 9.5 per cent in Assam, 4.2 per cent in Mizoram, 32.2 per cent in Nagaland and 26.7 per cent in Tripura. Unfortunately, 1 per cent women in Tripura had no tradition of studies in their families.

We have attempted to find out the reasons of non-enrolment which can be defined as responsible for negative response towards education. In simple terms, non-enrolment means that children has not been given in formal education and official recognition to the children from educational institution is totally absent. Non-enrolment can occur from both individual and official apathy towards the students to enroll their names for education. In India, many social factors inhibits education of the children and even adults in educational institutions, Indian Social structure has not allowed the bottom placed caste groups and their children not to receive education and discouragement is always put on them. Even in higher studies, these caste groups are looked down upon on many bases. Instances of educational organization based on power hierarchy and caste hierarchy can be found. To monopolize power and authority in the educational power and administrative structure, often becomes a centre for rivalry between caste affiliations. External political power holding, which is also a reflection of the caste. People's organizations evident in the functioning sometimes. However it should not occur from legal point of view. But despite the notion of mutuality, which very often exists only in black and white, monopolize of power and authority happens. Some kind of imposition take place in order to

Table 4.7: Per 1000 distribution of drop-out of female (age 5-24 years) by reasons for dropping out in Urban areas

States	*Reasons for dropping out #*													
	01	02	03	04	05	06	07	08	09	10	11	12	13	Total
(1)	(2)	(3)	(4)	(5)	(6)	(7)	(8)	(9)	(10)	(11)	(12)	(13)	(14)	(15)
Arunachal Pradesh	–	160	–	245	–	–	–	595	–	–	–	–	–	1000
Assam	–	271	22	399	–	–	–	2	34	–	22	156	95	1000
Manipur	–	92	44	29	92	–	–	88	93	61	60	424	–	1000
Meghalaya	–	200	–	85	–	–	–	374	87	–	104	–	–	1000
Mizoram	–	392	–	198	–	14	74	22	74	9	18	145	42	1000
Nagaland	–	–	–	360	–	–	–	–	–	–	–	318	322	1000
Tripura	10	273	126	282	–	13	03	23	20	6	14	79	267	1000

\# 01 = No tradition in family.
02 = Child not interested in studies.
03 = Parents not interested in studies.
04 = Inability to cope with or failure in studies.
05 = Unfriendly atmosphere at school.
06 = Education not consider useful.
07 = Schooling/higher education facilities not convenient.
08 = Has to work for wage/salary.
09 = Has to participate in other economic activities.
10 = Has to look after younger siblings.
11 = Has to attained other domestic activities.
12 = Financial constraints.
13 = Others.

retain supremacy. As a result, universal motive of education suffers and the social category makes its prominence in Indian situation. To keep the people under dark and observation sometimes affect educated people's mind. Hence, scientism does not flourish in the minds, which, what to use education as a tool for enlightenment. Moreover, for our purpose, we have found out 13 reasons, which encourages non-enrolment in education. The seriousness of this affects females most in rural areas. But that does not mean that non-enrolment do not take place in urban area.

Statewise variation, in the non-enrolment of females in rural areas of North East in also noticed. Plenty of reasons have been identified for non-enrolment. Frequency of non-enrolment is shown in Table 4.8. The table shows that frequency of non-enrolment enters around reasons number 02 and 03, which indicate first children not interested in studies and parents, are also not interested in studies. A larger frequencies can be observed at reason number 13 which is others comprising a variety of factors. Some interesting answers were found of reasons of non-enrolment. Some reasoned that education not considered useful by some sections of population. Most important of these is that schooling/higher education facilities are not convenient and do not provide equal access to at least, who want it. Other impediments are a learner has to work for wages first and then think over education. A larger number of females have to participate in other economic activities. Some learners have very personal-familial obstacles such as older learner has to look after younger siblings in the house. This is true for female learners particularly. In addition, another contributing factor involves is that, female has to attend other domestic activities, and after completing those she can go to attend school or colleges. In case of male, domestic activities is not an impediment as domestic works are basically undertaken by the women. Then there is the financial constraints of the family.

One can think that urban area is not so affected by non-enrolment phenomenon. But our data suggests that even in north-eastern states urban women also are victim of non-enrolment. Table 4.9 indicates that variety reasons were attributed to phenomenon of non-enrolment among the females. States of Manipur and Meghalaya have registered some women, who did not enroll due to having no tradition of female education in their family. Most of the non-enrolment occurred due to financial constraints and other factors conspiring multiple reasons. From Table 4.9 it is observed that two reasons have been prominent of

Table 4.8: Proportion (per 1000) of never enrolled female (age 5-24 years) and their per 1000 distribution by reasons for non-enrolment in Rural areas

States	*Reasons for non-enrolment #*														*Proportion of never enrolled*
	01	02	03	04	05	06	07	08	09	10	11	12	13	*Total*	
(1)	(2)	(3)	(4)	(5)	(6)	(7)	(8)	(9)	(10)	(11)	(12)	(13)	(14)	(15)	(16)
Arunachal Pradesh	2	187	131	–	–	2	16	2	47	40	37	37	519	1000	408
Assam	1	113	366	–	–	24	6	0	22	–	16	85	366	1000	259
Manipur	17	61	141	–	–	14	13	–	53	1	70	64	565	1000	176
Meghalaya	–	197	160	–	–	2	–	–	253	12	85	79	211	1000	179
Mizoram	–	44	381	–	–	–	13	–	–	–	–	–	562	1000	186
Nagaland	–	264	87	–	–	–	–	–	125	31	6	275	212	1000	125
Tripura	–	253	227	–	–	–	33	24	18	–	14	187	137	1000	210

\# 01 = No tradition in family.
02 = Child not interested in studies.
03 = Parents not interested in studies.
04 = Inability to cope with or failure in studies.
05 = Unfriendly atmosphere at school.
06 = Education not consider useful.
07 = Schooling/higher education facilities not convenient.
08 = Has to work for wage/salary.
09 = Has to participate in other economic activities.
10 = Has to look after younger siblings.
11 = Has to attained other domestic activities.
12 = Financial constraints.
13 = Others.

Table 4.9: Proportion (per 1000) of never enrolled female (age 5-24 years) and their per 1000 distribution by reasons for non-enrolment in Urban areas

States	*Reasons for non-enrolment #*														*Proportion of*
	01	02	03	04	05	06	07	08	09	10	11	12	13	*Total*	*never enrolled*
(1)	(2)	(3)	(4)	(5)	(6)	(7)	(8)	(9)	(10)	(11)	(12)	(13)	(14)	(15)	(16)
Arunachal Pradesh	–	183	55	–	–	–	–	–	32	–	–	–	731	1000	118
Assam	–	314	124	–	–	11	–	29	–	–	33	164	326	1000	157
Manipur	14	147	102	–	–	–	–	–	24	–	176	170	368	1000	123
Meghalaya	154	–	120	–	–	–	–	–	204	–	–	132	391	1000	24
Mizoram	–	–	31	–	–	–	–	–	–	–	–	–	969	1000	154
Nagaland	–	14	–	–	–	–	–	12	28	–	12	264	670	1000	98
Tripura	–	107	189	–	–	–	–	24	47	–	–	32	602	1000	–

# 01 = No tradition in family.
02 = Child not interested in studies.
03 = Parents not interested in studies.
04 = Inability to cope with or failure in studies.
05 = Unfriendly atmosphere at school.
06 = Education not consider useful.
07 = Schooling/higher education facilities not convenient.
08 = Has to work for wage/salary.
09 = Has to participate in other economic activities.
10 = Has to look after younger siblings.
11 = Has to attained other domestic activities.
12 = Financial constraints.
13 = Others.

non-enrolment in many states in north east India. First, is children not interested in studies and secondly, parents are not interested in studies. It may be an additional burden on the family income and budget. Moreover female has to participate in other economic activities. As in rural area, urban women also have to do domestic activities, which encourages non-enrolment. Very few consider education not useful as observed in Assam. In Assam, Nagaland and Tripura, 2.9 per cent, 1.2 per cent and 2.4 per cent of women respectively had to work for wages and hence they could not enrol themselves. In Assam, 3.3 per cent, in Manipur 17.6 per cent and in Nagaland 1.2 per cent have to do domestic chores; hence they have not enrolled themselves in schools. It may be noticed from Table 4.9 that 16.4 per cent urban female in Assam, 17.0 per cent in Manipur and 13.2 per cent in Meghalaya, 26.4 per cent urban female in Nagaland and 3.2 per cent in Tripura have not enrolled themselves in school due to financial constraints or such.

Conclusion

Characteristically, North East are physically and morphologically different places for outsiders. We have found some common problems of women's education, for which, drop out occurs at primary and secondary levels. Other problems of women education may be the economic engagement of women in north east India for their sustenance of the family and livelihood. As women in that area take many responsibilities in the household maintenance and tackle socio-economic problems, they are more likely to enjoy superior status than their male folks. But too much importance on economic activities, educational achievement and improvement does not take place as expected. That is why, lag in literacy of the women in north east is occasionally observed. But the most crucial impediments to women education are the management of entire domestic chores by them. Also the physical feature of the hilly terrain sets the education on the backseat. It hinders their educational development and consequent social development as well. We don't suggest that they will not do the task, which the long drawn habit has bestowed upon them. On the contrary, male to some extent may share the heavier domestic task and if possible, machine-driven domestic appliances may be used to reduce the drudgery of the work. So no one would argue that traditional habit of women's work pattern is the major constraints to women's development.

Some recommendations may be formulated here to solve the problems associated with the education of women in North-East. Some of them are common characteristics of the recent disparities of educational achievement on the basis of gender. We can arrange them accordingly.

1. Access to education and quality of learning is important. The education of children, particularity the girl child, has to be viewed within the larger context of development. In addition to the socio-economic and cultural factors the education of girls is in a very real sense linked to the availability of water, fuel, fodder and child care facilities to individual families. There is a crucial link between the easy access to water, fuel and fodder and schooling of girls. This understanding needs to be explicitly reflected in the policy of government and be concretized in operational designs.
2. Local area planning with regard to education may be taken into consideration and it must take into account the above linkage while planning for programmes relating to forestry, drinking water and greening of common lands.
3. *The availability of Schooling* – The availability of schooling facilities within easy reach is crucial for access to and retention of girls in school. About one-fifth of the country's rural populations do not have primary schools. These includes habitations having population of more than 300 persons and almost 95 per cent of the rural population are served by primary schools either within or up to walking distance of 1 km. But it should not be a matter of complacency as far as girls' education is concerned. That is why, it is necessary to recognise that the socio-cultural constraints may make even 1 km. beyond walking distance for them.
4. *Early childhood care and education*—It is crucial for an easy access to organised and holistic early child care, if families, especially among the underprivileged, are expected to relieve girl children of this responsibility and spare them for schooling. Without providing full-fledged day care services, particularly for baby, no school programme can hope to become accessible to older girls in the 6-14 age groups.

5. While the Integrated Child Development Scheme (ICDS), *e.g.* Anganwadi etc. should continue to be given importance; other models, which are sensitive to local needs, should also be encouraged. In order that child care facilities and pre-school and primary education of girls are prioritised in the village and the community Anganwadi management should be decentralized and their workers and poor women's groups should be represented in the village and education committees.

5

Educational Planning in the 21st Century North East India

T.B. LAHIRI

Profile of Present National Scenario

School Education

India's Total Literacy Campaign (TLC) aims at complete eradication of illiteracy by 2005.

Achievements had been substantial. The gross enrolment ratio in the Primary stage (Class I to V) has increased from 42.61 per cent in 1950-51 to 90.5 per cent in 1996-97. At the Upper Primary stage (Class VI-VIII) enrolment growth was from 12.7 per cent to 62.3 per cent over the same period. This progress contributed to the rise in literacy rate in the country from 18.3 per cent in 1951 to 65.49 per cent in 2001.

Efforts towards universalisation of elementary education have given India the 2nd position in the world in absolute sense with 151.5 million children in the age group of 6-14 years enrolled in 1996-97. Thus about 81 per cent of the children in this age group had been covered.

On the whole, school education has registered substantial progress at all levels, *viz.* Primary (I to V), Upper Primary (VI-VIII), Secondary (IX-X) and Higher Secondary (XI-XII).

Higher Education

Higher education is dominated by undergraduate courses, which

Table 5.1: Percentage of Girls enrolled at various school levels in North-East India

State	Area	I – V		VI – VIII		IX – X		XI – XII	
		All	*ST*	*All*	*ST*	*All*	*ST*	*All*	*ST*
India	R	41.96	40.96	36.43	34.04	32.23	29.88	29.76	26.29
	T	43.16	41.45	39.62	35.77	36.47	32.10	35.93	27.62
1. Assam	R	45.28	47.00	44.45	44.47	44.59	44.40	37.00	35.62
	T	45.46	47.03	49.81	44.55	44.99	44.26	36.97	37.33
	(R+U)								
2. Manipur	R	46.46	45.44	45.47	44.34	45.47	42.47	35.29	42.13
	T	46.91	45.55	46.49	44.79	46.66	44.34	35.88	40.43
3. Meghalaya	R	49.97	50.28	47.91	48.84	45.59	46.72	29.82	40.00
	T	50.14	50.46	48.56	49.62	46.88	48.38	41.87	55.80
4. Mizoram	R	46.53	46.58	47.13	47.25	47.48	47.48	00.00	00.00
	T	47.36	47.39	48.30	48.39	49.97	50.05	00.00	00.00
5. Nagaland	R	48.00	48.07	48.45	48.50	44.39	44.30	00.00	00.00
	T	47.90	48.02	49.11	49.24	46.26	46.24	38.33	38.33
6. Tripura	R	45.53	43.33	43.58	40.39	40.91	36.61	30.75	21.59
	T	45.75	43.45	44.63	40.90	43.06	37.31	36.19	26.06
7. Arunachal Pradesh	R	43.10	44.01	39.32	39.53	34.22	34.31	24.57	22.46
	T	43.28	44.26	40.53	40.90	37.13	36.50	30.25	26.21

Class I – V: Primary — All States above
Class VI – VIII: Upper Primary — National average
Class IX – X: Secondary
Class XI – XII: Higher Secondary

Source: 6th All India Educational Survey, N.C.E.R.T., July 1998.

Ref. Data: September 1993, Jointly conducted by N.C.E.R.T. and National Information Centre, Planning Commission.

account for 88 per cent of enrolment followed by post-graduate courses with 9.5 per cent and research activities covers only 1.10 per cent.

Unlike school education, decennial growth rate of higher education is declining in the country. Decadal growth rate, which was 12.4 per cent from 1950 to 1960 came down to 4.7 per cent during the period from 1981 to 1989. This trend is continuing.

Re-orientation of higher educational courses is being seriously considered, in view of changing nature of job market. Employment scope for candidates with humanities, social sciences and other arts qualifications is dwindling. On the other hand, demand for those having technological, scientific, managerial and entrepreneurship skills are growing. Such skills development is costly. In general, per student recurring cost for Science and Technological education is much higher than arts and social sciences.

The present policy of the government is to encourage self-financing of higher educational institutions. This implies reversal of the current funding pattern. Now institutions heavily depend upon the government funding, which covered 57 per cent of the expenses in 1950-51 and rose to 88 per cent in 1990-91. Share of fees collection in total revenue of the institutions has sharply fallen from 20 per cent to 4 per cent during the same period. So, constraints for imparting necessary courses in higher educational institutions are quite explicit.

Literacy Performance in N.E. States of India

Literacy percentage in all north-eastern states barring Arunachal Pradesh, Meghalaya and Assam was higher than national average of 52.20 in 1991 and also higher than the national average of 65.49 per cent in 2001.

Though in all the north-eastern states literacy rate has increased during 1991 to 2001, but except Tripura, which has improved its literacy rank in 2001, and Mizoram, which could retain 2nd position both in 1991 and 2001, rest of the north-eastern states have slided down in the ranking of all states of India. Sharp fall is recorded in Nagaland from 13th position to 21st position.

Two factors seem to be responsible for downward creep in ranking in terms of literacy rate:

1. Heavy population growth rate (64.41 per cent in Nagaland during 1991 to 2001 — highest in the country). Only Tripura

and Assam showed a lower growth rate of population than national average of 21.34 per cent.

2. Tremendous upsurge in literacy in Maharashtra, Gujarat, Himachal Pradesh, Tamil Nadu, Uttaranchal, Punjab and Sikkim have pulled down the literacy rank of north-eastern states.

So, strategy for educational development in north-eastern states in the 21st country, would be first to regain literacy status as was prevalent during 1981-91 and to move up the ladder.

Status of School Education in North-Eastern States of India

General Scenario

Generally level of literacy, percentage of enrolment in 4 stages of school education in north-eastern states is higher than national averages. Meghalaya shines in the area, though in the rural areas of Maghalaya unlike other states (when tribal and non-tribal students are combined), percentage of enrolment in Class XI-XII is much lower, but if only tribal students are considered, percentage of enrolment is observed to be high. It shows relative reluctance of other non-tribal communities for education in rural areas of Meghalaya.

Problem of Drop-outs

If enrolment in Class I is taken as 100, at Class X it slides down to only 1/5th on an average in north-eastern states. Meghalaya in particular shows a grim picture in this respect. However, Manipur is the solitary exception with more than 1/3rd enrolled students continuing up to Class X in tune with national average.

Role of Schools under Different Managements

It is interesting to note, how the tribal students are being educated at schools under different managements. Role of government schools is better than the national average, but contribution of Local Bodies and private aided schools are far from national average. Only the share of Private Non-Aided Schools in the north east India is higher than the national average (generally missionary schools).

Table 5.2: Percentage of Enrolment of Classes 1-X
Vis-à-vis enrolment in Class I (R+U) in North-Eastern States

Sl. No.	*State*	*Sex*	*I*	*V*	*X*
1.	Arunachal	Boys	100	41.48	18.30
		Girls	100	40.34	13.29
2.	Assam	Boys	100	36.76	17.67
		Girls	100	34.48	16.91
3.	Manipur	Boys	100	56.50	36.32
		Girls	100	55.10	34.72
4.	Meghalaya	Boys	100	34.33	12.72
		Girls	100	33.91	11.03
5.	Mizoram	Boys	100	45.24	15.98
		Girls	100	44.22	16.81
6.	Nagaland	Boys	100	45.71	20.08
		Girls	100	48.32	19.47
7.	Tripura	Boys	100	45.49	20.41
		Girls	100	44.16	17.64
	All India	Boys	100	56.76	28.50
		Girls	100	51.90	20.57

Teachers' Residential Pattern, Their Training and Capacity Utilisation

If the teachers live in the town or village, where the school is located, that helps improving education in better ways. From the residential pattern of the teachers for 4 levels of school education, it is seen:

Arunachal Pradesh has provided accommodation for most of the teachers.

Accommodation provided to the teachers in rest of the states is low.

No teacher is staying outside village/town in Nagaland and only a few in Mizoram. Largest number of teachers in Assam stay outside the area of institution.

Condition of the rest of the states are in between Arunachal Pradesh and Assam.

In all the states of north-eastern India, percentage of trained teachers fall far short of national average of above 80 per cent. Only in Mizoram and Tripura percentage of trained teachers is high. Position is same in respect of both male and female teachers of the north-eastern states.

Table 5.3: Scheduled Tribes: State-wise Enrolment in Classes I-V under Different Managements in North East India

Sl. No.	State	Total	Govt.	Local Body	Pvt. Aided	Pvt. Un-aided	Per cent of Pvt. Un-aided to Total Enrolment
1.	Arunachal	90,668	86,690	126	3038	814	0.89
2.	Assam	5,62,283	4,96,533	56,898	5,332	3,520	0.62
3.	Manipur	1,07,286	50,392	0	10,685	46,209	43.07
4.	Meghalaya	2,59,084	16,993	1,30,061	91,289	20,741	8.00
5.	Mizoram	1,13,112	93,934	769	12,581	5,818	5.14
6.	Nagaland	1,32,299	82,440	5,046	24,101	20,694	15.64
7.	Tripura	1,33,524	61,396	70,827	977	324	0.24
	Total	**13,98,256**	**8,88,378**	**2,63,745**	**1,48,013**	**98,120**	
	All India	**88,09,631**	**46,79,424**	**33,29,810**	**6,16,938**	**2,83,459**	

Source: 6th All India Education Survey, Vol. IV.

It is indeed surprising that in the north-eastern states, capacity utilisation of teachers is low. A large number of teachers with science and mathematics qualifications are not teaching these subjects. Assam has the largest number of such under-utilised teachers.

Use of Mother Tongue as Medium of Instruction at Primary and Upper Primary Stages

In Arunachal Pradesh, mother tongue is hardly used as medium of instruction in schools.

However in Assam, Manipur, Mizoram and Tripura mother tongue is the principal medium of instruction.

Meghalaya registers a sharp change in the use of mother tongue as medium of instruction from Primary to Upper Primary stages. Nagaland follows Meghalaya, but here shift is not so significant.

However national average figure shows the predominance of mother tongue as medium of instruction.

School Infrastructure

Quality of teaching and learning is also related to school infrastructure, which is very poor in north-eastern states.

Table 5.4: State-wise Teachers staying pattern *vis-à-vis* school location in North-East India

Sl. No.	State	Primary School			Upper Primary School			Secondary School			Higher Secondary School		
		WNT	*Staying outside*	*Accommodation Provided*	*WNT*	*Staying outside*	*Accommodation Provided*	*WNT*	*Staying outside*	*Accommodation Provided*	*WNT*	*Staying outside*	*Accommodation Provided*
1.	Arunachal	2505	189	1750	1929	107	1350	1138	18	958	1444	12	1304
2.	Manipur	10781	2434	116	7175	1932	303	8241	2238	369	1236	342	150
3.	Meghalaya	8625*	1849	211	3942*	997	240	4825	885	547	236	18	67
4.	Mizoram	3459	71	15	4118	150	43	1998	56	25	N.A.	0	0
5.	Nagaland	5821	0	409	3735	0	547	2974	0	466	112	0	10
6.	Tripura	8817	3554	1135	5340	2159	687	7455	3049	713	6077	1531	592
7.	Assam	69297	26757†	426	47745	17316†	671	32746	11133†	302	17660	5008†	277

* More persons working than number of sanctioned posts (8156).
† Assam Staying outside in bulk.
WNT = Actual No. of Working teachers.

Source: 6th All India Education Survey, Vol. III.

Table 5.5: Schools with Mother Tongue as the medium of Instruction at Primary and Upper Primary Stages

Sl. No.	*States*	*Per cent at Primary Stage*	*Per cent at Upper Primary Stage*
1.	Arunachal	2.67	2.89
2.	Assam	99.53	98.42
3.	Manipur	65.40	63.94
4.	Meghalaya	90.01	42.03
5.	Mizoram	97.91	95.60
6.	Nagaland	53.68	43.01
7.	Tripura	80.40	79.31
	All India	**91.65**	**88.64**

Source: 6th All India Education Survey, Vol. II.

Table 5.6: Schools and their type of Building in North-Eastern States of India

Sl. No.	*State*	*Pucca*	*Partly Pucca*	*Kaccha*	*Thatched Huts*	*Tents*	*Open Space*	*Total*
1.	Arunachal	524	347	427	263	0	2	1563
2.	Assam	5628	15220	11592	5800	373	729	39342
3.	Manipur	435	1209	1886	686	10	14	4240
4.	Meghalaya	1273	2208	1089	761	4	2	5337
5.	Mizoram	74	893	752	85	0	0	1804
6.	Nagaland	227	686	797	87	0	1	1798
7.	Tripura	580	422	1616	294	3	37	2952
	All India	**547608 (66.57 per cent of all Schools)**	**158226**	**68438**	**20744**	**2352**	**25118**	**822486**

Notes: 1. Hardly 15.32 per cent of School Buildings are pucca.
2. In general 2-3 rooms are available for instructional purpose at Primary Stage.

Source: 6th All India Education Survey, Vol II.

Against national average of 66.57 per cent, north-eastern states in aggregate, has only 15.32 per cent *pucca* school buildings. In Assam, *kutcha* and thatched huts are mostly used as school buildings. At primary stage, hardly 2-3 rooms are available for teaching in all the north east Indian states.

Table 5.7: Schools having basic utilities and its percentages in North East India

States	*Per cent having Drinking water*	*Per cent having Urinals*	*Per cent having Separate Urinals for Girls*	*Per cent having Lavatory*	*Per cent having Separate Lavatory for Girls*
Arunachal	46.96	22.20	9.34	14.91	6.46
Assam	28.60	21.93	9.20	5.38	2.05
Manipur	24.03	29.98	13.92	19.98	9.43
Meghalaya	16.23	19.02	8.47	7.91	3.92
Mizoram	39.80	82.15	28.60	45.18	11.03
Nagaland	22.69	35.26	23.64	14.35	10.40
Tripura	29.95	24.76	9.01	11.21	3.90
All India	**52.59**	**31.52**	**19.48**	**20.35**	**12.01**

Source: 6th All India Educational Survey, Vol. II.

Table 5.8: Underutilisation of Secondary and Higher Secondary Stage Teachers in North-Eastern States

		Total No. of Teachers with Science Qualifications bu not teaching Science		*Total No. of Teachers with Mathematics Qualifications but not teaching Mathematics*	
Sl. No	*States*	*Total*	*Female*	*Total*	*Female*
1.	Arunachal	6,480	1,470	6,699	1,486
2.	Assam	1,55,511	38,949	1,56,725	39,531
3.	Manipur	25,803	8,537	26,140	8,791
4.	Meghalaya	16,760	7,602	16,840	7,678
5.	Mizoram	9,071	2,934	9,108	2,962
6.	Nagaland	12,113	3,930	12,150	3,960
7.	Tripura	25,311	6,746	25,531	6,968

Source: 6th All India Educational Survey, Vol. VII.

Table 5.9: Estimated Number of Trained Teachers: Primary + Upper Primary + Secondary + Higher Secondary Teachers Combined in North-Eastern States

Sl. No.	*States*	*Total No. of Teachers*		*Total No. of Trained Teachers*		*Per cent of Trained Teachers*	
		Total	*Female*	*Total*	*Female*	*Total*	*Female*
1.	Arunachal	7012	1507	3196	514	45.57	34.10
2.	Assam	168086	41101	72743	17122	43.27	41.65
3.	Manipur	27429	9018	11603	2884	42.30	31.98
4.	Meghalaya	17626	7787	7424	3415	42.11	43.85
5.	Mizoram	9574	3012	7215	2378	75.36	78.95
6.	Nagaland	12642	4013	4154	1014	32.95	25.26
7.	Tripura	27688	7193	15825	3874	57.15	53.85
	All India	**4197521**	**1411234**	**3640294**	**1238193**	**86.72**	**87.73**

Source: 6th All India Educational Survey, Vol. VII.

Table 5.10: Source of Income of all Educational Institutions in India

(Percentage)

Year	*Govt. Fund (Centre & States)*	*Local Funds*	*University*	*Fees*	*Others*	*Total*
1950-51	57.06	10.93	—	20.39	11.60	100
1980-81	81.70	4.71	1.37	8.20	4.03	100
1990-91	87.87	6.22	0.01	3.53	2.37	100

Source: Ministry HRD published in Economic Survey, 1997-98, Economic Division, Ministry of Finance, Government of India.

Table 5.11: Decennial Growth Rate of Enrolment in Higher Education (Degree + University) in India

	Growth Rate (per cent)
1950-51 to 1960-61	12.4
1960-61 to 1970-71	13.4
1970-71 to 1980-81	3.5
1980-81 to 1988-89	4.7

Note: Since 1980s, the need to shift emphasis from 'degree' oriented education to capability oriented education was recognised in view of mounting unemployment. Required inputs of the market for scientific and technological capabilities re-oriented educational policy.

Share of affiliated colleges in higher education enrolmentwise, is around 83 per cent.

Source: *Higher Education in India* (Ed.) Moonis Raza, Association of Indian Universities, 1991.

In respect of other important amenities, like percentage of schools having facilities of drinking water, urinals, separate urinals for girls, lavatory etc., all the north-eastern states fall far short of national standards. Only Mizoram is a shining example in north east India, having by and large such basic amenities and, Arunachal Pradesh is outstanding in respect of only drinking water facility.

Table 5.12: Ranking of North-Eastern States in terms of Literacy Rate and Population Growth Rate (1991-2001)

State	*Rank in Literacy*		*Per cent Decadal Growth of Population*
	2001	1991	1991-2001
Mizoram	2 (88.49)	2 (82.27)	29.18
Tripura	12 (73.66)	15 (60.44)	15.74 (in 81-91 it was 34.30)
Manipur	19 (68.87)	16 (59.89)	30.02
Nagaland	21 (67.11)	13 (61.65)	64.41
Assam	24 (64.28)	23 (52.89)	18.85
Meghalaya	27 (63.31)	24 (49.10)	29.94
Arunachal Pradesh	32 (54.74)	30 (41.59)	26.21
India	**(65.49)**	**(52.20)**	**21.34**

Notes: Figures in brackets indicate literacy percentages. Maharashtra, Himachal Pradesh, Tamil Nadu, Uttaranchal, Gujarat, Punjab, Sikkim, showed very high improvement 2001.

Source: Census of India, 2001.

Strategy of Development

Following above narrations and analyses, broad consensus may emerge about the realistic strategy for meaningful educational development in north-eastern states:

- To maintain and improve literacy rankings of north-eastern states in the country.
- The scope of higher technical and scientific education is slipping out of the hands of ordinary students due to sharp rising costs. So improvement and diversification of school education should get top priority, which after Higher Secondary may give self-sustaining ability to common students.
- The problem of using mother tongue *vis-à-vis* alien languages as medium of instruction is to be resolved.
- Drop outs in schools to be arrested .

- Education should have a vision and students should be capable of understanding other people with different languages and customs and should not hurt each other in ignorance — a worst form of blindness (Tagore).

Principal Languages of North-Eastern States and Problem of using Mother Tongue as Medium of Instruction

1.	Arunachal	Monpa, Miji, Aka, Tajin, Apatani etc. a total of 13 Languages
2.	Assam	Assamese
3.	Manipur	Manipuri
4.	Meghalaya	Khasi, Garo, Jaintia and English, 4 Languages
5.	Mizoram	Mizo and English
6.	Nagaland	Ao, Konayak, Chang, Sangtam, Angami, Sema, Lotha, total of 7 Languages
7.	Tripura	Bengali, Kakborak, Manipuri

Source: India 1990, Publication Division, Government of India.

REFERENCES

Aizazuddin Ahmed (1999), *Social Geography,* Rawat Publications, Jaipur & New Delhi.

Census of India (2001), Provisional Population Totals.

Moonis Raza (Ed.) (1991), *Higher Education in India : Retrospect and Prospect,* Association of Indian Universities, New Delhi.

Ministry of Finance Economic Division Government in India (1997-98), *Economic Survey..*

Mridula (1987), *Educational Statistics at a Glance*, Association of Indian Universities, New Delhi.

NCERT (National Council of Educational Research and Training) (1998), *Sixth All India Educational Survey,* New Delhi, (Vol. II) *Schools and Physical Facilities.*

NCERT (1998), *Sixth All India Educational Survey,* New Delhi, (Vol. III) *Teachers in Schools.*

NCERT (1998), *Sixth All India Educational Survey,* New Delhi, (Vol. IV) *Enrolment in Schools.*

NCERT (1998), *Sixth All India Educational Survey,* New Delhi, (Vol. VII) *Qualifications and Service Conditions of Teachers.*

Visva Bharti and Its Institutions (1961), Visva Bharti Santiniketan.

6

Universal Education is Still a Far Cry in North-Eastern States of India

SUBHENDU CHAKRABARTI & JADAB CHANDRA BHATTACHARYA

Introduction

The fundamental difference between a learned and an illiterate person lies in their attitude towards life and work. The former always takes a very positive, self-esteemed and self-confident approach towards his action, whereas self-esteem, confidence or, self-reliance are the rare characters in case of an illiterate one. Education plays the key role behind these differences of attitudes. Education not only increases knowledge, skill and a positive work attitude, but it also helps to develop a rationale of higher social value among the people. The prevalence of higher order social value system is a pre-condition for a course of rapid development.

Human resource is the most important among all resources because human brain has unbounded productive capacity. Education is a scientific process of developing one's brain in order to generate its productive capacity. Educational actually widens one's spectrum of outlook and helps to develop self-esteem and also the capacity to arrive at an unambiguous judgment. Skill, efficiency and productivity are the natural outcome of education. For the development of a country, an army of skilled, efficient and productive labour force is required and this can only be made available through the process of mass education.

Thus, the basic and intrinsic arguments in favour of universal education are:

(a) education can empower one who has so far been denied access to resources, politically and economically; and

(b) in order to exploit the economic opportunities as well as for sustainable development, an efficient workforce is required and this will only be possible through the introduction of universal basic education.

The importance of education is well recognised by our planners and policy makers. Giving education the status of the priority sector, the Government of India has introduced the Constitution (Ninety Third) Amendment Bill, 2001 in the Parliament to make free and compulsory elementary education for children of the age group of 6-14 years a fundamental right. Planners and policy-makers rightly understood that education is the only way to survive in a globalized market economy. Free and compulsory education for the children of the age 6-14 years and the country-wide adult literacy programmes are the stepping stones to build up efficient workforce to exploit the economic opportunities. Education thus becomes a national priority.

In spite of national priority the elements of impotency that are crept in teaching of elementary schools has been identified by various research studies. The results of the studies [NCERT (1994), Bashir (1994), Sharma (1997)] presented a dismal picture in teaching children, basic reading, writing and numerical skills. All the studies clearly revealed the fact that even after completing four years of elementary school, an alarming percentage of children, by and large in all the states in India, cannot be called literate in real sense. So the task of proper implementation the educational mission and the challenge of imparting real education to children both are our national future course of action.

North-Eastern states are unique in geographical as well as socio-economic characteristics and until recently, the entire North-Eastern region had been out of the main stream development policies of India. In spite of being marginalized, the North-Eastern states with their limited resources have also been continuously revealing their development potentials. This was made possible only by their constant efforts to educate the people. Spread of education, among the people of North-Eastern states, specially among the tribal groups, entirely transformed the socio-cultural as well as economic structure of these states.

In this paper we try to assess the educational status of the North-Eastern states in the beginning of the 21st century. Keeping in mind the task of imparting real education under the present globalized market economy, we also try to focus on some of the emerging challenges.

National Educational Policy in the 21st Century

Now-a-days education is recognised as a central component of 'human capital'. Economists also agreed on the point that the social rates of return on investment in all levels of education much exceeds the long run opportunity cost of capital.

The impact of education on population control, life expectancy, infant mortality etc. as well as its role as a contributor to economic growth is well recognised. Our national planners and policy-makers also realised the dire importance of education in every step of development. Both the Central and the State governments have given special drive to eradicate illiteracy from the country as well as to educate the mass through launching Nationwise Literacy Campaign. Several schemes, like Operation Blackboard (OB), District Primary Education Programme (DPEP), Shiksha Karmi Project, Mid-day Meals etc., have also been launched by the Central government to meet the needs of the educationally disadvantaged and for strengthening the social infrastructure for education. However, in spite of all the efforts, universal primary education is still a far cry even after more than five decades of planned development in India.

For achieving the goal of "Education for All", Ninety-third Amendment of the Constitution was passed in the Lok Sabha on November 28, 2001 to make the right to free and compulsory education for children of age group 6-14 years, a Fundamental Right and also, to make it a Fundamental Duty of the parents/guardians to provide opportunities for education to children in the same age group.

In 2001-02 the Central government in partnership with the State governments has taken a significant step towards achieving the goals of education through launching a time bound integrated approach 'Sarva Shiksha Abhiyan' (SSA). The SSA plan is a decentralised one, where the highest priority accorded to community ownership and monitoring. The goals of SSA are:

(i) All children of age 6-14 in Schools/Education Guarantee Centres/bridge course by 2003,
(ii) All children of age 6-14 to complete to five years primary education by 2007.
(iii) All children of age 6-14 to complete eight years of schooling by 2010,
(iv) Focus on elementary education of satisfactory quality with emphasis on education for life,

(v) Bridge all gender and social category gaps at primary stage by 2007 and at elementary education level by 2010, and
(vi) Universal retention by 2010.

This SSA programme will subsume all existing programmes in due course within its overall framework, with district as the unit of programme implication. However, our experiences during Total Literacy Campaign were not always very happy. The success of the SSA heavily depends on the sincere initiative and monitoring by both the Centre and State governments. But that will go against the new economic policies of the government.

We have discussed above in brief, about our national policies and schemes of education and before going to discuss in details the danger and the challenge ahead of education in the 21st century, it would be worth examining the status of education in the North-Eastern states *vis-à-vis* India.

Educational Status of North-Eastern States

North-Eastern states situated in a geographically handicapped region are inhabited by numerous communities having diverse languages and culture. Even then, these states are relatively advanced in education compared to many other states in India. Except for Arunachal Pradesh, Assam and Meghalaya, all other states of the North-Eastern region have been enjoying the benefit of greater literacy than in All India, since the last four decades (Table 6.1). Among the North-Eastern states the highest rate of literacy is in Mizoram, which is eventually be the second highest in India according to 2001 Census Report.

To get an in-depth picture of literacy it would be worthwhile to see the district level literacy rates. Table 6.1(a) shows the number of districts according to literacy percentages in each of the North-Eastern states. It is clear from the Table that there is not a single district in any of the North-Eastern state having 90-100 per cent literacy rate (there are only 9 districts in India in 1991 where 90-100 per cent were literate). Mizoram having the second highest literacy rate in India, has only one district having 80-90 per cent literacy rate. In terms of literacy, Arunachal Pradesh depicts a very dismal picture, where, out of 11 districts in 1991 not a single district attains the distinction of more than 50 per cent literacy rate. This is mainly due to very poor female literacy rate.

When we compare the North-Eastern states with all other states in India, in terms of literacy rates over various censuses (Table 6.2), we would find that the position of North-Eastern states varies from 2nd (Mizoram) to 24th (Arunachal Pradesh) with respect to total population. In the last 40 yeas the literacy status of North-Eastern states underwent significant changes. Previously the rank varied between 9th and 20th. Of them Assam moved from 10th to 17th position and Manipur from 6th to 13th position (a dismal performance). The performance of Tripura and Nagaland are better than any other states in North East region (Tripura went up from 15th to 7th position and Nagaland went up from 20th to 15th).

Table 6.1: Literacy rates in the North-Eastern States by Sex and Overall over Various Censuses

Category	*Year*	*Arunachal Pradesh*	*Assam*	*Manipur*	*Meghalaya*	*Mizoram*	*Nagaland*	*Tripura*	*All India*
(1)	(2)	(3)	(4)	(5)	(6)	(7)	(8)	(9)	(10)
Total Population	1971	11.3	28.7	32.9	29.5	–	27.4	31.0	29.5
	1981	20.8	–	41.4	34.1	59.9	42.6	42.1	36.2*
	1991	41.59	52.89	59.89	49.10	82.27	61.65	60.44	52.21
	2001	54.74	64.28	68.87	63.31	88.49	67.11	73.66	65.38
Male Population	1971	17.8	37.2	46.0	34.1	–	35.0	40.2	39.5
	1981	28.9	–	53.3	37.9	64.5	50.1	51.7	46.9*
	1991	51.45	61.87	71.63	53.12	85.61	67.62	70.58	64.13
	2001	64.07	71.93	77.87	66.14	90.69	71.77	81.47	75.85
Female Population	1971	0.37	19.3	19.5	24.6	–	18.7	21.2	18.7
	1981	11.3	–	29.1	30.1	54.9	33.9	32.0	24.8*
	1991	29.69	43.03	47.60	44.85	78.60	54.75	49.65	39.29
	2001	44.24	56.03	59.70	60.41	86.13	61.92	65.41	54.16

Note: * Excludes Assam and the population of those areas which are illegal occupation of Pakistan and China where census could not be taken.

Source: Statistical Abstract (various issues), Government of India.

Table 6.3 presents the distribution of persons of age 15 years and above by levels of education. It is apparent from the data that the percentage of persons decreases monotonically as one goes from lower to higher levels of education. This is however expected but one interesting point to note here is that at below primary and primary levels of formal schooling, the rural sector has significantly higher percentage of persons than that of urban sector, in all the North-Eastern states.

Table 6.1(a): No. of Districts According to Literacy Percentages—Total Population, Male Population and Female Population

Category	*Literacy slabs in percentage*	*States*							
		Arunachal Pradesh	*Assam*	*Manipur*	*Meghalaya*	*Mizoram*	*Nagaland*	*Tripura*	*All India*
Total Population	0-10	–	–	–	–	–	–	–	–
	10-20	–	–	–	–	–	–	–	1
	20-30	2	–	–	–	–	–	–	26
	30-40	2	1	–	2	–	1	–	88
	40-50	7	8	2	1	–	1	–	121
	50-60	–	11	4	1	1	–	1	91
	60-70	–	3	1	1	–	3	2	76
	70-80	–	–	1	–	1	2	–	28
	80-90	–	–	–	–	1	–	–	12
	90-100	–	–	–	–	–	–	–	9
	Total	11	23	8	5	3	7	3	452
Male Population	0-10	–	–	–	–	–	–	–	–
	10-20	–	–	–	–	–	–	–	–
	20-30	–	–	–	–	–	–	–	1
	30-40	1	–	–	1	–	–	–	19
	40-50	3	2	–	1	–	1	–	59
	50-60	7	8	3	2	–	1	–	114
	60-70	–	10	3	1	1	–	2	116
	70-80	–	3	1	–	–	3	1	90
	80-90	–	–	1	–	1	2	–	38
	90-100	–	–	–	–	1	–	–	15
	Total	11	23	8	5	3	7	3	452

Table 6.1(a) (*Contd.*)

Category	*Literacy slabs in percentage*	*States*							
		Arunachal Pradesh	*Assam*	*Manipur*	*Meghalaya*	*Mizoram*	*Nagaland*	*Tripura*	*All India*
Female Population	0–10	–	–	–	–	–	–	–	2
	10–20	3	–	–	–	–	–	–	71
	20–30	2	1	–	–	–	1	–	104
	30–40	6	9	4	2	–	–	–	92
	40–50	–	10	2	2	–	1	–	74
	50–60	–	3	2	1	1	2	1	56
	60–70	–	–	–	–	–	2	2	27
	70–80	–	–	–	–	1	1	–	12
	80–90	–	–	–	–	1	–	–	11
	90–100	–	–	–	–	–	–	–	3
	Total	11	23	8	5	3	7	3	452

Source: Census of India, PCA, General Population, Part II (B)(I), Vols. I and II, 1991.

Most of the official educational statistics are based on enrolment. But it may happen that a person, who is enrolled is not currently attending the institution. So to get the current status of education, we are interested to examine the current attendance status with the implicit assumption that a person who is attending an educational institution is necessarily enrolled in that institution. In this connection we present data on gross attendance ratio and age specific attendance ratio in general education in Tables 6.4 and 6.4(a) respectively.

Table 6.2: All India Ranks of North-Eastern States by Sex and Overall Population over Various Censuses

Category	*States*	*1971*	*1981*	*1991*	*2001*
Total Population	Arunachal Pradesh	24	24	23	24
	Assam	13	–	17	17
	Manipur	8	10	11	13
	Meghalaya	12	17	18	20
	Mizoram	–	3	2	2
	Nagaland	14	7	8	15
	Tripura	11	9	10	7
Male Population	Arunachal Pradesh	24	24	25	25
	Assam	14	–	18	19
	Manipur	6	7	9	11
	Meghalaya	16	21	23	23
	Mizoram	–	3	2	2
	Nagaland	15	11	13	20
	Tripura	11	9	10	8
Female Population	Arunachal Pradesh	24	24	21	23
	Assam	13	–	17	18
	Manipur	12	13	12	14
	Meghalaya	7	12	15	12
	Mizoram	–	2	2	2
	Nagaland	14	6	5	10
	Tripura	9	9	10	7

Source: Statistical Abstract (various issues), Government of India.

It is clearly evident from Table 6.4 that the gross attendance ratio in secondary and higher secondary level is very poor in all the North-Eastern states. It is apparent from Table 6.4(a) that in Arunachal Pradesh for the 6-10 age group, age specific attendance ratio is 65 per cent but for the 11-13 age group, it is 82. The corresponding figures for Assam, Manipur, Meghalaya, Mizoram, Nagaland and Tripura are

73 & 80, 69 & 87, 69 & 94, 71 & 88, 71 & 85 and 81 & 84 respectively. One interesting observation is that, when we see gross attendance ratio and age specific ratio together we would easily find out the incidence of the presence of over aged children in the primary and middle levels.

Table 6.3: Per 1000 Distribution of Persons of Age 15 years and above by Level of Education

States	*Sector*	*Level of Education*									
		01	02	03	04	05	06	07	08	09	10
Arunachal Pradesh	R	615	28	91	128	74	31	16	–	6	4
	U	238	16	72	90	168	202	111	16	70	17
	T	549	26	88	122	91	61	33	3	17	6
Assam	R	327	16	155	174	186	85	37	1	18	1
	U	136	25	63	137	247	161	111	6	104	10
	T	307	17	146	170	193	93	44	2	26	2
Manipur	R	385	6	81	154	171	110	43	–	47	1
	U	245	3	19	87	209	181	121	6	123	6
	T	353	5	67	139	180	126	60	1	65	2
Meghalaya	R	257	32	154	331	148	49	21	–	10	0
	U	43	8	95	152	248	155	134	7	156	3
	T	229	29	146	307	161	63	36	1	29	0
Mizoram	R	162	57	175	337	236	25	4	–	4	–
	U	29	13	100	248	357	147	56	6	38	6
	T	116	42	149	306	278	67	22	2	16	2
Nagaland	R	224	21	130	254	228	101	23	1	17	0
	U	112	33	48	152	300	195	79	6	68	6
	T	191	25	106	224	249	128	40	3	32	2
Tripura	R	305	34	177	184	197	54	16	2	27	4
	U	115	10	87	130	264	145	95	13	134	8
	T	281	31	166	177	205	65	26	3	40	4
All India	R	536	14	79	133	128	65	26	2	14	2
	U	230	12	65	138	190	154	89	9	92	20
	T	457	13	76	134	144	88	42	4	35	7

01 = not literate, 02 = literate without formal schooling, 03 = below primary, 04 = primary, 05 = middle, 06 = secondary, 07 = higher secondary, 08 = diploma/ certificate, 09 = graduate, 10 = post-graduate.

Source: NSS Fifty-second Round (July 1995-June 1996).

Drop out is a serious phenomenon in our educational system. So while studying the educational status of a state it becomes imperative to study the proportion of drop out and their distribution at which they drop out. The overall drop out in India is 56 per cent (Table 6.5). Among the North-Eastern states, Arunachal Pradesh has the highest percentage of drop out (75.6%), followed by Mizoram (75%), Tripura (71%), Assam (61.9%), Manipur (55.4%), Nagaland (42.9%), and Meghalaya (36%). The literacy rate of a state is highly dependent on the number of never enrolled persons and the percentage of drop out at the primary level. It is clearly evident from Table 6.5 that Arunachal Pradesh where the literacy rate is lowest has the highest primary level drop out (55%) and Mizoram where the literacy rate is second highest in India has the lowest primary level drop out (12.6%). All the North-Eastern states, except Mizoram and Nagaland, have higher percentage of drop out in the rural sector than that of urban sector. The percentage of drop out monotonically decreases from primary to higher levels of education.

Table 6.4: Gross Attendance Ratio by Broad Class Group in General Education

State	*Rural/Urban/Total*	*Broad class group of education*			
		I-V	*VI-VIII*	*IX-X*	*XI-XII*
Arunachal Pradesh	R	87	59	11	13
	U	112	98	82	48
	T	90	65	27	22
Assam	R	90	71	75	41
	U	102	77	70	68
	T	91	73	78	43
Manipur	R	87	91	93	54
	U	103	100	106	133
	T	91	93	97	68
Meghalaya	R	108	84	36	3
	U	133	97	85	53
	T	111	86	44	11
Mizoram	R	96	101	25	–
	U	117	120	97	56
	T	102	108	46	23
Nagaland	R	105	114	93	34
	U	103	92	142	60
	T	105	107	105	42
Tripura	R	110	80	54	17
	U	116	99	81	65
	T	110	82	57	22
All India	R	81	59	44	24
	U	100	83	70	51
	T	85	65	51	32

Source: NSS Fifty-second Round (July 1995-June 1996).

Table 6.5(a) gives the proportion of drop out by sex and their distribution by levels at which they drop out. It is evident from the Table that with respect to both male and female, Mizoram has the highest urban overall drop out (male and female drop outs are 839 and 751 per thousand respectively). Arunachal Pradesh has the highest rural overall drop out (male and female drop outs are 794 and 831 per thousand respectively). Rural female drop out at the primary level is highest in Arunachal Pradesh (614) and lowest in Mizoram (129) and in Manipur, Nagaland and Arunachal Pradesh the rural female drop out at the primary level is higher than that of their male counter part.

Table 6.4(a): Age Specific Attendance Ratio by Broad Age Group in General Education

State	*Rural/Urban/Total*	*Broad age group of education*			
		6-10	*11-13*	*14-17*	*18-24*
Arunachal Pradesh	R	61	82	54	18
	U	92	81	82	37
	T	65	82	61	21
Assam	R	72	79	64	23
	U	83	90	76	40
	T	73	8	65	25
Manipur	R	66	86	71	38
	U	78	91	86	64
	T	69	87	74	44
Meghalaya	R	67	93	70	13
	U	88	97	96	57
	T	69	94	74	19
Mizoram	R	60	83	76	6
	U	96	98	78	44
	T	71	88	77	18
Nagaland	R	69	86	83	35
	U	78	84	74	49
	T	71	85	81	40
Tripura	R	81	83	59	20
	U	88	94	85	33
	T	81	84	62	22
All India	R	65	67	45	10
	U	83	85	65	23
	T	69	72	50	14

Source: NSS Fifty-second Round (July 1995-June 1996).

Table 6.5: Proportion (per 1000) of Drop outs (age 5-24 years) and their per 1000 Distribution by level at which Dropped out

States	*Sector*	*Proportion of drop out*	*Level at which dropped out*						
			Primary	*Middle*	*Secondary*	*Higher Secondary (HS)*	*Above HS*	*n.r.*	*All*
Arunachal Pradesh	R	810	563	240	122	43	14	19	1000
	U	383	361	42	334	263	–	–	1000
	T	756	550	227	135	57	13	18	1000
Assam	R	623	370	231	302	58	22	17	1000
	U	564	225	221	348	99	107	–	1000
	T	619	361	230	305	60	28	16	1000
Manipur	R	575	323	296	303	54	11	12	1000
	U	426	104	274	393	90	112	27	1000
	T	554	299	293	313	58	23	14	1000
Meghalaya	R	359	432	403	142	12	–	10	1000
	U	373	497	233	116	154	–	–	1000
	T	360	438	388	140	25	–	10	1000
Mizoram	R	733	153	442	373	32	–	–	1000
	U	795	59	256	490	175	12	8	1000
	T	750	126	388	407	73	3	2	1000
Nagaland	R	368	295	240	389	53	16	8	1000
	U	594	220	366	339	63	11	–	1000
	T	429	267	287	371	56	14	5	1000
Tripura	R	721	424	243	264	38	–	32	1000
	U	620	288	234	404	74	–	–	1000
	T	711	413	242	276	41	–	29	1000
All India	R	581	332	269	269	71	22	38	1000
	U	513	222	242	339	109	67	22	1000
	T	562	304	262	287	80	33	34	1000

Source: NSS Fifty-second Round (July 1995-June 1996).

Table 6.5(a): Proportion (per 1000) of Drop outs (age 5-24 years) and their per 1000 Distribution by Sex and Levels at which Dropped out

State	Sectors	Proportion of drop out		Level of which drop out											
				Primary		Middle		Secondary		Higher Sec. and above		n.r.		All	
		M	F	M	F	M	F	M	F	M	F	M	F	M	F
Arunachal Pradesh	R	794	831	519	614	239	241	153	85	57	55	2	5	1000	1000
	U	513	290	454	245	75	–	–	755	472	–	–	–	1000	1000
Assam	R	669	562	433	273	222	245	261	366	65	102	19	14	1000	1000
	U	596	534	296	149	156	291	340	356	208	204	–	–	1000	1000
Manipur	R	623	521	230	449	297	295	426	138	47	89	–	29	1000	1000
	U	306	512	22	139	329	250	462	363	187	208	–	39	1000	1000
Meghalaya	R	408	296	478	350	380	444	115	192	19	–	8	15	1000	1000
	U	399	357	489	502	324	174	186	71	–	253	–	–	1000	1000
Mizoram	R	757	713	180	129	435	448	368	378	17	44	–	–	1000	1000
	U	839	751	85	31	222	294	492	487	186	187	15	–	1000	1000
Nagaland	R	341	386	279	304	259	229	348	414	94	53	20	–	1000	1000
	U	673	405	221	219	458	–	257	665	64	116	–	–	1000	1000
Tripura	R	748	694	463	382	223	263	233	298	63	12	19	45	1000	1000
	U	563	652	120	369	320	193	398	407	162	31	–	–	1000	1000
All India	R	605	551	304	369	274	264	287	245	105	75	31	47	1000	1000
	U	546	475	224	219	238	246	340	338	176	175	22	22	1000	1000

Source: NSS Fifty-second Round (July 1995-June 1996).

It would be worthwhile to study the reasons behind drop out. In the NSS fifty-second round (1995-96) thirteen reasons were identified for such drop out and are presented in Tables 6.6, 6.6(a) and 6.6(b). It is evident from Table 6.6 that both economic and non-economic factors are responsible for such drop out. A closer examination will reveal that the economic reasons are quite dominant in the urban sector, whereas in the rural sector non-economic reasons are dominant. If we pull rural and urban sectors together then the non-economic (may be social or political) are rather dominant over economic reasons. This pattern is observed in all India as well as in all the North-Eastern states except in Arunachal Pradesh, where economic reasons are very much dominant both in the rural and urban sectors.

Tables 6.6(a) and 6.6(b) present the reasons of drop out by sex in rural and urban sectors respectively. Lack of interest of both the child and the parents and inability to cope with or failures in studies become the major reasons behind the all India rural and urban sectors' drop out irrespective of sex. Among the North-Eastern states, in Arunachal Pradesh, irrespective of sex and sectors, economic reasons are predominant behind drop out. In Assam, Mizoram and Nagaland the reasons behind the rural male and female drop out are non-economic, whereas in Tripura and Manipur the reasons behind female drop out are mostly economic. But in the urban sectors the reasons of drop out for both male and female are predominantly economic. We could not gain further insight into the reasons of drop out because of the limitation of handling secondary data.

In the NSS fifty-second round data are also available for the reasons why the children are never enrolled, which are presented in Table 6.7. The same reasons as in Table 6.6 were attributed for non-enrolment. The reasons for individual states in the North-Eastern regions as well as all India are almost similar as in case of drop out.

Conclusion

The 21st century has begun at a challenging phase of our economy, *i.e.* under the era of globalisation or structural adjustment. Under the new economic policy both the Central and the State governments decided to exit and hence relinquish their responsibilities of public sector undertakings including educational sector into the hands of profit-making private concerns.

Table 6.6: Per 1000 Distribution of Drop outs (age 5-24 years) by Reasons for Dropping out

State	*Sector*	*Reason for dropping out**															
		01	*02*	*03*	*04*	*05*	*06*	*07*	*08*	*09*	*10*	*11*	*12*	*13*	*14*	*15*	*Total*
Arunachal Pradesh	R	8	62	118	46	–	24	7	16	84	5	472	19	–	–	123	1000
	U	–	189	–	150	–	–	–	526	135	–	–	–	–	–	–	1000
	T	8	70	111	53	–	23	6	49	87	5	441	18	–	–	115	1000
Assam	R	–	218	253	184	5	11	5	15	106	4	38	68	–	–	67	1000
	U	–	180	93	237	–	–	–	45	92	13	11	263	–	–	67	1000
	T	–	215	243	189	5	10	5	17	105	4	36	80	–	–	67	1000
Manipur	R	1	267	5	419	–	–	5	–	33	–	63	92	–	–	119	1000
	U	–	78	31	109	64	–	–	62	103	43	42	448	–	–	9	1000
	T	1	246	8	384	7	–	5	7	41	5	61	132	–	–	103	1000
Meghalaya	R	–	179	47	314	8	–	–	–	156	–	32	195	–	–	18	1000
	U	–	122	–	89	–	–	–	455	180	–	63	–	–	–	–	1000
	T	–	174	43	295	7	–	–	40	158	–	35	178	–	–	16	1000
Mizoram	R	–	445	13	247	1	–	–	12	160	2	–	77	–	–	24	1000
	U	–	464	9	196	–	22	35	26	109	4	8	92	–	–	29	)00
	T	–	451	12	232	1	7	10	16	145	2	2	81	–	–	25	1000
Nagaland	R	–	189	16	399	2	–	–	46	50	8	74	135	–	–	81	1000
	U	–	161	6	230	–	–	–	7	–	–	–	466	–	–	130	1000
	T	–	179	12	336	1	–	–	31	31	5	47	259	–	–	99	1000

(*Contd.*)

Table 6.6 (*Contd.*)

	Sector	*Reason for dropping out**															
		01	*02*	*03*	*04*	*05*	*06*	*07*	*08*	*09*	*10*	*11*	*12*	*13*	*14*	*15*	*Total*
Tripura	R	3	211	127	199	–	–	–	8	125	4	59	123	–	–	138	1000
	U	–	296	27	125	–	–	–	27	88	16	9	119	–	–	224	1000
	T	3	218	124	19	–	–	–	9	122	5	55	123	–	–	145	1000
All India	R	5	253	102	215	5	19	20	41	82	14	46	121	–	–	60	1000
	U	6	220	69	256	4	13	8	69	65	10	43	133	–	–	67	1000
	T	5	244	94	225	4	17	17	48	78	13	46	124	–	–	62	1000

Code: 01 = no tradition in the family, 02 = child not interested in studies, 03 = parents not interested in studies, 04 = inability to cope with or failure in studies (n.a.), 05 = unfriendly atmosphere at school (n.a.), 06 = education not considered useful, 07 = schooling/higher education facilities not available conveniently, 08 = has to work for wage/salary, 09 = has to participate in other economic activities, 10 = has to look after younger siblings, 11 = has to attend to other domestic activities, 12 = financial constraints, 13 = completed the desired level, 14 = awaiting admission to the next level, 15 = other (incl. 'n.r.' cases).

Source: NSS Fifty-second Round (July 1995-June 1996).

Education, especially the universal primary education has been given utmost priority since independence. But the performance reflected in the data above is very much unsatisfactory. This is due to the fact that even after 55 years of our independence 35 per cent of the people of India are still illiterate and the process of imparting real education is proved to be absent in our system of education [*viz.*, studies by Bashir (1994), Sharma (1997), NCERT (1994) etc.].

Table 6.6(a): Reasons for Drop out by Sex in the Rural Sector

State	*Sex*	*Rural : Reasons for drop out*												
		01	*02*	*03*	*04*	*05*	*06*	*07*	*08*	*09*	*10*	*11*	*12*	*15*
Arunachal	M	12	109	75	84	–	41	12	29	47	–	454	18	93
Pradesh	F	4	7	172	–	–	5	–	–	129	11	493	21	157
Assam	M	–	239	257	156	–	15	9	25	164	5	7	60	38
	F	–	186	247	230	12	5	–	0	16	1	86	80	113
Manipur	M	–	408	2	445	–	–	–	–	–	–	–	73	72
	F	3	77	8	383	–	–	12	–	78	–	148	119	172
Meghalaya	M	–	151	74	214	12	–	–	–	206	–	44	225	12
	F	–	230	–	494	–	–	–	–	66	–	13	142	27
Mizoram	M	–	625	11	114	–	–	–	26	97	3	–	109	12
	F	–	288	14	364	2	–	–	–	215	–	–	48	43
Nagaland	M	–	294	42	261	1	–	–	89	81	20	–	211	76
	F	–	126	–	482	2	–	–	19	32	2	119	90	130
Tripura	M	–	297	90	221	–	–	–	11	200	–	24	125	32
	F	7	120	165	175	–	–	–	4	46	9	96	120	251
All India	M	1	285	56	241	4	16	9	61	114	6	12	136	41
	F	11	210	163	180	6	22	35	14	39	25	92	102	86

Source: NSS Fifty-second Round (July 1995-June 1996).

By this time, our planners and policy-makers realised the fact that without direct supervision and monitoring by the government the goals of education cannot be achieved. For this reason, we find that while launching the SSA, a time bound scheme, it was clearly stated that the Central government in partnership with the State government has taken steps to achieve the goals of education. There is no doubt that the fate of SSA depends heavily on the sincere initiative and monitoring by both the Central and the State governments. But this will go against the new economic policy of the government. Since our past experiences during Total Literacy Campaign were not very happy. As a result, the government's role here in SSA programme will be always under suspicion.

From 1970s onwards, the government at the Centre and States built-up a new culture of blindly implementing recommendations of some foreign advisory bodies without care and caution as recommended by our Educational Commission appointed after 1947 (*e.g.* Mudaliar Commission, Radhakrishnan Commission). Now the government is trying to privatise the educational sector. Again, the fate of most of the educational programmes are dependent on aids and loans from abroad, like District Primary Education Programme (DPEP) from British Development Fund, Mid-Day Meals and many others from UNICEF etc. These facts simply imply how vulnerable our educational programmes.

Table 6.6(b): Reasons for Drop out by Sex in the Urban Sector

States	*Sex*	*Urban : Reasons for dropout*												
		01	*02*	*03*	*04*	*05*	*06*	*07*	*08*	*09*	*10*	*11*	*12*	*15*
Arunachal	M	–	213	–	75	–	–	–	472	241	–	–	–	–
Pradesh	F	–	160	–	245	–	–	–	595	–	–	–	–	–
Assam	M	–	96	159	86	–	–	–	85	146	25	–	362	40
	F	–	271	22	399	–	–	–	2	34	–	22	156	95
Manipur	M	–	47	–	294	–	–	–	–	128	–	–	503	29
	F	–	92	44	29	92	–	–	88	93	61	60	424	–
Meghalaya	M	–	–	–	95	–	–	–	580	324	–	–	–	–
	F	–	200	–	85	–	–	–	374	87	–	104	–	–
Mizoram	M	–	527	17	193	–	29	–	30	141	–	–	46	17
	F	–	392	–	198	–	14	74	22	74	9	18	145	42
Nagaland	M	–	202	8	197	–	–	–	9	–	–	–	504	81
	F	–	–	–	360	–	–	–	–	–	–	–	318	322
Tripura	M	–	264	43	115	–	–	–	45	144	49	–	203	137
	F	–	311	121	130	–	–	–	18	61	–	14	79	267
All India	M	2	239	42	267	6	13	3	99	96	5	8	149	45
	F	12	194	106	240	2	13	14	28	24	16	91	111	98

Source: NSS Fifty-second Round (July 1995-June 1996).

Given the peculiarities and diversities within and between the North-Eastern states, for achieving the goals of universal primary education, a strategy should be formulated in such a way so that all the children belonging to all ethnic groups as well as to each of the religions can get the advantage of education.

Table 6.7: Proportion (per 1000) of Never Enrolled Persons (age 5-24 years) and their per Thousand Distribution by Reason for Non-Enrolment

States	*Sector*	*Proportion never enrolled*	*Reasons for non–enrolment**															
			01	02	03	04	05	06	07	08	09	10	11	12	13	14	15	Total
Arunachal Pradesh	R	380	1	174	114	–	–	4	20	1	39	10	32	125	–	–	479	1000
	U	139	–	215	16	–	–	–	–	26	66	–	–	83	–	–	593	1000
	T	344	1	177	108	–	–	4	19	3	41	10	30	122	–	–	486	1000
Assam	R	231	3	140	362	–	–	23	5	5	23	1	9	78	–	–	351	1000
	U	118	–	308	170	–	–	7	–	18	4	–	20	147	–	–	326	1000
	T	221	3	148	353	–	–	23	5	5	22	1	9	81	–	–	349	1000
Manipur	R	142	10	59	108	–	–	22	10	–	42	1	47	65	–	–	637	1000
	U	95	8	141	79	–	–	–	–	–	19	–	104	181	–	–	467	1000
	T	130	10	74	103	–	–	18	8	–	38	0	57	86	–	–	606	1000
Meghalaya	R	167	–	246	119	–	–	2	–	2	204	6	58	76	–	–	286	1000
	U	22	74	–	58	–	–	–	–	–	.98	–	–	64	–	–	707	1000
	T	146	2	241	118	–	–	2	–	2	202	6	57	76	–	–	295	1000
Mizoram	R	232	16	44	484	–	–	–	4	–	1	–	–	–	–	–	450	1000
	U	24	–	112	52	–	–	–	–	–	–	–	–	–	–	–	836	1000
	T	167	16	47	464	–	–	–	4	–	1	–	–	–	–	–	468	1000
Nagaland	R	108	–	295	53	–	–	–	–	–	138	18	3	224	–	–	268	1000
	U	95	–	10	–	–	–	–	–	9	32	–	9	331	–	–	609	1000
	T	104	–	218	38	–	–	–	–	2	109	13	5	253	–	–	361	1000
Tripura	R	169	–	242	176	–	–	–	26	24	55	–	11	104	–	–	362	1000
	U	85	–	111	117	–	–	–	–	61	112	–	–	30	–	–	570	1000
	T	160	–	234	173	–	–	–	25	26	58	–	11	99	–	–	374	1000
All India	R	315	39	173	326	–	–	28	22	14	36	13	27	146	–	–	176	1000
	U	120	38	179	265	–	–	15	4	13	25	12	15	197	–	–	244	1000
	T	268	39	173	318	–	–	27	20	14	35	13	26	151	–	–	184	1000

Code: Same as in Table 6.6. ** Children of age 5 not included in the school going age-group classification.
Source: NSS Fifty-second Round (1995-1996).

Hence, under the regime of globalization and structural adjustment our prime task is to implement the universal primary education properly and sincerely and at the same time it is the right time to take the challenge to impart real education to our children.

REFERENCES

Bashir, S. (1994), *Public versus Private in Primary Education: Comparison of School Effectiveness and Cost in Tamil Nadu*, Ph.D. thesis submitted in London School of Economics, London.

The Census of India, Government of India (various issues).

Sharma, R. (1997), 'Dynamics of Learning Three R's in Madhya Pradesh', *Economic and Political Weekly*, Vol. XXXII, No. 17, April 26.

Shukla, Snehlata *et al.* (1994), *Attainments of Primary School Children in Various States*, National Council for Educational Research and Training (NCERT), New Delhi.

NSS Fifty-second Round (July 1995-June 1996) (1998), Attending an Educational Institution in India : Its Level, Nature and Cost.

Statistical Abstract, Government of India (various issues).

7

Literacy Scenario in North East India

N.N. BHATTACHARYYA

Introduction

Literacy is the ability to read and write and the Census of India defined someone as literate who could write and read with understanding in any languages. Generally literacy is considered as one of the indicators of educational development and education is an integral part of the country's development process. Thus literacy and education have been accorded a high priority in the process of development in India. Some progress has been taking place in the field of education in the country, since Independence. It is to be mentioned that the literacy rate increased from 18.3 per cent in 1951 to 65.37 per cent in 2001 and the number of primary school increased from 2.09 lakh in 1951 to 5.73 lakh in 1994. Similarly, the number of universities increased from 27 to 169 in the said period.

In 1993 UNESCO ranked India 50th in primary education among the developing nations of the world. The country has the largest number of illiterates in the world which shares 32.3 per cent of the illiterates of the world. Its major concern is the gender-wise difference in literacy and the illiteracy percentage among women today is about 60 per cent.

The literacy rate of India is not only low but also very much uneven across the different states of India. Kerala has the highest literacy rate, *i.e.* 91 per cent followed by Mizoram 88 per cent and the lowest one 48 per cent is that of Bihar.

The National Policy on Education has been approved by the Parliament in 1986 and its aim was to make education an effective tool for taking India into the 21st Century. The policy has been modified in Parliament on May 7, 1992 for making the "Plus two Stage" part of school education throughout India. It accorded a very high priority to the programme of universalisation of elementary education and it is made compulsory and free for all children up to the age of 14 years. The policy lays down that educational transformation, reduction of disparities, adult education, universalisation of elementary education, scientific research etc. would be accepted as national responsibilities, for which adequate fund and resources would be provided. According to this policy, a programme entitled "Operation Blackboard" has been operated to improve the basic infrastructure of primary schools to provide three class rooms and three teachers to every schools. Such programmes have failed to create desired results because poor families prefer to involve children in the process of earning livelihood rather than sending them to their schools.

North-Eastern Scenario

North EastIndia is educationally one of the least developed regions of India. The literacy rate of the region was 55.63 per cent which was less than the national average of 65.37 per cent in 2001. This burden of illiteracy does not permit them to contribute much to the development processes. In 2001 the gap of literacy rate between the male and female were wide with 61.47 per cent and 48.58 per cent respectively. But this male-female disparity in literacy is low in certain areas among certain Hindu communities. For example, the caste Hindus constitute the overwhelming majority of the village Ichadagharia under Rangia Police Station of Assam. The position of literacy among the children of the village up to the age group 6-14 is very good, *i.e.* 100 per cent, but the number of drop outs are higher among the female children than among the males beyond this age group. According to Annual Report, Ministry of Human Resources Development, Government of India, 1994-95, the drop out rate at the primary stage was only 39 per cent but it increased to 77 per cent when they reached Class X in Assam. Thus the problem of literacy gets more complicated because the drop out rates are quite high in all the states of North EastIndia (Table 7.1).

There has been some progress in literacy and the change in the literacy rates between 1991 and 2001 as shown in Table 7.2.

Table 7.2 indicates that except Mizoram, the overall literacy rate of the states of North EastIndia is rather low. Such low level of literacy in the region may be due to existence of schools without adequate infrastructure, including physical facilities like drinking water, urinals,

Table 7.1: Drop out rates from Class I to Class V, 1994-95

Arunachal Pradesh	60.52
Assam	39.05
Manipur	68.26
Meghalaya	32.06
Mizoram	57.58
Nagaland	31.65
Tripura	63.49

etc., lack of educational awareness among the people, poverty, uninteresting school curriculum and others. The region has disparities in the level of literacy. Thus Mizoram (88.49%), Nagaland (76.11%), and Tripura with 73.66 per cent from the high literate area while Assam (64.28%) and Meghalaya (63.31%) form lower category, marginally below the national level (65.37%) and finally, Arunachal Pradesh with 54.74 per cent forms the very low level of literate area.

Table 7.2: Literacy rates between 1991 and 2001

States	*Literacy Rates, 1991*	*Literacy Rates, 2001*
Mizoram	82.27	88.49
Nagaland	61.65	76.11
Tripura	60.44	73.66
Manipur	59.89	68.87
Assam	52.89	64.28
Meghalaya	49.10	63.31
Arunachal Pradesh	41.59	54.74

Conclusion

Various governments try to remove such disparities in literacy since Independence. Still there are 11 lakh children of the age group 6-14 years out of the school boundaries excluding large number of illiterates and drop out children. Thus, this is a very serious problem, which requires government aids, physical facilities, qualified teachers, communications, skilful efforts and a high degree of motivation on the part of students and teachers. Substantial disparities in educational infrastructure exist in the plains and hills of North East India in the manner in which educational institutions operate. It is seen that pupil-teacher ratio also varies from low to high in different areas of North East India, which should be nationalised. The existing uninteresting school curriculum should be modified with including new activities like basic computer knowledge, drawing, dancing, physical fitness, making flower, toys etc. The isolated areas of the plains and remote hills of the region demand more schools even though the number of school children is small. The improvement of education and literacy appears to be very difficult because India is spending less than 2 per cent of her total annual budget on education in comparison 20 per cent spent by USA, 19.6 per cent by Japan, 17.3 per cent by Canada etc. Thus the Government must increase the total annual budget on education.

REFERENCES

Ahuja, R. (1992), *Social Problems in India*, Rawat Publications, Jaipur.

Annual Report (1994-95), Ministry of Human Resource Development, Government of India, Department of Education.

Panda, B. (2002), *Levels of Disparity in Literacy and Education in North East India: A Geographical Analysis*, Unpublished Ph.D. Thesis, NEHU.

Raza, M. (1990), *Education, Development and Society*, Vikas Publishing House, New Delhi.

8

School Education in North East India
Issues and Prospects

J.P. SINGH

Education, an essential requirement of a good and enlightened life, is an important component of the human resource development. After its inclusion in the Concurrent List of the Constitution of India, we now have an all-India policy in the field of education. The Ministry of Human Resource Development in consultation with the states formulated the National Policy on Education (NPE) in 1986. The NPE envisages free and compulsory education for all citizens up to the age of 14 years. The Government has earmarked about six per cent of the Gross Domestic Product (GDP) for education sector and fifty per cent of the outlay now is to be spent on primary education. School education comprises the following four stages: Primary, Upper Primary, Secondary and Higher Secondary. The Pre-Primary Education is not a compulsory educational ladder, but it forms a part of the Integrated Child Development Scheme (ICDS). It runs in three forms: Anganwadi/ Balwadi, Independent Pre-Primary School and Pre-Primary classes attached to a school. Each state of India compiles data on school education for various purposes, but they often lack in comprehensiveness.

The First All India Educational Survey was conducted by Government of India in 1957. The Fifth All India Educational Survey was conducted in 1986 with 30 September 1986 as the reference date. The Sixth All India Educational Survey was conducted in 1993 and its date of reference was 30 September 1993. the Seventh All India School Education Survey is being conducted with the reference date of 30 September, 2002. The detailed data of the Sixth All India Educational

Survey were published during 1997-99. The data obtained in the Educational Survey reveal some interesting facts about school education.

North-Eastern India

North-Eastern India comprising states of Arunachal Pradesh, Assam, Manipur, Meghalaya, Mizoram, Nagaland, Sikkim and Tripura contains an area of 262,179 km^2 (7.98 per cent of India) and shares according to 2001 Census a population of 40.2 millions (3.91 per cent of India). The north-eastern region is smaller than several states like Andhra Pradesh, Madhya Pradesh, Maharashtra and Rajasthan, both in area and population. Occupying a strategic location in the country, the region is rich in agriculture, forest and mineral resources. In majority of the states, the people are tribal, and are employed primarily as cultivators and agricultural labourers.

In terms of area, Arunachal Pradesh is the biggest state in the region, Assam is the second biggest and Sikkim is the smallest. The first two shares about 62 per cent area of the region. In terms of population, Assam is the giant with over 66 per cent of the regional population (Table 8.1). The growth of population has been higher than the all-India average; only recently Assam and Tripura have recorded a low growth of population (Table 8.2). In Arunachal Pradesh, Meghalaya, Mizoram and Nagaland, the tribal population ranges between 64 and 95 per cent of the state population. The region is less urbanised (except Mizoram) than the national average. The over-all literacy in the region is good, better than the all-India average; only Arunachal Pradesh, Assam and Meghalaya have the literacy rate a little less than the national average. Except Arunachal Pradesh, all the states of the region have a low male-female gap in literacy (Table 8.3).

School Facilities

As a result of the efforts made by the Central and State Governments, 94 per cent of the country's rural population have primary schools within one kilometre and 85 per cent of the rural habitations have upper primary schools within a distance of 3 kilometres. In predominantly tribal and scheduled caste habitations, this percentage is 89 and 91 in case of primary schools and 69 and 83 in case of upper

Table 8.1: North-Eastern India : Basic Geographical Data

States	*Area*		*Population in Thousands*				*No. of Districts*	
	km²	%	*1991*	%	*2001*	%	*1991*	*2001*
Arunachal Pradesh	83,743	31.94	865	2.71	1,091	2.71	11	13
Assam	78,434	29.92	22,414	70.14	26,638	66.26	23	23
Manipur	22,327	8.52	1,837	5.75	2,389	5.94	8	9
Meghalaya	22,429	8.44	1,775	5.55	3,474	8.64	5	7
Mizoram	21,081	8.04	690	2.16	891	2.22	3	8
Nagaland	16,579	6.32	1,210	3.79	1,989	4.95	7	8
Sikkim	7,096	2.71	406	1.27	540	1.34	4	4
Tripura	10,486	4.00	2,757	8.63	3,191	7.94	3	4
North-Eastern India	262,179	100.00	31,954	100.00	40,203	100.00	64	76

Source: Census of India 2001, Provisional Population Total, Paper I of 2001, Supplement, District Totals.

Table 8.2: *North-Eastern India : Composition of Population (%)*

State	Population Growth		1991(%)			Urban 2001	Main workers 1991		Cultivators 1991		Agricultural Labourers 1991	
	1981-91	1991-2001	ST	SC	General		Male	Female	Male	Female	Male	Female
Arunachal Pradesh	36.83	26.21	63.66	0.47	35.87	20.41	53.5	35.6	47.0	83.8	5.1	5.1
Assam	24.24	18.85	12.82	7.40	79.78	12.72	48.4	12.6	50.9	50.9	12.1	12.0
Manipur	29.29	30.02	34.41	2.02	63.57	23.88	44.2	32.7	58.6	66.2	4.6	9.6
Meghalaya	32.86	29.94	85.53	0.51	13.96	19.63	49.5	30.7	68.7*	83.5*	—	—
Mizoram	39.70	29.18	94.75	0.10	5.15	49.50	49.6	34.0	57.8*	78.3*	—	—
Nagaland	56.08	64.41	87.70	—	12.30	17.74	46.7	37.3	59.8	90.8	1.7	1.0
Sikkim	28.47	32.98	22.36	5.93	71.61	11.10	50.8	28.6	51.0	71.7	8.0	7.4
Tripura	34.30	15.74	30.95	16.36	52.69	17.02	47.0	10.1	38.2	37.5	21.9	30.5
India	23.86	21.34	8.08	16.48	75.44	27.78	50.9	15.9	39.9	34.6	20.8	44.2

* Including agricultural labourers, forestry and fishing.

Source: Census of India 1991, *State Profile 1991 India*, Delhi: Controller of Publications; Census of India 2001, *Provisional Population Totals*, Paper 1 of 2001, Supplement, District Totals; Paper 2 of 2001, Rural-Urban Distribution. ST—Scheduled Tribes, SC—Scheduled Castes.

primary schools (Table 8.4). The table shows that Mizoram ranks first in case of primary schools, and Arunachal Pradesh the last. Almost a similar pattern exists in case of tribal habitations for primary and upper primary schools.

Table 8.3: North-Eastern India : Literacy Percentage, 1991, 2001

States	*1991*				*2001*			
	Total	*Male*	*Female*	*M-F Gap*	*Total*	*Male*	*Female*	*M-F Gap*
Arunachal Pradesh	41.59	51.45	9.69	21.76	54.74	64.07	44.24	19.83
Assam	52.89	61.87	43.03	18.84	64.28	71.93	56.03	15.90
Manipur	59.89	71.63	47.60	24.03	68.87	77.87	59.70	18.17
Meghalaya	49.10	53.12	44.85	8.27	63.13	66.14	60.41	5.73
Mizoram	82.27	85.61	78.60	7.01	88.49	9.69	86.13	4.56
Nagaland	61.65	67.62	54.75	12.87	67.11	71.77	61.92	9.95
Sikkim	56.94	65.70	46.76	18.94	69.68	76.73	61.46	15.27
Tripura	60.44	70.58	49.65	20.93	73.66	81.47	65.41	16.06
India	52.21	64.13	39.29	24.84	65.37	75.85	56.16	19.69

M-F Gap—Male Female Literacy Gap.

Source: Census of India 2001, *Provisional Population Totals*, Paper 1 of 2001, Supplement, District Totals.

Table 8.4: North-Eastern India : Statewise Rural habitations with Primary Schools (%) within 1 km. and Upper Primary Schools (%) within 3 km. for all habitations, tribal habitations and scheduled caste habitations

State	*Primary Schools*			*Upper Primary Schools*		
	All	*ST*	*SC*	*All*	*ST*	*SC*
Arunachal Pradesh	77.87	78.13	97.61	54.39	52.87	59.75
Assam	88.61	87.36	91.50	87.16	79.87	88.95
Manipur	94.12	92.44	98.37	82.24	68.85	81.44
Meghalaya	87.27	87.93	—	69.50	68.87	—
Mizoram	95.77	96.22	—	83.38	84.24	—
Nagaland	95.05	95.05	—	74.54	74.54	—
Sikkim	83.44	79.62	97.69	79.01	79.15	89.04
Tripura	85.00	78.75	89.16	85.89	70.08	94.32
India	93.76	88.55	91.32	85.00	68.95	82.54

Source: The Sixth All India Educational Survey 1993, National Tables, Vol. 1, Educational Facilities in Rural and Urban Areas.

Seventy-eight per cent of the rural habitations of India have secondary schools within a distance of 5 kilometres. Except Assam and Tripura, where this percentage is higher than the national average all other states of the region have this facility for a lower percentage of rural habitations. In Arunachal Pradesh, not even 45 per cent of the rural habitations have secondary schools within a distance of 5 kilometres. For the tribal habitations, however, this facility is better in the region, except in Arunachal Pradesh, Manipur and Nagaland. For scheduled caste habitations, this percentage is lower in Arunachal Pradesh and Sikkim than the all-India average. Fifty-seven per cent of the rural habitations in India have higher secondary schools (including intermediate, junior colleges and pre-university course) within a distance of 8 kilometres. Tripura has this facility for 82 per cent habitations and Mizoram only for 8 per cent habitations. This facility is better in tribal habitations of Manipur, Tripura and Assam than the all-India average. The position of scheduled caste habitations is good to very good in Assam and Tripura (Table 8.5).

Table 8.5: North-Eastern India : State-wise Rural Habitations with Secondary Schools (%) within 5 km. and Higher Secondary Schools (%) within 8 km. for all habitations, tribal habitations and scheduled castes habitations, 1993

State	*Secondary Schools*			*Higher Secondary Schools*		
	All	*ST*	*SC*	*All*	*ST*	*SC*
Arunachal Pradesh	41.70	38.53	63.43	30.66	29.20	58.44
Assam	87.40	80.54	88.24	75.19	60.44	70.07
Manipur	73.57	51.26	86.12	57.68	73.48	50.04
Meghalaya	59.18	58.63	—	20.12	19.28	—
Mizoram	58.99	60.26	—	8.13	8.40	—
Nagaland	50.48	50.48	—	22.05	22.05	—
Sikkim	68.35	61.55	65.78	41.25	38.38	37.71
Tripura	88.62	72.66	97.34	81.53	62.10	90.09
India	77.91	59.14	78.03	56.96	43.38	67.03

Source: *The Sixth All India Educational Survey 1993*, National Tables, Vol. 1—Educational Facilities in Rural and Urban Areas.

Only 30.24 per cent villages in India have pre-primary facilities. In north-eastern region these facilities are better than the national average. The percentage of villages having pre-primary facilities in the states of the region are as follows: Arunachal Pradesh (30.80),

Assam (9.81), Manipur (84.11), Meghalaya (47.91), Mizoram (55.43), Nagaland (78.75), Sikkim (86.82) and Tripura (83.51).

Enrolment

Between 1986 when the Fifth All India Educational Survey was conducted and 1993 when the Sixth All India Educational Survey was conducted, there has been an overall increase in the number of schools of different categories. The percentage increase in the number of schools of different categories during the period is given in Table 8.6. The table shows that the increase in the number of primary schools in the north-eastern region, in general, was more than the national average. Only in Mizoram and Tripura it was less; in Arunachal Pradesh the increase was about 3 times. In case of upper primary schools this increase was lower in Sikkim and Tripura, while in Manipur and Arunachal Pradesh it was more than 3 times. Almost a similar pattern existed for secondary schools. In Nagaland the increase in secondary schools was more than 3 times, while in Arunachal Pradesh and Mizoram it was more than 2 times. The increase in the number of higher secondary schools in Manipur and Meghalaya was 5 to 7 times.

Table 8.6: North-Eastern India : Percentage Increase in the Number of Schools in Different Categories in 1993 over 1986

State	*Primary Schools*	*Upper Primary Schools*	*Sec. Schools*	*Hr.Sec. Schools*	*All Schools*
Arunachal Pradesh	20.38	52.20	58.00	96.77	28.64
Assam	11.66	39.11	30.58	63.56	17.58
Manipur	9.64	61.01	29.75	260.00	18.90
Meghalaya	11.02	23.31	42.01	350.00	14.85
Mizoram	-6.17	31.32	58.13	—	10.81
Nagaland	8.31	32.30	93.68	—	18.52
Sikkim	11.97	-2.48	20.00	76.92	11.23
Tripura	5.29	3.58	20.36	52.00	8.29
India	7.89	17.11	24.74	53.00	11.79

Source: *The Sixth All India Educational Survey*, Selected Statistics.

Along with the increase in number of schools, the enrolment between 1986 and 1993 also increased. While the average increase in primary classes for India was 13 per cent, it was 42 per cent for Arunachal Pradesh and 49 per cent for Manipur. This increase was less than 10 per cent for Mizoram, Nagaland and Sikkim. Assam, Meghalaya and Tripura matched with the all-India average (Table 8.7).

Table 8.7: North-Eastern India : State-wise Percentage Increase in Enrolment in 1993 over 1986

States	*Primary Classes*	*Upper Primary Classes*	*Sec. & Hr. Sec. Classes*
Arunachal Pradesh	42.23	84.76	99.97
Assam	12.36	28.24	32.76
Manipur	48.73	54.60	55.13
Meghalaya	12.03	18.20	35.50
Mizoram	9.33	36.75	30.81
Nagaland	7.28	54.08	58.76
Sikkim	3.96	28.94	104.14
Tripura	13.51	11.44	39.55
India	12.94	24.93	37.63

Source: *The Sixth All India Educational Survey*, Selected Statistics.

The average increase in enrolment in upper primary classes for the country during the period was 25 per cent. It was more than 2 times in Manipur and Nagaland, and more than 3 times in Arunachal Pradesh. Except Meghalaya and Tripura, which recorded a low increase, all other states had more than the national average. So far as the enrolment in secondary and higher secondary classes are concerned, the increase was more than 2 times in Arunachal Pradesh and Sikkim and less than the national average in Assam, Meghalaya and Mizoram (Table 8.7).

In India, boys outnumber girls in enrolment. The percentage of girls' enrolment to the total in India in primary classes is 43 per cent; all the states of the region have this percentage more than the national average (Table 8.8). In upper primary classes the girls' percentage is 40 whereas all other states of the region have more than this. In secondary classes the percentage share of girls' enrolment is 37; and other states have more than this. Only in case of higher secondary classes, the position is a little different. In Arunachal Pradesh the percentage of girls' enrolment is about 30, against the national average of 36. In Mizoram there was no higher secondary school. All other states had almost the same share of girls' enrolment as that for the national average.

Table 8.8: North-Eastern India : State-wise and Stage-wise Percentage of Girls' Enrolment to Total Enrolment, 1993

States	*Classes I-V*	*Classes VI-VIII*	*Classes IX-X*	*Classes XI-XII*
Arunachal Pradesh	43.28	40.53	37.13	30.25
Assam	45.46	44.81	44.99	36.97
Manipur	46.91	46.49	46.66	35.88
Meghalaya	50.14	48.56	46.88	41.87
Mizoram	47.36	48.30	49.97	0.00
Nagaland	47.90	49.11	46.26	38.33
Sikkim	46.82	48.80	47.90	41.22
Tripura	45.75	44.63	43.06	36.19
India	43.16	39.62	36.47	35.93

Source: *The Sixth All India Educational Survey*, Vol. IV – Enrolment in Schools.

Drop out

Out of hundred children enrolled in class one, in India, only 55 per cent reach class five. The rest 45 per cent drop out. Except Manipur, where the drop out rate is 44 per cent, all other states of the region have it higher, which increases to 66 per cent in Meghalaya. By the time school children reach class 8, 64 per cent drop out. This rate is very high in all the states, ranging from 81 per cent in Meghalaya to 56 per cent in Manipur. The dropout rate increases with the increase in school stage. By the time students reach class 10, most of them drop out. The average drop out rate in India is 75 per cent. It is 64 per cent in Manipur, but in Meghalaya it is 82 per cent. All other states have a very high dropout rate (Table 8.9).

The drop out rate is more among the girls than the boys. While the average drop out rate of girls in class 5, in India, is 41; it is more in all the states except Nagaland and Sikkim (Table 8.10). It is more than 50 per cent in Manipur, Meghalaya, Mizoram and Tripura. Meghalaya tops with 64 per cent drop out among girls. By the time girls reach class 8, 59 per cent in India drop out. Except Nagaland, where the drop out is 36 per cent, in all other states it is higher. It is more than 70 per cent in Manipur, Mizoram and Tripura. The high rate of drop out of girls is a big challenge for educationists. When the drop out rates among girls of different social categories are taken into account, it, however, does not show a much difference among the states of the region (Table 8.11). The drop out among the scheduled tribes is more than the general and scheduled caste population.

Table 8.9: North-Eastern Region : State-wise Enrolment in Classes I-X as Percentage of Class I, 1993

States	*Class I*	*Class V*	*Class VIII*	*Class X*
Arunachal Pradesh	100.00	40.98	25.57	16.10
Assam	100.00	35.71	25.15	17.32
Manipur	100.00	55.84	44.18	35.56
Meghalaya	100.00	34.12	19.26	11.88
Mizoram	100.00	44.76	29.55	16.37
Nagaland	100.00	46.95	37.85	19.79
Sikkim	100.00	50.98	27.67	16.30
Tripura	100.00	44.88	26.08	19.14
India	100.00	54.63	36.27	25.03

Source: *The Sixth All India Educational Survey*, Vol. IV – Enrolment in Schools.

Table 8.10: North-Eastern India : Percentage of Girls Drop out Rate at Primary (Classes I-V) and Upper Primary (Classes I-VIII) Stages 1997-98

States	*Primary*	*Upper Primary*
Arunachal Pradesh	45	67
Assam	42	69
Manipur	54	72
Meghalaya	64	47
Mizoram	52	71
Nagaland	35	36
Sikkim	37	68
Tripura	54	74
India	41	59

Source: *India Education Report : A Profile of Basic Education, 2002*, p. 40.

Teacher-Pupil Ratio

As the number of schools and students increased between 1986 and 1993, the number of teachers also increased. The number of students per teacher in India is 40 in primary classes, 36 in upper primary classes, 30 in secondary classes and 34 in higher secondary classes. In all the states of the region the number of students per teacher is less than the national average. In primary classes of the region, the teacher-pupil ratio ranges between 12 in Nagaland and Sikkim and 35 in Assam. In upper primary classes this ranges between 14 in Mizoram and Nagaland and 24 in Arunachal Pradesh, while the national average is 36. The teacher-pupil ratio in the region in secondary classes ranges between 16 in Mizoram and 24 in Arunachal Pradesh. In higher secondary classes this pattern changes a little. In Nagaland there are 30 students per teacher and in Sikkim 18. The teacher-pupil ratio is better in rural areas (that is less number of students per teacher) than in urban areas (Table 8.12).

Table 8.11: North-Eastern India : Community-wise Drop out Rates (%) in Classes V and VIII in Rural Areas, 1993

States	*Admi-ssion Class I*	*Boys/ Girls*	*General*		*Scheduled Castes*		*Scheduled Tribes*	
			Class V	*Class VIII*	*Class V*	*Class VIII*	*Class V*	*Class VIII*
Arunachal	100	B	49.01	68.34	60.58	63.46	63.97	78.68
Pradesh		G	52.16	70.21	73.44	78.12	65.10	83.16
Assam	100	B	66.29	80.45	59.57	71.73	70.25	80.54
		G	67.66	80.45	61.73	73.53	74.26	83.20
Manipur	100	B	30.63	45.52	56.70	62.27	65.48	77.73
		G	35.39	50.76	45.40	60.51	66.41	79.08
Meghalaya	100	B	38.05	67.77	38.93	63.36	71.04	86.18
		G	53.08	81.29	50.42	78.15	71.37	87.42
Mizoram	100	B	NA	NA	92.31	NA	58.63	81.44
		G	NA	NA	NA	NA	60.92	81.15
Nagaland	100	B	17.81	38.36	67.65	77.46	62.61	71.40
		G	00.00	24.55	66.67	73.91	60.42	70.93
Sikkim	100	B	49.06	73.60	66.29	87.72	56.85	77.50
		G	45.84	73.75	63.65	85.46	41.72	64.72
Tripura	100	B	46.42	69.00	55.80	76.10	79.10	84.33
		G	48.34	69.43	59.86	80.82	73.35	87.71
India	100	B	42.86	62.87	54.46	75.63	65.33	82.35
		G	48.35	72.49	63.91	84.61	72.19	88.77

Source: Calculated from *The Sixth All India Educational Survey*, Vol. IV – Enrolment in Schools.

On an average, majority of the school teachers in India are of general category at all stages of school education. In states populated primarily by the tribal population, the teachers in primary and upper primary classes are mostly tribals. In urban schools, both in primary and upper primary classes, however, majority of them are female. In rural areas the pattern is different. This is different also in secondary and higher secondary classes (Table 8.13).

Table 8.12: North-Eastern India : Teacher Pupil Ratio in Different Categories of Schools, 1993

State	*Primary*			*Upper Primary*			*Secondary*			*Sr. Secondary*		
	R	*U*	*T*	*R*	*U*	*T*	*R*	*U*	*T*	*R*	*U*	*T*
Arunachal Pradesh	27.65	19.93	26.57	23.80	29.63	24.49	23.74	23.87	23.75	24.14	27.52	25.17
Assam	35.25	30.92	34.80	19.67	20.89	19.77	20.92	25.27	21.66	23.67	23.41	23.58
Manipur	14.25	13.26	14.03	14.36	17.40	15.17	17.38	20.28	18.50	22.88	18.67	19.99
Meghalaya	23.42	25.38	23.60	18.56	20.73	18.85	19.93	23.50	21.47	23.19	21.68	22.33
Mizoram	24.60	21.18	23.03	11.83	16.85	13.63	13.32	19.12	16.47	–	–	–
Nagaland	11.63	11.39	11.61	12.40	17.97	13.63	20.52	33.83	25.73	–	29.92	29.92
Sikkim	11.49	–	11.49	14.56	–	14.56	17.90	27.81	18.21	18.51	14.13	17.87
Tripura	22.79	24.47	22.95	21.43	19.49	21.18	22.60	21.02	22.36	22.87	20.44	21.83
India	40.94	36.57	40.00	35.84	36.61	36.07	29.33	31.78	30.21	33.57	34.65	34.21

R—Rural, U—Urban, T—Total.
Source: *The Sixth All India Educational Survey*, Vol. IV – Enrolment in Schools.

Table 8.13: North-Eastern India : Teachers Position in percentage in 1993

State		*Primary*				*Upper Primary*			
		SC	*ST*	*OBC*	*Females*	*SC*	*ST*	*OBC*	*Females*
Arunachal Pradesh	(R)	0.88	51.79	3.71	14.90	1.06	37.45	3.59	15.17
	(U)	0.29	42.86	1.43	73.43	0.00	46.05	3.07	65.79
	(T)	0.80	50.54	3.39	23.07	0.93	38.47	3.53	21.15
Assam	(R)	6.00	17.03	32.37	24.48	4.74	10.98	33.67	15.24
	(U)	6.30	10.86	20.59	67.25	3.98	3.15	21.77	43.62
	(T)	6.03	16.40	31.17	28.85	4.68	10.37	32.74	17.46
Manipur	(R)	1.39	43.95	0.20	26.00	1.50	46.62	0.99	27.45
	(U)	5.07	3.51	0.58	46.77	3.30	15.85	1.47	47.35
	(T)	2.20	35.07	0.29	30.56	1.98	38.44	1.11	32.74
Meghalaya	(R)	0.46	95.21	0.93	43.07	2.17	84.20	3.47	33.25
	(U)	0.76	79.65	2.78	80.53	3.54	69.65	5.50	67.60
	(T)	0.49	93.79	1.10	46.50	2.36	82.22	4.29	37.92
Mizoram	(R)	0.37	98.50	0.32	34.21	0.35	97.60	0.62	18.60
	(U)	0.69	97.93	0.69	61.72	0.85	97.01	0.72	32.44
	(T)	0.52	98.24	0.49	46.86	0.53	97.38	0.66	23.77
Nagaland	(R)	1.74	92.97	1.92	28.04	3.92	71.64	6.46	21.14
	(U)	3.88	87.26	1.66	78.67	2.18	74.58	3.63	64.65
	(T)	1.87	92.61	1.91	31.18	3.53	72.29	5.84	30.76
Sikkim	(R)	2.69	22.45	1.49	31.04	2.36	25.08	1.77	32.68
	(U)	—	—	—	—	—	—	—	—
	(T)	2.69	22.45	1.49	31.04	2.36	25.08	1.77	32.68
Tripura	(R)	8.66	47.25	1.29	17.05	8.32	27.41	1.01	17.60
	(U)	5.70	5.81	0.12	65.23	5.44	3.29	0.14	59.23
	(T)	8.37	43.21	1.18	21.75	7.94	24.25	0.90	23.05
India	(R)	12.49	9.01	28.20	23.50	9.88	7.84	29.70	25.40
	(U)	7.06	2.65	21.90	61.29	6.82	3.18	24.15	60.60
	(T)	11.32	7.65	26.85	31.61	8.96	6.44	28.03	35.97

		Secondary				*Sr. Secondary*			
		SC	*ST*	*OBC*	*Females*	*SC*	*ST*	*OBC*	*Females*
Arunachal Pradesh	(R)	0.60	24.10	3.40	20.40	1.20	10.47	2.79	17.15
	(U)	5.07	23.91	2.17	42.03	2.27	4.99	6.12	20.63
	(T)	1.14	24.08	3.25	23.02	1.52	9.14	3.81	18.21
Assam	(R)	4.13	9.94	32.99	19.85	4.11	7.88	27.56	20.49
	(U)	3.45	4.34	21.28	44.36	3.31	4.70	19.79	38.47
	(T)	4.01	8.98	31.00	24.02	3.83	6.77	24.85	26.76
Manipur	(R)	1.34	30.27	1.68	28.43	1.03	20.88	0.26	33.25
	(U)	2.02	16.97	0.22	46.98	0.94	7.31	2.83	36.91
	(T)	1.60	25.14	1.12	35.58	0.97	11.57	2.02	35.76

(Contd.)

Table 8.13: (*Contd.*)

States		*Secondary*				*Sr. Secondary*			
		SC	*ST*	*OBC*	*Females*	*SC*	*ST*	*OBC*	*Females*
Meghalaya	(R)	3.50	57.74	8.63	30.27	2.97	8.91	4.95	58.42
	(U)	1.78	57.54	7.16	62.98	2.96	38.52	6.67	62.96
	(T)	2.76	57.70	8.00	44.37	2.97	25.85	5.93	61.02
Mizoram	(R)	3.72	89.61	2.63	11.60	—	—	—	—
	(U)	2.40	88.75	2.40	28.14	—	—	—	—
	(T)	3.00	89.14	2.50	20.57	—	—	—	—
Nagaland	(R)	2.87	61.73	9.55	25.84	—	—	—	—
	(U)	4.04	94.36	7.14	46.95	2.68	53.57	10.71	31.25
	(T)	3.33	57.89	8.61	34.10	2.68	53.57	10.71	31.25
Sikkim	(R)	2.11	24.60	0.45	40.15	3.14	21.19	11.43	49.66
	(U)	6.98	11.63	41.86	69.77	3.27	17.65	0.00	58.82
	(T)	2.27	24.20	1.75	41.08	3.16	20.67	9.76	51.00
Tripura	(R)	8.21	15.68	1.65	22.78	9.70	6.82	1.47	25.40
	(U)	3.79	4.14	0.53	55.59	4.50	2.54	0.38	41.98
	(T)	7.54	13.92	1.48	27.78	7.47	4.99	1.00	32.50
India	(R)	7.15	4.09	24.33	23.09	7.59	3.24	28.86	17.84
	(U)	5.23	2.64	19.13	55.45	5.37	1.78	19.55	43.52
	(T)	6.46	3.57	22.46	34.68	6.26	2.37	23.30	33.18

R—Rural; U—Urban; T—Total.

Source: *The Sixth All India Educational Survey*, Vol. III – Teachers in Schools (Govt., Local Body, Private, Private unaided).

The number of primary schools with 3 or more teachers in India is 31 per cent. The rest, 69 per cent of the primary schools, have less than 3 teachers. In comparison to this, the position of Manipur, Mizoram, Nagaland, Sikkim and Tripura is very good as the percentage of primary schools with 3 or more teachers ranges between 60 and 92. Arunachal Pradesh, Meghalaya and Assam have shortage of teachers in primary classes; the percentage of schools with 3 or more teachers in these states is 19, 25 and 30 respectively (Table 8.14).

Physical Facilities

Eighty six per cent of school buildings in India are pucca and partially pucca. In comparison to this, the school buildings in the region is worse. In Manipur and Tripura, less than 40 per cent of the school buildings are pucca and semi-pucca; in other states, this percentage is more than 50.

Table 8.14: North-Eastern India : State-wise Distribution of Primary Schools according to Teachers Position, 1993

States	*Schools with three or more teachers(%)*
Arunachal Pradesh	19.00
Assam	30.01
Manipur	59.76
Meghalaya	24.86
Mizoram	64.56
Nagaland	78.91
Sikkim	92.16
Tripura	66.23
India	31.18

Source: *The Sixth All India Educational Survey*; selected statistics.

While 53 per cent of the school buildings in India have drinking water facilities, and in the region this percentage is very low. Except Sikkim, Arunachal Pradesh and Mizoram, where more than 40 per cent of the schools have drinking water facilities, in rest of the states this percentage is very low, particularly in Meghalaya (Table 8.15). So far as urinal, separate urinal for girls, lavatory and separate lavatory for girls are concerned, the position of the region in general is bad. Majority of the schools in the region do not have separate urinals and lavatory for girls. The situation is the worst in Assam, Meghalaya and Tripura. In urban areas, the facilities are far better than in rural areas.

Other physical facilities like almirah/box, playground, blackboard, furniture for students and teachers, also, matter much in development of an appropriate learning situation. So far as the number of usable blackboards in primary schools are concerned, the situation in the region is better than the national average. Only in Arunachal Pradesh, Assam and Tripura the percentage number of usable blackboards is less than the all-India average. In upper primary, secondary and higher secondary schools of the region this is somewhat better. So the problem of blackboards and furniture for teachers and students remain mainly with the primary schools located in rural areas.

Quite a good number of primary schools in rural areas do not have almirahs or boxes to keep teaching-learning materials and other necessary papers related to schools and students. The situation, however better in upper primary and secondary schools.

Table 8.15: North-Eastern India : State-wise Schools having Ancillary Facilities(%), 1993

States	*Total Schools*	*Pucca and partially pucca buildings*	*Drinking water*	*Urinal*	*Separate Urinal for girls*	*Lavatory*	*Separate lavatory for girls*
Arunachal Pradesh	1563	55.73	46.96	22.20	9.34	14.91	6.46
Assam	39342	52.99	28.60	21.93	9.20	5.38	2.05
Manipur	4240	38.77	24.03	29.98	13.92	19.98	9.43
Meghalaya	5337	65.22	16.23	19.02	8.47	7.91	3.92
Mizoram	1804	53.01	39.80	82.15	28.60	45.18	11.03
Nagaland	1798	50.78	22.69	35.26	23.64	14.35	10.40
Sikkim	731	78.11	59.78	40.49	17.37	19.84	8.48
Tripura	2952	33.94	29.95	24.76	9.01	11.21	3.90
India	822486	85.82	52.59	31.52	19.48	20.35	12.01

Source: *The Sixth All India Educational Survey*, Vol. II – Schools and Physical Facilities.

Educational Inputs and Facilities

Proper education demands certain inputs and facilities particularly at secondary and higher secondary stages. Home science in majority of the schools is taught without laboratory. Some schools do not have this facility at all (Table 8.16). Laboratory is essential for teaching science. Only in Arunachal Pradesh and Sikkim, over three-fourths of the secondary schools have science laboratory (Table 8.17). In rest of the states, this is available in less than 50 per cent of the schools; the national average is 60 per cent. At this stage of school education students have a variety of physical and educational problems for the solution of which they need guidance and counselling. But majority of the schools, do not have this facility (Table 8.18).

Table 8.16: North-Eastern India : State-wise Secondary and Higher Secondary Schools teaching Home Science and having Home Science Laboratory, 1993

States	*Number of Secondary Schools*		*Number of Hr.Sec. Schools*	
	Teaching Home Science	*Having Laboratory (%)*	*Teaching Home Science*	*Having Laboratory (%)*
Arunachal Pradesh	1	100.00	1	100.00
Assam	36	8.33	19	52.63
Manipur	98	33.67	8	62.50
Meghalaya	9	11.11	0	00.00
Mizoram	6	16.67	0	00.00
Nagaland	61	25.54	2	50.00
Sikkim	3	33.33	2	100.00
Tripura	2	00.00	6	00.00
India	4500	36.78	3477	64.65

Source: *The Sixth All India Educational Survey*, Vol. V – Educational Inputs and Facilities in Secondary and Higher Secondary Schools.

Library is an important place of activities in schools, but in many cases, it does not exist. Wherever it exists, even there it remains non-functional in the absence of a librarian. There is an acute shortage of both trained and untrained librarians in the schools of the region. High cost of books make the availability of library facilities more difficult for students.

A study of enrolment of students at higher secondary shows that majority of the students in rural areas opt for arts and humanities and the percentage of girls opting for this course is very high. Science, commerce and vocational courses have a declining preference both by boys and girls, both in rural and urban areas (Table 8.19). This trend, however, has changed recently with the upsurge in information technology.

Table 8.17: North-Eastern India : State-wise Secondary Schools Teaching Science and having Laboratory Facilities, 1993

States	*No. of Sec. Schools*	*Having Science Laboratory*	*%*
Arunachal Pradesh	140	110	78.57
Assam	3447	213	6.18
Manipur	503	254	50.10
Meghalaya	418	100	23.92
Mizoram	253	115	45.45
Nagaland	118	59	31.38
Sikkim	89	80	89.89
Tripura	489	69	14.11
India	87238	52105	59.73

Source: *The Sixth All India Educational Survey*, Vol. V – Educational Inputs and Facilities in Secondary and Higher Secondary Schools.

Educational Initiative During Last Decade

During the last decade of the 20th century, a number of school improvement programmes were initiated by the State and Central governments. Some of them were meant to check drop out and some to improve the level of achievement in schools. Some elements of the programmes have been the creation of parental awareness and mobilisation of communities, involvement of communities and Panchayats, economic incentives, improvement in infrastructural facilities in schools, DPEP initiatives, national programme of nutritional support to primary education in the form of mid-day meals scheme, non-formal education scheme and teacher's education scheme.

The Operation Blackboard (OB) scheme was launched in 1987-88 with the aim to improve human and physical resources available in primary schools of the country. The scheme was to provide at least two rooms, two teachers and essential teaching-learning materials to every existing primary school. During 1993-94, the scheme was extended to cover upper primary schools. It provided 3 rooms for primary schools, an additional teacher for upper primary schools and a third teacher for primary schools, where the enrolment was more

Table 8.18: North-Eastern India : State-wise Secondary and Higher Secondary Schools with Guidance Services and Librarians, 1993

States	*Number of Sec. Schools*	*Guidance Services (%)**	*Having Librarian (%)***	*No. of Hr. Sec. Schools*	*Guidance Services (%)**	*Having Librarian (%)***
Arunachal Pradesh	79	7.59	11.39	61	34.43	50.82
Assam	2912	14.70	8.38	597	38.19	28.14
Manipur	471	43.10	29.72	36	77.78	66.67
Meghalaya	409	24.69	16.14	9	77.78	66.67
Mizoram	253	69.17	7.11	0	00.00	00.00
Nagaland	184	48.37	21.20	4	17.39	25.00
Sikkim	66	15.15	27.27	23	52.17	65.21
Tripura	337	1.19	2.37	152	13.95	17.11
India	65564	41.50	17.30	23662	67.11	51.00

* Includes Guidance services, Guidance Counsellors, Teacher Counsellors and Career Masters.
** Includes Full time, Part time, Trained and Untrained Librarians
Source: *The Sixth All India Educational Survey*, Vol. V – Educational Inputs and Facilities in Sec. and Hr. Sec. Schools.

Table 8.19: North-Eastern India : Enrolment of all Communities According to Type of Course in Percentage at + 2 Stage, 1993

State		*Arts*		*Science*		*Commerce*		*Vocational/Technical*	
		Total	*Girls*	*Total*	*Girls*	*Total*	*Girls*	*Total*	*Girls*
Arunachal Pradesh	R	73.45	71.27	25.68	19.95	0.75	0.61	0.00	0.00
	U	63.29	71.27	34.51	27.03	2.20	1.70	0.00	0.00
Assam	R	94.24	96.83	4.22	2.19	0.94	0.51	0.36	0.20
	U	84.10	92.54	11.12	5.45	3.81	1.34	0.97	0.67
Manipur	R	46.26	62.14	49.02	34.98	4.72	2.88	0.00	0.00
	U	46.44	54.67	34.26	29.38	5.93	4.71	1.88	3.37
Meghalaya	R	20.48	34.34	72.89	65.66	6.63	0.00	0.00	0.00
	U	58.13	59.63	37.02	39.13	0.00	0.00	4.84	1.24
Mizoram	R	0.00	0.00	0.00	0.00	0.00	0.00	0.00	0.00
	U	0.00	0.00	0.00	0.00	0.00	0.00	0.00	0.00
Nagaland	R	0.00	0.00	0.00	0.00	0.00	0.00	0.00	0.00
	U	71.67	82.61	28.33	17.39	0.00	0.00	0.00	0.00
Sikkim	R	61.35	68.64	32.86	27.94	5.51	3.41	0.17	0.00
	U	40.29	43.45	41.43	37.13	10.57	8.02	7.71	11.39
Tripura	R	78.09	88.72	11.13	7.92	10.78	3.36	0.00	0.00
	U	69.29	81.38	21.43	16.04	14.28	2.58	0.00	0.00
India	R	59.03	63.44	22.49	18.95	10.25	9.63	1.80	4.35
	U	41.11	48.00	30.88	25.99	19.63	17.63	5.03	5.20

R—Rural, U—Urban.

Source: *The Sixth All India Educational Survey*, Vol. V – Educational Inputs and Facilities in Secondary and Higher Secondary Schools.

than 100. The scheme is implemented through State governments with 100 per cent assistance for teaching learning equipment (TLE) and for salary of teachers during the plan period (GoI, 2002, p. 84).

The District Primary Education Programme (DPEP) was launched in 1994 as a major initiative to achieve the objective of Universalisation of Primary Education (UPE). The programme takes a holistic view of primary education development and seeks to operationalise the strategy of UPE through district specific planning with emphasis on decentralised criteria. DPEP, a centrally sponsored scheme, was introduced only in Assam state of the region. Other schemes also made a dent in the improvement of school education in different states. This is well reflected by improvement in literacy rate of the states, of the region.

Issues Summarised

In spite of the fact that enrolment has increased recently, still a large number of children remain outside the school. Drop out rates for both boys and girls have declined at the primary stage. The gap of the drop outs for boys and girls has also narrowed down. Now more children are studying in the system for a longer number of years (Govinda, 2002). More drop outs in girls, however, is a serious problem. Schools have to be provided with ancillary facilities in the form of drinking water and separate urinals and lavatories for the girls. Educational facilities have improved, but still in many secondary and higher secondary schools, science and home science are taught without laboratories. Libraries are in bad shape, and guidance and counselling services are not available in several schools. State-wise position and requirement are given below:

Arunachal Pradesh: Improvement in school facilities at primary and upper primary stages are required. Encouragement for girls enrolment in primary, upper primary and secondary classes are essential. Drop out rates particularly, among girls should be reduced at primary and upper primary levels. Ancillary facilities in the form of urinals, lavatories for boys, separate urinals and lavatories for girls are needed. Guidance services and libraries also demand special attention.

Assam: Girls enrolment needs special notice. Drop out rate should be controlled. Efforts to check drop out among girls need extra care particularly at the primary stage. Special attention should be given for lavatories, separate urinals and lavatories for girls. Laboratories for teaching home science, and science at the secondary stage need urgent consideration. Guidance services and library facilities demand improvement.

Manipur: Drop out rates in primary and upper primary classes need to be controlled. Improvement in ancillary facilities are needed, particularly separate urinals and lavatories for girls.

Meghalaya: Special care are needed to control drop out rates in primary, upper primary and secondary classes. Drop out rates are high both among tribal boys and girls; efforts are needed to check them. Extra effort should be made for construction of urinals and lavatories both for boys and girls. Laboratories for science and home science are also essential and libraries also require improvement.

Mizoram: Mizoram has better facilities in school education. But the drop out rate demands attention. Ancillary facilities in school of Mizoram are the best in the region. Laboratories for teaching science and home science, however, need improvement. Libraries are also required special attention.

Nagaland: Comparatively lower drop out rates exist even among girls. Ancillary facilities demand attention particularly lavatories. Laboratories for science and home science are needed.

Sikkim: School facilities are good. Drop out rate is high particularly at the upper primary stage. This needs special attention. Ancillary facilities are better but improvement in separate urinals and lavatories for girls demand special notice.

Tripura: Drop out rate is very high particularly at upper primary and secondary stages. Girl's drop out rate is high both at primary and upper primary stages. Drop out rates are high among the tribals. Ancillary facilities are poor. The state has to make extra provision for separate urinals and lavatories for girls. Science and home science laboratories have to be provided in several schools. Libraries and guidance services require proper care.

Prospects

Education is a prerequisite for progress and development. The main thrust of educational activities should be promotion of quantity, quality and excellence, all at a time. The Sarva Shiksha Abhiyan (SSA) launched by the Government of India to universalise elementary education through community ownership of the school system may remove many of the problems associated with primary and upper primary schools (NCERT, 200,1 p. 11). The goals of SSA are : (i) to have all children in schools by 2003, (ii) to ensure that all children complete 5 years of primary education by 2007 and 8 years of elementary schooling by 2010, (iii) to make education relevant, (iv) to remove social and gender gaps, and (v) to achieve universal retention by 2010. The basic features of the SSA are : (i) to undertake institutional reform, (ii) sustainable financing for the programme, (iii) to provide community ownership of the programme, (iv) to decentralise the process of education up to sub-district and habitation levels. The SSA will cover the following types of districts: Non-DPEP states and low female literacy districts, and unconcerned districts of DPEP states. This would benefit all the states of the north-eastern region. The states must ensure full utilisation of resources under the *abhiyan*.

Vocational education, which is not in good shape in the region must find a suitable place in the school system. This is important to provide learners with some kind of livelihood. Vocations should be related to available natural and human resources. This may generate employment opportunities for the people and reduce various kinds of tensions and anti-social activities, which are digressing the developmental efforts of the governments within the region.

Large scale erosion of human values in recent years has given birth to various kinds of social evils. For inculcation of human values, we have to make a concerted effort. This must be given weightage in education, and social, economic, and political life of a person. The system of evaluation of educational achievement and human personality will also have to be changed to include components of values.

Economic development is generally defined in terms of national income and its rate of growth, but this concept have to be changed. As all economic development programmes affect society, we should emphasise socio-economic development, rather than economic development (Singh and Agrawal, 2002). Socio-economic development demands well informed society, which knows the difference between good and bad aspect of a development.

REFERENCES

Census of India, 1991 (1998), *State Profile 1991 India*, Delhi: Controller of Publications.

Census of India 2001 (2001), *Provisional Population Totals*, Paper 1 of 2001. *Supplement, District Totals*, Delhi: Controller of Publications.

Census of India 2001 (2001), *Provisional Population Totals*, Paper 2 of 2001, *Rural-Urban Distribution*, Delhi: Controller of Publications.

Govinda, R., (Ed.) (2002), *India Education Report: A Profile of Basic Education* (NIEPA); New Delhi: Oxford University Press.

Government of India (2002), *India 2002: A Reference Annual*, New Delhi: Publications Division.

NCERT (1998), *The Sixth All India Educational Survey*: National Tables, Vol. I.

— (1997), *Educational Facilities in Rural and Urban Areas*; Vol. II—(1998) – *Schools and Physical Facilities*; Vol. III (1998) – *Teachers in Schools*, Vol. IV.

— (1998), *Enrolment in Schools*; Vol. V (1998), *Educational Inputs and Facilities in Secondary and Higher Secondary Schools*; Vol. VI (1998) – *Age-wise Enrolment, Repeats, Incentive Scheme etc. in Schools; Main Report.*

— (1999), *Selected Statistics* (1998), New Delhi: NCERT.

— (2001), *Sarva Shiksha Abhiyan*: Orientation on Appraisal and Supervision, New Delhi: NCERT.

Singh, Y.P. and Agrawal, A. (2002), Role of Education for Economic Development and Social Transformation, *Employment News*, 19-25 January, New Delhi.

9

Population and Development Education
A North East Indian Perspective

SIBY K. GEORGE

Introduction

India as a nation has been facing the population problems which is well known. However, whether this same problem is encountered with the same gravity in the north-eastern region of India is debatable. In the early 20th century, this region of India was said to be a land of scattered populations, who lived on the isolated hilltops and in the Brahmaputra, Barak and Imphal valleys. This perception of the region as a plenty of land, where space is not really a problem, has not radically changed over the years. But a close observation will reveal that the demography of the region in fact has radically changed and the quality of living conditions, especially in the rural/interior areas, is deplorable and inhuman, to say the least. The quality of life of people living in the far off pockets of the region cannot be masked for too long under the garb of affluence in the urban areas. This once again brings us face to face with the fact that availability of space/land is not the only or chief measure of the optimum size of population. All types of resources and social factors for sustainable development needs to be considered as a whole, while considering population problems. Mass education on the various aspects of Population and Development Education (PDE), then, is the best bet against population problems of the region.

A Word on the Need for Mass Education

When we use the term 'education', very often we think of 'formal education', that includes schooling, university education and technical and professional education. Now-a-days we hear a lot about non-formal education and vocational courses. This once again is largely perceived as technical and vocational courses offered to school and college drop outs with the aim of making them employment-friendly. What about the illiterate, semi-literate and neo-literate masses — are they outside all educational programmes? Cannot the masses be educated? A time has come when we, in India — country where the teeming millions (we are more than a billion now!) can tear down all that the educated class living in a high-tech 21st century, boast of as progress, development and advancement — should reflect with a sense of urgency on the need for mass education. Until the progressive human goals like literacy for all and better health facilities for all penetrate the Indian villages, can we really say the country is marching ahead? 'The soul of India', as Gandhiji said, 'lives in the villages'. Many of India's persistent difficulties can be solved only if we reach out to the masses with the message. A highly educated elite cream and the highest number of computer professionals and such other superlatives are mere myths that we need to come to terms with by looking deeply out into the masses.

Population Education : Concept

Population Education (PE) is a newly evolved and dynamic concept. The population science of 'demography' is not what is meant by 'PE'. In the present scenario, however, the need for PE is felt keenly. Implications of the changes in population for the quality of life of families and societies and the role individuals play in determining the nature of population change have given rise to the concept of PE. It is not easy to give a precise universally acceptable definition of this concept since population related beliefs and customs vary according to cultures and communities. However, it may be, with reservations, defined as that education process, which informs people about processes, characteristics and causes of population change and about the real picture of the population situation, so that, they may responsibly and reasonably comport themselves towards those changes and situations. Hence, PE has two important components: (i) population growth, dynamics and policies, including relation of population to economic and social development and population policies of governments, (ii) population growth, development and quality of life, including effects of population growth on sustainable development, educational development and quality of life, and relation of population growth to the environment and natural resources, and the emergent cross-cultural scenario.

Though issues relating to quality of life formed an important component of PE, the bias towards controlling the numbers, as if, it were an end in itself could not be avoided in the early stages of the development of the concept. Later the emphasis on sustainable development became pronounced and overgrowth of population was seen as a problem due to the pressure of the soaring numbers on limited resources.

The Population Explosion Concern in India

India's ever-soaring population is a matter of national concern. Statistics show that on an average, 16 million people are added each year to the country's already multitudinous population. We have crossed the 1-billion mark on 11 May 2000. India's diversity and complex nature and its strong democratic tradition do not allow the government to take any quick, drastic measures to control population. Though our policy makers regularly set national targets for containing the numbers, the gap between the target and the actual population growth situation has always been embarrassing. In this context, the cases of states like Kerala and Tamil Nadu suggest that increase in general awareness through literacy will have a positive impact on population control measures. It was also clear that education is the best bet against uncontrollable population explosion and unhealthy population conditions. Hence, the Ministry of Human Resources Development (MHRD), Government of India, in collaboration with the UNFPA undertook three PE projects in 1986 for three different target groups: (i) school-going population, (ii) college and university going population, and (iii) the community in general.

Of these three projects, the third one has special significance. It particularly strives to integrate PE in adult literacy programmes. Since adult illiterates generally are not favourably disposed to population control measures due to their beliefs and customs, educating the illiterate adults, enrolled at literacy programmes about population issues was visualised as the best way of improving the results of population control programmes. This is especially vital because the target learners of the adult literacy programme generally belonged to 15-35 years age group, which is the most reproductive group of the population. Even though it is important to educate school going youth and those in higher education on the population concerns, I think, the real target group for PE programmes should be the ordinary masses. Family size and quality of life among the educated class is increasingly becoming reasonable, but not among the vast majority of our people, who live in the villages or migrate to the towns for small jobs. Until the message reaches them, we, as a nation, will not be able to grapple with the population explosion reality. The original goal of the PE project was: "to enhance knowledge, awareness and understanding of learners of adult literacy programmes about core population issues, in order to develop attitudes favourable for appreciation of problems of over population and 'demand' for measurers to control it."

The three phases of the programme have already been completed and the fourth phase is presently going on. Some of the core issues that were originally treated in the PE programmes of this project were family size, spacing of children, responsible parenthood, right age of marriage, population related beliefs and customs and population and development, and the messages of these components became integral part of the adult literacy programmes. However, the number-mania could not be avoided in the early years of the project.

Population and Development

The PE programme in India underwent a constructive change after the shift of focus made by the International Conference on Population Development (ICPD), Cairo, in September 1994, from mere numerical control issues to population as a problem related to development. After this, the PE project in India was itself re-named as population and development education or PDE. With this change the emphasis was straight on issues like reproductive health and reproductive rights, fostering human dignity, gender equality and women's empowerment, adolescent reproductive health and sex education, family life education, and preventive and curative education for STDs, RTIs and HIV-AIDS. The empowerment of women both as an end, in itself and as a means to population stabilisation, became the key issue in the successive phases of the PDE national project. Though the PE project of the Government of India would continue with the originally conceived core concerns of the project, since ICPD, the content and methodology of the project would be saturated with the ICPD objectives, which are:

(a) to achieve equality and equity based on harmonious partnership between men and women and enable women to realise their full potential,
(b) to ensure women's contribution to sustainable development through their involvement and participation in policy and decision-making, employment, production, education, health, science and technology, sports, culture etc. as active decision makers, participants and beneficiaries, and
(c) to ensure that all women and men are provided with the education necessary for them to fulfil their basic human needs and to exercise their human rights.

It is believed that this shift of emphasis from containing the numbers to contributing to the quality of life of the population by primarily empowering women, by educating both them and men is the best bet, against the problem of population explosion and its ill effects.

Key Population and Development Education (PDE) Issues

There are several issues in PDE on which training is given to literacy and NGO functionaries, in order that they in turn instill these messages to the neo-literates, who are primarily within the age group 15-35. Some of these key issues are:

(a) family life education
(b) gender equality and equity
(c) adolescent and reproductive health
(d) Health and education
(e) Sustainable development
(f) Urbanisation and migration

The North East

When the reports of the 2001 Census of India began to be published, the north east had little to cheer about. North East India as a region has the highest rate of growth of population. The state of Nagaland and its Wokha district top the list of states and districts with the highest rate of growth of population respectively. However, what is alarming is not just the swelling numbers. In fact, if there were enough resources the great numbers would not have been a problem. The bulging population of the north east, especially in the interior, far off regions, lives under inhuman conditions. Despite the fact that most of the north-eastern states have a literacy rate above the national average, population here is overgrowing the limits. Hence, the urgency to impart sound PDE to the educated, literate, semi-literate and neo-literate populations of the north east needs to be felt all the more.

Let me briefly dwell on certain specific issues in relation to PDE, which have special relevance for the north east region.

Sustainable development

With the advent of globalisation and all that modernity brings, development is seen as consumerism in the region. Instead of reckless consumption in imitation, we need to promote sustainable consumption in the region. Optimum level of consumption as a middle path between under-consumption by the vast majority and over-consumption by a few should be encouraged. For this we have to revert to consumption that is affordable for the people of the region in accordance with available resources rather than recklessly imitating and importing consumption styles and items. This was adequately emphasised specifically for the north east Indian context, during the discussions of United Nations Development Programme in Itanagar from 20 to 21 September 1998.

Population concern

According to the 2001 Census report north east India as a region has the highest rate of growth of population. Nagaland state and its Wokha district are topping the list. If the swelling members had enough resources to live with dignity, there would have been no problem. However, this is not the case. People in the villages are living under inhuman conditions. *Jhum* cycles are being reduced and alternative methods of cultivation are not easily introduced. Though four out of the seven north east Indian states have a literacy rate above the national average, basic population and development issues like family planning and maternal and child health have not been accepted on a mass scale. Using all available medium (radio, television, posters and especially newspapers and all print media, adult literacy programmes, street dramas, health camps etc.) for championing the cause of addressing the population concern as a development problem, is the need of the hour in the region.

Migration

All observers of north east Indian society know that migration is one of the reasons for the high rate of growth of population in the region and the root cause of social turbulence here. It has changed the demography of the border districts of Assam and the social structure of Tripura. Sanjoy Hazarika poignantly remarks in his *Strangers of the Mist*: "Tripura is one of the few places in the world where, in the 20th century, indigenous people has been transformed from a numerical majority and ruling community into a minority, dependent on the goodwill and largesse of immigrants, who have seized economic and political influence" (p. 32). In 1999 unofficial estimates claimed that, if the present trend of migration continues in Nagaland, the Nagas will be a minority in less than 25 years in their own land (*North East Sun*, Dec. 1-14, p. 13, "A Silent Incursion" Krishna Das, Cover Story – "Welcome to Working Guests"). Hence migration is a serious issue that PDE needs to address so that indigenous people themselves do not become complacent promoters of migration but may socially and under legitimate means discourage the trend.

Urbanisation

North East has one of the highest urbanisation rates in the country. According to 1991 Census, Aizawl, the capital of Mizoram, topped the list. This is the chief reason for a masking sense of affluence in the region. A surge in urbanisation masks the reality of life in the rural areas. Again, if the rural areas are bereft of enough population, there development would not speed up. A balance in urbanisation levels in another PDE issue specially relevant for the north east.

Women's reproductive health and child care

While the women of most of the north east Indian communities seem to live in more freedom than their counter-parts in others parts of India, due to the easy mingling of the sexes here, are women truly empowered here? Most of them live under inhuman conditions and work much more than their men. Their health conditions are awful and their babies are not properly cared for. Vaccination, immunization, post and pre-natal care, awareness of sexually transmitted diseases and reproductive tract infections need to improve a lot among them. Rural development can be effectively achieved only if women become enlightened and empowered. This is an uncontradicted global experience, and needs to be given special attention in the context of the north-eastern region of the country.

Adolescence education

Most of the communities of north east India are undergoing transitional phase. There are a lot of uncertainties and anxieties. There is the break-up of traditional authority. Young people, especially in tribal societies, who once enjoyed freedom and social control in a balanced way, are today increasingly taking up bohemian youth culture of violence, experimenting with dangerous substances, youth movements, illicit sex and the like. This scenario needs to be checked very urgently for the future of the north east Indian society itself. Hence, adolscene education looms large as a significant and relevant component of PDE in north east India. We should not see young people as villains but as victims of a particular transitional social situation. This is an important message for PDE programmes here.

Sanctity of marriage

Though this cannot be universally applied, the relevance of the institution of marriage and family life are increasingly threatened in the region. Divorce is a common problem now-a-days, especially in towns. This is yet another PDE issue that has special relevance for the region. Among the tribal societies of the north east, where familial bonds were once very strong, the threat to these ties is felt more keenly as a result of the crosscurrents of sweeping transitions and changes. Hence, family life education needs to be taken up in a massive scale in the region.

Early marriage and spacing of children

Early marriage is the most significant cause of high rate of growth of population in north east India besides migration. This is almost a universal phenomenon in rural north east. Spacing of children is at the same time a means and an end. When children are born with sufficient intermediate break, there is all the possibility of smaller family size. It is also necessary for the health of the mother and child. These issues also need special attention in PDE programmes of the north east India.

Conclusion

The above discussion is only about what is good for future programmes of PDE in the region. Here I have not adequately dealt with how the MHRD programme itself is faring in north east India. In most of the north east Indian states, there are no State Resource Centres into which the PDE programme for mass education is incorporated in the country. It exists only in Meghalaya and Assam, however, the error is with a programme approach, though the action plan drawn out for the years is well monitored through two national projects progress review meetings every year. Even though the action plan is faithfully carried out, I think, we care little about the people, for whom the programmes are conducted, whether their lives have been improved or not. We need to choose for a *person approach* to a mere *programme approach*, whereby the effects of the programmes are timely evaluated by quantifying the improvement of the quality of life of the persons, who benefited from the programmes. At the close, it may be re-emphasised that the PDE message needs to reach to every nook and corner of north east India, before the population problem here grows into volcanic proportions.

10

Perceived Self-efficacy and Academic Achievement of Primary School Students

ANJALI GHOSH

Introduction

People's beliefs about their personal efficacy constitute a major aspect of their self-knowledge. Bandura (1977) describes self-efficacy as "the belief in one's capability to organise and execute courses of action required to produce given attainments". Efficacy beliefs influence the particular courses of action a person chooses to pursue, the amount of effort that will be expended, the willingness to persevere in the face of challenges and failures, resilience to adversity, and the ability to cope with the demands associated with the chosen course.

Bandura (1986), in his theory of self-efficacy, contended that students, accepted challenges when they believe that they have a reasonable chance of success. This would occur more often in non-competitive environments, because these situations can permit more students to experience success. He has suggested that self-efficacy judgments can vary along the dimension of level, generality and strength. People's efficacy perception may involve only simple and easy tasks or include even the most demanding ones within a particular domain (level); individuals may judge themselves to be effective only in a restricted range of domains or consider themselves to be effective only in a restricted range of domains or consider themselves efficacious across a wide range of activities and situations (generality). Persons with a strong sense of personal competence remain steadfast on occasional failures, whereas those with weak percepts of efficacy are quick to resign with self-deliberating expectations (strength).

Academic self-efficacy is often conceptualised as a domain-specific construct, and its relationship with various indices and achievement have frequently been studied in the context of carrying out a specific task of interest (Bandura and Schunk, 1981). Students with a strong sense of academic self-efficacy have been proven to expend greater effort for accomplishing a given task (Schunk, 1983, Salomon, 1984), persist longer in the presence of difficulties (Bandura and Schunk, 1981; Schunk, 1982), use more effective learning strategies (Pintrich and De Groot, 1990) and self-regulate better than others (Zimmerman and Martinez-Pons, 1990). A meta-analysis of self-efficacy research in educational settings (Multom, Brown and Lent, 1991) found that self-efficacy was related both to academic performance (average correlation = .38) as well as persistence (average correlation = .34).

Most academic self-efficacy studies have used measures that focus on the strength of efficacy beliefs. Several researchers have recently began to think that academic self-efficacy perception possesses a certain degree of generality across similar activities or domains (Schunk, 1991; Pajares, 1996). The generality of academic self-efficacy judgments was found to be depended on the degree of perceived similarity among tasks (Bong, 1997). Self-judged efficacy has proved to yield significant impact on many facets of students' academic quest. It is also interesting to find out whether and how much students, with firm or weak percepts of efficacy in one domain of academic functioning, face another domain with equal certainty.

The objective of the present study is to investigate the role of self-efficacy judgments on academic achievement in two groups of primary school students from West Bengal and Tripura. The study also tries to explore whether perception of efficacy in one domain is transferred across similar activities. Academic achievement is measured here in the areas of reading comprehension (language) and arithmetic.

Methodology

Subjects

The subjects of this study were 128 students, selected from West Bengal and Tripura. There were 64 boys and 64 girls. All of them were studying in class IV. There were 42 boys and 36 girls selected randomly from two schools of Birbhum district, West Bengal, and 22 boys and 28 girls selected randomly from two schools of West Tripura district of

Tripura. Most of the students were from lower-middle socio-economic class. Both the states have similarity with respect to language and other social customs.

Measures and Procedures

Self-efficacy judgments

Children's perception of self-efficacy for reading comprehension and for solving arithmetic problems were measured. Children were shown one passage for reading comprehension for five minutes followed by six questions — each question was shown for 10 seconds. For arithmetic also, six questions were shown — each for ten seconds. The efficacy judgment for each student was taken on a four-point scale — ranging from 1 to 4 with verbal descriptors as 1 = Not sure, 2 = Maybe, 3 = Pretty sure, and 4 = Real sure. The children were shown the problems in such a way that they could judge their capability to solve a problem. However, they were asked not to solve the problems at that time.

Achievement measures

Achievement measures were constructed in the area of reading comprehension (language) and arithmetic. The tests were out of the textbooks used in the school, but based on the syllabus.

In the reading comprehension test, one passage was given and then six questions were to be answered. Arithmetic test contained six problems, two each from subtraction, division and simplification. Students were provided sheets of paper for solving the problems.

School Performance Record

Marks obtained by the students in the last examination for language and arithmetic were also collected. Besides these, some biographical information like age, gender, socio-economic condition of the family etc. were also taken from the students.

Data from the students were collected individually. Initially rapport was established with the students and then data were collected.

Results and Discussion

Analyses were conducted on the scores of academic achievement (reading comprehension and arithmetic), and self-efficacy beliefs. Achievement in the area of reading comprehension and arithmetic was scored as 1 for correct answer and 0 for wrong answer. Then the scores were summed up for the six items for reading comprehension and arithmetic separately. Composite self-efficacy score was obtained by summing up the self-efficacy belief across each item. The maximum possible score for achievement (reading comprehension and arithmetic) was 6 and for self-efficacy belief 24. The means and standard deviations for all the variables were obtained for the two groups of students separately and the values are presented in Table 10.1.

Table 10.1: Means and Standard Deviations for self-efficacy beliefs and academic achievement of two groups of students

*Measures**	*West Bengal (N =78)*		*Tripura (N = 50)*	
	Mean	*S.D.*	*Mean*	*S.D.*
SERC	20.18	3.15	21.58	2.18
Ach. RC	3.60	1.52	4.42	1.39
SEAR	20.35	3.09	15.44	2.53
Ach. AR	2.69	1.70	1.16	1.04

* SERC = Self-efficacy (Reading Comprehension).
Ach. RC = Achievement (Reading Comprehension).
SEAR = Self-efficacy (Arithmetic).
Ach. AR = Achievement (Arithmetic).

From the values presented in Table 10.1 it is clear that there is difference in the mean scores of students of the two states. Significant difference was observed with respect to self-efficacy judgment of arithmetic (t-value = 9.82, $p<.01$), achievement in arithmetic (t-value = 6.38, $p<.01$) and achievement in reading comprehension (t-value = 3.15, $p<.01$). Students of West Bengal scored significantly higher in self-efficacy judgment of arithmetic and also in arithmetic achievement test, whereas students of Tripura scored significantly higher in reading comprehension.

Correlation analyses were conducted to gain information about the relationship among the different variables for the two groups of students. The values are presented in Table 10.2.

From Table 10.2, it is clear that there is significant positive relationship between student's perception of self-efficacy beliefs in reading comprehension and arithmetic with subsequent achievement in that area for the students of West Bengal, but in case of students of

Tripura this relationship of self-efficacy belief was found to be significant only for reading comprehension.

Table 10.2: Intercorrelations among self-efficacy beliefs and achievements measures[a]

	SERC	*Ach. RC*	*SEAR*	*Ach. AR*
SERC	—	.40**	.32**	.33**
Ach. RC	.29*	—	.24**	.42**
SEAR	.33*	-.06	—	.47**
Ach. AR	.14	.31*	.22	—

[a] Values in the upper half of the table are for West Bengal and in the lower half are for Tripura.

* Significant at .05 level.

** Significant at .01 level.

Relationship of self-efficacy judgments with school examination marks in the area of language and arithmetic were also done. It was observed that for the students of West Bengal, self-efficacy perceptions for the specially constructed achievement tests are also significantly related with marks obtained in the school examination (language: r-value = .39, p<.01), (arithmetic: r-value = .35, p<.01). But for the students of Tripura this relationship was not found to be significant. It shows that efficacy perception of students of Tripura were not so firm and for that their judgments were not found to function with equal certainty with other related domains.

Congruence Between Self-efficacy Judgment and Academic Achievement

This analysis is based on agreement measures between self-efficacy judgments and accuracy in achievement of reading comprehension and/or arithmetic. It was envisaged that the more efficacious judgments the students could give, the more correct answers they would provide subsequently. For measuring this, self-efficacy judgments of students at and above the median value were designated as efficacious. Similarly, achievement scores at and above the median in the respective field were designated as accurate. Congruence was observed when students judged themselves as efficacious *i.e.* capable of solving a problem or question and subsequently solved or answered that accurately or *vice versa*. Incongruence measure may be either overestimation or underestimation. Overestimation was found when a student judged that he/she could solve a certain problem but subsequently failed. And underestimation was observed when a student judged that he/she would not be able to solve a problem but subsequently solved that. Table 10.3 presents the percentages of congruence and incongruence between self-efficacy judgments and academic achievement.

Table 10.3: Percentage distribution of congruence and incongruence between self-efficacy judgment and achievement measures for boys and girls of West Bengal and Tripura

Congruence Index	*West Bengal*				*Tripura*			
	Reading comprehension		*Arithmetic*		*Reading comprehension*		*Arithmetic*	
	Boys	*Girls*	*Boys*	*Girls*	*Boys*	*Girls*	*Boys*	*Girls*
Congruence	69.0	73.0	64.3	47.2	41.0	82.1	45.0	60.7
Over estimation	19.0	13.5	33.3	27.8	45.4	3.6	45.0	25.0
Underestimation	12.0	13.5	2.4	25.0	13.6	14.3	10.0	14.3

It is revealed from Table 10.3 that 60 per cent and above students correctly judged their capabilities both in reading comprehension and in arithmetic except in case of girl, students of West Bengal in reading comprehension and boy students of Tripura in both the subjects. The boys have not given much efficacious judgment, instead 45 per cent of them overestimated their self-efficacy judgments. Girls underestimated their judgments more than boys both in reading comprehension and in arithmetic in both the States. They also overestimated their judgments for arithmetic. It may be a fact that most of them were first generation learners, who have low self-confidence level and thus could not accurately judge their capabilities.

Conclusion

It can be concluded from the findings of the study that self-efficacy perceptions of students are positively related with their achievement in reading comprehension and arithmetic. The findings also reveal that perceived efficacy in one area is transferred to other similar tasks.

It is observed from the results that the boys have overestimated their efficacy judgments more than girls. This overestimated judgment was found more for the boy students of Tripura. And the girls of West Bengal have underestimated their judgments, more in case of arithmetic.

This can be explained by self-worth theory (Beery, 1975; Covington and Beery, 1976). It may be that both the boys and the girls have demonstrated self-serving biases in judging their capabilities (Covington and Omelich, 1979; Schunk, 1981). To lessen the sense of failure, students might have judged their expectations unrealistically high. Conversely, they might have judged their expectation unrealistically low in some cases, thereby guaranteeing success.

Thus, the present investigation supports the idea that students' self-perceptions about their capabilities have an important effect on subsequent achievement. This relationship was not found to be very strong for the students of Tripura. The reason may be that the sample size was small and most of them were first generation learners having low self-confidence. It can be said that students' efficacy judgments can be enhanced through proper guidance and counselling. Parents and teachers can play an important role in fostering this important aspect of school learning.

REFERENCES

Bandura, A. (1986). *Social foundations of thought and action: A social cognitive theory*. Englewood Cliffs, NJ: Prentice Hall.

Bandura, A. (1997). *Self-efficacy : The exercise of control*. W.H. Freeman & Company, New York.

Bandura, A., & Schunk, D.H. (1981). Cultivating competence, self-efficacy and intrinsic interest through proximal self-motivation. *Journal of Personality and Social Psychology*, 41, 586-98.

Berry, R.G. (1975). Fear of failure in the student experience. *Personnel and Guidance Journal*, 54, 190-203.

Bong, M. (1997). Generality of academic self-efficacy judgments : Evidence of hierarchical relations, *Journal of Educational Psychology*, Vol. 89, No. 4, 696-709.

Covington, M.V. & Berry, R.G. (1976). *Self-worth and school learning*. New York : Holt, Rineheart & Winston.

Covington, M.V. & Omelich, C.L. (1979). Effort : The double edged sword in school achievement. *Journal of Educational Psychology*, 71, 169-182.

Multon, K.D., Brown, S.D. & Lent, R.W. (1991). Relation of self-efficacy beliefs to academic outcomes : A meta-analytic investigation. *Journal of Counselling Psychology*, 38, 30-38.

Pajares, F. (1996). Self-efficacy beliefs in academic settings. *Review of Educational Research*, 66, 543-578.

Pintrich, P.R. & Degroot, E.V. (1990). Motivational and self-regulated learning components of classroom academic performance. *Journal of Educational Psychology*, 82, 33-40.

Salomon, G. (1984). Television is "easy" and print is "tough" : The differential investment of mental effort in learning as a function of preconceptions and attitudes. *Journal of Educational Psychology*, 76, 647-658.

Schunk, D.H. (1982). Effects of effort attributional feedback on children's perceived self-efficacy and achievement. *Journal of Educational Psychology*, 74, 548-556.

Schunk, D.H. (1983). Ability *versus* effort attributional feedback : Differential effects on self-efficacy and achievement. *Journal of Educational Psychology*, 75, 848-856.

Schunk, D.H. (1991). Self-efficacy and academic motivation. *Educational Psychologist*, 26, 207-231.

Zimmerman, B.J. & Martinez-Pons, M. (1990). Student differences in self-regulated learning : Relating grade, sex, and giftedness to self-efficacy and strategy use. *Journal of Educational Psychology*, 82, 51-59.

11

Education in India and Its North East
Some Unpopular Thoughts

GORKY CHAKRABORTY

Introduction

Whenever the early *homo sapiens* learnt, discovered or deciphered certain things or traits, which were new, their first task must have been to preserve the new found knowledge and secondly, to impart it to the younger generations, so that they could carry it forward for the generations to come. Whether the discovery of fire or the process of preservation of food or say the use of letters, in all cases the finer nuances of these skills were passed on to children as the common wisdom of mankind. The process of learning or education thereby began its journey and in the process new facts were unearthed, which enlightened newer generations. Later, with the evolution of human civilization certain aspects emerged concerning education and the process of imparting it, namely (i) who is to educate a child — the family or society; and (ii) for whom a child is to be educated — for itself or the society. It seems that the methodology and framework of the education system has revolved around these two principal contradictions. Nations and societies have attempted to resolve them within their own ideologies and world-views. The present era of globalisation has also been dealing with these contradictions and now attempts are being made to resolve them within the redefined parameters.

The Athenian semi-egalitarianism dealt with these contradictions under the tutelage of Plato. According to him 'a child should be given over to society; it may be reared by his mother in so far as she is a good wet-nurse, but then it passes into the hands of the specialists, who develop it into a real man'.[1] Similarly, the Greeks placed society before the individual and pleaded that a child should be educated for the society. 'Every Greek teaches : do not try to elevate yourself above others. When people become too eminent — never mind whether it may be a famous general or famous statesman — he is driven out of the state, he is punished with ostracism, because such a large, overgrown individually may be noxious to democracy'.[2] They encouraged the growth of individuality but discouraged individualism. Athenian democracy has been in that sense quite clear regarding resolving the contradictions between the child, family education and society.

In Greek democracy, Spartan aristocracy or Indian caste system the model of education[3] has been followed on above lines and if not fully homogenous the major elements of those systems were common. But in all forms of ancient societies, education has been by and large limited to the ruling elite, who formed the dominant minority in their respective socio-political and economic set-up, whereas the vast majority remained outside the ambit of the education system. This particular pattern of socially restrictive education continued over a long period of human history. Later the era of enlightenment along with its democratic ideals started changing the situation in Europe, which took some centuries more to reach the Indian shores. It has been slowly realised that democratisation of the educational system by encompassing the subdued majority is necessary for the development of the society.

During the 18th century there has been a realisation that political power and equality before law were not enough, if lack of knowledge persist among the masses. Thomas Jefferson[4] in 1786, *i.e.* three years before the start of French Revolution wrote to his great predecessor 'I hold it to be axiomatic that out freedom can be safe only in the hands of the people themselves, and then only if the people have attained a certain level of education. That is why the introduction of education on a common plain is the first charge of the state.' However it has not been realised in the 18th century that equally, any educational and cultural programme would remain a good intention only, unless it is based upon the transference into society's hands of the means of production. The Bolshevik Revolution of 1917 carried this message to its logical conclusions. Lunacharsky[5] stated after the Revolution 'the struggle of the people for its freedom and its well-being proceeds along three lines. The people can account itself victorious, as having attained full power of the people, when it is in possession of the means of production and in possession of knowledge.' So political power (by capturing the state), economic power (by socialising means of production) has been added with transmission of knowledge to every man, *i.e.* wide educational network resulting in maximum consciousness of the masses.

Today both the models are under severe strain, while one has collapsed in its own weight, the other is continuously modifying itself for survival and therefore the contradictions raised in the beginning of this section remains unresolved. In the next section, this paper deals with these contradictions within the Indian educational framework in its historical continuum.

Indigenous *vis-à-vis* Macaulian Educational System[6]

The contradictions raised in the previous section has also been found in India. How different patterns of educational systems have responded to it, is discussed in this section. The indigenous, Macaulian and reformer's agenda of education has been considered here.

There has been a deliberate attempt by colonial historiography to destroy and negate the indigenous institutions in order to replace them by colonial organisations. It was undertaken so that the roots of colonial administration gets firmly rooted in the consciousness of those emerging classes, who would help in nurturing the colonial framework. Without denying the importance and role played by western education in changing social consciousness in India, it can also be said that the indigenous institutions too played an equally important role in building a base for education during pre and early colonial period. Paucity of data and written text hampers the process of evaluation regarding the role played by these institutions. Yet, from the reports of various colonial administrators, their role can be assessed to a great extent. Thomas Munro's Report in 1822 for Madras Presidency, Mountstuart Elphinstone's Report in 1823 for Bombay Presidency and the most elaborate Report of William Adam in 1835-38 for Bengal Presidency are valuable treasures. These Reports helps in understanding the role, efficacy and importance of indigenous educational institutions, which has been just brushed aside by colonial historiography.

Indigenous educational institutions can be broadly categorised as elementary schools and institutions of higher learning. Among the elementary school category there were two types — one, which derived their principal support from the patronage of a single wealthy family and the second, which was depended upon the general support of the community, where they were established. In the schools run by wealthy families not only the children of these families were taught but children from neighbourhood were also drawn into them. These institutions were broadly included under the domestic system, which played an important role in the indigenous framework. The other category of schools were maintained by the pupils themselves and these institutions were attached to the temples, mosques or to the charitable institutions. Other than this, several centres of higher learning in Sanskrit, Arabic and Persian flourished during the 18th century.

These Reports also provides an insight into the number of students served, nature of curriculum etc. Adam came to the conclusion that there was a village school for every 400 persons or every 73 children of school going age or one for every 30 to 32 boys. In Madras, Munro found one primary school in every village, for approximately 1,000 people. So according to Munro's assessment, one child out of every three of school going age received education. John Malcom observed similarly in Central India, where every village with a hundred houses had an elementary school. Although there has been debates and disagreements among scholars who cited that the number of institutions and population served as myth and exaggeration; a careful analysis of these Reports and contemporary chronicles reveals that they were exaggerated but in no way related to myth.

In terms of curriculum, these schools emphasised on memorising literary texts and on studying grammar and metaphysics, science and mathematics remained out of the students pursuit. Surprisingly, Adam remarked in his Report that "my recollections of the village schools of Scotland do not enable me to pronounce that the institution given in them has a more direct bearing upon daily interests of life than that, which I find given or proposed to be given, in the humble village schools of Bengal." Thus the dark period (as emphasised by colonial historiographers) had its own indigenous educational system, which sustained the Indian population within its traditional socio-cultural framework. It might have been dimly lit but certainly far from dark.

Instead of reforming the then existing shortcomings of the indigenous educational system, the colonial administrators imposed an alien educational policy, which suited their colonial administration. Through the dissemination of colonial ideology, the colonial administrators seeked to create a class who were 'Indian in blood and colour but European in taste and manners'. The colonial rule has been proposed to be maintained not simply with the help of the police and the army, but also by an illusion created by ideological influences. In creating this illusion, education had the dominant role. Thus the colonial or Macaulian system of education emphasised only on the requirements of politico-administrative framework of colonial administration leaving aside mass education.

The Indian reformers on the other hand were able to understand various changes that were occurring during early colonial period particularly concerning with fragmentation of caste, occupational mobility, sanskritization etc. and could put forward an educational system, which were in tune with the evolving scenario yet not alien to the indigenous framework of educational practices. In spite of individual preference patterns, there were marked similarities in the scheme of education as forwarded by Indian reformers. Prominent among them were Rammohan Roy, Mahadev Govind Ranade, Sayyid Ahmed Khan, Veeresalingam, Dayanand, Vidyasagar, Kesab Chandra Sen and Akshay Kumar Dutt. The reformers realised the inadequacies of the traditional methods and content of education and therefore proposed a system, which they thought will help in the process of India's regeneration. They were against both the then existing traditional system and the imposed colonial system and pleaded for 'a liberal and enlightened system of instruction, embracing Mathematics, Natural Philosophy, Chemistry and Anatomy with other useful Sciences.'

This alternative system of education had three major focal points, namely free and compulsory education, education through vernacular languages and a proper emphasis on scientific outlook and knowledge. Both the traditional pattern and the colonial one, redirected education for a small section of the society, which was strongly opposed by the reformers. Majority of reformers emphasised upon free and compulsory education, *e.g.* Akshay Kumar Dutt pleaded for free and compulsory education, whereas according to the suggestion of Dayanand, their should be a government order and national custom that nobody should keep their children at home, once they attained the age of eight. Anyone, who violated the order should be strictly punished. The reformers pleaded for mass education to enlighten and awaken the masses against oppression, superstition and exploitation. Similarly, instead of Sanskrit or English they preferred vernacular medium of instruction. Oriental classics and scientific knowledge were sought to be translated into Indian languages for the benefit of the masses. Many reformers published journals in vernacular languages, namely Rammohan's *Sambad*

Kaumudi, Young Bengal's *Gyananveshan*, Debendranath's and Akshay Kumar's *Tattwabodhini Patrika*, Kesub's *Sulabh Samachar*, Bal Shastri Jambekar's *Dig Darshan*, Bhau Mahajan's *Prabhakar*, Naroji's *Rast Goftar,* Veeresalingam's *Vivekvardhini* to name a few. The lack of knowledge of the vernacular languages has been identified as one of the major reasons for the misery and degradation of India.

The reformer's emphasis on science education has been due to the result of a growing realisation that scientific knowledge is crucial to the progress of the country and its culture. Even in schools run by Arya Samaj, where there seemed to be an obsession with Vedic knowledge, scientific subjects found a place in their curriculum. The establishment of various scientific and technical institutes as well as journals were a step forward in that direction. Society for Translating European Sciences, Mechanical Institute, National Institute for the Cultivation of Sciences and journals such as *Vigyan Sebadi*, *Bigyan Sar Sangraha* etc. were some of the glaring testimonies.

So the agenda of reforms of education both in terms of content and instruction has been different from the traditional and colonial system of educational framework. It has been neither restricted in 'approach' nor limited in 'access' for the masses. But the success of their programme were depended upon various inter-related factors and as the politico-administrative reality in India has been sharply different from their ideals, the scope for their success remained limited. On the other hand, the Macaulian system, which seeked to destroy the indigenous forms and create a comprador class best suited to the colonial administration and therefore received full patronage. The reformers ideals of national reawakening, mass education and scientific knowledge has never been in the colonial agenda as a result of which, those ideals never transformed into reality. To quote Gramsci[7] from a different context it was right to struggle against the old school, but reforming it was not so simple as it seemed. The problem was not one of model curricula but of men, and not just of the men who are actually teachers themselves but of the entire social complex, which they express. The prevailing social complex resulted in the ultimate success of the Macaulian System over the indigenous system of learning and the process, which started, then continue till date giving rise to confused identities and contradictory mental frameworks.

Education Since Independence

Our 'tryst with destiny' ushered in a new era of reawakening, regeneration and a process of nation-building for transforming the ideals of our reformers into reality, which was earlier impeded due to the contradiction between British imperialism and the interest of the Indian masses. It also provided with an opportunity to our policy-makers to frame an education policy, which will be rooted to our soil and serve the purpose of the Indian people. But the contradiction within the ruling elite who held the reigns of power in independent India proved to be an obstacle in this direction. Among the policy formulators, those who were tutored under the Macaulian System gained prominence over their indigenous counterparts due to which, mass education (by emphasising on primary education) through vernacular medium of instruction did not gain prominent. On the other hand, modern education became synonymous with English medium educational system, which by and large like the colonial system, kept the masses away from the entire set-up. The ghost of Macaulay haunted our nation-builders and the words of Rabindranath and Gandhiji fell on deaf ears. Rabindranath[8] expressed boldly 'true modernism is freedom of mind, not slavery of taste, it is independence of thought and action, not tutelage under European schoolmasters'. Similarly Gandhiji's[9] statement 'my resistance to Western civilization is really a resistance to its indiscriminate and thoughtless imitation based on the assumption that Asiatics are fit only to copy everything that comes from the West' was never heeded to and both Rabindranath and Gandhiji's views regarding indigenous education were thrown into the dustbin of history. Therefore, the crisis of self-identity, contradiction in world-view and lack of participatory nature of development approach ushered in an educational framework, which lacked the elements of mass content and appeal respectively. Accordingly, the instructions of white *sahibs* prevailed with minor modifications to create a class of brown *sahibs* in India.

The contradictions within the ruling elites became evident when we consider the issue of mass education in India. It unmask the duality of words and deeds of our power-brokers. While Akshay Kumar Dutt[10], Dayanand[11] and other reformers pleaded for free and compulsory elementary education, it has been Goakhle[12] in 1910, who introduced a bill in the Imperial Legislative Council recommending that a beginning must be made in the direction of making elementary education free and compulsory. Although the bill stood rejected yet the nationalist always pressed for its re-introduction. Consequently, Primary Education Act has been passed in various Provinces and Presidencies for introduction of compulsory education. But under the colonial rule, primary education has been largely neglected and it remained mostly in private hands. In 1936-37, 62 per cent of the primary schools were private schools, 37 per cent were local board schools and just 1 per cent were government schools.[13] Similarly, during 1890 to 1920[14], the expenditure on primary education remained more or less a constant proportion of the total educational expenditure from local board and government funds, namely 30 to 35 per cent.

The Sargeant Committee[15] in 1944 recommended achievement of free and compulsory education by 1960. The nationalist opposed it on the ground that 1960 was far too distant and that Sargeant wanted to keep India backward. Interestingly when the nationalists in the Constituent Assembly got the opportunity to make primary education free and compulsory, they retreated and instead of an Act in the Constitution, it was included in the Directive Principles. Here also the contradiction of our ruling elites, while framing the laws and Constitution for an independent India, came to the forefront. It has been at the beginning of the 21st century or 54 years after independence that free and compulsory primary education became a fundamental right through the 93rd Constitution Amendment Bill.

In the latest endeavour concerning free and compulsory education, our ruling elite have once again side tracked various related issues and therefore have given rise to more questions than it has seeked to answer through the Bill. When on November 28, 2001 the Indian Parliament passed the 93rd Constitution Amendment Bill[16], it contained several loopholes, which in its ultimate analysis might defeat the purpose of free and compulsory education in India.

Firstly, the age group for which elementary education has been made compulsory is 6-14 years. Here the guarantee of education for 6-14 years age group is meaningless without the state taking responsibility for Early Childhood Care and Education (ECCE). So while elementary education has been deemed to be a fundamental right under the Constitution, the same right has been placed under Directive Principles for the age group of 0-6 years. So 93rd Constitution Amendment Bill (read Article 21A of the Constitution) through its enactment nullified Article 45 under which, there has been a provision for early childhood care and education for all children.

Secondly, the clause that 'the state shall provide free and compulsory education to all children of the age of 6-14 years in such a manner as the state may, by law determine' leaves the entire promise of free and compulsory education wide open for varied interpretations.

Thirdly, by denying fundamental right of elementary education for children below 6 years of age, the state has placed the onus of education on the parents and in a country like India the success of this endeavour leaves us far from the desired. In a classic example of double speak M.M. Joshi, Union Minister for Human Resource Development, announced that the amendment is a 'revolutionary step as it would make it the duty of the parents to send their children to school but will not penalise them for not doing so'.

Fourthly, the 93rd Amendment dilutes the previous commitments to universalise elementary education. In 1993, in *J.P. Unnikrishnan* vs. *the State of Andhra Pradesh*, a five member bench of Supreme Court had laid down that the right to education is fundamental right that flowed from the Right to Life (Article 21). Therefore it held that free education up to the age of 14 is a fundamental right for every child.This has been jeopardised by including only children belonging to 6-14 years age group.

Lastly, the financial memorandum attached to the 93rd Amendment Bill states that an additional sum of Rs.9,800 crores, per year will be provided for the next 10 years for free and compulsory education. Since Rs. 3,800 crores has already been allocated for elementary education in budget 2001-02, an additional sum of Rs.6,000 crores a year will be allocated accordingly. This comes out to be 0.35 per cent of our G.D.P. Contrary to it Tapas Mazumdar Committee constituted by the N.D.A. government stated in its Report in 1999 that an additional sum of Rs.14,000 crores a year on average would have to be spent for the next 10 years in order to provide school education to half the children in the 6-14 years age group, who are out of the school today. This additional investment work out to be 0.78 per cent of G.D.P. This is nothing but more than double, compared to what has been proposed by the latest Bill. The reality is that the government wants to push its agenda through low quality parallel streams for the poor children in the name of ensuring a fundamental right.

It is, therefore, observed that even after five and half decades of planning and nation-building our ruling elite have failed to transform primary education into a mass based educational system. We have somewhat retained the colonial structure with minor changes and so the inherent contradiction remains unattended, which ultimately results in depriving at least 7 million children out of our 20 million children from basic education. Still now more than one-third of our population are illiterate according to the latest census figures (Table 11.1).

Table 11.1: Literacy Rates in India, 1991-2001

State/Nation	*Literacy percentage*	
	1991	2001
Kerala	89.81	90.22
Mizoram	82.27	88.49
Goa	75.51	82.32
Maharashtra	64.87	77.27
Himachal Pradesh	63.86	77.13
Tamil Nadu	63.66	73.47
Nagaland	61.65	67.11
Gujarat	61.29	69.97
Tripura	60.44	73.66
Manipur	59.89	68.87
Punjab	58.51	69.95
West Bengal	57.70	69.22
Sikkim	56.94	69.68
Karnataka	56.04	67.04
Haryana	55.85	68.59
Assam	52.89	64.28
INDIA	52.21	65.38
Meghalaya	49.10	63.31
Orissa	49.09	63.61
Madhya Pradesh	44.20	64.11
Andhra Pradesh	44.09	61.11
Uttar Pradesh	41.60	57.36
Arunachal Pradesh	41.59	54.74
Rajasthan	38.55	61.03
Bihar	38.48	47.53
Jammu & Kashmir	- N.A. -	54.46

Note: Uttaranchal (72.28); Chhatisgarh (65.38); and Jharkhand (54.13) were not in existence in 1991, therefore three States have not been included in the table.

Source: *Frontline,* Dec. 7, 2001.

Thus, instead of social and national regeneration our education system has chosen personal aggrandisement for the children of elite and those surrounding them, leading to schism and discontent among the masses at large.

The North-Eastern Scenario

The scenario in India's north east is not much different from that of the rest of India. However there are certain specific problems, which are unique to the north east India. In this section we will discuss about two related problems and its link with the overall educational frame work, one similar to the all India scenario and another which is unique to the north east. As is evident from the discussion in the earlier section that India suffers from a deep-rooted problem of mass illiteracy, even after five decades of planning and nation building, this problem is also found in the north-eastern region. Secondly, due to various factors ranging from socio-economic to ethnicity and nationality, insurgency is a burning problem in the north east, which in many ways is unique to this region. We will try to analyse the link between education and insurgency in the north-eastern region of India.

Lack of Mass Literacy

There has been a significant rise in literacy level in all the eight north-eastern states including Sikkim, yet other than Mizoram, the rest are far from achieving near universal literacy. The overall literacy rate increased from 57.97 in 1991 to 68.80 in 2001 (See Table 11.2). This

Table 11.2: Literacy Rates in North-Eastern Region

Sl No.	*State*	*1991*	*2001*
1.	Mizoram	82.27	88.49
2.	Nagaland	61.65	67.11
3.	Tripura	60.44	73.66
4.	Manipur	58.89	68.87
5.	Sikkim	56.94	69.98
6.	Assam	52.89	64.28
7.	Meghalaya	49.10	63.31
8.	Arunachal Pradesh	41.59	57.74
9.	N.E.R.	57.97	68.80
	India	52.21	65.38

increase in literacy in terms of percentage points has been lower in north-eastern region as compared to the all India level. This region (other than Mizoram) has to improve a lot to reach the desired levels of literacy (Table 8.3).

Among the north-eastern states, highest increase in literacy during the decade, 1991-2001 has been in Meghalaya, followed by Tripura and Arunachal Pradesh. Both Meghalaya and Arunachal Pradesh have started from a lower base.

Table 11.3: Percentage Rise in Literacy in NER, 1991-2001

	State	*Per cent*
1.	Meghalaya	14.21
2.	Tripura	13.22
3.	Arunachal Pradesh	13.15
4.	Sikkim	12.74
5.	Assam	11.39
6.	Manipur	8.68
7.	Mizoram	6.22
8.	Nagaland	5.46

In terms of position, Mizoram is most literate State in the region and is the second most literate state in India, after Kerala. Tripura has moved up to the second position from its third position in 1991 among the north-eastern states. The position of Nagaland fell from the second in 1991 to fifth in 2001. Sikkim has moved up the ladder from fifth to third position during the same period. For all the other states (Manipur, Assam, Meghalaya and Arunachal), their respective position in terms of literacy in the north-eastern region has remained unchanged.

Despite a rise in overall literacy levels several islands of mass illiteracy remains, which not only pulls down the average for the states but also creates division, discord and disenchantment among the masses. Here we deal with one such area, namely the *char* areas of Assam. *Chars* are nothing but geological formations in the river Brahmaputra, which are formed due to the abrupt differences in slope and gradient of the river. They have an unique eco-system and geo-morphological pattern of their own. There are no recorded evidence regarding the history of their formation but human habitation in these stretches are over hundred years old. They are settlers from erstwhile East Bengal (now Bangladesh), who have settled in *chars* for number of generations. These settlers played an important role in developing the agricultural sector in the state and by dint of sheer courage and hard work these barren stretches have been turned into revenue yielding fields from the days of colonial rule. The livelihood pattern of these settlers have remained similar although their habitats are under constant threat of erosion during the floods in Brahmaputra.

The *chars* stretch over 14 districts in Assam. There are 2,089[17] *char* village in the state, where 16,00,244, people are inhabited. Agriculture is the main source of livelihood of the *char* dwellers but due to rampart feudal relations and practices, majority are poor, illiterate and have a pathetic plight. According to estimates more than 50 per cent of the *char* dwellers are below official poverty line. These areas have the dubious distinction of being the islands of illiteracy too. The following Table 11.4 illustrates the fact.

Table 11.4: Educational Status of the *Char* Areas in Assam

Districts	*Literacy (%)*
Darrang	10.12
Barpeta	12.90
Kamrup	16.85
Nalbari	7.90
Bongaigaon	12.85
Goalpara	8.38
Dhubri	19.06
Morigaon	8.02
Nowgaon	9.44
Dhemaji	14.44
Lakhimpur	14.01
Sonitpur	12.63
Tinsukia	14.20
Jorhat	31.90
Total	15.45

Source: Socio-Economic Survey Report 1993-94, Directorate of *Char* Areas Development, Assam, 1992-93.

Thus after half a century of independence we couldn't assure basic minimum right to the *char* dwellers. Rampant illiteracy and poverty adds fuel to the fire of discord, which is aptly exploited by the power brokers to retain their hold over our democratic power structure.

Insurgency[18]

The North East Assam Plains came under British rule in 1826, Cachar plains in 1830, Khasi Hills in 1833, Jayantia plains in 1835, the then Mikir Hills in 1838, the North Cachar Hills in 1854, the Naga Hills during 1866-1904, Garo Hills in 1872-73, the then NEFA from 1875 and the then Lushai Hills came under British rule finally in 1890[19]. This period between 1826 and 1890 witnessed a gradual expansion and consolidation of the colonial rule over a number of traditional societies having their own system of economy (which has been basically subsistence economy), training of youth (which we call education) to make them relevant for their concerned economy and also their own traditional political arrangements. About the pre-British political arrangements and also the economic patterns of these societies, much dependable data and analysis are available by now though a relative silence is observed among the scholars about the pre-British education system. There is no denying of the fact that the focus of the pre-British education system was mainly concentrated in the highlander societies and also partly in the societies of the plain that has been guided by the necessity to lead a collective life and not the individualistic education and training that constitute the core of so-called modern educational agenda.

In the hill societies, the traditional training for the youth has been almost compulsory for everyone. In a sense, that has been their very own variety of universal education. But with the increasing consolidation of the British rule as also the spread of modern education, primarily, with the help of Christian missionary through there missionary institutions, a new model of education and training were sought to be imparted to the youth. The content of this model was not only far away from the pre-British model of universal education but also in its scope, it has been more Euro-centric than inward looking. It has been an attempt of negating whatever has been there in the past and a value crisis in the minds of the young got embedded from the very beginning. Neither they could totally dissociate themselves from the traditional setting, nor they could desist themselves from the temptation of a so-called modern training that opened up newer varieties of career opportunities for them. This dilemma has been latent from the very beginning, which was manifested sometimes in aggressive forms in later periods.

On the other hand, with each single dose of modern education a sense of relative deprivation got concretised in the younger minds. Earlier societies were more or less isolated with occasional exposure to neighbouring societies. British administration brought the neighbouring world closer to them making them aware about levels of material development in various societies of the north east India. This awareness shaped the base of the agitated mind that got manifested again in the later periods.

Again in pre-British political arrangement each clan, each tribe and every single ethnic group particularly in the highlands of north east either had there own decision-making system or a fair representation in the decision-making process. With a gradual consolidation of the modern rational-legal political arrangement the participatory practices of the traditional societies got affected and that too contributed towards aggravating the mental agony that, in its turn, contributed towards a sense of political deprivation and alienation. The process, that has been initiated during the British period in the spheres of education and training or political administration has been almost *in toto* accepted by the Indian Government after 1947 of course with more emphasis on spreading the bases of education with higher degree of intervention from the government. This can be observed from the figures available for north east showing literacy rates over decades.

However we must not loose sight of the fact that only literacy rate does not indicate the degree of integration of the individuals with the system. The history of the north east since 1940s indicates that more education, more so-called development doses, more penetration of administration led to lack of integration not only from the present politico-economic arrangement but also from their very own social arrangement that stood continuously at the crossroads — neither traditional nor modern. A curriculum that fails to incorporate the positive elements of traditional curriculum, a curriculum that fails to appreciate the collective thrust of traditional curriculum that is probably destined to create this mental chaos to belong or not to belong. Those who could solve the dilemma by deciding to belong, they were problem saved by opting for a agony free life. But those more conscious section or people of the traditional societies who for their own reasons decided 'not to belong' — for them, life has not been so peaceful or stable. Their primary decision of 'not to belong' moved them out of their normal family situation and in the terrains and turning hilly roads they began their search for freedom — that rightly or wrongly is the true path for them while the same is visualised by the people, who stood for the 'system' as disruptive. In any case the modern education opened up newer vistas, newer realisation, new awareness and newer dreams that can never be denied.

Education in the 21st Century

The 21st century will surely be the Age of Information, where sustainable development, information, technology and communication will be the key areas along with bio-technology and genetics. Both evolution and decay in all the fields of human activities will be at an unbelievable speed. This ephermal nature will increase the schism between the structure and superstructure leading to newer contradictions as well as synthesis in the time to come. Changes in both 'form' and 'content' of educational curriculum and framework will be rapid and a generation of learners will have to update themselves several times, in order to be efficient and competitive, else they become obsolete automatically. The prospects of the present century along with its difference with the earlier ones has been subtly presented by Indiresan[20] in Table 11.5.

Table 11.5: Various Changes over the Centuries

Item	*Past*	*Present*	*Future*
Tools of Production	Agriculture	Machinery	Information
Half-life of skills	Generations	Decades	Less than a decade
Economic Ambitions	Inheritance	Salaries	Competitive careers
International Linkages	Few	Limited	Overwhelming
Cultural Privacy	Extensive	Limited	Virtually non-existent
Cultural Identity	Local tribe	Nation	Globalisation(?)
Environmental Attitude	Preservation	Development	Sustainable development

The present era of globalisation has pushed the world into a global village in terms of communication linkage and network, yet vital differences remain culturally, socially and economically, which in turn experience the pulls of localisation. Those people either in terms of group, class, ethnicity or nationality, who are unable to change themselves with the ephermal production dynamics and value system, feels betrayed and stand against the present model of globalisation. Resistance to the neo-liberal globalisation process has entered a sporadic and spontaneous phase globally but resistance in an organised manner will emerge in future accordingly.

The present model of globalisation furthers inequality and those enjoying the cream, consider themselves as global citizens, while other 'breeds reptiles in their mind'. Jobless growth patters increases G.D.P. but fails to satisfy the basic human requirements, which in turn creates further inequalities both locally and globally. It naturally gives rise to immigration into those areas, where there are better prospects for income and employment on a global scale. However, the overall recessionary trend often creates economic mirages for the immigrants on one hand and hatred and xenophobia on the other for the locals. The rise of far-right in Europe (particularly in France, Denmark, Britain, Russia and Austria), religious fundamentalism in Asia and in parts of Africa, as well as, economic upheavals in Latin America[21] bears testimony to these postulates.

Education in the 21st century is passing through a critical phase and educational reconstruction at present has two major areas — firstly, the technical aspect concerning curricula, organisation, coordination, extension and efficient supervision; and secondly, the role of educationists to evolve a strategy to meet the ever-rising aspiration of our people and integrating them with the global system. While the question regarding curricula is a technical one, where its modification and concurrent evaluation will be an on-going process. There are other issues related to content and its missing links in the educational system, which can be analysed so that the future educational framework can include them after thorough debate and deliberations. In this section four related issues are discussed, while have become important point of discussions among educationists both during the later half of the 20th century and the early years of 21st century. This is by no means is an exhaustive list nor a final judgment of these issues but rather an attempt to initiate a debate so that the learners of 21st century do not feel exasperated, as we did in the 20th century.

Moral Education[22]

People of all shades grudge — the present day world is immoral and devoid of values. In order to change it, we should teach morality to our children. Interestingly although the aspect regarding immorality is understood, yet it is very difficult to define morality. If, at all, it is defined then the question remains, can morality be taught? In an open-ended fashion it can be said that 'morality constitutes of those ideas, which helps us to hold society together as a basis for a good life for individuals constituting society'.

Morality plays an important role in 'building up and strengthening habits and values to ensure the continuance of social framework within which productive and useful activities take place'. If one accepts morality within these precincts then the question remains how to impart it within our educational framework.

Religion happened to be the chief vehicle of imparting moral education earlier and it still continues in some institutions, yet, leaving aside the theist and atheist divide morality through religion provides certain problems due to which, it becomes unconvincing, particularly regarding choice among various communities. Secondly, theocracy or state religion could solve the problem but that will lead to totalitarian state, which by itself becomes immoral. Thirdly, nationalism can be regarded as a vehicle of morality but again morality in terms of humanity as a whole when considered, through the prism of nationalism might lead to political slogan-mongering. Fourthly, there are people who advocate teaching morality by preaching the ideals of great souls — but considering the stark discrepancy between what is preached and practised, this method is always a doubtful one.

Leaving aside the above inhibitions, morality can be the simple art of learning about group formation and its synchronisation with individual activities. It is work-centric to a large extent, where students are divided in small groups discussing and designing a task among themselves. The group-identity is maintained at all stages and individual brilliance merges with the brilliance of the group. The teacher here acts as a facilitator to achieve the goal of group functioning. Similarly, moral education must focus on physical education, namely sports, which helps to build team spirit and also channelises energy in a constructive way at a tender age. In this way, the student rises above all discriminations and through moral education accepts 'victory without pride and defeat without bitterness'.

If this pattern of moral education is imparted at the childhood it forges the ideals of group formation, which strengthens the habit and value of maintaining a social framework afterwards in life. This will stand in contradiction against crass individualism of modern era.

Universalism vis-à-vis Neo-Liberal Globalisation

Communication technology has undoubtedly turned the world into a global village and various analyst have termed the process of globalisation as the limitless and frictionless Stage of human civilization. However various manifestations of the present model of globalisation have shown that, for the majority the world has turned into a 'global-jungle' with shrinking opportunities of livelihood, food, bio-diversity and cultural subjugation. Due to its sporadic and spontaneous nature, the world view and counter culture to the present neo-liberal globalisation is yet to emerge on a global scale and so various thoughts and ideals can be considered at this juncture of history, which finally will be an anti-thesis to the present model. Here Rabindranath's approach to universalism is considered accordingly.

Tagore's[23] approach to universality has three major aspects:

universality through the approach of sciences, universality through a cosmopolitan approach and universality through the cosmic approach. In the first approach, Tagore emphasises the universal appeal of sciences. Science through reason and rational approach ameliorates the condition of the people and cleanse the human mind of blind superstition. Science by its universal appeal tries to create self-confidence in man through reasons and uplifts humanity. Thus this universal appeal of science tries to forge a bond among people around the world and bring human minds closer. Modern day science has no doubt brought human beings closer, yet the forces of market and its rampant profit-motive has erected an artificial division, which acts as a stumbling block for Tagore's notion of universality through sciences.

Second is the cosmopolitan approach of universality[24]. Living in an era of strong nationalist upsurge Tagore has always been opposed to nationalism. He has been a patriot the core but never a nationalist. In his words, nationalism, a modern concept is always connected with the organised power of the state, which is nothing but a collective pursuit for power. It organises people for power. On the other hand, one's love for nature, neighbour or country is a silent power, by which, people are knit together. There is no boundary to the circle of neighbourhood and it is an even expanding-circle, where the entire world is considered as a single neighbourhood. Interestingly, as a real tribute to Tagore, the universalist, the national anthem of both India and Bangladesh are composed by Tagore. Perhaps the only instance in the world. In an era of re-emergence of parochial nationalism this approach can reopen an alternative path.

The third approach is the cosmic approach, which is a logical extension of the earlier approach. Here Tagore seeks to raise the inner-self to link oneself to the universe or cosmos. He attaches fundamental importance to the personal testimony in matters of religious experience rather than basing one's faith on a book or preached rigid ideals. Tagore uses personal testimony and the call of the inner-self to unite oneself with the universe in its wholeness, *i.e.* 'Unity through joy and through sorrow'.

Thus through these three approaches Tagore wants to construct a model of universalism, where the inner urge of the self of a person is united with that of another irrespective of national boundaries and then with the cosmos as a whole in a mutually scintillating way to pave the way for unity by retaining individual uniqueness throughout the world.

Rootless Modernity

Modernity has been interpreted in a number of ways by scholars of all discipline. Parameters have varied from one set of analyst to another. Some have emphasised upon modernisation of the economic base while the others have pleaded for scientific modernisation. Similarly some has focused on cultural modernisation, while others stressed on modernity of mind without imitation. Without going into the debate of modernity and its forms, here we try to analyse the problem with our form of modernisation.

After 1947 we embarked on a path of modernisation, where secularism, science and technology have been important corner stones and removal of poverty, illiteracy and hunger has been the avowed goals. But in our tryst with modernity, our ruling elite portrayed the same sort of contradictions as has been evident in the earlier section of this paper, particularly in case of universalisation of education. Our modernisation programme while creating a material base for its sustenance has been unable to create a cultural tradition rooted to the soil, which could provide a different value and meaning for life, for our ordinary individuals. Nehru[25] once stated 'in our efforts to ensure the material prosperity of our country, we have not paid any attention to the spiritual element in human nature. Therefore, in order to give the individual and the nation a sense of purpose and something to live for and if necessary to die for, we have to devise some philosophy of life and give in the wider sense of the word, a spiritual background to our thinking'. What Nehru could realise in his later years were completely missed by others among his ruling elites. So our modernisation programme remained trapped in the pursuit of material interest by completely negating the cultural elements. This cultural vacuum has resulted in rootless modernity, which gave birth to a cultural backlash in the form of religious fundamentalism and cultural revivalism.

Our modernisation project (may unintentionally) has not been rooted to the culture and tradition of the soil. Moreover, it has been carried forward by the much publicised 'new middle class' or the anglicised, English educated, urban classes. In their pursuit to modernity they imitated and aped the Euro-American style of life and offered a market for cultural and economic goods and services of the affluent countries who themselves were caught in deep moral crisis[26]. Again this pattern of modernity has never been mass based, as a result of which, it created further schism and fissures within our society. It provided the base for discontent among the masses, which has been aptly exploited by the religious fundamentalists to further their cause.

Our model of modernity therefore provided a limited basis for modernisation through science and technology and has been devoid of any cultural values. This directed attention to things oppose to values. Material pursuit (read consumerism) became the only sign of modernisation and in words of Russell[27] 'science as technique overshadowed science as philosophy or values'. This alienated the masses who were rooted to their cultural traditions. Due to the absence of people's culture, our modernisation programme remained devoid of mass appeal and philosophical touch, which always, instead of uniting divided the masses. Again to quote Russell[28] 'knowledge is power, but it is power just as much for evil as for good. It follows that unless men increase in wisdom as much as in knowledge, increase in knowledge will be increase in sorrow'. Similar is our case with modernity, which has therefore been rootless and valueless devoid of the wisdom about which Russell emphasises.

Commercialisation and Privatisation

Due to major charges and upheavals in the global political economy there has been a paradigm shift in economic management in various countries, particularly the developing countries around the world. The major advocates of these changed methods of economic management have been the International Monetary Fund and the World Bank and through the Structural Adjustment Policies, these two institutions forced the way for change in every aspect of life and livelihood in these countries, where their policies were implemented. Education, particularly higher education has been under constant threat for which, an on-going process of change seems imminent. The present move in education has been towards commercialisation and privatisation, which is a major fall out under the SAP. Andrew Noss[29] have aptly summarised the effects of SAP on the educational scenario in the third world countries and according to him 'adjustment measures affect education through changes at the macro and micro level of the economy.' Adjustment at the macro level often implies a combination of budget containment measures for public education and higher user fees for education services at the secondary and tertiary levels. At the micro-level, changes in household incomes and prices directly influence the demand for education by altering the opportunity cost of attending school. Household incomes also affect health and nutrition status, and thus indirectly influence attendance and learning. Finally, adjustment affects education through changes in markets and infrastructure that affect supply of education services and the opportunity cost of attending school.

Another avowed goal of SAP is to make for such changes in the production structure, which would make the country 'competitive, which will help to integrate it with the global market'[30]. However this process of integration is to be attempted by making space for private initiative and enterprise as opposed to government intervention and participation. This principle thereby works under the guise that 'apparently anything connected with government is by definition inefficient, the market system is *ex hypothesis* more efficient'[31]. Thus it brings the private players to the forefront through reduced budgetary support, increasing commercialisation ultimately leading to privatisation.

It is universally agreed now that in India, there is tremendous inequality of education, where the richers have greater access to higher education than the poorer and socially backward sections of the population. Similar is the case of scholarships and financial assistance forwarded by state and private agencies. Again, there is a bias towards higher education *vis-à-vis* primary education in terms of intra-sectoral allocation of education funds. However, the question remains, if this is the ground reality, what will be the implication, if the state deny its role in social sectors? Do the markets concern about equity? The answer certainly lies not in negating one sector of the educational framework but by harmonising resources among them.

The first step towards improving education is to increase the overall allocation of education instead of counter posing expenditure on higher education, which seems nothing but a ploy to divert attention of inadequate allocation to education sector as a whole. The Indian government's policy towards higher education seems to be tailor-made according to the IMF/WB prescriptions to suit rampant privatisation through commercialisation mainly to (i) 'facilitate entry of private operators with the logic that, since social returns are lower so user changes should be raised and running and managing this sector should be left in the hands of private operators; (ii) secondly, developing credit market for education, together with selective scholarship, especially in higher education.'[32]

Now the pertinent question remains, can we globalise successfully with the above logic and if so at what terms. A study[33] on 'levels of education among workforce observed that in India, mean level of education for the workforce is 1.9 years of schooling. It has also been found that 66.6 per cent of the workforce is illiterate, 14.5 per cent has incomplete primary schooling and 6.9 per cent only has complete primary schooling'. Under these circumstances, we obviously would not succeed in 'globalising' the Indian economy without creating a domestic base of industrial growth based on high level of scientific and technological skills. In the absence of such development, the 'globalisations' of our production structure will be tantamount to accepting that India should remain a backward society, producing and exporting only primary products and depending on imports for all sophisticated manufactured goods, particularly those value added ones.

Conclusion

Education in the 21st century has double tasks to perform. On the one hand, it has to get rid of the problems of rootlessness and crass consumerism and on the other will have to renovate its time tested humanistic values embedded within the human civilization. The ephermal nature of the 21st century will place an enormous importance on preservation of our heritage ranging from language to bio-diversity, while on the other, the educational framework should also be flexible enough for concurrent evaluation and constant upgradation. It is a difficult but challenging task to which, educational policy-framers and implementers should be dedicated too. Globally any island of poverty, illiteracy and under nourishment will be a threat to the humankind and educational policies should formulate itself in such a way that these marginalized are assimilated and not annihilated in our onward march of human civilization.

During the end of the last century David Crystal[34] drew the attention that 'of the world's estimated 6,000 languages, 3,000 would be gone in the next 50 years as the last speakers of those languages die'. Can we as sincere human beings allow this to happen? We should preserve our culture, identity and language from this continuous onslaught. But while doing so we should never sound parochial or suffer from cultural xenophobia. The importance of education in preparing the mind for multiculturalism lies there. If left otherwise it will lead to a cultural backlash facilitation only the reactionary elements for their petty political gains as is evident in present day India and various other countries globally.

D.P. Mukherji[35] explained this backlash in his own words, 'as days passed by, Indian culture became less concerned with such affairs of the spirit as the person's soul and its discovery and made instead a religion of politics, which culminated in transforming India into a mother-goddess, saints into political leaders and leaders into saints and heroes. Education in 21st century can go a long way in resolving these contradictions of the earlier centuries along with creating newer vistas for hope, life and livelihood for the humankind.

NOTES

1. For a detailed discussion *see The Republic and the Dialogues of Plato*, Vol. 3 (Oxford : Clarendon Press, 1875).
2. *Op. cit.* n. 1.
3. Plato presupposes the existence of three estates and the Indian caste system states about four castes in their respective social orders. Education in both the social orders were restricted within the dominant minority whereas the voiceless majority remained outside its purview. Although belonging to the same age, Plato and Buddha's view of education has never been restrictive in nature mainly due to the negation of caste system in his preaching and philosophy. Buddhism and Jainism (to a great extent) has been in that way more open and democratic in terms of access to education for the masses.
4. Thomas Jefferson as quoted in the notes of Lunacharsky, Anatoli. *On Education : Selected Articles and Speeches* (Moscow : Progress Publishers, 1981).
5. Anatoli Lunacharsky has been one of the leading figures among the educationists in post-Revolution Russia and has contributed substantially to the growth of education in U.S.S.R.
6. This section is based on 'An Overview' and Cultural Trends in Pre-Colonial India in Panikkar, K.N., *Culture, Ideology, Hegemony : Intellectuals and Social Consciousness in Colonial India* (New Delhi : Tulika, 2001).
7. Gramsci, Antonio, *Selections from the Prison Notebooks* (Chennai : Orient Longman, 1998).
8. Tagore, Rabindranath, *Nationalism* (London : Macmillan & Co., 1950).
9. Gandhi, M.K., *Young India*, January 12, 1928.
10. *Op. cit.* n.6.
11. *Ibid.*
12. Nair, Gopinath, Primary Education, Population Growth and Socio-Economic Changes as quoted by Pushpendra in 'From the Editor's Desk'

in *The Administrator*, Vol. XLI, No. 3, July-September, 1996.

13. *Op. cit.* n. 12.
14. *Ibid.*
15. Tilak, J.B.G., *Education for Development in Asia* (New Delhi : Sage Publications, 1994).
16. For details see Rajlakshmi, T.K., 'A Regressive Bill', *Frontline*, Vol. 18, No. 25, December 21, 2001, Sadgopal, Anil, '93rd Amendment and Policies', Surya, Vasantha, 'For the right to learn'. *Frontline*, Vol. 18, No. 26, January 4, 2002.
17. For a detailed analysis see Hussain, Ismail (Sr.) and Hussain, Anowar, *Char-Chaporir Jiban Charyya* (Guwahati : Natun Sahitya Parishad, 2000).
18. This section is based upon an impromptu discussion with Dr. P.S. Datta, eminent scholar in ethnicity and currently Editor, *Daily Bhumiputra*, Dibrugarh.
19. Datta, P.S., 'Karbi-Dimasa Autonomy Movement' in Datta, P.S. (ed.), *Ethnic Movements in Poly-cultural Assam* (New Delhi : Vikas, 1990).
20. Indiresan, P.V., 'Education for Development in the Twenty-First Century', in *Liberalisation with a Human Face*, Vol. 3 (Mussoorie : L.B.S. National Academy of Administration, 1994).
21. The rise of far-right has been a characteristic feature in Europe particularly in Austria, Denmark, Britain, France and Russia over last couple of years. Cultural xenophobia and attack against immigrant population has been a major part of this campaign. Recently the victory of the far-right Presidential candidate in the Columbian elections has set the trend in Latin America, which is already troubled with U.S. imperialism and economic bankruptcy due to Fund-Bank Programmes. Asia (including India) and parts of Africa is also showing similar tendencies.
22. For a detailed analysis see 'Teaching of Morals' in Datta, Amlan, *On the Edge of a Century* (Calcutta : Subarnarekha, 1999).
23. 'Tagore and Three Approaches to University', in Datta, Amlan, *On the Edge of a Century* (Calcutta : Subarnarekha, 1999).
24. Tagore's Cosmopolitan approach to Universality is also similar to the concept of 'Metta' in Buddhist philosophy.
25. Jawaharlal Nehru, *Letters to Chief Ministers, 1958-64* (Delhi : O.U.P., 1989).
26. For a detailed analysis on issues related to modernisation, secularisation and rootless modernity see Joshi, P.C., *Secularism and Development : The Indian Experiment* (New Delhi : Vikas, 1995).
27. Bertrand Russell, *Unpopular Essays* (New York : Simon & Schuster, 1962).
28. *Op. cit.* n.27.
29. Noss, Andrew, *Education and Adjustment*, World Bank Staff Paper, 1992.
30. Ghosh, Arun, 'Structural Adjustment and Education's in *Liberalisation with a Human Face* (Mussoorie : L.B.S. National Academy of Administration, 1994).

31. *Op. cit.*, n. 30.
32. Upendranath, C., 'Structural Adjustment and Education : Issues Related to Equity', in *Liberalisation with a Human Face* (Mussoorie : L.B.S. National Academy of Administration, 1994).
33. Psachraopoulos, George and Arrigada, A.M., 'The Educational Composition of the Labour Force : An International Comparison', *International Labour Review*, Vol. 125, No. 5, September-October, 1986.
34. Crystal, David, 'The death of language', as quoted by Watson, C.W., *Multiculturalism* (New Delhi : Viva Books Private Limited, 2002).
35. Mukherji, D.P., *Diversities* (New Delhi : People's Publishing House, 1958).

12

21st Century Problems and Issues of Higher Education in North East India

P.C. DUTTA

> "The only service to be done for our masses is to give them education to develop their lost individuality. They are to be given ideas, their eyes are to be opened to what is going on in the world around them, and them they will work out their own salvation."
>
> —Swami Vivekananda

Education plays a very important role in the formation of a progressive society for which its importance has been realised by eminent philosophers like Plato, Aristotle, Locke, Rousseau, Diewey, Mahatma Gandhi etc. In a religion oriented world, it is regarded as a means for spiritual emancipation from the ills of Mundane existence. All round development of society needs a scientific educational system from which scientific discoveries and technological advancements can be resulted. The Indian Nationalist Movement in 19th and 20th centuries has been led by the people who had received school and university education. Our leadership during the freedom struggle was overwhelming and predominantly in the hands of western-educated classes. The school, colleges, and universities are the important agencies of political socialization because they promote those attitudes and values which can be oriented towards strengthening the political system. Political development demands that the educational institutions are available for the inculcation of values and criteria which can enhance growth and lessen social stratification. In the economic sphere the importance of education is being increasingly recognised and India's

Five Year Plans have emphasised the pursuit of educational policies which lead to the development of these areas in education which have immediate relevance in strengthening the economic foundation of the state. Human values like equality, liberty, justice, fearlessness etc. demand a strong educational system for the development of human personality in a pluralistic society like India. Increasing trend of modernisation, urbanisation, industrialisation, liberalisation, privatisation and globalisation in 21st century require a good amount of specialised knowledge to which our system of education is going to challenge.

Realising the importance of higher education, Jawaharlal Nehru once said, "A university stands for humanism for tolerance, for reason, for progress, for adventure of ideas and the research for truth. It stands for the onward march of the human race towards ever higher objectives. If the universities discharge their duties adequately, then it is well with the nation and the people." Universities and colleges are institutions of higher education which play a pivotal role for socio-cultural and economic development of nation. Laying emphasis on high ideals as the aims of higher education, the University Education Commission (UEC) observed, the greatness of country does not depend on the extent of its territory, the length of its communication or the amount of wealth, not even on widespread education or equitable distribution of wealth important as all these things are. If we wish to bring about a savage upheaval in our society, a *Rakhsasraj*, all that we need to do is to give vocational and technical education and starve the spirit. We will have a number of scientists without conscience, technicians without taste who find a void within themselves, a moral vacuum and a desperate need to substitute something, anything for their lost endeavour and purpose. Society will then get what it deserves. If we claim to be civilised we must develop thought of the poor and the suffering, regard and respect for women, faith in brotherhood regardless of race or colour, nation or religion, love of peace and freedom, abhorrence of cruelty and ceaseless devotion of the claims of justice.

The National Policy on Education (NPE) defines education in 1986 in terms of empowerment of man through knowledge, acquisition of skills and values, social and economic mobility, leadership in all spheres of human endeavours, social, political, religious, moral and ethical. Generation, preservation and dissemination of knowledge, skills and values, teaching, research and extension service are the primary functions which higher education intends to undertake. To accomplish the objective of higher education, the Programme of Action (POA) 1986, suggests consolidation and expansion of institutions, re-designing courses relevance to productivity and organising faculty training programme. This would increase the excellence of the system. The system of higher education needs to be more dynamic and responsive to the need of the country. According to the estimate of the Society for Education and Economic Development (SEED) 1993, more than 80 per cent of the total students in higher education get enrolled in colleges. It is hoped that the Indian Collegiate System would improve both the quantity as well as quality of higher education if this standard will be maintained. Quality control in higher education has been the main concern of the New International Economic Order (NIEO) and of the 21st century.

Education promotes development in all the sectors of the economy and yield high social and economic returns. Sustainable development cannot take place without investments being made in people. It is now widely accepted that improvements in the quality of people as productive agents must be a central objective of development policies (Prabhu, 1996; Malhotra, 1997).

The social sector expenditure plays an important role in supporting economic growth and reducing poverty. Education plays a very important role in promotion of economic, social, political and institutional development. Education promotes development of all the sectors including agriculture, industry and social sector. Rather the social returns to education far more out weigh the economic returns and the social rate of return is highest in case of primary education followed by secondary and higher education (Procharopouclus, 1994).

Higher levels of education may have greater direct impact on economic development but the primary and middle-level education are important because they widely distribute the conditions conducive to development. In order to have desired results, there has to be threshold level of investment. Such investments have long gestation period but they also yield returns over a long period because of durability of human Capital and its wider implications (World Bank, 1997).

High teacher-pupil ratio affects the quality of education which is one of the dampening factors in educational decision (Bhatty, 1998). Low levels of educational attainment at primary level in rural areas are particularly due to low quality of education, which is party due to over-crowding of primary classes (Malhotra, 1999).

The rate of return criterion is a useful tool for evaluating investment in education at different levels. There is abundant research to support the proportion that investment in lower levels of education contributes more to income redistribution and reduction in poverty, besides contributing to economic growth, than investment in higher education (Tilak, 1989). Elementary education has suffered severe setbacks, one of the most important ones being insufficient allocation of financial resources (Tilak, 1998).

The priority accorded to education can be assessed by the shares of educational expenditure in total expenditure provided for in the national budget. The priority given to education in government budgets declined in most of the states from 1980-81. The relative share of elementary education in the total educational budget has also declined overtime in most of the states. About 60 per cent of Indian population live in the lowest income group (less than Rs. 20,000.00 per annum). More than half of them have no resources to spend on education at the given price of education. It comes to luxury goods to them which is the main reason for enrolment of their kids for schooling (Dutta, 2000).

Even after more than 50 years of independence, India spends less than 4 per cent of Gross National Product (GNP) on education and less than half this amount (1.8 per cent) on elementary education (Shariff & Ghose, 2000).

In the year 1857, first three universities — Calcutta, Madras and Bombay were set-up under the British rule. Today there are 242 universities and equivalent institutions of which 146 are General universities, 18 are of Science and Technology, 5 are Woman universities, 8 are Open universities, 30 are Agricultural, 17 are Medical universities and 18 language universities. As on today, there are 16 Central universities, 169 State universities, 40 Deemed universities and 11 Institutes of National importance. Out of 10,600 Colleges, 1260 are for Women, 119 are Autonomous, 700 Teacher Education/Training Colleges, 110 Polytechnics, 600 Management Institutions, 550 Colleges of Engineering and Technology and 170 Medical Colleges. Enrolled strength of students in higher education is around 7.5 million and the teachers number to 3.21 lakh. At present our educational system is neither relevant nor effective (Gautam, 2000).

There is an increasing air of indiscipline and irreverence leading to an increasing sense of disenchantment with the higher educational institution. Erosion of ethical values and moral standard among the teachers, students and society as a whole has undermined the standards of higher education. Work culture in the institutions has been vitiated which is to be repaired cautiously. Merit has been consistently ignored in most of the institutions. Non-recognition of talent and entry of non-serious students are disturbing the educational atmosphere among the students in the institutions. Thus in higher educational course, admission of students should be selective. Ingress of politics in academics at the time of appointment of teachers ignoring merit etc. applying back door process, internal examination system in the Colleges like B.Ed., Technical etc. inbreeding and growing indiscipline due to cross interference of corrupt political leaders for their self-interest have been impeding the quality of education.

Since family is the first unit of educational environment, where mother plays the vital role, to get a good child, proper environment of the house must be maintained. In our country, where around 90 per cent of the women folk are not properly educated and qualified to be a housewife, min canker remains in the basic education in the under educated family environment dominated by the parents preferably by the mother.

The survey of higher education by the National Commission on teachers in higher education in India notes with concern that the regions with high enrolment in general (that is men and women together) have low enrolment of women, a majority of whom are in Arts faculties. Moreover, in most regions, a lesser proportion of women are enrolled in universities than in the colleges. About two-thirds of women enrolled in Arts and concentrated in educationally backward states. Factors that inhibit female access to higher education are both quantitative and qualitative which are rooted in the socio-cultural context.

If women have to contribute as full members of society, their potential must be harnessed especially when they have demonstrated their capability to succeed in the educational system. It is up to the colleges and universities to build their self-confidence, to harness their capacities and provide the opportunities and choices that they deserve and contribute towards gender equality.

Trends in the development of education in the states of North East India are also reflected to some extent in the unit cost of education that is the annual expenditure by the government per student. What is legally is very often politically untruth in India, more particularly in North-eastern Region (NER). There is a vast gap between the theory and practice.

Deliberated attempts of the governments in the states of NER to reduce the expenditure on higher education make emphatically clear that the challenges of the new millennium cannot be by the higher education. Without studying the present socio-economic situation of the country they formulate the plans and policies by harassing the people involved in higher education in the region.

In this context, an enquiry is deemed to be necessary to examine the multi-dimensional and complex relationship among some socio-economic variables of the north-eastern region of India and Assam in particular as it is located in backward area and in disadvantageous position due to its physical geography as social and political conditions prevailing in the region. The purpose of the study is to explain the ill-effects of globalisation and mis-matching policies of the state governments in NER. Care has also been taken to analyse the issues and problems of higher education in the region as a result of globalisation and the study ends with some viable suggestions for improvements of the quality of higher education in the region. The study is based on secondary sources of statistical data and the analysis of the study have been completed under different sections.

Education and Socio-Economic Development

Education is the main instrument on social change. It is an important human activity. It was born with the birth of the human race and shall continue to function till the human race exists. Education fashions and models man for society. It signifies man's supreme position in societies. Normally, it has been considered an agency helping economic production through the development of skills and efficiency highly necessary for the said production. Economic development is usually defined as the maximisation of national income and its rate of growth. Intellectual development is the aim and function of education. Education is a social instrument which functions as a vital agent of socio-cultural change. The main aim of education is to preserve, transfer and enrich culture. Culture symbolises the society and consequently education emerges as an instrument of social transformation. In modern societies, education tends to become the master determinant of social mobility and social transformation because it alone leads to higher occupational achievements. The entire culture, including values, norms, ideals, beliefs, customs, skill techniques etc., is transmitted through education from one generation to another. Thus education is one of the most powerful tools in shaping our future. It is striking to note that except Arunachal Pradesh (42 %) and Meghalaya (49 %), the literacy level of the region's population is a above the national level (52 %) according to 1991 census, while in 2001, percentage of literacy rate in the state of Assam (64.28 %) has also been included along with Meghalaya (63.31 %) and Arunachal Pradesh (54.74 %) which are below than the national level (65.38 %)[1].

The female literacy rate is highest in Mizoram (95 %) followed by Nagaland (77 %) and lowest in Arunachal Pradesh (48 %)[2]. There is a big gender gap in literacy which is one if the major obstacles in attaining total literacy. Enrolment in various stages of education is growing at a fast rate, but the proportion of girls is low and declines sharply at higher stages of education. The highest gender gap has been found in the states of Manipur (24.03 % points), Arunachal Pradesh (21.76), Tripura (20.93) and lowest in Mizoram (7.01) followed by Meghalaya (8.27). However, all the states of NER are below all-India (24.84 % points) level. Almost same trend is continued in 2001 also. Low female literacy has strong repercussions on other aspects like enrolment of children, population growth, care and acceptance of family welfare measures.

It is striking to note that per capita expenditure on education in 1997-98 in highest of smaller states of Mizoram (Rs. 1210), followed by Manipur (Rs. 984), Arunachal Pradesh (Rs. 951) and Tripura (Rs. 836) while it is lowest in Assam (Rs. 537) among the states of NER[3].

Health is a social goal and considered as an integral component in over-all socio-economic development. The majority of health problems are the product of illiteracy, poverty, ignorance, overcrowding, poor environmental conditions and uneven distribution of health manpower and institutions. It is observed that there are only 4.32 per cent of Public Health Centres in the states of NER (958 Nos.) as compared to India's figure and only in Assam there are 64 per cent Public Health Centres among the states of NER, while less than 10 per cent are in each of other states of the region. The same patterns are observed in case of Sub-centres and Community Health Centres. Thus, it is high time to make an effort to increase the number of health centres in backward states of NER so that health problems can be minimised to some extent.

Dutta (2002) concluded that food security is a matter of great concern not only to the people of NER but also to the policy makers and planners of NER. While economic poverty and inequality are nothing new for people in the Third World or for people in India and more particularly it is for the people of NER. It has been accepted by them as a cultural heritage, thus showing cultural poverty. On the other hand, people of NER are indifferent regarding quality of education and health. While water is the life blood of the environment, it is striking to note that only 16.21 per cent of total households of Mizoram, a state with highest literacy rate, can drink safe water. All the states of NER, except Arunachal Pradesh, a state with lowest literacy rate, are less than the national average (62.3 %) in regard to safe drinking water facilities.

One of the important problems which creates the hindrances on the way of socio-economic development is the problem of population explosion in the region. The total population of the region is about 38.5 million representing 3.75 per cent of India's total population in 2001. The region's growth rate of population is much higher than the national average. Population explosion creates food shortage, poverty, unemployment, illiteracy, crimes etc. Dutta & Roy (1998) observed that urban population significantly affects the literacy rate. Positive significant correlations are observed for literacy rate with per capita expenditure and mean age at marriage. Again Female-work participation rate is significantly negatively correlated with percentage growth rate. Thus it can be suggested that in controlling fertility, schooling of females in the age group 6-14 plays a vital role.

Education and Administration

Coming to the administration of the educational system, we are all aware of the fact that higher education was a state subject under the Constitution of India till 42nd Constitutional Amendment Act passed in the year 1976. After this Amendment higher education became a concurrent subject and both centre and state can pass laws on the subject. However, the Union law will have precedence over the state law for all practical purposes of higher education. Here, the dual control over the higher education in the state cannot be easily avoided. To maintain the minimum educational standard, U.G.C. devised different rules and regulations, such as U.G.C. norms, National Education Test (NET) etc. for appointment of teachers in colleges and universities. But in some states of NER, the state government have relaxed the conditions led by U.G.C. for causes better known to them. As a result of which neither minimum standard nor all-India parity in higher education is maintained in the states of NER which is clearly visible from the performance in NET examination conducted by U.G.C. at all-India level. Hence NER is always lagging behind.

In some states of NER, the politicians at the helm of administration want to change the system of higher education for their political interest. In Assam, major state of NER, despite of good number of commissions on educational reforms headed by great educationists and social scientists, the government is stick on executing the recommendation of H.N. Das Commission's report without discussing it on the floor of legislature. Instead of educationalising politics, the administrators are trying to politicizing the education. Many relevant issues related to higher education such as absence of appropriate academic administration, ensuring of quality education, introduction of new course and syllabus in tune with the needs of time, providing social security to the educationists etc. are pending before us. But without going through all the above, the governments of NER are hurry to implement self-styled restrictions by reducing the grants to the institution of higher education.

The macro-economic policy of the country always has a cascading effect on the micro-economy of the state because our Constitution has been so designed that a state government is incapable of going ahead with its own planning and execution process without centre's approval or fund allocation[4]. The imbalance in the matter of devolution of power between the state and the centre makes it an uphill task even for a sincere state government to mobilise enough resources on its own to extend higher education in the state. The non-plan expenditure of the state has been mounting day by day because the government jobs created during execution of a plan become a liability for the state once the plan period expires. The successive state government of the state did not make any definite strategy to mobilise additional revenue to cater to the future demand on account of such job transferred from plan head to non-plan head. Consequently, the state government has become more and more dependent on the centre for non-plan expenditure also. There is Central Finance Commission (CFC) which for every five years makes an assessment of such gap in non-plan expenditure gap of the state by awarding its sanction. Further, there are innumerable leakage point in our system of governance through which precious resources leak into wilderness. It is evident, in the states of NER, that the politicians and bureaucrats divert funds appropriated for the purpose to some other heads. In the name of fiscal reforms and curtailment of government expenditure the society and social sectors have been deliberately neglected. This is anti-people educational policy which the state governments have been following against the interest of masses.

Globalisation and Education

The foreign imperialists dictated a new economic order which made the Union government bound to its responsibility in the matter of imparting higher education in order to pave the way for privatisation of our educational system. Contrary to the imperatives of the National Policy on Education (NPE), 1986 and 1992, government institutions in crowded urban areas are being closed down. The official strategy is to let the quality of these government institutions deteriorate over a period of few years. The parents, guardians including the poor parents, get the message and start shifting their children to nearby private institutions and there is marked mushroom growth of the private institutions. Several private institutions of higher education are also taking huge amount of money as capitation fee in the name of quality education in the region, where a lower middle class or a poor student cannot hope to obtain a seat. Hence, U.G.C. support to higher education is going go be threatened by the elements such as LPG (Liberalisation, Privatisation, Globalisation of New Economic Order). Such measures will be in violation of the spirit of the Indian Constitution which emphasised equality and social justice.

The New Economic Policy giving primacy to the market forces in national development and integrating India into the global economic order was enunciated by the government of India in July 1991.[5] Thus, the government managed to avoid taking steps in fulfilment of the constitutional directives and to keep the doors open for international intervention in Indian education. The political and economic framework for subjugation by the global forces in the educational sector emerged soon after the announcement of the New Economic Policy (NEP) when the Indian government was persuaded by the International Monetary Fund (IMF) and the World Bank to accept the twin concepts of Structural Adjustment and Social Safety NET in Planning and Budgeting for social sectors. These twin concepts implied that the government will successively reduce public spending on social sectors such as health, education and social welfare (Structural Adjustment). Recognising that such a reduction can lead to severe socio-political tensions, the IMF and the World Bank offered loans for the social sector on certain terms and conditions to create social safety NET. Hence, the Ministry of Human Resource Development, Planning Commission, National Policy on Education shall pay no more role in educational decision-making since educational decisions are being dictated either by World Bank Head Quarter in Washington D.C. or the Corporate Capitals of the northern hemisphere. Thus, the people of India are again return back to the atrocities of the East-India Company of early 19th century. Like Macauley's approach to education, globalisation also aims at using education as a tool for building up various skills and capacities that are useful to the global economy. In this paradigm, knowledge in science, social science and humanities would need to be divested of its philosophical, historical, ethical, socio-cultural and aesthetic roots.

If Japanese have not lost their culture by modernizing themselves in the modern world and by bringing advancement in technological fields to make a progressive society of their own why the people of NER, in particular and India, in general, will loose their culture, tradition custom language and traditional occupation of their own in the 21st century to establish a New Economic Order. The people of NER do not want such advancement in technology and skills which would increase number of semi-educated and educated unemployed youth in the society. They do not allow industries to come up at the cost of their environment, which nurtured them well since their birth. They do not want such education which would promote criminal activities like communalism, extortions, murders, kidnappings etc. Insecurity, injustice, self-destruction, corruption, absence of felling of nationalism, drug trafficking and AIDS have a free play in the hill areas of NER. Inter and intra-ethical conflicts will further divide the states of NER into few sub-divisions by loosing its ancient glory in 21st century, Thus, what is needed in 21st century is a healthy and enlightened education for the people of NER. Then only the scientific discoveries and technological advances in the region will be regarded as sustainable development. The people of NER want a civil society to be created by the proper education in which peace would reign supreme.

Education and Environment

Another emerging issue in 21st century which will swell to great importance is the environment. Global warming, climate change, species extinction, soil erosion etc. are products of man's thoughtless exploitation of nature and natural resources without taking proper care of its environment. The NER has a unique environment compared to the rest of the country but we can say with certainty that this region is the worst victim of pollution and environmental degradation. Thus the need of the hour is sound educational system which would include the environmental education as compulsory in its curriculum from early childhood till the completion of higher education. The United Nation's Conference on the Human Environment held at Stockholm in 1972 made the first concerted attempt to focus on the Global Environmental Problems. This Conference produced an Action Plan resulting in the establishment of United Nation's Environmental Programme. In October 1975, the UNESCO organised an International workshop on Environmental Education at Belgrade in which the historic document known as "Belgrade Charter" was produced.

The New Education Policy (NEP) of 1986 in India has emphasised the importance of Environmental Education and stated that "there is a paramount need to create a consciousness of the environment. It must permit all the ages and all the sections of the society." The NEP of 1992 also led stress on environmental education for all categories of people in the society but environmental education is still in the process of becoming. Hence, the main task of our education is to face the challenges of new millennium relation to environmental degradation. The task before the policy makers and the planners on education to integrate environmental education with the curriculum at all levels highlighting the measures for protection and care of air, water and earth in all respects. Specially at under-graduate and post-graduate level environmental education may be offered as a separate discipline. An inter-disciplinary approach may be most fruitful for providing Environmental Education to the students in institutions of higher education in all the streams. Personnel involvement is the best effort to solve the environmental problems for its degradation and hence through picnic, excursion etc., environmental education may be imparted. Since the Indian psyche is deeply rooted in spiritual values and cultural heritage environmental study should contain the values in various religions for the promotion of environment. For examples, Hindu rituals of worshipping trees, *neem, tulsi* etc. and animals like cows, snakes and others will establish a good relationship amongst the human beings, plants and animals. Also, these plants have economic values as medicinal plants. The text books should be published reflecting cultural and economic values which would protect and care the environment. However, any new innovation in education of the region cannot be fruitful without caring the tribal way of life and old age traditions. Through proper environmental education and sincere effort of the different NGOs blind faiths among the tribals can be removed. Researches should be made for conservation of the soil from its degradation, preservation and protection of environment from its destruction. Only theoretical education is not enough to solve the environmental problems of the region but all should come forward to save the environment and environmental education should be a continuous process.

Education and Women

As human development moves centre stage in the global development debate on gender equality and gender equity are emerging as major challenges from Mexico to Copenhagen, on to Nairobi and to Beijing in 1995 is merely 2 decades of contemporary social history.[6] However, if one looks at the history of the struggle for the women's rights, both in India and the world, it constitutes one of the most eventful and momentous in recent times. A pluralistic society like India has a lot of contribution in different respect to the global women's debate and the principle of gender equality has been basic to Indian thinking for over a century. The Constitution of India not only grants equality to women but also empowers the state to adopt measures for affirmative discrimination in favour of women. The Constitution further imposes a fundamental duty on every citizen to renounce practices derogatory to the dignity of woman. In 1971, the government appointed a committee on the status of women in India. A significant outcome of these in the seventies was a shift in recognition from viewing women as targets of welfare policies in the social sector to regarding them as critical groups for development. This recognition was clearly reflected in the Sixth Five Year Plan which contained for the first time a chapter on women and development. A separate Development of women and Child Development was set up in 1985 under the newly created Ministry of Human Resource Development.

The National Policy on Education (1986) emphasised that education will be used as an agent of basic change in the status of women. It will foster the development of new values through re-designed curriculum text books, training and re-orientation of teachers, decisions makers and administrators. Women studies will be promoted as part of various courses and educational institutions encouraged to take up active programmes to further women's development. So far as the above target is concerned, the National Council of Educational

Research and Training (NCERT) has achieved the goal to some extent by preparing a framework for National Curriculum for Elementary, Secondary and Higher Secondary Education. They have also prepared Handbooks for the teachers regarding "Status of Women through Curriculum". Through various subjects and contents they have also tried to shift sex-bias in favour of girls. But the question is, how many states are in a position to follow this curriculum with a vast geographic, regional and socio-cultural disparities.

North-Eastern Region of India (NER) bears a clear testimony of the fact that although women's education is squarely on the development agenda of the country it is not translated into reality in the states of NER due to different reasons. Further, higher education for women is a distant dream in the region. The major obstacles of women's education are psychological, socio-cultural and economic factors. A close study to some of the indicators of socio-economic development of the region (Dutta, 2002) such as child-care, health, family nutrition, population explosion and education for the entire family clearly brings the attention of social scientists and economists that women's education is essential for the region. For want of special schools for girls with women teachers in rural areas, the women education is discouraged further. *Anganwadis, Balwadis* etc. meant for pre-school educational provisions for girls are absent in the region. Socio-cultural tradition of the society of the region denies women's education to some extent.

In NPE emphasis is laid on women's participation in vocational, technical and professional courses and to promote women's participation in non-traditional occupations as well as in existing and emerging technologies. NER lives in villages and only the urban elite of women's section has started taking advantage of such benefits and rural mass women are deprived of it. Under this circumstances no one can think of developing new values and for the promotion of women education. Very few and negligible attempts have been made so far to prepare women oriented new text books. The Orientation Programme for teachers and administrators for the upliftment of women's status at the level of their education is yet to be implemented. Women's education in higher educational system has always been a neglected area. The courses are not enriched with women-studies. Although there are women study centres at some particular universities of the region, most of these are confined to organisation of seminars and workshops within the campus where there is no need of women education. The outcomes of the deliberations in these seminars does not reflect in the women's studies as such. The educational institutions are not actively taking up programmes for further women's development. So far as the role of politicians and administrators are concerned, there is no bothering at all of them towards the problem of women. Their concern is only to earn money in the name of development without going into the details of the real meaning of the development. Since education is the most potent method to fight against evils like illiteracy and poverty at grass-roots level, women education seems to be the only way of hope. As north-eastern society is largely agricultural, women's education should involve skills and crafts, according to the aptitudes and needs of the learners. Patriarchal mind set of the policy makers and planners should be changed. This can be achieved through orientation programmes "India's heart lies in villages" and hence vocational, technical and other specialised women institutions having girls' hostel should be established in rural areas for the benefit of the women in larger scale.

The rising trend of feminist movement in many parts of the world persuaded Indian Policy makers in 1986 to include a special section called "Education for Women's Equality" in the NPE and accordingly the policy built up pressure on both the society as well as government to at least designed programmes which purportedly attempted to make education accessible to the girl-child, transform the ethos of higher educational institutions in favour of women and subject curriculum and text books to securing from the stand point of gender equality. Women's education is already in the agenda of globalisation. However, liberalized Economic Policy paved the way for the mushroom growth of private educational institutions. Hence, NIEO is self-contradictory and government is deliberately neglecting the higher education and indirectly encouraging privatisation of higher education in future. Under this situation it seems that real development in women's studies is not possible in future unless special attention be paid by the government for the same.

Education and Teacher

In the era of globalisation, one of the most important challenges the higher education is going to face is role of the teachers in the changing society. The very pertinent question before us is how to equip our students to face the ill-effects of the NIEO and hence the role of the teachers in higher education is very crucial.

The International Commission on Education's report popularly known as Delor's Report, has also given meaningful emphasis on the role of teachers in the changed society[7]. Actually, nobody can replace a teacher, but unfortunately, many of our teachers are not very serious about the role which they should play not only in moulding their own lives but also in giving a direction to the future generation of the society as a whole. It is only through the teachers that a society can resolve its conflicts of being and becoming. It is through the teachers only that a society can transform itself and reach newer heights. Long ago, Plato, the Greek philosopher highlighted the role of the teachers in his system of education. But unfortunately, there are teachers in different higher educational institutions who lack in seriousness and commitment to their job. To many teachers, teaching has been taken as a business. Some of the teachers always come late to the class room and leave off the class room earlier than the schedule time. They are not at all serious about their job and interested in teaching. Some of the teachers remain busy in private tuition for their material benefit and forget that teaching is a noble profession. Nepotism in teacher's recruitment process is most prevalent in NER. Politicisation of educational institutions made the recruitment policy further worse. Non-committed teachers are entering through back door as a result of which in many institutions there is teacher-taught conflict. Emergence of teacher-politicians in different educational institutions of NER made education a play-thing. They induct party-politics, groupism and lobbying into the arena of the holy academic atmosphere. The bulk of their time they spent in attending party politics by visiting seldom to the institutions where they are working. Without preparing for class-room lectures, they deliver the lectures without establishing any link with course curriculum. No creativity could be seen among the teachers engaged in higher education. Hence, pulling and pushing of the politicians into the academic environment of the institutions should be stopped. Professional academicians should obstructed to enter into the institutions. Intense inbreeding in appointments and promotion in favour of "Songs of the Soil" has taken away the Indianness of the system, leave aside globalisation. People with tunnel-vision and parochial interest are occupying positions of power. They are against migration of talent and excellence from one state to another or even one district to another. Windows for fresh and futuristic ideas, intelligent and innovative dialogues, constructive and creative dissent are shut off.

Periodic refresher course and orientation course should be arranged not only for their career advancement but also to refresh their skill and knowledge in the real sense that the student community will be greatly benefited. A teacher in higher education should be a scientist as well as an artist. The great task of interpretation of values will be wholly vitiated unless he can view incidence and events without the coloured spectators of bias and prejudice. He must be above sectarian, communal and even national narrowness. He must be a cultural person. In short, a teacher in higher education should approach the ideals of a skillful teacher, a student leader, a worthy colleague, a good citizen, a participant in community affairs, and a scholar who keeps abreast of education and contemporary affairs to deliver the goods of proper quality.

Conclusion and Suggestion

The present analysis is a clear indication of the fact that our educational system has failed to cope with New Socio-Economic Order introduced by the government. We live in a highly competitive world in which creative original thinking is absolutely essential. We live in an age of fast changes of computers and information technology and we cannot continue the educational system of the 20th century any longer. We have to make our education adaptive and to make all our students and teachers innovative, creative and original.

We must adopt a completely objective, transparent continuous internal assessment system where everybody will be accountable to everybody else. The teachers will be accountable to the students for the grades they give. They will have to show the answer books to the students and satisfy them individually and collectively that the grading is completely fair. On the other hand, the teachers will have to be ready to be assessed by the students. The teachers will be responsible to educational administrators for producing original thinkers and the government will be responsible for providing all facilities to the teachers and educational institutions for creating a real academic climate and by absolutely refusing to interfere in appointments and promotion of teachers. Nobody should be able to exploit the educational system for his personal and party benefits as high quality of higher education will introduce our nation as dignified nation in the modern world. Higher educational institutions of our country should be able to attract students from abroad because of the quality of education they provide.

Improvement in the real education tends to reduce fertility, infant mortality and gender inequality. To improve the quantity and quality of the education, the government should curb the wastage of public money and improve the rate of return. The reward for education has to be known to the pupils to make their life better. As education is the backbone of any development of a society, state and ultimately of the nation, the government should take proper care honestly and sincerely for its upliftment and not by vertical interference with it. The government must desire a system which ensures equal opportunities to the poor and the rich in obtaining higher education and training on in getting a start in trade and industry on securing employment. Another important measure is the introduction of a comprehensive social security scheme guaranteeing to each individual a minimum standard of living. Government should provide various social services like education, medical aid, labour welfare and other services for social and economic security of the weaker sections of the population.

Today's world is based on Science, Technology and fast Communication of Information. It is a very fast changing world in which we are lagging behind and the teachers are not the only source of knowledge. One has to learn from libraries, CD ROMs, Internet and through deep thinking. One has to know where knowledge is available and one should have the curiosity to avail this knowledge. Hence, adequate steps should be taken by providing funds to develop infrastructural development of educational institutions. The policy-makers and planners of the country should be equally concerned with removing intellectual poverty as more attention is paid to remove economic poverty. We are still miles away from the situation where our knowledge mission will be trying to persuade our people to acquire knowledge in depth. Hence, top most priority should be given to remove illiteracy and to upgrade the educational system till higher secondary level.

After 54 years of Independence we are thinking about to develop the quality of our human resources. During these years we have developed only very few institutions to give quality education in original thinking. In science, we have got no Nobel prize, in science, after independence for work done in India. There are almost no front line researches, which have been done for the first time in India and possibly further developed by other countries. If some Indian names have been enlisted there for awards and prizes, they may be non-resident Indians. Thus, a very small percentage of our human resources is prepared for original creative thinking. Unless we change the system of education we cannot compete in the modern world and even other regions of Indian Union.

In the coming years some new commerce based vocational areas world have to be added to in this region to enable the students of higher classes to compete with their counterparts in other parts of the country. However, the present vocational courses in different schools and colleges are not matching with the allotment of subjects. As vocational stream has a tremendous potentiality and slogan of globalisation is "Vocational Education for All", our appeal to the governments of North-Eastern States for re-examining their policies. If specialised institutions will be established for vocational courses it may solve the problem of unemployment by providing opportunities for self-employment.

The economic evidence in the developed countries shows that relatively higher income and comfortable level of living depends to a very large extent on good education and health care coupled with ease of mobility. But unfortunately, in India adequate attention has not been paid to universal educational and health care to all even after 54 years of Independence. It is a matter of great regret to clarify that the expenditure on education is hovering around 3 per cent and on public health 1.4 per cent of the Gross Domestic Product (GDP) for the last 5 years. This is in sharp contrast to other countries where social expenditure as percentage of GDP is much higher compared to India. Based on the Human Development Report more than 15 per cent of our population have no access to health services, 18 per cent have no access to safe drinking water while 48 per cent of the adult population is illiterate.

We are a country of more than one billion people which has a large. Reservoir of technical manpower. But the number of technical personnel available per 1000 population is awfully inadequate. For every 1000 population, we have in India only 3.5 persons while in the U.S. they have 55 technical persons, in Germany 76, in South Korea 46 and in Japan it is 110. At the outset, we don't have enough young boys and girls at schools level entering the vocational educational stream. There are nearly 4 crores of people in the young age group of less than 14 years, who are not able to either join any school or forced to drop out due to economic compulsions which is not at all desirable. Of the 20 millions of people born every year, only 10-15 per cent are able to have 10 years of education. It is shocking that, at this moment nearly 90 per cent of Indians have not passed class X level. It is further shocking when one of the state governments of NER accepts education department as non-productive. It also proves when we go through the statistical reports on education in NER. According to latest data, the percentage of population below poverty line in India is 35 per cent as against 5 per cent in China. There are 2 doctors in China per 1000 population as against 0.4 in India. In America, the investment in education contributed 23 per cent of the growth of real income and 42 per cent of the growth of real income per person employed during 1929-57. Thus the Government of India, in general and the state governments of NER, in particular, should spent honestly relatively more funds for the real development of education and health of the people for the development of the society in real sense.

Commercialisation of higher and technical education has been promoted in the present era under the false argument that resources need to be shifted from this sector to the school sector. It needs to be emphasised that knowledge is produced and communicated in institutions of higher learning. The quality of school education, teachers, administration etc. of school sector is highly depending upon the success of higher education in the region. If public expenditure in higher education will be reduced, the lower middle class and weaker sections of the society are likely to be deprived of this knowledge. The entire higher education system will become oriented to only utilitarian goals, while any knowledge that might lead towards social development or transformation will be marginalised. However, mushroom growth of institutions of higher education should be checked as those gives only quantity but not quality. Hence, the government should increase the expenditure on higher education for real socio-economic development of the region. It may be noted here that the responsibility cannot be fixed at one man but as a whole, the students, guardians, teachers, principals etc. and above all the government can bear this responsibility to make a healthy academic atmosphere.

Education holds the key for increasing awareness of the population of the methods for improving their quality of life through appropriate utilisation of available resources, opportunities and facilities. Further, investment in education to women and girl children can play an important role in improving and sustainable on-going developmental efforts. Thus necessary thrust should be given at the time of planning and allocating funds by creating adequate opportunities for higher education as it is necessary for meeting the human resources required for the tasks of economic and social development. For proper manpower planning there is need to focus on skill development of the workers in the weaker sections of the society. There is a need for vocational and technical institutions for rural women.

The need of the hour is to concentrate on reforming reorienting, rejuvenating reinvigorating the entire education system to meet the emerging needs and challenges of the new century and the new millennium.

However, to conclude the paper, our slogan should be think globally and act locally.

NOTES

1. J.C. Aggarwal (2001). "Census of India", Population Policy of India — Population and Progress in Global Perspective. Doaba House, Delhi.
2. Govt. of India. "Census of India 2001, Series 1", Provisional Population Totals, Registrar General and Census Commissioner, India.
3. P.C. Dutta (2001). "Regional Disparity and its Consequences in NER" paper presented in the 33rd Regional Science Conference, 19-20 October, NEHU, Shillong.
4. A. Dutta (2002). "Are College Teachers on the Warpath?" – 6th May, 2002, *The Assam Tribune*.
5. A. Sadgopal (2000). Guest Speaker lecture on the theme " The Challenge to quality of Education in the Age of Globalisation" on the Occasion of Council Foundation Day Lecture on 01-06-2000, organized by Assam Higher Secondary Education Council, Bamunimaidam, Guwahati.
6. 4th World Conference on Women, Beijing, 1995 Country Paper India (draft): Report Submitted by the "Department of Women and Child Development", Govt. of India, 1994.
7. Baroowa, D.C. (2000). Presidential Remarks made on the occasion of the Council Foundation Day Lecture, 2000, Guwahati.

REFERENCES

Dutta, P.C. (2000). *Role of Education in Socio-economic Development in North East India* – Paper Presented in the Seminar of 39th Annual Conference of All Assam College Employees Association, 23-25 June, Hailakandi.

Dutta, P.C. (2000). "A Study on the Impact of Socio-economic Development In North East India with Special Reference to the Problems of Population Growth and Urbanisation on Environment" — Report on the U.G.C. Sponsored Minor research Project submitted to the U.G.C. on 18.03.2000.

Dutta, P.C. & N. Roy (1998). "Socio-economic Development of North East India with Special Reference to the Problems of Urbanisation" – Paper presented in the Seminar on Environmental Problems in North East India, Assam University, Silchar, 6-7 November.

Gautam, H. (1999). The Objective of Our Education, *University News*, 38(26), June 26.

Malhotra, N. (1999). "Human Development in India and Inter State Pattern", *Indian Regional Science*, 31(1), 31-45.

Malhotra, R. (1997). "Incidence of Poverty in India — Towards A Consensus on Estimating the Poor", *The Indian Journal of Labour Economics*, Vol. 40, No. 1, 67-102.

Prabhu, K.S. (1996). "Social Sector in Economic Development: Some Issues", Paper Presented in 79th Annual Conference, Indian Economic Association, Guwalior.

Procharopouclus, G. (1994). "Returns to Investment in Education — A Global Update", World Development, pp. 1325-43.

Shariff, A. & P.K. Ghose (2000). "Indian Education Scene and the Public GAP", *Economic and Political Weekly*, April 5.

Tilak, J.B.G. (1989). "Education and its Relation to Economic Growth, Poverty and Income Distribution: Past Evidence and Further Analysis", Discussion Paper No. 46, Washington DC, World Bank.

Tilak, G.B.G. (1994). "Education for Development in Asia", Sage Publication, New Delhi.

World Bank (1997). "Primary Education in India, Development in Practice Series", Washington D.C.

13

Quality and Excellence in Higher Education
Some Thoughts

SUMANA PAUL

Higher education in any society is of vital importance, in the whole education system. In India higher education has been an integral part of education system since time immemorial. An overview of the higher education system of our country reveals that there are about 240 universities, 9700 colleges with an enrolment of approximately 70 lakh students under total faculty strength of about 3.5 lakhs. In the ladder of higher education system, university education has its own importance and place in almost all the societies of the World. Pandit Jawaharlal Nehru once said, "A university stands for humanism, for tolerance, for reason, for progress, for the adventure of ideas and for the search of truth. It stands for the onward march of the human race towards even higher objectives."

By now, India has sufficient number of universities engaged in various educational pursuits. In spite of these phenomenal growth in the field of higher education, for quite sometime now a general feeling has been growing that the standards of higher education has been declining. The need of the hour is to arm India with higher quality education. Universities and colleges are institutes of higher learning, which intends to equip the learners with confidence so that they would face the unknown future. Higher education has to play pivotal role for socio-cultural and economic development of a nation. The National Policy on Education (NPE, 1986) defines education in terms of empowerment of man through knowledge, acquisition of skills and values (scientific and democratic values, *viz.*, dignity of labour, tolerance etc.), and social and economic mobility, and leadership on all spheres of human endeavours — social, political, religious, moral and ethical. Generation, preservation and dissemination of knowledge, skills and values, teaching, research and extension services are the primary function, which higher education intends to undertake. To accomplish the objectives of higher education, the Programme of Action (POA, 1986) suggests consolidation and expansion of institutions, redesigning courses relevance to productivity and organising faculty-training programmes. This would increase the excellence of the system. The system of higher education needs to be made dynamic and responsive to the desired need of the country. Society for Education and Economic Development (SEED), 1993, reveals that more than 83 per cent of the total students in higher education in India get enrolled in colleges. It is hoped that the Indian collegiate system would impart both the quality high education as well as the quality of life, if its standard is maintained.

While delivering the 93rd convocation of University of Pune, Dr. Hari Gautam, Chairman, University Grants Commission (UGC) said, "An effective quality control, monitoring of academic performance to maintain the standards of education, examination and research in all the institutions should constantly be undertaken. The quality assurance is a key and which is to be seriously applied to the system of higher education. Accreditation, assessment and academic audit are the basic components and should be enforced on the institutions to provide the desired information and status of an institution." Quality control and achieving excellence in higher education has, therefore, been the main concern of the present century.

Efforts of UGC for Achieving Excellence and Assuring Quality in Higher Education

The UGC has introduced various educational programmes like College Humanities and Social Science Programme (COHSSIP), College Science Improvement Programme (COSIP), Social Assistance Programme in terms of Department of Research Support (DRS), Department of Special Assistance (DSA) and Centre of Advanced Studies (CASE) to improve the quality of the system, its excellence and efficiency.

Again for quality control of higher education, various supporting institutions have been established. Some notable institutions are Educational Media Research Centre (EMRC) for the countrywide classroom, Academic Staff Colleges (ASC) for staff development, University Science Instrumentation Centre (USIC) and Inter University Centre (IUC) for research in Nuclear Science, Astronomy and Astro-Physics. The creation of College Development Council (CDC) was intended to coordinate the academic planning of colleges and universities to evaluate the progress of college programmes financed by the UGC and to provide guidance and assistance to colleges for achieving their autonomous status. In spite of all its reforms in education, the UGC fails to achieve the expected goals.

An autonomous organisation — National Assessment and Accreditation Council more popularly known as NAAC, was established in 1994 by the University Grants Commission for the purpose of periodic assessment and accreditation of institutions of higher education or the units thereof. Unfortunately not many institutions so far have come forward to be accredited and assessed.

Steps Towards Achieving Excellence and Assuring Quality in Higher Education: Some Thoughts

1. It is the time that accreditation and assessment must be made compulsory for each and every institutions of higher education, so that the general public, progressive parents and inquisitive students should know the academic credibility of the institution, to which, they seek to take admission. In the 21st century autonomous status and accreditation grade points of the colleges should be the hallmark of quality and excellence.
2. Teaching and research should be more vibrant, modern, relevant and productive. Admission of students should be based on rigorous entrance examination followed by an aptitude test for higher education. Those who are less cut out shall be encouraged to have either a diploma or a degree through distance education mode. In respect of faculty, not only their qualifications have to be evaluated at the time of recruitment but also their competence and commitment have to be judged by means of proper tests. A non-committed teacher fails to motivate students in his/her class. Teachers should be encouraged to engage in research and this should be reflected through their publications of high order.
3. Mushroom growth of universities and colleges should be

checked. There has to be a policy decision regarding the opening of a new educational institutions and this be taken only after examination of its need and feasibility.

4. It is distressing to see that colleges are opened with the same traditional courses in humanities, which have no relevance in the present day job market. Teachers teach what they know rather than what they ought to know. It is necessary to restructure the curricula as per the job requirement in the market. Necessary modifications, innovations and changes have to be brought in the existing universities to generate better relevance and quality education. Introduction of new courses keeping pace with the developments and updating the curriculum should help in maintaining the quality.
5. A college or a university can also think of increasing the resources through consultancy, project work and so on. Alumni association should be strengthened and those past students, who have done well in life, must be involved in various academic and developmental programmes.
6. Most of the college and university teachers lack seriousness and commitment to their jobs. It is observed that one remains serious till he/she gets a job in a college or a university. Most of the teachers come late to the class and leave off the class earlier than the scheduled time. Some teachers remain busy in private tuition and earning a good income. Teaching is a noble profession and a teacher is a public figure and a social reformer. So a teacher ought to give up this money-making attitude. The Government may consider the feasibility of giving allowance to teachers for not taking private tuitions, and then the Principals of colleges and the Vice Chancellor of the university will have to check private tuition undertaken by teachers. The Government should also empower the Head of the Institutions to take proper action against such teachers.
7. It is important to note that higher education is to be qualitative and must not be cheap. It is also necessary to hike students' fee. This would help laboratories and libraries to be well equipped.

   We have basically two categories of students: one, who can afford to pay the increasing cost of higher education, and the other who really cannot afford to pay because of the weak economic status. In order to enable those students who cannot afford to pay, but who are bright, scholarship and stipend should be given.

8. Indiscipline in the present education system in the form of malpractice, attaches low values to college and university degrees. It is very peculiar to note that most of the students usually prepare 8-10 topics for examination and that to within the last two months before the examination. It has been noted more in humanities than in science or commerce subjects. Examination has become an instrument for the test of memory only. Other objectives such as Bloom's Taxonomy of Educational Objectives are hardly realised. According to Dr. Radhakrishnan the Chairman of University Education Commission 1948-49, if we have to suggest one single reform in the university system, it would be that of examination. The present system of examination fails to facilitate continuous feedback on the performance of both the students as well as the teachers. Teaching is delivered mostly through lecture method. There is less comprehensive internal assessment. Today's examination does not intend to develop regular study habit among the students. In order to make examination a useful tool for protecting the credibility and validity of the degree awarded to the students, examination phobia should be removed from the minds of students and it is possible only when internal assessment is done frequently. Moreover continuous assessment of the students throughout the whole academic year would ensure students' proficiency by inculcating in them regular study habit on the basis of continuous feedback of their performance.

Therefore in order to properly train students to accept the challenges of the 21st century we have to think seriously about the achieving excellence and assuring quality in higher education. Our system of higher education will have to respond to the challenges, which are now thrown up. In this regard, it is desirable that the three basic responsibilities of higher education — teaching, research and extension must be reflected in all the institutes of higher learning.

14

Assessment and Accreditation of Higher Institutions of Learning

Quest for Quality Assurance

SUJIT SIKIDAR & PADMALOCHAN HAZARIKA

Introduction

The National Policy on Education (NPE) 1986, Section IX states "No Person in the Society should rise above the status of a teacher", putting a great onus on the dedicated service of the teachers to humanity in the process of learning for self and make other also to learn. Assessment and accreditation by the National Assessment and Accreditation Council (NAAC) is also an attempt through institutional arrangement for quality improvement in higher education.

As per the World Bank prescription, for the Reforms in higher education, the National Policy on Education (Higher) 1986 called for the "Creation of a system of performance appraisal of institutions according to standards set at the national or state level". On this basis, the UGC constituted a committee headed by Dr. Vasant Gowarikar to make recommendation regarding setting up of NAAC. The Gowarikar Committee submitted its report in 1987. Its recommendations were basically based on "Accreditation Hand Book" published by the commission on Institution of Higher Education in USA. The features of the American system were taken as "Benchmark in establishing a system of institutional accreditation in Indian context". Further the Committee proposed that within five years of establishment of NAAC, all universities should delink their affiliated colleges. Besides, all universities and colleges should become autonomous as a pre-condition for accreditation, as it is said that "only accredited institutions will be eligible for central funding". The NAAC could take "painful decision" against the institution with unsatisfactory performance and it can take actions such as winding up or amalgamation or closure of the institution. Again accreditation once granted would be reviewed periodically for constant assessment.

NAAC is an autonomous body established by the UGC under Section 12-CCC of the UGC Act of 1956 and registered under the Karnataka Societies Registration Rules of 1961 on 16th September 1994 at Bangalore. It is an external Quality Assurance Agency like the Higher Education Quality Control Council of the U.K. and it is a member of the International Network of Quality Assurance Agency in Higher Education.

Criteria for Assessment

Criteria for assessment provided in the documents of NAAC reflect the different facets of functioning of the unit taken for assessment. These criteria embrace the activities of the assessee in totality. NAAC has pin-pointed the following seven criteria for assessment:

(1) Curricular aspects
(2) Teaching, learning and evaluation
(3) Research, consultancy and extension
(4) Infrastructure and learning resources
(5) Organisation and management
(6) Student support and progression
(7) Healthy practices

However, on the basis of above criteria NAAC has formulated three stages in the process of assessment and accreditation such as:

(1) Preparation of self-study report by the institution to be submitted to the NAAC.
(2) Ratification of the self-study report by the peer team visit.
(3) Final decision of NAAC based on the report of the peer team.

Grading of the Institutions

After scrutinising the report, the NAAC offers grades to the institution of higher education on a five-point scale as follows:

Grades		*Institutional (Score in per cent)*
A *****	....	75 and above
A ****	....	70-75
A ***	....	65-70
A **	....	60-65
A *	....	55-60

Institutions getting rank 5 star, 4 star and 3 star would be rated outstanding, very good and good. But those institutions getting 2 star and 1 star would be under watch or special watch respectively. If those institutions do not improve in due course they would face severe action such as cancellation of affiliation or closure of the institution.

Mandatory Provision of UGC

Originally the process of NAAC was voluntary. It was stated that NAAC would access and accredit only those institutions, which volunteer to undergo the process. Assessment and accreditation by NAAC was made as "without interfering in their autonomy and funding". The entire process of NAAC was made voluntary and NAAC could assess only those institutions that apply for assessment and pay prescribed fees.

Contrary to the above original provision of NAAC, UGC in its 388th meeting held on 29th-30th November, 1999 resolved that "the accreditation and assessment by NAAC be made mandatory and compulsory to start with for all the Universities in India. It was further decided that all the Universities in India be accredited and assessed by December 31, 2000." It was further stated that the colleges are to be assessed and accredited by 31st December, 2003. This provision was stated in its document "Relevance of Assessment and Accreditation in the Indian context".

In addition to the above, it was made clear by the Memorandum of Association of NAAC that it would also assess institutions "on the request of the UGC and/or Ministry of HRD or State Government".

It is a clear indication that the UGC or the concerned State Government could ask the NAAC to assess a particular institution for the purpose of funding. Assessment and accreditation is a necessary per-condition for the improvement of quality of education. It is a matter of concern for us that assessment and accreditation be linked with funding and grants. It amounts to a threat to the autonomy of higher educational institutions. It appears that the UGC going to implement the proposal of the Gowarikar Committee in a piecemeal manner, in the shape of regulation.

Scope of New Subjects in N.E. Region

The Arunachal University has introduced a Course on Himalayan Bio-Diversity in April 2002. The Ministry of Human Resource Development through UGC has sanctioned a grant of Rs.8 crore for the purpose to introduce graduate and post-graduate degree on the subject. A course curriculum has been approved by competent authorities. The same University in its Academic Council and Executive Council meetings has agreed to introduce some language programmes to award degree in Chinese, Thai, Bhutanese and Tibetan languages, which have some avenues for placement of the students.

Manipur University has a small section imparting teaching in Japanese language and the government of Japan often offers financial support for this course of study. Owing to financial crisis the university could not run a full-fledged degree course although it has some potentiality. The cordial relation between Manipuri people and the Japanese people goes back to the Second World War when with the help of Japanese army Netaji Subhas Chandra Bose had landed at Mairang in Imphal and Japanese Government provided financial support to the people of the state.

Similarly the Ahom community has urged the Dibrugarh University to include Thai and French languages in its curricula as a necessity to bridge the communication gap between the North-East and South-East Asian Countries. In a memorandum submitted to the Chancellor on May 12, 2002, it was argued that owing to opening of Guwahati-Bangkok route, learning of those languages would usher a new era of people's contact besides in trade and commerce. Apart from Thailand, variations of the Thai languages are spoken in Myanmar, Laos, Cambodia, Vietanam, and Yunan province of China. French is a legacy of colonial rule in South-East Asia. It is considered an added qualification for participation in global exchange programmes and employment in foreign services, international airlines, export and import business, foreign embassies and missions, and border trade centres located in different parts of India. Dibrugarh University thus had introduced a two-year diploma course in Tai in 1974. The memorandum demanded the change in nomenclature to make it known and identified as Ahom and not Tai.

Growth of Educational Institutions

There has been an exponential growth of institutions of higher learning. Number of Universities with 19 in 1947 went upto 275 in 2001; number of colleges little over 600 in 1947 increased to over 9,000 in 2001; number of teachers in Universities and colleges will be around 3 lakhs in 2001; enrolment of students increased from 0.2 million in 1947 to over 7 million in 2001. There was only one college in 1903, *i.e.* Sydanam College of Commerce in Mumbai. There are 43 Higher Secondary Boards in the country in May 2002.

Growth of education cannot be viewed in isolation, rather it may be looked into from total sectoral growth of the national economy. For instance, primary sector's contribution to GDP declined from 56 per cent to 26 per cent; Secondary sectors contribution to GDP was 15 per cent in 1950-51; it rose to 27 per cent in1990-91 and then again came down to 21 per cent in 1998-99, Tertiary Sector or Service sector contribution to GDP has registered an increase during the period of economic reform. It makes us to rethink in making budgetary allocation for higher education and also in emphasising on professional and technical education.

Vocational course and curriculum of studies was introduced in 1994 to remove the imbalance in educational sphere at first at degree level. In 1976 the UGC organised a model vocational course at +2 level of education, to groom our students and to diversify general students to entrepreneurship. While designing course curriculum, we give emphasis on core subjects; tertiary subjects and integrating them in certain proportion to a coherent synchronised course of studies.

Vocationalisation of course at first at degree level was launched by UGC in 1994; its primary objective was to check migration from rural areas; make it relevant to the society, increase self-employment opportunities; to encourage employment avenues of the students and enhancement of self-employment. 35 subjects were originally introduced in colleges all over the country.

Reviewing and Updating of Curriculum

The UGC Chairman in its UGC Model Curriculum 2001 observed "Reviewing and updating of the curriculum is the essential ingredient of a vibrant university system. There ought to be a dynamic curriculum with necessary addition and changes introduced in it from time to time and also providing therein inputs to take care of fast paced development in the subject concerned." For the purpose standardisation of academic curriculum is inevitable along with test of relevance, maximisation of student capability. This should be legitimate, reasonable, existential, epistemological. The exercise has five components, namely: (a) Syllabus: formulation and implementation; (b) Teaching: teacher's training, trainer's training, refresher course, orientation course; (c) Examination: question system; (d) Evaluation: grading, rating of teachers and students; (e) Placement of students in real life situation. Curriculum development is a continuous process and there cannot be a universal curriculum. It must be subject to review and refinement from time to time.

Revamping of the College Machinery

Celebration of alumni meet aims to make a record of the students who have passed out from the institution, their alma mater, many of whom have brought laurels for the state as well as the country. The alumni covered under one umbrella to be united and to stand as one family. The NAAC has issued directive to have an active alumni association to all the educational institutions. The NAAC has also made it mandatory for the colleges to submit themselves for an assessment to check whether they are at par with the standard norms. According to the standard norms, each college is required to take into account its alumni for implementation of changes and other development work. Another clause of the UGC is that each college should strive for self-sufficiency in terms of resource generation and be able to support itself. Hence, there is a major revamping of the college machinery to comply with the new rule, like all other colleges in north east India.

The revamping becomes necessary to secure a decent ranking by the NAAC. The college is required to facilitate an education policy that combines academic knowledge and practical skills. The parameters generally adding strengths and plus points to a college are:

1. Additional classes engaged beyond routine hours to help financially poor, academically poor, SC, ST students to bring them at par with advanced students,
2. Hostel facilities for boys and girls are specially for girl students,
3. Conducting of PG classes along with undergraduate classes,

4. Hi-tech biotechnology department; fully computerised teaching departments with internet connection; audio-visual unit and teaching aid in each department,
5. Students, guidance centre; career counselling centre for students under distance learning mode and correspondence mode,
6. Refresher course, orientation course attended by the college teachers,
7. Students-teachers ratio subject-wise as well as college-wise,
8. Publication of the teachers in national and international journals; referred journals,
9. Peer review system of evaluation performance of teachers,
10. Industry-college collaboration,
11. Patent right, copy right applied and created,
12. Innovative practices such as semester programme, regular evaluation of students' performance, creation of students' guidance centre,
13. Providing extension service such as adult education centre, providing education in catchment areas during vacation or recess to improve adult literacy, women literacy, alleviating rural poverty, rural health care facility,
14. Evaluation of teachers by students,
15. Preparation and submission of self-assessment report by the teachers periodically,
16. Implementing a year long learning and evaluation programme and taking feedback of the students into account to improve teaching skills.

The main reason to secure a good NAAC ranking is financial. Most government and semi-government colleges, government aided colleges depend on UGC for financial grants. According to the new UGC directive on self-generation of funds by the colleges, it is mandatory for the institutions to provide for themselves and sustaining their existence in future.

Apart from the tuition fees, the college may plan to meet its expenses by introducing vocational courses; other income generating courses other than traditional courses. This would enhance employability of the students and contemporary areas of operation. Such extra courses may be on taxation, insurance, computer operation, internet server facility, electronic typing, office management and secretarial practice, banking, fishery.

Girls college may opt for spoken English, receptionist, sales girl, marketing executive, pre-marriage counselling courses, which will impart lessons on baby care, housekeeping and so on.

Another step towards fund generation will be the selling of educational video cassettes that will be made available in the college. There is a tentative possibility of introducing paid seats in the various courses run by the college.

Human Factor in Economic Development

Economic development in some of the states, notwithstanding their abundant material resources, has been very slow, while a few others with far less natural endowment have achieved remarkable progress. The differentiating factor is human factor. The knowledge, skill, attitude can contribute substantially in translating human capability into productive asset. Unfortunately for Assam, at the lower level, the indicators convey a reverse message as may be realised from the following:

	Primary Class	*Middle Class*	*Secondary Class*
	I–V	*VI–VIII*	*XI–XII*
Drop out rates (%)			
Assam	76.55	69.81	76.80
All India	65.44	54.33	68.28
No. of teachers			
Assam	87,009	57,079	65,812
All India	19,19,340	12,97,805	17,20,430
Student-teacher ratio			
Assam	46	26	13
All India	59	32	16

Source: Annual Report of Ministry of HRD 2000-2001. Assam has done better in terms of student-teacher ratio but that has been negated by higher drop out rates, which is alarming.

Quality of education and total quality management (TQM) of education has become a strategy of the new millennium. Our survival in the present competitive world depends on our ability to attain TQM in education.

15

Adult and Continuing Education Programme in North East India

Need for Community Participation

B. LALTANPUIA

Elimination of illiteracy has been one of the major concerns of our government since independence. An ambitious programme of social education was launched in the first five year plan. This was integrated with community development programme in the Second Five Year Plan. Eventually, several significant programmes of the state level as well as the national level were launched. Farmers' Functional Literacy Programme and non-formal education programme was launched during the Fifth Plan. Yet these programmes did not result in any significant changes in the living and working conditions of the people. An unfortunate aspect of these campaigns was the lack of attention to levels of learning. It was considered sufficient if learners could write their names, the names of their children and the name of the village, in which they lived. And indeed, within a span of few years the people who had been declared literate had relapsed into illiteracy. The euphoria, the excitement and the sense of involvement unleashed during the campaign also became a distant fading memory.

In 1978 the National Adult Education Programme was launched and under this, the programme of Rural Functional Literacy Programme (RFLP) was activated with an attempt to impart functional literacy to the adult illiterates. In 1986 the National Policy on Education was adopted by the Parliament. In pursuance of the directions of the National Policy on Education, a comprehensive programme of action known as National Literacy Mission (NLM) was formulated on 5th May, 1998. The aim is to impart functional literacy to the adult illiterates in the age-group of 15-35 years. Functional Literacy for the Adult learners implies[1]

- — Achieving self-reliance in literacy and numeracy;
- — Becoming aware of the causes of their deprivation and moving towards amelioration of their condition through organisation and participation in the process of development;
- — Acquiring skills to improve their economic status and general well-being;
- — Imbibing the values of national integration, conservation of environment, women's equality, observation of small family norms etc.

From 1999 onwards the National Literacy Mission adopted the Total Literacy Campaign (TLC) approach. This campaign is by nature and implementation area-specific, time-bound, volunteer-based, cost-effective and outcome oriented. The TLC has been launched in many districts of the country including some districts in the North-Eastern states. The following figure indicated the number of districts, which has launched the Total Literacy Campaign in the North East[2].

1.	Assam	:	in 14 districts
2.	Arunachal Pradesh	:	N.A.
3.	Mizoram	:	Continuing Education Programme launched in 8 districts
4.	Meghalaya	:	6 districts
5.	Manipur	:	1 district
6.	Nagaland	:	N.A.
7.	Tripura	:	4 districts

Source: Literacy campaign in India — Annual Report, 1997-98 prepared by NLM, Government of India.

The Total Literacy Campaign is delivered through community participation on voluntary basis. Its success also largely depends upon the level of community participation. Peoples' participation on voluntary basis implies that a large number of functionaries contribute to their own capacity time, energy and resources without any expectation of awards or incentives, NCERT says "Community means a group of people with common interest and needs, participating in promoting the cause of education within a particular area/village/locality". The most effective organised community in the present day is the church community or the religious communities. We can also think of other communities like the village community, teaching communities, NGO's, the community of the elite or the educationists.[3]

As has usually been said that "Education is a key to development", the success of the Adult and Continuing Education Programme can be considered as an indicator of progress and development of a community, a society and also that of the state and the nation.

It has been observed that the success of Adult and Continuing Education Programme in the North East is a result of the contributions made by different communities in various stages of the programme. For instance, Mizoram's high literacy percentage can rightly be accredited to the untiring efforts made by the church communities, the NGO's, the teaching communities and the students under the NSS. The relentless and united efforts of these communities has promoted the literacy position of the state to 89.49 per cent (2001 Census), which stood second in the all India literacy race. Similarly, in Meghalaya, the Total Literacy Campaign went through successfully in Ri-Bhoi district and East Khasi Hills districts. The success can be attributed largely to the collective contribution made by different communities. The religious communities like the India Every Home Crusade, The World Vision of India, NGO's, Youth Organisation known as the Seng Samla, NSS etc., had participated actively in the Total Literacy Campaign, which marked to its success. In the Garo Hills of Meghalaya we have also seen tremendous participation of NGO's, student communities, and even the politicians like the MDCs spared no efforts for the success of the literacy campaign. Assam, Manipur, Tripura and other north-eastern states are also witnessing active community participation in the literacy campaign. Experiences have revealed that those areas or districts or states, where literacy drives have been successful, the participation and involvement of school and college teachers, students, women, social organisation, the church and para-church organisations, government servants, traditional village bodies was crucial. However, in some areas there has been instances where the level and volume or peoples' participation subsidies gradually and the programme came to a standstill. Sustained and continuous participation of the community with a mission mode can only ensure the success of this programme.[4]

Therefore, in order to achieve real success in the Adult and

Continuing Education Programme, the people or the communities must be continuously persuaded or exhorted or challenged to take active part in this noble venture with the true spirit of voluntarism for the good of the society. Active involvement of the institutions of higher learning like the universities can also strengthen the programmers by way of providing structural, academic and technical resource support to the programme functionaries especially in the field of research, curriculum development, training, documentation, monitoring and evaluation, and various other extension programmes.

NOTES

1. *Adult Education – Its implementation in Mizoram* published by Directorate of School Education, Adult Education Wing, Government of Mizoram.
2. *Literacy Campaigns of India – Annual Report-1997-98.* Published by the National Literacy Mission, DAE, MHRD, New Delhi.
3. *Total Literacy – UEE Campaigns – Guidelines for Project Formulations,* Published by the MHRD, Government of India, New Delhi.
4. *Guidelines for Post-Literacy and Continuing Education.* Published by MHRD, Government of India, New Delhi, 1995.

Education for the Challenged Children

K. PRAFULLA REDDY

A challenged child may be defined as one, who suffers from any continuing disability of body, intellect or personality, which is likely to interfere with his normal growth and development or capacity to learn. His disability may be the result of unfavourable factors in his heredity or of disadvantageous environmental circumstances in prenatal or postnatal life. An understanding of normal child development can guide us in planning activities that will help the disabled child progress. Every child develops in three main areas:

- Physical (body), which includes gross and fine motor skills and vision;
- Mental (mind), which includes hearing, language, comprehension and concept development; and
- Personal-social development, which includes self-help and communication skills.

In each area, skills develop step by step in a certain order. At that time a child should be given stimulation, which would lead to a variety of opportunities to experience, explore and play with things around. It involves body movement and the use of all the senses especially seeing, hearing and touching. Early stimulation is necessary for the healthy growth of ever child's body and mind. For a normal child, stimulation often comes naturally and easily, through interaction with people and things. But it is often more difficult for the challenged child to experience and explore the world around him. For his mind and body to develop as early and fully as possible, he will need extra care and special activities that provide easy and enjoyable ways to learn. The younger the child is in the beginning of a stimulation programme, the less retarded or delayed he will be when he will become older.

The child's ability to see, makes her see things and wants to reach for things and explore. Seeing stimulates her to try to learn and do more. If a child cannot see, this basic part of early stimulation is lacking. To prevent her falling behind, we must look for other ways to encourage her to learn and do things. We can do this through touch and sound, adapting the type of stimulation, we use to the child's particular stage of development. A child who is born deaf but whose brain is normal will have difficulty in understanding what people say, and in learning to speak. As a result, she is often left out of exchange of ideas and information. Because language is so important for the full development of mind, in some ways she may seem mentally slow for her age. However, if the child is taught to communicate her wishes and thoughts through 'sign-language' at the age when other children learn to speak, her thinking power (intelligence) will often develop normally.

However, a child who has a disability, needs special help to keep progressing. Whatever the cause of their disablement, the vast majority of these children suffer from a number of functional impairments, which affect abilities such as comprehension, speech, sight hearing, mobility and fine motor control. These disabilities can in turn lead to handicaps. The presence of a handicap and its degree of severity depends upon the interaction between abilities (or disabilities) and the social and physical environment. For instance, a school building with steps, stairs, long corridors and unsympathetic pupils would create considerable handicaps for a child who is unable to walk. Those handicaps could, on the other, be prevented or reduced by the presence of ramps, lifts and willing wheelchair pushers.

'Education for All' has long been one of the cherished goals of national development reflected both in constitutional and policy commitments since Independence. Despite planned concerned efforts this goal remains elusive due to certain disadvantaged groups remaining out of the fold of the formal educational system. One such group is the '*challenged children*' who have been considered peripheral for almost three decades of planned development. It is obvious that universalisation of elementary education cannot be achieved unless all children are brought into schools, retained and provided quality education, that is equitable.

It has been well established that adequate social and cultural environment is an essential pre-requisite for normal intellectual development of a child. Poor socio-economic environment and emotional deprivation can therefore lead to apparent mental deficit in such cases as may be attributable to delayed maturation. Moreover, as our competitive society becomes more complex and fast moving, the demands for intellectual capacity and for adaptability increase. Thus in our age of automation, individuals with minimal skills and abilities become double handicapped. Not only do they face an increasingly competitive society, they are forced to keep pace with people of increasingly higher capacities.

All children and young people of the world, with their individual strengths and weaknesses, with their hopes and expectations have the right to education. It is not our education system that has a right to a certain type of children. Therefore, it is the school system of a country that must be adjusted to meet the needs of all its children.

All children need help in order to adjust to life, but some children are so obviously deprived of the usual requirements for normal learning that their need for special help is immediately seen. Whatever be the degree of impairment, the developing personality is always involved to some extent and the child is generally unable to profit fully from the general education, which is offered to normal children. Normalisation of the handicapped requires different types of educational methods. For this reason, special educational programmes have evolved in many places with different methods and equipments, which supply compensatory education for specific defects and which attempt to let the handicapped share in the store of common knowledge, so that they can play an independent and participative role in the society.

For children with disabilities and special educational needs, most countries have created a parallel school system called 'special education'. It is often an arrangement that so far has been of no particular concern to the rest of the educational system and reaching very few (1-2 per cent) of all those, who are in need of some extra help.

In 1936, the International Conference on Public Education convened at Geneva recommended, "It is the duty of educationists to concern themselves with conditions by which, both the physically defective and the mentally defective may, by suitable courses of education, be enabled to live an economic and social life more profitable to themselves and to society, and be trained like other children to profit by the moral, artistic and intellectual riches, which give to human life, its true value. Although children with disabilities are briefly mentioned in the final report from the Jomtien Conference, Thailand, 1990, as well as in the World Declaration on Education for All, little information is available on new initiatives to include them in the implementation of national plans for Education for All. There is also very little reference to the needs of disabled children in the Education for All Summit of Nine High populated countries (New Delhi, December, 1993) or in the International Consultative Forum on EFA.

There are many United Nations initiatives for the disabled. These include:

- The International Year of Disabled Persons (1981),
- The subsequent Decade of Disabled Persons (1983-1992),
- The World Programme of Action in Favour of Disabled Persons (United Nations 1983),
- The Convention on the Rights of the Child (1989),
- The Asian Decade of Disabled Persons (1993-2002), and
- The recent adoption by the United Nations General Assembly of the standard rules on the Equalisation of Opportunities for Disabled Persons.

All these initiatives have educational implications. In addition, they all encourage a multi-disciplinary, multi-sectoral approach to the planning and delivery of services to enable disabled people of all ages to become full citizens of their society. Before having the World Conference on Special Needs Education in Salamanca, UNESCO with the support of the Swedish government had organised a series of five regional seminars. They are in:

- Botswana (eight countries),
- Venezuela (five countries),
- Jordan (six countries),
- Austria (five countries), and
- China (twelve countries).

The purpose of these seminars was to mobilise policy and professional support for pupils with special educational needs, within the regular school system. The Salamanca Declaration (1994) states that "the learning needs of the disabled demand special attention" within the framework of Education for All. The Salamanca Conference thus provided the first significant international opportunity to ensure that children with special educational needs are included from the outset in national and local plans to open schools to all children and to ensure that schools become enjoyable and challenging learning environments. The right of every child to an education is proclaimed in the Universal Declaration of Human Rights and was forcefully reaffirmed by the World Declaration on Education for All. Every person with a disability has a right to express their wishes with regard to their education, as far as this can be ascertained. Parents have an inherent right to be consulted on the form of education best suited to the needs, circumstances and aspirations of their children.

Article 41 of the Indian Constitution directs the state "to make effective provision for securing the rights to work, to education and to public assistance in case of unemployment, old age, sickness and disability". So the disabled being the citizens of India, have the right to an adequate means of livelihood and have the right to secure education and work. The recent legislation passed in India relating to challenged children, the Persons with Disabilities Act, 1995, which also stresses the need of free education till 18 years of age, integration of students with disabilities in normal schools and also establishing special schools in governmental and private sector for those in need of special education.

With the advent of compulsory schooling, the need for special schools and other institutions for children, who were unable to attend ordinary schools became increasingly obvious. All handicapped persons, 'with the possible exception of those, who lack all capacity to respond to stimulation' are capable of learning and should be educated in ways, which increase self-sufficiency and reduce dependency. There is no need of expensive and sophisticated programmes for the challenged children. A well-organised school can provide many opportunities for its students to participate in self-initiated projects and social activities. Proficiency in the fundamental tools of learning should be achieved in classroom situations, which stimulate the child not only to gain skills and knowledge but also to develop attitudes of cooperation, both with adults and with young persons of his/her own age. It has been realised that costly special schools and centres which in any case foster segregation, cannot meet the education and training needs of the majority of children with disabilities. Regular schools must play a much bigger role. They need to re-design their objectives, teaching and curricula and apply an "inclusive education" that would cater to a great diversity of pupils, including children with disabilities. Within the total spectrum of services for the retarded, nursery and pre-school training must occupy a primary position.

Education is one of the vital components of rehabilitation. The framework for Action on Special Needs Education adopted at the World Conference in Salamanca, 1994, stresses that "Integrated Education and Community Based Rehabilitation represent complementary and mutually supportive approaches to serving those with special needs. Both are based upon the principles of inclusion, integration and participation and represent well tested and cost effective approaches to promoting equality of access for those with special educational needs as part of a nationwide strategy aimed at achieving Education for All".

A school system emphasising Education for All should ensure the right of all children to a meaningful education based on individual needs and abilities. Education should proceed, at any age or level, by finding out the stages of development that the child has reached and the skills, which he has achieved in the relevant areas, and by working forward from these baselines. The slower rate at which the handicapped child progresses through the developmental and learning stages involves the need for more repetition, greater reinforcement and more individual pupil-teacher contact than is found in the nursery school. For an educator the focus should be on the current level of functioning of the child, which would help her to further develop programme for training the child towards social competence to be as independent as possible in the society. It is important that a teacher is aware of the various characteristics so that she can plan her educational programming accordingly.

The regular schools have to play a major role in making provision for children with special educational needs available nationwide. Making the school system flexible and adopting an inclusive approach may, however, prove the most challenging task of all. It might lead to reforming the school system as a whole from a traditional, examination oriented approach to an inclusive child oriented approach.

17

Education for the Challenged Children
Issues, Prospects and Challenges in the 21st Century

ZEENAT ARA ALI

As we passed a century and begin a new one, it is always felt that good progress will be met in the next 100 years. Despite the many upheavals in an era we do know that success and achievements have made the World, what it is today. Though turmoil seems to have ushered in this new century, we hope that development will move at a greater pace to overshadow the calamities. "Education for All" is probably the core of advancement.

A little historical background before we talk of challenges and how we could try to meet them. We in India, have come a long way in the area of disability rehabilitation since Independence. The lifestyle of people with disabilities has shifted from charity to rights. Now it is the RIGHT of a disabled person to receive appropriate support and not be at the mercy of the provider. We are proud of our progress despite our social, economic, linguistic and cultural variations. However many things need to be done if disabled persons are to receive equal opportunities and access.

Before Independence there were few Special Schools and generally a disabled person used to be admitted to a Mental Asylum. During post-Independence period there has been a gradual increase and since the 90s a steep rise has been observed, which includes manpower development. This is significant as special children receive professional assistance.

The National Policy on Education 1986 for the first time, included disability and kept provision for the children with mild disability to be included in regular schools. Severely disabled children were to be admitted in special schools. Vocational Education was to be given. Teacher Training Programmes were to be reoriented, which would include education of the disabled children. The Department of Education implemented this policy and Integrated Education of Disabled Persons gained momentum. This however was not beneficial for the intellectually impaired.

The Rehabilitation Council of India was established in 1992. This is a statutory body under the Ministry of Social Justice and Empowerment, which is to assure quality education, training and management of the disabled.

The Persons with Disabilities (Equal Opportunities Protection of Rights and Full Participation) Act, 1995 is responsible for bringing about major changes. Seven kinds of disabilities are covered and this Act aims to improve the quality of life of a disabled person at the literacy level, employment, social security, suitable assistive devices and a barrier free environment.

The National Trust for Welfare of Persons with Autism, Cerebral Palsy, Mental Retardation and Multiple Disabilities Act of 1999, is the answer to the query of many parents, who have children, who will require lifelong care. The Trust has made provisions to help guardians by facilitating organisations to develop residential services.

Many, many schemes have been developed to enhance the quality of life of the disabled. The latest being the Composite Rehabilitation Centres and the District Rehabilitation Centres. These have been created to fulfil the needs of the disabled persons in villages and remote areas.

With so much being done, have we been earnest to implement these legislations! This we feel, is one of the greatest challenges we face.

Integration is a central issue around the World. It is indeed a moral issue, revolving round the right of the individual and the society's attitude towards acceptance. Let us now ponder as to why special schools began at all. The concept of community based rehabilitation is not a new concept in India. At the time of joint family system, there was always help at hand. Neighbours, who were a great support system are no longer able to fulfil little deeds of kindness, as they have to face the stress of the modern world to fulfil the needs of their own homes. Traditional joint family system has eroded to give way to the nucleus family. Special schools were the answer to the need of the new family system. Regular schools were unable to accommodate special needs of the children due to the lack of supportive infrastructure. High quality work is done in special schools with well planned individual programmes, strategies developed to teach according to the abilities. Now it is debatable whether this segregation is good for the child or whether he learns better with his peer group in regular schools. It is this that concerns us the right to quality of educational opportunity and the right to participate in society.

Let us review the difficulties faced by the disabled group –

1. Limited few attend any form of schooling.
2. General schools unwilling to accept the disabled.
3. Special school only in urban areas.
4. Resources in terms of finance and trained manpower is limited.
5. Lack of awareness.
6. Stigma attached.
7. Lack of professional infrastructure in rural areas.
8. Negative attitude of parents and community.
9. Limited exposure of girl child and more so of the disabled girl.
10. Parents believe that unless education leads to income generation it is not worthwhile.
11. Learning difficulties (moderate/severe) cannot be met by education alone.

Considering the problems, there are disadvantages in planning for the successful implementation of a model integration system and more so for the severely disabled. Our work is not simplified as we do not have accurate statistics or sufficient research done. The challenges we face are many. However, it is not impossible, considering the fact that man has gone to the moon.

We may look into the work done in some developed countries and probably adopt ideas and adapt them to our needs. In these countries an extensive programme has been planned, special schools are centres of competence and expertise. Together with staff of regular schools, they are able to provide opportunities in the least restrictive environment, so that the disabled may enjoy the best possible quality of life. Every school is seen as a 'School for All' based on Individual Educational Programmes where parents play a crucial role.

In India most primary schools are given to rote learning, which may be quite meaningless. So while considering an integrated education, the curriculum should be functional and relevant. Though many models have been suggested, implementation of those models in our country has been sporadic and superficial. The two possible models often given are, a resource room with a resource teacher to enable the disabled students to participate wherever and whenever possible in a regular school. The other is when a disabled student is included into a regular classroom and is supported by a resource teacher. Either way there has to be carefully planned programmes. While talking of integration, it may not be possible to do away with special schools till proper provisions are made to suit the special child in the regular school. We must remember that special schools have withstood the test of time. The future change must definitely be better. The quality service given in special schools must be maintained in regular schools along with all plus points that go with mainstreaming. At present the District Primary Educational Programme includes children with special needs. Models must be selected and adapted to suit the existing schools.

Hence to meet these challenges we must have—

1. integrated delivery of services.
2. multidisciplinary collaboration.
3. early detection/identification.
4. parental involvement.
5. professional staff.
6. in service training at regular intervals.
7. a curriculum adapted to the individual needs, which should reflect human variances and give educational service in accordance.

For rural areas the Community Based Rehabilitation Services should be more structured to reach more people and quality of work to be attained and maintained. We are fortunate to have the services of the Anganwadi workers under the ICDS Programme. These Anganwadi workers should receive training in disability so that prevention, early detection and intervention can take place and the severity of the condition can be reduced. Public awareness, referral services and treatment must be imparted by the PHC doctors — as they are held in high regard by the people of the villages.

Before concluding my paper it would be wise for us to weigh the pros and cons of this issue, as the question of integration is highly debatable. We have reached a turning point, where we must make decisions about value, direction and expenses. What kind of future do we want for our children? How do we get there?

Those who support exclusion state the following, that we are not equal in capacity, it is not possible to give equal opportunity, we must strengthen a few to take care of the rest and the weaker section will benefit from the support system that is created. To oppose this, those who support inclusion, state that we are unique each having certain capacities, all people can learn, all people have contributions to make, we have a responsibility to give everyone a chance to make a contribution. The criterion for inclusion is not about IQ, income, race, language or colour, it is about living. Here again the supporters of exclusion say integration is expensive, they can't learn and they do not know what is good for them and that inclusive education is quite impossible to achieve. The critics of exclusion insist special schools are expensive, people can learn and are able to respond when given a chance. Inclusion is possible and it is totally unethical to write off marginalised people in our society.

The Story

We want to believe in a value based system, where everyone belongs, we must make time to listen to the struggle, pain and frustration of the less privileged. We must find hope in the future. This choice is entirely ours. When we talk of integration and inclusion we talk of the efforts to give the best education within the diversity, remembering that social skills and peer relations are the basic foundations for a secure adulthood.

REFERENCES

Jayanthi Narayan, *Intellectual impairment in India, Government policies and Legislation.* Deptt. of Human Resources, Spastic Society of India, Network Seminar on Integrated Education for Children with Special needs.

Sandhya Paranjpe, *A community based model of integration for primary education in India.*

Seamus Hegarty, *The Education of children and young people with disabilities.*

18

Strategies of Education for Under-privileged Children of Guwahati

A Case Study

JAYASREE BORAH

Illiteracy is the major hurdle to development. It is associated with ignorance, poverty, ill health, crime, drug addiction, juvenile delinquency, etc. In case of the underprivileged children like street children, children living in slum areas and the child labour, low level of education adds more their misery. Due to population explosion haphazard growth of urban centres and lack of employment opportunities among the adults, the number of child labour and street children are increasing along with different other problems. In Guwahati city also this problem is not a new phenomenon. With the increasing poverty, the problems of education and proper training of these under-privileged children has been increasingly rapidly. The present study is an attempt to assess the problems of these children in Guwahati city and suggest strategies for education and proper training with a sociological perspective.

Objectives

The main objectives of the present work are:

(i) to study the demographic characteristics of the urban poor having child labour.
(ii) to find out the causes of different problems of these families.
(iii) to assess the awareness of the children and their families regarding education.

(iv) to find out strategies for education and vocational training programmes to attract and aspire these children.

(v) to formulate a model of education for the underprivileged children of Guwahati city.

Methodology

This is a descriptive study based on primary data collected by using a survey schedule. The sample population is chosen by selected sampling from the Harijan colony near Dispur and slum areas of Ganeshguri Market, Paltan Bazar and Bamunimaidan Railway Colony. The sample constitutes of 50 child labours and 50 street children are respondent. They are interviewed through informal discussion. The collected data have been analysed to indicate percentages. Then strategies are formulated on primary education and vocational training programme for these children.

Study Area

It is already mentioned that social problems like poverty, illiteracy, crime, child abuse, child labour are more common in urban areas due to population explosion and haphazard and unplanned growth. Guwahati, being the largest urban centre of the entire North East India, also has experienced similar types of problems. At present, it is the lone city of this region where huge flow of poor, uneducated and unskilled people has created a number of social problems like growth of slum areas and increase of child labour, child abuse, juvenile delinquency etc. The present study will explore the problem of these underprivileged group of children of Guwahati city.

Findings

The sample consisting of 100 drop out school children (50 child labours + 50 street children) in the age group of 8 to 15 years and about half of them are of rural background, *i.e.* formerly they were engaged in agricultural fields. All the surveyed child labours do not live with their parents. One-third of them are illiterate while only around one-third have their education up to primary level. Number of girl children are very limited in the child labour group and they are mostly engaged in household works, as domestic helpers. Boys are mostly engaged in hotels and garages. Various reasons were stated by the respondents for selection of their present job. The most common reason is that they are interested in hotel or garage jobs, which is less tiring than the agricultural work or construction work. All the job-places provide free meals. Almost 50 per cent of them do not get any salary. They had to work from 6.30 a.m. to 7.00 or 8.00 p.m. in the evening. Hotel workers even sometimes prepare food, tea etc.

Majority of these child labours and street children are school drop outs and poverty is the main reason of leaving school. Ninety per cent of the respondents would like to resume schooling, if they are provided that opportunity. Most of them, who had lost interest in education felt that they would no longer be able to cope with studies since their minds were at work. A few of them even enjoyed the economic independence acquired through employment. Even some of their parents also prefer to send them to work than to school. Here they feel that even if the child goes to school, there is no guarantee of a job at the end of it. Whereas, if the child, even though he may not be earning anything, is trained, which is an advantage for his future career. However, almost all these child labours are unskilled and untrained and they are more susceptible to various infectious diseases. Child labour working in garages and markets are also constant threat of traffic accidents and street violence.

Two years back the Government of Assam issued directive to all Deputy Commissioners of the districts to conduct a survey on child labour. It is learnt that a sum of Rs.1.50 lakh were also allotted to conduct the survey and make arrangement for these children. During the process, the then Deputy Commissioner of Kamrup asked the employers of the child labour to pay Rs.50 per child for their education. Many NGOs came forward to render social service to educate these children through "*Pohar* Schools", which were arranged particularly for these child workers. However, due to the negligence of the Labour Department, lack of monitoring from the administration and non-cooperation of the employers, the whole idea of educating these poor children came to an end. Thus the Government has undermined the attempt suitable for these needy child workers.

Strategies

1. A scientific non-formal educational programme is required to make studies attractive, easy and also practical so that it

will reduce the number of school drop outs and will help the neo-literates to acquire skills to improve their mental as well as physical ability.

2. Certain facilities should be provided to read and write and thus developing abilities of the learners.
3. The Education Department should encourage production of books and other learning materials, especially for these children.
4. Various attractive schemes should be implemented by government organisations and NGOs to create awareness among these underprivileged children, about their rights and benefits which they can draw from educational programmes and vocational trainings.
5. NGO's can provide necessary free and compulsory education and training.
6. Programme can be adopted involving both students and teachers of the schools and colleges to educate these under-privileged children. Here we can follow the principle of 'each one teach two' motto.
7. In the process of Mass Programme of Functional Literacy (MPFL) a master trainer can be selected to train the volunteers and motivate and mobilise those who are genuinely and sincerely committed to such schemes. There will be a group of teachers and educationists for training and monitoring the whole process.
8. By conducting a camp or workshop for these children and their parents, their attitude towards education can be changed that it will help them to earn more, if they learn more.
9. Provision of short-term stipend through social welfare department, to the families of the child labour will encourage them to send their children to school.
10. Lastly, effective monitoring of the entire chain is necessary by the government officials, specially by the Labour Department.

Conclusion

In conclusion it can be said that though poverty is the root cause of poor educational background of the child labour and street children at Guwahati city, lack of awareness and proper educational scheme at free of cost also behind such poor education. So their parents should be motivated to send their children to the school, instead of sending them to labour market, street or Railway Station. They should be made aware of the importance of education, emphasising its long-term benefits like increasing efficiency, development of personality, morality etc. Polities should be geared to educate women folk towards improving the environment for educating their children. The employers of the child labour also can play a positive role by encouraging the children to go to the school, at least for two hours a day. They should be treated as a component of the society, not as an easy prey to exploit. Only a humanitarian approach by the employers, NGOs and government organisations can solve their problem. It is already mentioned that during 1998, some non-formal schools (*Pohar*) had been started at Guwahati city for the child labour with the help of a number of NGOs, which miserably failed. It is only due to the non-cooperation of the employers and lack of monitoring from the Labour Department. Proper survey, awareness programme and training of the teachers is the other part of this scheme. The vocational training after completion of the general education programme is most essential, so that these children get better job opportunities or they may become self-employed. Non-formal educational scheme (ex-*Pohar*) is thought to be of great help in bringing the desired awareness for education and consciousness about the evils of illiteracy. In conclusion, a model has been tried to formulate the strategies for educating these under-privileged group of children.

19

Higher Education in Tripura

MAHADEV CHAKRAVARTI

Like many other states of North-east India, higher education in Tripura had a late start. Although as early as 1901, Radhakishore Manikya made an attempt to establish a degree college at Agartala, but the then authorities of the University of Calcutta did not approve of the idea. The first degree college (Maharaja Bir Bikram College), affiliated to the University of Calcutta, was founded in 1947 at Agartala, when Bir Bikramkishore Manikya acquired about 234 acres of land and initiated the *Vidyapattan Scheme* for this purpose. Today, with a population of about 32 lakh, there are 1 University, 14 Degree Colleges, 10 Professional Colleges along with ITI, Pharmaceutical Institute, Nurses Training Centres etc. in Tripura. The colleges for general education conduct under-graduate courses in Arts, Science and Commerce streams. The student population at present of the professional colleges like the Engineering College, College of Education, Music College, Law College, College of Art and Crafts at Agartala and the College of Physical Education at Panisagar etc. are no less impressive.

It would become evident from Table 19.1, how among the 14 General Degree Colleges, the first was established in 1947, the second in 1950, then four colleges in the 60s, three in 1979, two in 1987 and two in 1988 and the last in 1991. All the colleges of Tripura today are Government Colleges and there is virtually no scope of private initiative in the field of higher education. The student population in all the fourteen Degree Colleges is 17,694 with 10,515 boys and 7,179 girls. Table 19.2 shows the scheduled tribes and scheduled castes (boys and girls) students, whose numbers compared to general category students are far less.

Table 19.1: Tripura – Profile of Government General Degree Colleges as on 1-1-2002

Sl.No.	*Name of the College*	*Year of Establishment*	*Number of Teachers*			*Number of Students*		
			Total	*Full time*	*Part time*	*Total*	*Boys*	*Girls*
1.	M.B.B. College, Agartala	1947	148	87	61	3762	2546	1216
2.	R.K. Mahavidyalaya, Karipashahar	1950	51	15	36	1042	718	324
3.	Belonia College, Belonia	1964	71	25	46	2094	1554	540
4.	Women's College, Agartala	1964	89	60	29	2485	—	2485
5.	Ramthakur College, Agartala	1967	89	32	18	1891	1151	740
6.	B.B. Evening College, Agartala	1969	54	28	26	1707	1707	–
7.	Netaji Subhash Mahavidyalaya, Udaipur	1979	44	19	25	1411	837	574
8.	Dosarath Deb Memorial College, Khowai	1979	41	15	26	1014	668	346
9.	Dharmanagar College, Dharmanagar	1979	48	13	35	1051	631	420
10.	Sabroom College, Sabroom	1987	15	5	10	162	102	60
11.	Kamalpur College, Kamalpur	1987	21	5	16	392	219	173
12.	Kazi Nazrul Mahavidyalaya, Sonamura	1988	18	4	14	435	278	157
13.	Amarpur College, Amarpur	1988	14	3	11	86	34	52
14.	Ambedkar College, Fatikroy	1991	15	2	13	162	70	92
	Total		679	313	366	17,694	10,515	7,179

Source: Directorate of Education, Government of Tripura, Agartala, 2002.

However, the present trend is encouraging and more and more S.T. Students (boys and girls) are coming forward to take admission in the premier college of the state, *i.e.* M.B.B. College, Agartala (Table 19.2), compared to previous time. The total number of S.T. students in the fourteen Degree Colleges is 1,373 (809 boys and 564 girls) and the number of S.C. students is 2,677 (1,550 boys and 1,127 girls), the number of S.T. and S.C. teachers (including part times) are 12 and 33 respectively. In the Degree Colleges, there are 5 Principals belonging to the S.T. category and 3 (including in-charge) to the S.C. category.

Tables 19.1 and 19.3 show the number of teachers in all the above-mentioned fourteen Degree Colleges with full time and part time, male and female and S.C. and S.T. break-up. The part time teachers in the degree colleges outnumber the full timers and higher education in Tripura today, is mainly dependent on the performance of the part timers. A lot of vacant teaching posts could not be filled by the Tripura Public Service Commission (TPSC) because of the non-availability of the NET/SLET qualified candidates particularly belonging to the reserved categories. As the reservation quota is meticulously maintained in Tripura, the question of de-reserving the sanctioned teaching posts may raise controversy in the society. As a result, a number of colleges are run without a single full-time teacher in the respective subject. For example, 8 subjects are offered in Sabroom and Kamalpur Colleges, but the member of full time teachers are only 5 each, in Kazi Nazrul Mahavidyalaya there are only 4, in Amarpur College only 3 and in Ambedkar College only 2 full time teachers respectively. The quality of education in those colleges can easily be imagined. Many part time teachers do not have the requisite qualifications as prescribed by the UGC. Hence, their absorption as full-time teachers may not be possible. Again, most of the sub-divisions of Tripura are today provided with a Government Degree College; but the student population in some colleges (particularly serial Nos. 10 to 14) are abnormally low (Table 19.2). Still, there are demands for more Degree Colleges in other areas, although for the last one decade no new degree college has been established in Tripura, as the question is now one of consolidation, rather than expansion.

Today, about 17 per cent of the total budget of this tiny state of north east India is spent on education and the total literacy rate now is 73.66 per cent (Male : 81.47 and Female : 65.41), the second highest in the north-eastern region, still the desired effect is yet to be achieved.

Table 19.2: Tripura – Enrolment of different categories of students in General Degree Colleges during 2001-2002

Sl.No.	*Name of the College*	*Total No. of Students*	*Boys*			*Girls*		
			S.T.	*S.C.*	*General*	*S.T.*	*S.C.*	*General*
1.	M.B.B. College, Agartala	3762	488	365	1693	121	111	984
2.	R.K. Mahavidyalaya, Karipashahar	1042	41	109	568	13	38	273
3.	Belonia College, Belonia	2094	41	223	1290	9	143	388
4.	Women's College, Agartala	2485	–	–	–	335	412	1,738
5.	Ramthakur College, Agartala	1891	3	152	996	4	86	650
6.	B.B. Evening College, Agartala	1707	45	238	1424	–	–	–
7.	Netaji Subhash Mahavidyalaya, Udaipur	1411	34	170	633	10	109	455
8.	Dasarath Deb Memorial College, Khowai	1014	56	89	523	45	63	238
9.	Dharmanagar College, Dharmanagar	1051	39	86	506	14	52	354
10.	Sabroom College, Sabroom	162	27	11	64	1	8	51
11.	Kamalpur College, Kamalpur	392	26	37	156	9	29	135
12.	Kazi Nazrul Mahavidyalaya, Sonamura	435	2	49	227	1	49	107
13.	Amarpur College, Amarpur	86	6	8	20	2	11	39
14.	Ambedkar College, Fatikroy	162	1	13	56	0	16	76
	Total	17,694	809	1,550	8,156	564	1,127	5,488

Table 19.3: Tripura – Number of Teachers (Male, Female, S.C. and S.T.) and Number of Subjects offered in General Degree Colleges as on 01-01-2002

Sl. No.	*Name of the College*	*No. of Teachers*					*No. of Subjects Offered*	
		Total	*Male*	*Female*	*S.C.*	*S.T.*	*Total No.*	*No. of Honors Subjects*
1.	M.B.B. College, Agartala	148	81	67	1	0	19	17
2.	R.K. Mahavidyalaya, Karipashahar	51	35	16	3	1	10	8
3.	Belonia College, Belonia	71	55	16	6	0	15	11
4.	Women's College, Agartala	89	18	71	2	3	15	12
5.	Ramthakur College, Agartala	50	34	16	4	0	13	6
6.	B.B. Evening College, Agartala	54	54	–	0	0	10	6
7.	Netaji Subhash Mahavidyalaya, Udaipur	44	25	19	5	2	11	6
8.	Dasarath Deb Memorial College, Khowai	41	23	18	4	0	12	4
9.	Dharmanagar College, Dharmanagar	48	34	14	4	2	12	4
10.	Sabroom College, Sabroom	15	10	5	1	0	8	Nil
11.	Kamalpur College, Kamalpur	21	14	7	0	2	8	2
12.	Kazi Nazrul Mahavidyalaya, Sonamura	18	7	11	1	1	5	Nil
13.	Amarpur College, Amarpur	14	10	4	2	0	6	Nil
14.	Ambedkar College, Fatikroy	15	11	4	0	1	5	Nil
	Total	679	411	268	33	12		

Source: Directorate of Education, Government of Tripura, Agartala, 2002.

The supply of educated manpower under general category from the higher education system in Tripura during the 8th and 9th Five Year Plan period is more than the projected demand for this course. As a result, there is an acute unemployment problem of educated youth of the general categories. The hopes and fears of the educated youths of Tripura are centred mainly with the chances of gaining employment. Like many other states of north-eastern region, there is virtually no industry in Tripura. The scope of employment in fields, other than education service and government offices, is very limited. There is very little relation between higher education and agriculture and/or forestry etc., although the economy is based on agriculture and forest. There are 10 professional colleges in Tripura at present, among which, the picture of 4 colleges are shown in Tables 19.4 to 19.7. Most of the students after having Bachelor of Engineering opt for service outside the State as there is very little opportunity within. In the Law College, the girl students in the general category outnumber the boys, which is an indication of women today are more conscious about their rights than in the past.

In the College of Teachers Education, the Master Degree Course is opened. The Bachelor of Visual Art (Honors) course in the College of Art and Craft, the Bachelor of Music in Vocal, Instruments and Dance in the Music College, the Diploma and Bachelor of Pharmacy Courses in the Regional Institute of Pharmaceutical Science and Technology, the Certificate and Bachelor Courses of Physical Education in the Regional College of Physical Education at Panisagar have attracted students from many other states of the north east India. In fact, the overall situation in the professional colleges of Tripura is no less encouraging, but due to the dearth of employment opportunity, the society today is facing a lot of complex problems.

University Education

There is only one university in the state, named Tripura University. Before the foundation of Tripura University on 2 October, 1987, all the colleges of Tripura had been affiliated to the University of Calcutta and for long ten years there was a Post-Graduate wing of Calcutta University at Agartala, known as Calcutta University Post-Graduate Centre (CUPGC). Consequent upon the merger of the CUPGC in the Tripura University in 1987, all the colleges of Tripura came under the charge of Tripura University. At present, there are only twelve post-

Table 19.4: Tripura Engineering College – Number of Teachers and Students (2002)

Number of Teachers						*Number of Students Enrolled (2001-2002)*						
Total	*Male*	*Female*	*S.C.*	*S.T.*	*General*	*Total*	*Boys*			*Girls*		
59	56	3	4	7	48		*S.T.*	*S.C.*	*General*	*S.T.*	*S.C.*	*General*
						110	8	15	36	2	8	41

Courses Offered : Bachelor of Engineering.
Branches : Civil, Electrical, Mechanical and Computer Science.

Table 19.5: Tripura Law College – Number of Teachers and Students (2002)

Number of Teachers								*Number of Students enrolled (2001-2002)*						
Total	*Male*	*Female*	*Full Time*	*Part Time*	*S.C.*	*S.T.*	*General*	*Total*	*Boys*			*Girls*		
22	21	1	3	19	0	0	22		*S.T.*	*S.C.*	*General*	*S.T.*	*S.C.*	*General*
								110	8	15	36	2	8	41

Course Offered : LLB (Honors).

Table 19.6: Tripura – College of Teacher Education : Number of Teachers and Students (2002)

Number of Teachers								Number of Students enrolled (2001-2002)						
Total	Male	Female	Full Time	Part Time	S.C.	S.T.	General	Total	Boys			Girls		
									S.T.	S.C.	General	S.T.	S.C.	General
21	15	6	12	9	0	0	21	121	23	11	33	12	13	29

Table 19.7: Regional Institute of Pharmaceutical Science and Technology — Number of Teachers and Students (2002)

Number of Teachers					Number of Students Enrolled (2001-2002)			
Total	Male	Female	Full Time	Part Time	Total	S.T.	S.C.	General
14	12	2	7	7	115	44	19	52

Courses Offered : Bachelor of Pharmacy, Diploma in Pharmacy.

graduate departments (English, Bengali, Sanskrit, History, Political Science, Philosophy, Economics, Physics, Chemistry, Mathematics, Life Science and Commerce) and two Certificate Courses (in Computer application and Kak-Barak language each) in the University. Also there is a system of Distance Education (two-year B.Ed. course and three-year B.A. course). In the M.B.B. College alone 19 subjects are taught and the total number of subjects offered in different under-graduate colleges come up to 22; but the post-graduate education is limited to only 12 subjects. Thus, in spite of having their own University, students of 10 subjects are even today denied the opportunity to have their post-graduate education. Table 19.8 shows the teacher and student strength of the University.

The Tripura University Act, 1987 envisages that the objects of the University shall not only be "to disseminate and advance knowledge by providing instructional and research facilities", but to make special provisions for studies in tribal life and culture as well as to promote study of vocational subjects, with a view to provide employment opportunities to the students. The Act specifically enjoins the Tripura University to organise specialised diploma, degree or post-graduate courses in forestry, fishery, agriculture, horticulture, tribal languages, rural and urban planning, ecology, environmental studies etc, *i.e.* the introduction of new subjects having been relevant to the demand of the society. Although the focus in the 10th Plan will be on the establishment of schools in Management Studies, Information Technology, Computer Studies, Biological Studies, Natural Sciences and Environmental Studies, Tribal Languages etc. The dream is yet to be achieved.

Trade in Education and Society

Recently, National Institute of Educational Planning and Administration (NIEPA) has sent one document to various state governments, including Tripura, seeking their opinions on the background notes as prepared by the Ministry of Human Resources Development (MHRD), regarding General Agreement on Trade in Services (GATS) mentioning that education is one of the services covered under GATS for progressive liberalisation. The name of the document of the NIEPA (Higher Education Unit) is: 'Trade in Education Service under WTO Regime – An Indian Response'. The intention is quite clear from the name. Prior to the emergence of the World Trade Organisation (WTO came

Table 18.8: Tripura University – Number of Teachers and Students in 2002

Number of Teachers							*No. of Students Enrolled during 2001-2002*						
Total	*Male*	*Female*	*Full Time*	*Part Time*	*S.C.*	*S.T.*	*Total*	*Boys*			*Girls*		
								S.T.	*S.C.*	*General*	*S.T.*	*S.C.*	*General*
57	49	8	51	6	2	3	923	46	113	334	34	69	327

No. of Courses offered in M.A.		7
No. of Courses offered in M.Sc.		4
No. of Courses offered in M.Com.		1
Total		12
Plus	*	Ph.D.
	*	Certificate course in Kak-Barak Languages.
	*	Certificate course in Computer Application.
	*	B.Ed. (2 years course) under Distance Education.
	*	B.A. (3 years course) under Distance Education.

into existence *w.e.f.* 1-1-1995), there was no multilateral agreement on services, but GATS in general covers all the services including education. In this age of liberalisation, privatisation, globalisation it is urged that trade liberalisation must go hand-in-hand with domestic reforms in all countries who have signed the agreement. The definition of higher education is proposed to be expanded by covering training, testing and out of University education for skill development, for leisure or for any other activity, where market access is to be allowed. It does not distinguish between general education and professional education or within professional education say, medical, law, engineering and so on.

The WTO has identified four main modes of trade in education:

(i) *Cross Border Supply* of a service, which includes any type of course that is provided through distance education or the internet, which can cross national boundaries.

(ii) *Consumption Abroad*; that involves the education of foreign students.

(iii) *Commercial Presence*, *i.e.* presence of foreign investors/ foreign universities in a host country.

(iv) *Presence of Natural Persons*; refers to the ability of people to move between countries to provide educational services.

In the face of the above mentioned challenges, we are to review the scenario of higher education in Tripura. Whether market access of profit-making institutions be allowed or not? Whether it is desirable to further define higher education? What are those areas, where we may limit the entry of the foreign suppliers? In a state like Tripura, where education is virtually free and majority of population live below the poverty line, should education be treated as a profit-making tradable service? Should education service come under the category of commercial service? What would happen to those who have virtually no purchasing power? What would be the fate of present colleges of Tripura as all colleges are government colleges? These are some of the important questions we are confronting today.

20

Secondary Education in Manipur
An Overview

N. TEJMANI SINGH

Introduction

The society due to technological and scientific developments all over the world has advanced much beyond the expectation of common man. The common man in turn will have to be wiped out with the changes and emergence of new society. Manipur, on the contrary, being the underdeveloped state, is characterised with the high rate of superstitions, rigidity, and other several things. Naturally, therefore, Manipur in order to go hand in hand with other advanced states of India, needs speedy improvement in the education of people. At the present juncture, the social, political and economic conditions of India were changing fast, new problems are coming up. It becomes all the more necessary to re-examine carefully and restate the aims of education of this important state.

Education for Leadership

For a large majority of secondary students, education marks the completion of their formal education and therefore, it could be viewed primarily as a stage, complete in itself with its won ends and special purposes. On passing out of the secondary schools such students, who do not propose to join college or technical institutions, should be able to enter various walks of life and fill the role of leadership.

Development of Personality

The aim of education should be (i) to release the sources of creative energy in students so that they may be able to appreciate their cultural heritage, and (ii) to cultivate right interests, which they can pursue in the leisure and so contribute in latter life to the development of this heritage.

Therefore, in our educational programme a pace of honour should be given to subjects like art, craft, music, dance and development of hobbies.

Growth of Secondary Education in Manipur

Before 1906, the provision of secondary education in Manipur was zero. The system of secondary education came into picture only when the Middle School was established in the year 1885, which could not provide higher studies to its students. The provision was possible when the Middle School was upgraded into a High School in 1921 and got affiliated to Calcutta University. The progress of secondary education in Manipur got a set-back with the outbreak of World War-II (1936-1945). It was only after India achieved its Independence that the secondary school began to expand. And the Secondary Education Act of 1973 was passed. Under this Act, the Board of Secondary Education Manipur (BSEM) was set-up, in order to regulate, supervise and develop secondary education in the state.

Table 20.1 shows the growth of institutions at the secondary stage during the period from 1949 to 2000. From Table 20.1 it is evident that there were only 8 secondary schools in the state during 1949-50. Among them 7 were for boys and only 1 was for girls. In this connection, one may rightly points out that girls education is much neglected even after independence. Further, from the table the rate of increase in secondary school during 1971-72 to 1980-81 is more than double. Here it may be remembered that Manipur was granted statehood in the year 1972. Soon becoming a full-fledged state, the state government at all stages, gave more stress on secondary education, which is evident from Table 20.1, during the period from 1971-72 to 1980-81.

Further, Table 20.2 indicates the yearwise enrolment in High/Higher Secondary Schools in Manipur during 1949 to 2000.

Table 20.1: Growth of Secondary Schools in Manipur During 1949-2000

Year	*Boys*	*Girls*	*Total*
1949-50	7	1	8
1951-52	11	1	12
1953-54	21	1	22
1955-56	22	1	23
1957-58	39	3	42
1959-60	50	4	54
1961-62	76	9	85
1963-64	105	17	122
1965-66	104	14	118
1967-68	103	16	119
1969-70	104	19	123
1971-72	104	19	123
1973-74	186	21	207
1975-76	187	25	212
1977-78	205	31	236
1979-80	233	31	264
1981-82	258	32	290
1983-84	289	40	329
1985-86	304	44	348
1986-87	332	41	373
1987-88	343	42	385
1988-89	345	42	387
1989-90	360	42	402
1990-91	375	55	430
1991-92	430	54	484
1992-93	446	51	497
1993-94	453	54	507
1994-95	474	51	525
1995-96	488	51	539
1996-97	503	53	556
1997-98	523	53	556
1998-99	526	56	528
1999-2000	549	56	605

Source: Directorate of Education, Government of Manipur.

It is evident from the observed data that from 1971-72 to 1987-88, there was gradual increase in the enrolment. During the period, enrolment of boys rose from 25836 to 67129, more than twice and for girls it increased from 13095 to 51325, almost became about four fold. Thus, by 1999 to 2000 there was sudden increase to the extent of 120314 enrolment for boys and 110311 for girls and altogether 230625 enrolment.

Table 20.2: Yearwise enrolment in High/Higher Secondary Schools in Manipur during 1949-2000

Year	*Boys*	*Girls*	*Total*
1949-50	4535	524	5059
1951-52	4272	756	5028
1953-54	7094	1247	8340
1955-56	8251	1572	9823
1957-58	12733	2869	15602
1959-60	16986	3940	20926
1961-62	20809	6084	26893
1963-64	25895	9935	35830
1965-66	25369	10108	35477
1967-68	23588	11046	34634
1969-70	24836	11395	35486
1971-72	25836	13095	38871
1973-74	34277	19677	53354
1975-76	37202	21643	58845
1977-78	39339	22998	62337
1981-82	47520	34350	81874
1983-84	5533	39183	94771
1985-86	58911	46935	105846
1986-87	58759	49296	108055
1987-88	67129	51325	118454
1988-89	68156	52134	120290
1989-90	71819	56951	128770
1990-91	71451	57811	129262
1991-92	94412	78139	172551
1992-93	100527	84060	184587
1993-94	98711	84212	182923
1994-95	104742	89031	193773
1995-96	106830	90332	197162
1996-97	111441	95504	260945
1997-98	117747	99932	217679
1998-99	119364	104554	223918
1999-2000	120314	110311	230625

Source: Directorate of Education, Government of Manipur.

Table 20.3 represents the growth of teachers serving secondary schools during the period from 1949-50 to 1999-2000.

It is observed that from 1949 to 1962 there was gradual increase in the number of teachers appointed but in 1963-64 there was sudden increase in the employment of teachers. One must not forget here that for female, there was a rather late start in education as well as a very slow growth in the number of scholars too. It is also evident from the preceding tables that during 1949 to 1988 the student-teacher ratio has decreased for both male and female. Lastly, the number of teachers' employment in 1988-2000 has increased for both male and female respectively.

Table 20.3: Yearwise Teachers in Secondary Schools in Manipur during 1949-2000

Year	*Boys*	*Girls*	*Total*
1949-50	137	8	145
1951-52	159	13	172
1953-54	34	18	332
1955-56	326	20	346
1957-58	497	29	526
1959-60	683	42	725
1961-62	987	62	1049
1963-64	1639	106	1745
1965-66	1429	139	1568
1967-68	1578	185	1763
1969-70	1621	217	1838
1971-72	1695	223	1918
1973-74	2349	345	2664
1975-76	2343	360	2703
1977-78	2521	348	2969
1979-80	2630	598	3228
1981-82	3059	721	3780
1983-84	3398	867	2465
1985-86	4196	1175	5371
1987-88	4635	1878	6413
1988-89	4895	2010	6888
1989-90	4963	2137	7100
1990-91	5230	2540	7770
1991-92	6073	3122	9195
1992-93	6323	3443	9766
1993-94	6103	3374	9477
1994-95	6259	3487	9746
1995-96	6226	3464	9690
1996-97	6724	3767	10491
1997-98	6365	3788	10153
1998-99	6593	4131	10724
1999-2000	6811	4179	10990

Source: Directorate of Education, Government of Manipur.

Secondary School Curriculum

The Board of Secondary Education, Manipur formulated the Secondary Education Curriculum in 1980, on the basis of the framework drawn up by the NCERT and the modifications made by the panel committee. The curriculum so envisaged, aims at preparing the students, who have inclination to undergo further specialised training in the fields, suitable to their aptitudes.

The subjects of studies that are found in the secondary curriculum are as follows:

1. First language – anyone of the following languages: Manipuri, Hindi, Assamese, Bengali and for those whose mother tongue is not only one of the above languages – Elementary Manipuri and anyone of the following languages: (i) Elementary Hindi, (ii) Addl. English, (iii) Punjabi, (iv) Nepali, (v) Lushai, (vi) Ao, (vii) Angami, (viii) Paite, (ix) Tangkhul, (x) Hmar, (xi) Thadou etc.
2. Second Language – English.
3. Science – Physics, Chemistry and Biology as one of the courses.
4. Socially useful productive works and physical and health education.
5. One of the following (i) Fine-Arts, (ii) Music, (iii) Dance, (iv) Home Science, (v) Urdu, (vi) Sanskrit.
6. Commerce.
7. Arts etc.

Conclusion

Though Secondary Education was neglected during the British rule, its expansion took place slowly after joining the Union and there has been rapid progress after achieving statehood to Manipur.

The definition of secondary education is to build-up one's character. It may be possible only through the implementation in order to have the re-oriented educational system. There should be provision for vocational and reconcile training so that every student can take up his/her own way of establishing and imparting entrepreneur's skill. To achieve the standard of education, the prescribed text books and syllabus, appointment of paper setter and examiner, conducting examination, publication of the results, for discipline and welfare of the students, for inspiration of institution, it is the Board of Education Body, which is responsible for controlling of secondary education.

REFERENCES

Annual report: Directorate of Education, Government of Manipur.

Statistical Hand Book: Directorate of Economics & Statistics, Government of Manipur.

21

Women and Higher Education in Manipur

KSH. BIMOLA DEVI

The importance of higher education has increased with the advancement of human civilization. A value based society and value oriented ideas can be originated only when, a person or persons receive higher education. The higher stage of human personality can also be developed by means of higher education. In brief, a person can develop fully when he/she receives higher education and can contribute in the establishment of a value based society.

The coming of higher education in Manipur may be traced back to the early 1970s with the attainment of statehood. Of course, there were few higher educational institutions before 1970. But the emergence of higher educational institutions on a large scale, giving an important impact on the society was from 1972 onwards. The people of Manipur both men and women have been receiving higher education for about three decades on a large scale.

Higher education plays a very important role in the empowerment of women. The real empowerment of women in the social, economic and political matters can be achieved only when women, who constitute half the population, receive higher education. Higher education can create skill, knowledge and awareness among the people and the achievements of human civilization among women. Through higher education, women can also possess basic scientific outlook and commitment to the ideals of patriotism, democracy, secularism, peace and development.

Growth of Higher Education among Women in Manipur

The educational institutions imparting higher education in Manipur came into existence for the first time in the middle of 1940s, before Independence. It was in 1946 that an intermediate college was established at Imphal. Very few women could come up at the intermediate level due to the lack of knowledge as well as the traditional social beliefs prevailing in those days. Parents were more guided by traditional social norms and beliefs. But from the beginning of 1950s, with the establishment of more colleges, girl students were enrolled and their number had increased slowly and slowly. In 1965-66, a separate college for women called Ghanapriya Women's College was established and also opened a girls' Hostel. With the attainment of statehood in 1972, the number of colleges had increased enormously. The Centre for Post-Graduate Studies under Jawaharlal Nehru University, New Delhi was also established in 1972. The number of girls attending colleges as well as Post-Graduate Studies was quite impressive. One important factor for the increase of girl students in the colleges and Post-Graduate Studies might be the fact that, equal treatment was given by the parents to both sons and daughters to pursue higher studies.

The number of colleges in Manipur University in 2000-2001 was 71. The colleges may be classified as follows[1]:

Female Students in Higher Education

Number of Colleges, Teachers and Students in Different Areas in 2000-2001

	Urban	*Rural*	*Hill*	*Total*
Colleges	23	30	18	71
Teachers	1035	1582	622	3239
Students	6042	5585	1290	20,558

In the next year, *i.e.* in 2001-2002 the number of students had increased from 20,558 to 21,979[2]. The total number of students enrolled in 71 colleges in Manipur in B.A./B.Sc./B.Com. and other equivalent courses may again be examined on the basis of gender:

Number of College Students in Manipur in 2001-2002

Number of Male Students	—	11,431
Number of Female Students	—	10,548
Total	—	21,979

The above figures show that female students in the graduate stage constitute nearly 48 per cent of the total number of students. In the Post-Graduate Studies in Manipur University the number of female students in 22 Departments is 547 out of about 1,600 students constituting 34.18 per cent. It shows that about 14 per cent of the female students are not able to come up to the higher studies of Post-Graduate level.

Female Teachers in Higher Education

From the records available in the College Development Council, Manipur University, it is found that there are 946 women teachers in June, 2002. The percentage is very low when compared with the men teachers. In twenty-two departments of Manipur University there are at present 26 women teachers. It may be remembered that during the last 2 decades the number had increased from one in 1980 to twenty-six in 2002. The percentage is 37.7, taking into account the existing faculty strength, *i.e.* 145[3].

In addition, there is sizeable number of women research scholars conducting research in different academic areas for their M.Phil. and Ph.D. degrees.

Problems Faced by Women

There are certain problems faced by women in getting the opportunities of coming up to higher education in Manipur. Let us examine some of the problems faced by the women in this regard:

1. Every community has its own traditional social norms and beliefs. The members are governed by these social norms in the conduct of their activities. The rural areas of Manipur have also its own social norms and customary laws. These social norms and customary laws do not encourage the rural women to receive higher education. It is believed that higher education is not meant for women.
2. Gender issues also form part of the traditional social norms and behaviour. There is demarcation of the duties and rules of both men and women by the tradition. Boys and girls are assigned separate duties right from their childhood. Girls are not allowed to perform their duties outside their families. They

are supposed to be confined within the four walls of the house. They are denied access to educational facilities, not to speak of getting higher education.

3. The financial position of the families may also be one important factor standing in the way of women coming up to higher educational level. Due to financial problems, most of the girl students tend to drop out at the primary and High School levels. Women or girls who have the chance to go for higher studies more or less belong to richer sections of the rural population.
4. The non-availability of higher educational institutions in the rural areas is another factor contributing to the problem of women. After passing High School or Higher Secondary stage, they don't find nearby college for study. They have to go a long distance or to stay in an urban or distant place, if they want to study further. This is not advisable in view of the social norms and prevailing law and order situation.
5. Sometimes personal likings or desires of the women or girls, decide the future of their studies. There are examples of some girls, who sacrifice their chance of getting higher education in order to promote their brothers to pursue higher studies. They even finance the higher education of their brothers by engaging themselves in traditional works like weaving, embroidery and other money-earning businesses suitable for them.
6. Lack of information regarding higher education may also be another factor for not allowing the rural women to receive higher education. The information of higher education in different areas of studies is not easily available in many rural areas.

Women in Higher Education and Social Unrest

It is important to examine the relationship between women in Higher Education and Social unrest in Manipur. Manipur has been experiencing a trend of social unrest since the early part of 1980s till date. The women of Manipur in groups called *Meira Paibis* are spearheading movements against the anti-social evils developed as a result of *alcoholism, drug addicts, rape cases, sexual abuses*, conflicts among the different ethnic groups of Manipur. Women could not participate in higher education actively due to the traditional duties at home as well as their duties and responsibilities at their working places. They do participate in Seminars, Conferences, Symposiums, Interaction Meets etc. to discuss the various social issues from time to time.

On the other hand, girl students at the graduate level are always found to participate in every social movement led by student bodies like *All Manipur Students Union, Manipuri Students Federation* and Voluntary organisations like *All Manipur United Clubs' Organisation* and *United Committee, Manipur*. It may also be mentioned that the unemployment of educated youths, both boys and girls may also be another contributing factor to the social unrest in Manipur.

Last of all, we have to remember that there is a close relationship between higher education and social unrest. The policy planners have to take into account the social factors, while framing the policies of higher education. At the same time, it is the concern of the State Government, specially the Education Department to see the effective and honest implementation of the policies so as to create a value based education, resulting in the emergence of a value based society, where women can discharge their duties peacefully without any disturbance.

NOTES

1. Records available in the College Development Council, Manipur University, 2002.
2. *Ibid.*
3. In 1994, the faculty strength was 161. The strength had decreased to 145 due to retirement of teachers and ban to fill up existing vacancies.

22

Women's Education in Manipur

M. RITA

Social progress is indicated by the level of intellectual development among the people. Educational backwardness is the main factor of social degradation. In this regard Laski expressed his view, 'the citizen who lacks education is bound to be slave of others...... He will go through life a stunted being whose impulses have never been ordered by reason into creative experiment. As a result it has become necessary to educate everyone especially women, who is the first teacher of a child. Moreover all over the world education is considered as the only way for raising the status of women as well as for the progress of the society. But the disparity in the level of education between male and female is still a worldwide phenomenon.

The women of Manipur have a distinct place in the socio-cultural, religious and economic life of the society. However, in spite of this, the door of education was not open to them during the Pre-British period. The traditional society assigned women only domestic duties like cooking, weaving, spinning, nursing the family members and looking after their children. Women did all the works except the heaviest. Education of women of some enlightened families was not of formal type. They received their education in their own household, as no school for girls existed in Manipur. They got lessons in rudimentary form of reading and writing. But knowledge of reading and writing was not accepted as qualification for a girl in the society. In Manipur skill in weaving, cooking, husking of paddy was considered greater accomplishment for a girl.

Women's Education during British Period

The role of English education, introduced by the British people in bringing social changes in the twentieth century cannot be denied. The

British introduced and encouraged education unfolded the Indian youths the vista of a new world.

English education came to Manipur very late in 1885 with the establishment of the first English school in Imphal by the then political Agent Sir James Johnstone. For the first time Manipuri women received education in 1898-99. In 1899 December one L.P. School for girls was established at Moirangkhom, Imphal and 12 girls were admitted in the school and the total enrolment of girls rose to 53 by 31st of March, 1900. But later no girl student came to school due to the rumour that as soon as the girls were satisfactorily taught to read, write and speak English, they were to be shipped off to England. Moreover, to be a good housewife, the qualifications that were required for a girl could be acquired from her mother and other elder members of the family. So, the guardians felt no necessity of sending their daughters to schools. Besides, the girls were in a great help in the household activities and to that extent it was considered a great loss for the family to send their daughters to the schools. English educated youths began to realise the need of womens' education and they advocated strongly for the introduction of women education for the welfare of the society. To remove prejudices of the people and to make them understand the necessity of womens' education for the welfare of the family and upliftment of the society, they took up pain. Thus women again started going to school. In 1913-14 Lady Earle Girls (Added) Middle School was established. In 1932-33 two L.P. Schools for girls were established and thus increased to 3 L.P. Schools. In 1934-35 a Private School for girls was established in the name of Princess Tamphasana. Sagolband Girls Added School was also established in the same year.

Before 1947 education of Girls and women in Manipur was completely neglected. This was not due to the prevalence of ill social customs but mainly out of ignorance of the people regarding the value of women's education.

Womens' Education in the Post-Independence Period

In the wake of Independence, new hopes and aspirations emerged and new avenues for women were opened declaring equality of both sexes. The Indian Constitution guaranteed equal status to both men and women. The Indian Constitution provides that there shall not be any discrimination against any citizen on the ground of religion, race, caste, sex and the place of birth .... There shall be equality of opportunity to all citizens, in matters relating to employment to any office. Under the State Article 45 of the Constitution of India provides that State shall endeavour to provide within a period of ten years from the commencement of the Constitution, free and compulsory education for all children till they complete the age of 14 years. It aims at the establishment of democratic set up based on adult franchise and where justice, social political and economic shall govern all activities of life with his aim.

From the historical, social and economic reason, education of girls has lagged behind considerably in Manipur. The overall picture of girls education at the beginning of the First Year Plan was very discouraging. However, there was a progress in development of womens' education in the state since 1951.

Table 22.1 shows the sharp increase of literacy rate of women in every decade. On the other hand, it also shows the disparity of literacy rate between the male and female in Manipur.

Table 22.1: Progress of Literacy in Manipur

Year	*Total Population*	*Total Percentage of Literacy*	*Male*	*Female*
1951	5,77,635	11.4	20.77	2.36
1961	7,80,037	30.4	45.12	15.93
1971	10,72,753	32.9	46.40	19.53
1981	14,20,953	41.3	53.29	29.06
1991	18,37,149	59.9	71.63	47.60
2001	23,88,634	68.87	77.87	59.70

Source: Census of India, 2001.

It may be the reason that earlier, most of the parents used to prefer to send their boys to school and daughters were asked to give up their education, if they cannot bear the expenditure and let them help in the family economy. There was lack of knowledge of the importance of giving education to girls.

Table 22.2 shows the ups and downs of number of institutions in Manipur. The causes of the decrease of number of institution may be due the conversion of the school as co-education, improper functioning etc. Moreover, giving higher education to girls is not considered necessary as they are going to live in the husband's house. As a result the number of girls going for higher education is less than the boys.

Here we also find the great differences in numbers of employees between men and women. Of course, when there is a lack of education, there will be lack of job opportunity also. It may be concluded that in

Table 22.2: Girls'/Womens' Institutions in Manipur 1950-51 to 1996-97

Year	Type of Institutions								
	Primary (Nursury+Primary+Middle)			Secondary (High+Higher Secondary)			Degree College		
		Girl's School			Girls' School			Girl/Women's College	
	Total Primary	Nos.	In % of Total	Total Secondary	Nos.	In % of Total	Total Colleges	Nos.	In % of Total
1950-51	526	28	5.32	11	1	9.90	1	–	–
1955-56	966	43	4.45	23	1	4.35	2	–	–
1960-61	1974	187	9.47	57	5	8.77	2	–	–
1965-66	2377	245	10.37	118	14	11.86	11	1	9.09
1970-71	2856	338	11.83	123	19	15.45	12	1	8.33
1975-76	3896	268	6.88	212	25	11.79	20	2	10.00
1980-81	3286	246	7.49	290	32	11.03	24	2	8.33
1985-86	3119	224	7.18	358	45	12.57	28	2	7.14
1990-91	3190	204	6.39	430	55	12.79	29	7	6.90
1995-96	3083	83	2.69	539	51	9.45	59	7	11.86
1996-97	2514	148	5.86	556	53	9.53	64	7	10.94

Sources: 1. Th. Mangoljao Singh, *Western Education in Manipur*, Vol. I &II, 1989, p. 115.
2. *Statistical Handbook of Manipur*, 1998.

Table 22.3: Women Employees in the Government Offices

Years	*Total Employees*	*Female Employees*	*Percentage of Total*
1960-61	6561	159	2.42
1965-66	17554	1443	8.22
1970-71	20428	1607	7.87
1975-76	–	–	–
1980-81	–	–	–
1985-86	–	–	–
1990-91	55622	8852	15.91
1995-96	78558	15840	20.16
1997-98	80588	17497	21.71

Source: Employment Exchange, Imphal.

Manipur, slow progress of women's education may be due to poverty or lack of economic condition, negligence of giving education to the girls in the beginning, early marriage and prejudices against girls' education etc.

It may be suggested to improve the educational condition of women like giving equal opportunities to both boys and girls in the family, giving scholarship to girls students, giving them the job opportunities and facilities for appearing at different examinations. The state government has been trying to popularize and encourage female education. A separate administrative machinery for expansion of girl's education was established in 1972 as a State Council for Women's Education. To improve the social, economic and political status of women, education to women is very important.

REFERENCES

Bose, Ashish (2001). *Population of India, 2001, Census Results and Methodology*, B.R. Publishing Corporation, Delhi.

Ghose, G.K. (1997), Shukla Ghose, *Women of Manipur*, A.P.H. Publishing Corporation, New Delhi..

Shanti, M. (2001). *Development of Education in Manipur*, Rajesh Publication, New Delhi..

Sircar, Manjushri Chaki (1984). *Feminism in Traditional Society*, Vikas Publishing House, New Delhi.

Statistical Abstract, Directorate of Economics & Statistics, Government of Manipur, Imphal, 1998.

Tayal, B.B. (1999). *Political Theory and Indian Democracy*, Arya Book Depot, New Delhi, pp. 18, 164.

Th. Manglojao (1989). *Western Education in Manipur*, Vols. I & II, Imphal, p. 17.

23

Higher Education in Barak Valley
With Special Reference to Assam University

J. SIDDHARTHAN

Introduction

Higher education plays a crucial role to meet the development of social sector and economic sector. So far as social sector is concerned universities were seen as institution, which provide degrees. However, the truth is that it provides not only degrees but also contributes towards human resource development higher quality of people. Moreover the University level education is the backbone of development process, which stimulates the academicians to undergo research works and develop know-how, these factors help the state to remove the drawbacks of former plans and formulate different plans of the Government; which lead to economic development of the people. Prof. Saha rightly pointed out that 'Undeniably the main objective of all the universities and other higher educational institutes of the North-East is the human resource development of the North-East.' In this view the present paper attempts to evaluate the status of higher education in Barak Valley with special reference to Assam University, Silchar. This paper is divided into two sections. Section I states the brief history of Assam University, and its development, Section II evaluates the affiliated colleges of Assam University and finally summary and conclusion are furnished.

I

Barak Valley consists of three districts, *viz.* Cachar, Karimganj and

Hailakandi. The populations of the districts are more than that of the states of Mizoram, Arunachal Pradesh, Nagaland, Meghalaya and Manipur.

Table 23.1: Population of Barak Valley

Population in Barak Valley	*1991 Census (in lakh)*
Barak Valley	24.9
Mizoram	6.9
Arunachal Pradesh	8.7
Nagaland	12.1
Meghalaya	17.8
Manipur	18.4

Source: Statistical Profile of Barak Valley and an agenda for Research on the Valley's economy 1998, Published by: Economic Research Division, North-Eastern Centre for Advanced Studies, p.3.

Table 23.1 shows that the Barak valley has larger population than many North-Eastern States. Barak valley has not only larger population but also higher-level literacy ratio. The male literacy in this valley in 1991 was 66.4 per cent and female literacy 46.1 per cent (Mazumder, A. *et al*, 1998). All India literacy rate 56.5 per cent in 1999 (*University News*, Vol. 13). This literacy rate instigates the people of Barak valley to demand further educational facilities. The fact says that in the early past of twentieth century, *i.e.* 1927 there were three high schools established and in 1935 the first college was installed in Barak valley that is Guru Charan College at Silchar. It was the first step to higher education in Barak valley (Chakravarty Archana, 2000). It was affiliated with Calcutta University.

During 1948 the Gauhati University was established at Guwahati, its jurisdiction was the entire North-Eastern Region. In the meantime number of colleges were established in this valley and were affiliated with Gauhati University, due to resolution passed in the Gauhati University Academic Council meeting regarding medium of instruction (must be English and Assamese) the people of Barak valley (Bengalees) went against the resolution, and urged the Central Government to establish a Central University. On 15th of May 1989 the Assam University Bill was passed in the Parliament on 21st January 1994 the Assam University came to an existence at Silchar (Kar Subir, 2000).

Development of Assam University Since 1994

The jurisdiction of Assam University comprises the five districts, namely Cachar, Hailakandi, Karimganj, Karbi Anglong and North Cachar, the first Vice-Chancellor was Prof. Jayanta Bushan Bhattacharjee. The total area of jurisdiction is 22,244 sq km. (Kar Subir, 2000).

In the year 1994-95 the University started with four schools, which consist of seven departments, few affiliated colleges and full capacity of roll strength (Table 23.2).

Table 23.2: Initial Establishment of Assam University 1994-95

Sl. No	*School of Studies*	*Departments*	*Roll capacity*	*Students strength*
1.	Languages	English	50	52
		Bengali	50	48
2.	Management Studies	Commerce	50	50
		Diploma in Management Studies	50	48
3.	Social Sciences	Economics	50	57
		History	50	44
4.	Physical Sciences	Mathematics	30	31
	Total		330	330

Source: Annual Report Assam University 1994-95. The Registrar, Assam University, Silchar.

Table 23.2 shows that the total capacity of students was tally with the total students strength. The students started their higher studies. In the departments like English and Economics, the roll strength of the students was more than capacity.

Meanwhile Assam University started some more schools; and more departments. As a result the University generated considerable human resource. The following table indicates the performance of Assam University (Table 23.3).

Table 23.3 indicates that the School of Languages and School of Social Sciences produced large number of students compare to other school of studies. The least number of students have admitted and passed out from the School of Environmental and School of Life Sciences.

Table 23.3: Performance of Assam University 1996-2001

Sl. No	*School of Studies*	*1996*			*1997*			*1998*			*1999*			*2000*			*2001*		
		App	*Pass*	*%*	*App*	*Pass*	*%*	*App*	*Pass*	*%*	*App*	*Pass*	*%*	*App*	*Pass*	*%*	*App*	*Pass*	*%*
1.	Languages	74	65	87.8	163	136	83.4	171	100	58.4	209	143	68.4	345	130	37.6	133	100	75
2.	Management Studies	33	28	84.8	21	21	100	NA	NA	–	60	54	90	50	39	78	41	38	92.6
3.	Social Sciences	59	39	66.1	172	124	72	207	120	58	281	135	48	237	110	46.4	155	87	56
4.	Physical Sciences	14	13	92.8	36	20	55.5	87	53	60.9	84	50	59.5	98	51	52	89	60	67.4
5.	Information Sciences	NA	NA	–	NA	NA	–	NA	NA	–	NA	NA	–	26	24	92.3	13	13	100
6.	Humanities	NA	NA	–	76	63	82.8	102	65	63.7	132	65	49	97	62	63.9	17	11	64.7
7.	Environmental Sciences	NA	NA	–	NA	NA	–	16	16	100	22	20	90.9	21	21	100	22	20	90.9
8.	Life Sciences	NA	NA	–	NA	NA	–	17	17	100	18	17	94.4	22	20	90.9	20	19	95

Note: App: Number of students appeared.
Pass: Number of students passed.
N.A. : Not available indicates that the course was not introduced till that year.

Source: Examination Section P.G. AUS.

Central Library of Assam University

The Library plays a significant role in the development of higher studies. Since Assam University is a infant University; the Library has got 51,595 books, 173 Journals, 14 Foreign Journals, 19 Newspapers, 11 magazines are readily available to the readers. There are two Officers and 22 full time staffs are working in the Library. The Library provides Internet, Photocopy facilities to the Researchers. This kind of inducement would stimulate the researchers to do research works in their fields. (*Source* : Central Library, A.U.S., 2002).

II

Development of Affiliated Colleges

During the initial stages of Assam University only nine colleges were permanently affiliated, eleven colleges were temporarily affiliated and twenty permitted colleges including Law, Professional, Medical and Engineering colleges. The academic profile of affiliated colleges is given below.

Table 23.4: Number of Students Passed out from Different Affiliated Colleges of Assam University

Year	*Stream*	*Appeared*	*Passed out*
1997	Arts	2215	1048
-Do-	Commerce	195	105
-Do-	Science	507	310
1998	Arts	3085	935
-Do-	Commerce	290	129
-Do-	Science	706	314
1999	Arts	4993	1286
-Do-	Commerce	400	118
-Do-	Science	884	372
2000	Arts	6010	1277
-Do-	Commerce	484	200
-Do-	Science	971	362
2001	Arts	6251	1331
-Do-	Commerce	506	168
-Do-	Science	1032	331
	Total	21838	6494

Source: Exam Branch, TDC, AUS.

The above table shows the students have got more attraction on Arts departments, Science and Commerce departments have got less number of students. The first reason may be that in Art group departments are more than other groups. The second reason perhaps that scoring pass marks in Science departments is more difficult than other departments. During 1997 to 2001, the total enrolled students were 21838, among them 6494 students have passed out. This indicates the human resource development is in increasing phase in this valley.

Further, this kind of development of Assam University in this valley led the University to step forward to affiliate more colleges, establish new departments.

Permanent affiliated colleges in 1994-95 were only nine and it increased to twenty-seven in 2000 (Table 23.5).

Table 23.5: Affiliated Colleges

Year	*Permanent Colleges*	*General Colleges*	*Permitted Colleges*	*Temporary Colleges*	*Total*
1994-1995	9	8	20	11	48
1999-2000	27	18	21	Nil	66

Source: Annual Report 1994-95 and 1999-2000 of Assam University. Published by the Registrar, Assam University, Silchar.

In 1994-95 the total number of colleges under the control of Assam University was forty-eight and it increased to sixty-six in 1999-2000. This shows the fast development of Assam University.

Summary and Conclusion

The study reveals that the establishment of Assam University has stimulated the youths to go for higher studies. It attracted the students not only from this valley but also from different parts of the country, such as Mizoram, Manipur, Nagaland and Arunachal Pradesh, Andaman Nikobar Islands and Southern region of the country.

The teacher's recruitment has also been made on the basis of National level. Teachers from different parts of the country are working therefore people belonging to different ethnic cultural categories have assembled at Silchar. Though the University gives lot of facilities to its students to do the research work, the infrastructure problems like transport, communication and drinking water, are the main blockade on the part of the researchers to spend more time in the University premises.

REFERENCES

Ahmed, Kamaluddin (2000), 'Assam University and Higher Education: The Suggested Agenda', Unpublished paper.

Annual Report of Assam University, various issues.

Choudhary, Nath P. (2000), 'The Assam University and Higher Education, Suggested Agenda for Future', Unpublished paper.

Chakravorty, Archana (2000), 'Process of Higher Education in South Assam during the Post-independence Period.' Unpublished Research paper.

Kar, Subir (2000), 'Problems of Higher Education in South Assam and the Backward of Assam University', Unpublished paper.

Mazumder A. *et al.* (1998), 'Statistical Profile of Barak Valley 1998 an agenda for Research on the Valley's Economy', Economic Research Division, North Eastern Centre for Advanced Studies. Silchar.

Saha, S.C. (2002), Vice-Chancellor, Assam University, Silchar, *University News* Vol. 40, No. 17, April 29-May 5.

University News, various issues.

24

Role of Voluntary Associations in the Educational Development of Manipur

TH. BINARANI DEVI

Education is a process of development and growth of a person from infancy to maturity. It displays the influence of one's vocation-home life, friendship, everything, which influences human personality of a society is going to develop as a successful democratic society, there will be proper education for the citizens of the society, because all the citizens are taking part in the decision-making process of the Government. The success of democracy depends upon proper training of citizenship. Education has to equip the young boys and girls for it.

In the post-Independence period Government of India is trying to develop education in all fields by any means. Not only the government, the non-governmental organisations or voluntary associations are playing a great role in this process. These associations have been acting for the changes and development as a whole. In the process of modernisation, several state governments are paying interest to voluntarism and ready to help as far as possible.

In Manipur, voluntary associations like the Clubs associations, organisations etc., came late when compared with other states of India and other countries of the world. Though late, they are playing important role in the educational matters.

Now-a-days, the tiny border state of India, *i.e.* Manipur witnesses a period of transition marked with day light murders, robbers, lootings, arm snatching, street fightings, ambush, and consequential army operations and alleged torture on the civil populace. There is not a day, for a considerable span of time in the recent past, that the front pages of many national and local papers missed reports on such ugly scenario, which simply made the law enforcing authorities a force. The whole functionary of the state was sometimes seemed to have been paralysed. The crimes were also committed even in the very centre of the city and security zones, what was imagined as the worst occurrence and a regular phenomenon in Manipur, resulting into confused state of affairs. At this juncture, the voluntary associations have been contributing a great valuable part in the normalisation of such situations.

As education helps in the building up of the personality of the individual through his/her physical, intellectual and moral development, the voluntary associations are giving more emphasis on the educational development of their local areas, specifically and state as a whole generally. If the citizens are physically, intellectually and morally developed, almost all the problems of the society can easily be solved. We can examine the performances and activities of some voluntary associations in matters relating to education.

The Youth Welfare Club, Langthabal, Imphal

This Organisation is ready to help the youths to become brave and good citizens of the motherland, subordinating personal interests to the needs of the country, to foster the habits of observations, thoughtfulness, self-reliance and obedience, to inculcate the qualities of leadership discipline, self-help, transprit, loyalty, tolerance, sacrifice and to promote their physical, mental and moral development. The aims and objectives of the organisation mentioned.

(1) To assist and supplement the work of existing educational institutions.
(2) To effort for setting up the non-existed requisite educational institutions (both in general and social) for the development and prosperity of the young people.
(3) To promote women and children welfare in all possible respects (both in general education and social education).
(4) To arrange and hold conferences, demonstrations exhibitions, meetings, lectures, debates, discussions and competitions of all acts and things necessary to promote physical, mental and moral development of the community and to abolish all kinds of social vices etc.

(5) To render possible help to the bereaved families of young learners of this locality and members of this Club at their premature death.[1]

They are conducting workshops, camps and seminars in connections with the educational development of the local area from time to time for achieving their aims.

Kuki Christian Association, Churachandpur

This missionary association was established in 1953 under the influence of the Evangelical Congregational Church of India. It has separate branches in Manipur and Assam. In the name of the Christian Mission, this association took up lot of works for the development of the society like:

(a) Establishment of Mission Schools.
(b) Community Development Programme etc.

It organises camps and seminars etc. for achieving their target. During that time they tried to highlight the value of education, its reactions towards the society etc.[2]

The Youth Cultural and Welfare Organisation, Heinoupok, Imphal

It was established in 1972. Just after one year of its inception, this organisation established a Balwadi Centre in its own premises for the educational development of the local small children, by providing nutrition, study materials, toys etc.[3] During the time of summer vacation, this organisation provided free coaching classes from class (III) to (X), taught by the local youths.

Shree Digamber Jain Samaj

This Association was formed by Jain Community, who are residing at Imphal. All the members are not the original people of the state. They came to Manipur for business purposes during the British period. As the association developed, it decided to establish a school in the bazar area and such a school in the name of "Shree Jain Vidyalaya" was established on 17th July, 1958. Earlier it was only upto Class VI and then upgraded to Class X in 1976 and to higher secondary (Class XII) in 1996. Even though the members of the school management committee belong to business section, the results of the school are just fantastic. In the Class X examination, the students got fine colour and in the Class XII Commerce almost all the first 10 position holders are from this school in the state.[4]

-1977 — 8th Position.
-1998 — 1st and 5th position.
-1999 — 3rd and 4th position.
-2000 — 4th, 8th & 9th position.
-2001 — 4th, 5th, 6th, 9th and 10th position.
-2002 — 2nd, 3rd and 4th position.[5]

The significant changes in the society can come only through strong and sustained public pressure and support. Given the overall democratic framework and magnitude of poverty and inequality, voluntary organisations have a vital and vigorous role to play. The activities of these associations are not less than the activities of the government and the parents of the students.

NOTES

1. Constitution, *The Youth Welfare Club*, Langthabal, Imphal, p.1.
2. Interview with Rev. T. Janglhun Haockip, Executive Secretary, K.C.A. Ccpur, dated 8-8-1991.
3. Annual report : The Youth Cultural Welfare Organisation, Heinoupok, Imphal.
4. Personally interview with Pramod Kumar Chhabra, Secretary School Management Committee, Shri Digambar Jain Samaj dated 11-6-2002.
5. Result records of the Council of Higher Secondary Education, Manipur.

REFERENCES

Rao, G. Laksharma (1977), *Internal Migration and Political Change in India.* National Publishing House, New Delhi.

Singh, Bhagat Puran (1985). What is wrong with work, All India Pingalwara Society, G.T. Road, Tehsilpura, Amritsar..

25

Literacy in Arunachal Pradesh
A Critical Analysis

R.P. BHATTACHARJEE

Introduction

Education helps man to improve his thought, expression and action. It also helps him to develop his talent and skills. Education is everyone's birth right. Without education it would become difficult to take an effective part in political and social activities. Education helps man to be aware of his rights and duties and is a panacea for all social evils. Illiteracy is a malady and must be eradicated through the spread of education.

Man is endowed with two qualities, which make him superior to the animal. These are his ability to think and his ability to express, what he has in his mind both in words and action. Air, water and food are essential for his body. Likewise for the mental development, knowledge is essential, and this knowledge can be obtained and increased only through education (Nagappa *et al.*, 1997).

Education has been defined differently by different scholars. Perhaps, the best definition of education is given by Vivekanand, who defined it as the "manifestation of perfection already in man". The aim of education is to help the individual to grow from all points of views. In everyone, there is some talent and under suitable conditions it blossoms. Education helps the individual in this regard. Education is closely connected with society, of which, the individual is an important component.

Bringing up children does not mean only feeding and clothing them. Imparting the right kind of education is also important. Educating the children is one of the important duties of responsible parents. Even the Governments have realised the importance of education of the children. As far back as 1883, Japan introduced compulsory primary education to all children of school going age. Within a span of fifty years, the country achieved cent per cent literacy. Denmark implemented universal compulsory education as early as 1814. India, even when it was under British rule considered the case of compulsory primary education. Gopal Krishna Gokhale introduced the Compulsory Primary Education Bill in the Imperial Legislative Council but unfortunately it evoked no response. If it was accepted, India would have had higher literacy rate than now. Even Baroda, a princely State, introduced compulsory primary education and set up rural libraries long before India achieved Independence.

After Independence, the Indian Government at the centre realised that education is the panacea for all social evils, and hence introduced compulsory primary education in 1961. But it was not successful as expected. The reasons are as follows:

(a) Ignorance of parents especially in rural areas.
(b) Poor parents, often prefer to send their children to work to augment their family income.
(c) Want of suitable teaching personnel.
(d) Want of accommodation to house the schools.
(e) Shortage of finance.

Illiteracy is a malady that haunts any nation. This can be effectively tackled in two ways, (i) by giving compulsory primary education to all children of the age group of 6-14 years, (ii) adult literacy and education to the illiterates aged 15-35 years. The fruits of primary education can be seen only after a few years but the impact of adult education is almost immediate. For example, in Mumbai a owner of a factory arranged for a literacy class in the factory premises after working hours. Many of the workers joined the classes. As a result, the illiterate employed became literate and their performances towards production improved and consequently their emoluments increased (Nagappa, *ibid.* 97). The benefit of literacy is observed in countries like Turkey, Pakistan, Thailand, Mali, Guatemala, Brazil, Iran, Morocco and Russia etc.

The advantages of literacy are as follows:

(a) Literacy makes a man efficient to discharge his duties.
(b) It broadens his outlook.
(c) It helps him to solve problems.
(d) It enables him to read receipts, bills, notices and governmental orders etc.
(e) It helps him to take care of his family, especially his children's health and education.

An illiterate person cannot be an effective citizen. He becomes a victim of exploitation. Hence education is necessary for everyone.

What is Literacy?

There is no unanimity on the definition of literacy in this world. But we can classify literacy in three categories:

(1) Those who put their signature instead of thumb impressions.
(2) Those having educational level equivalent to primary to fourth standard.
(3) Those, whose ability is equivalent to SSLC standard and above.

Literacy of the people, who come under first category will not serve any purpose. Then what should be the definition of literacy?

In 1949, Argentina conducted census of the country. It did not include persons who could just put their signature as literate. According to its view a literate person should be able to read and write, at least in one language well (Nagappa, *ibid.* 98). Sri Lanka considered that a man was literate only if he was able to read letters addressed to him and in turn could reply to the letters. In 1929 Belgium declared that a man would be literate, if he knew to read and write in his mother tongue. Japan included simple arithmetic under literacy. Thus the meaning of literacy differs from country to country. In India, a person aged 7 years and above, who can both read and write with understanding in any language is regarded as literate. All children of age 6 years and below are to be treated as illiterate even if the child is attending school and might have picked up reading and writing with understanding. Till 1981 census, all the children aged 4 years and below were treated as illiterates. But from 1991 census this definition has changed (Census,

2001:11). Many scholars in India terms literacy as acquiring 3 R's, *viz.*, to read, to write and to perform simple arithmetic.

Thus we find education and literacy is not same while the former means all-round development of human being, while the later as the capacity to read and write with understanding in any language.

Literacy in Arunachal Pradesh

Census in Arunachal Pradesh was held partially from 1901 to 1951 in Mishmi Hills, Abor Hills, Tirap Frontier Tract and Balipara Frontier Tract (Census of India, 1951:2). But it did not cover whole of present State. It was during 1961 that attempt was made to cover whole region by using two types of schedules, *viz.* All India Census Schedule and Simplified Census Schedule to count human population. The published literacy rate of Arunachal Pradesh is shown in Table 25.1 from 1961 to 2001.

Table 25.1: Literacy in Arunachal Pradesh

Year	*Literacy*
1961	7.13
1971	11.29
1981	20.79
1991	41.59
2001	54.74

Source: Census of India, 1961, 1971, 1981, 1991 and 2001.

While cross-examining the census reports of 1961, 1971 and 1981, it is found that the literacy rates estimated during the above three years for all the age groups were estimated without deducting the age group of 0-4 (RGCC, 1987). For example, number of literates in Arunachal Pradesh during 1961 was 24,013 out of total population of 336,558; total literates were 52,791 out of total population of 467,511 during 1971 and total literates were 131,511 during 1981 out of total population of 631,839 (DES, 1989:3). This has been observed for other States too. Due to this and due to change of definition let us compare the literacy of Arunachal Pradesh with neighbouring States and few other States for 1991 and 2001 in Table 25.2.

The literacy rate in Arunachal Pradesh was lowest during 1991 and 2001 censuses for total, male and female, as we find in Table 25.2

compared to neighbouring States, all-India and Kerala. The literacy was lowest among all the States except Bihar, Rajasthan during 1991 census and Jammu & Kashmir, Bihar and Rajasthan during 2001 census.

Table 25.2: Literacy of Arunachal Pradesh a comparative study

States	*1991*			*2001*		
	T	M	F	T	M	F
India*	52.21	64.13	39.29	65.38	75.85	54.16
Arunachal Pradesh	41.59	51.45	29.69	54.74	64.07	44.24
Assam	52.89	61.87	43.03	64.28	71.93	56.03
Manipur	59.89	71.63	47.60	68.87	77.87	59.70
Mizoram	82.27	85.61	78.60	88.49	90.69	86.13
Meghalaya	49.10	53.12	44.85	63.31	66.14	60.41
Nagaland	61.65	67.62	54.75	67.11	71.77	61.92
Tripura	60.44	70.58	49.65	73.66	81.47	65.41
Sikkim	56.94	65.74	46.69	69.68	76.73	61.46
Kerala	89.81	93.62	86.17	90.92	94.20	87.86

Note: T= Total, M=Male, F=Female, *Excluding Jammu & Kashmir.

Sources: (1) Census of India, 2001, Provisional Population Totals, Paper-1 of 2001, p. iv;

(2) Census of India, 1991, Series-1, Paper-2 of 1992, Final Population Totals, pp. 211-215.

The low literacy in the State is primarily due to historical reasons and lack of development both before and after Independence. Let us find the causes of low literacy in Arunachal Pradesh.

Causes of Low Literacy in Arunachal Pradesh

Literacy in Arunachal Pradesh is very low compared to other States during last 4 decades. There are various reasons for that. Some of these reasons are stated below.

Sparse Population

The inhabitation in Arunachal Pradesh is very sparse. The density is lowest which is 13 persons per square kilometre during 2001 census. It was lowest in earlier too. Maximum of the villages are nucleus villages. During 1991census there was 3649 villages but 151 villages were having population less than 10,878 villages were having population from 10 to 49, 868 villages were having population 50-99 and 796 villages with population 100 to 199. Thus about 74 per cent of villages were having population less than 200. These are shown in Table 25.3.

Table 25.3: Distribution of Villages According to Population Size (1991) in Arunachal Pradesh.

Population Size	*No. of villages*	*Percentage*
0-9	151	4.2
10-49	878	24.1
50-99	868	23.8
100-199	796	21.8
200-499	629	17.2
500-1999	299	8.2
2000-4999	24	0.7
5000-9999	3	N
10000 and above	1	N
Total	3649	100.0

Source: (1) *District Census Hand Books*, Arunachal Pradesh, 1991.
(2) Bhattacharjee, R.P. (2000), *Economic Development of Arunachal Pradesh*, p. 253.

Due to small size of villages and scattered in rugged terrain with a forest cover of 82 per cent or more it is impossible for any administration to reach each and every villages with educational facility specially with literacy programmes.

Lack of Administration

The British tool over the administration of parts of Assam in 1826 and the whole of Assam in 1838 and made it a non-regulatory province of the British India. The pre-British rulers of Assam "adopted policies of conciliation towards the tribal people supporting it by a display of force when it could be effectively engaged". The relation of Ahom King with the tribal people of the hills was a different story. Suffice it to say here that the main objective of the Ahom rulers was to contain the tribal people in the hills. So they had occasions to send expeditions in the interest of protecting the subject in the plains. The British largely followed the policies of the Ahom Kings. They established outposts only and conducted punitive expeditions. An Assistant Political Officer was appointed at Sadiya as late as 1882 (Bhattacharjee, 2000:29).

No attention had been given to education in this territory during the British rule. Till 1894, there was no impact on the people of government officials. In 1894, a political officer, Mr. J.F. Needham was appointed to study the languages and policies of the tribal people and try to win their goodwill by sympathy and contact. In 1911, Miri Mission in Northern Subansiri and in 1944 another mission in Siang made surveys. But these varied contacts had remarkably little effect on the life and culture of the people. They were probably too transient and occasional to have a deep effect, but they did succeed in slowly bringing the inhabitants to realize that the greater world outside their hills was not hostile to them but only wished them well (Rastogi, 1991:16). Thus there was no administration and the region was divided for the first time in 1914 with introduction of 3-sections and subsequent changes during 1921, 1937 and 1945. But these lackadaisical changes had no development in education or literacy.

Lack of Educational Institutions

Education in the simplest form always existed in Arunachal Pradesh among the local people. In the absence of formal education, traditional knowledge was orally transmitted from generation to generation to make the child fit in the physical and social environment. The ritual dances and incantations which were performed before a hunt, an expedition, harvest or sowing of crops, storing of food and religious worship provided informal education to the children. Under the British regime practically no effect was made to introduce any formal system of education in the erstwhile North East Frontier Tract.

According to Osik (1990), the Adis were in fact 'the first people to become conscious for the modern educational value in Arunachal Pradesh. The Adis had submitted to General Bower the commander-in-chief of the British armies in 1911 after a series of decisive battles (1830-1911). Soon after the general submission, the Adis demanded the Assistant Political Officer, Pasighat of a Government School at Pasighat. Unfortunately, the British policy in those days was to discourage education as most of the uprisings in India, they considered were due to education which made the native people conscious of their own rights. Being refused by the APO, Pasighat to provide a Government School, the local people opened a ventured school at Pasighat in 1918. Mr. Putiram Kaman, a Mishing was the first teacher of Pasighat School. The Adis of Dibang Valley also opened a similar school at Dambuk in 1922. Two Garos known to the local people as Marak babu and Sangma babu were the first teachers of Dambuk School. The villagers had to provide monthly rations (rice and vegetables) to the teachers. Besides they had to contribute money to make nominal monthly salary to the teachers. Thus educational development before Independence was negligible.

During Independence, there were only 3 schools with 50 children. This was the modest start of formal education. The Department of Education was established in the year 1947. Schools were opened on the basis of demand at the initial stage. The administration and supervision of schools was carried out from Sadiya. After the devastating earthquake in 1950, the Department shifted its headquarters to Margherita (*Arunachal News*, 1980).

The administration after Independence had to put in very hard work to see that this educationally backward region comes up to the level of the comparatively more advanced parts of the country at a faster pace. The main aim of the Department of Education was to extend facilities of primary education to the maximum possible number of children. Public enthusiasm was negligible at the beginning and problems regarding non-availability of trained teachers, housing for schools and teachers, hostel facility etc. retarded the expansion of education *vis-à-vis* literacy in the State. This can be attributed to the poor economic condition of the people. Various measures including persuading the people to offer co-operation in educating their children, provision of free education relaxation of rules and norms applicable to educational institutions elsewhere in respect of accommodation, enrolment, appointment, of teachers etc. were adopted by the Government. Free educational facilities included not only provisions for exemption from the payment of various school fees, but also supply of stationery, clothing etc. at free of cost. The scheme of inter-village schools with provision for ration worth Rs. 25 per month per boarder was considered. Subsequently when it was decided to open centrally located residential schools for a number of villages. For the first time, clothing also was supplied to the boarders and day scholars of the inter-village schools. To encourage girls education separate hostels for girls were run side by side with the boys hostels in the inter-village schools. Woman teachers were also appointed wherever possible to ensure high enrolment of girls in the educational institutions (*Arunachal News*, 1972).

Till 1971-72, education in this region was conducted in Assamese medium except for a short period of three years during 1958-59 to

1961-62 when Hindi was the medium of instruction. However in 1972-73 the medium of instruction was changed over to English. As the autochthons were not having any common language of their own or their mother tongue as medium of instruction, and regular change of medium of instructions made the people illusoned about education and literacy. It is surely an embarrassment to accept others language at pre-primary and primary level. The only tribes who have their own script are Monpas and Khamptis who use their script for limited purpose especially religious purposes.

After shifting of capita form Shillong to Itanagar (1974), the Department of Education along with other Departments started functioning from Naharlogun and at present it is bifurcated into two departments, *viz.* Department of School Examination at Naharlogun and Department of Higher Education at Itanagar. Let us find the trend of educational institutions in the State in Table 25.4.

We find herewith that educational institutions before 1971-72 was negligible and it started increasing during 1980s and 1990s. But for 3649 Nos. of villages scattered in whole of Arunachal Pradesh with geographical area 83,743 sq km, a mare 1303 primary schools are not sufficient to increase literacy in the State. Beside that, a large number of schools are concentrated in State capital and districts and other administrative centres. Due to shortages of Primary schools, it cannot be expected to have a high literacy rate in the State.

Lack of Enrolment

Enrolment is an essential indicator for spread of education and increase in literacy-rate. During 1950-51, there was 2278 students (Bulletin, 1957) but this has increased to 289,000 during 2000-2001 (DES, 2001:6). There are 9826 teachers in all educational institutions. But for increase in enrolment, number of schools and sufficient teachers are required. This will boost literacy rate in the State. A comparative enrolment ratio of the State (1999-2000) is shown in Table 25.5.

The recent enrolment ratio in the State is encouraging specially in Primary classes compared to classes VI to VIII. But this should be increased.

High Drop-out Rates

Drop-out rates from primary class or middle classes causes dissentment and discouragement in the literacy programme in any State. Our

Table 25.4: Trend of Educational Institutions in Arunachal Pradesh

Year	*Pre-Primary*	*Primary*	*Middle*	*Secondary*	*Higher Secondary*	*College*	*Technical Institutions*	*University*	*Total*
1947	—	2	1	—	—	—	—	—	3
1950-51	—	63	1	—	—	—	—	—	64
1960-61	—	129	14	5	—	—	—	—	148
1971-72	3	503	45	11	7	1	—	—	570
1986-87	28*	1253	181	47	29	3	2	1	1544
1990-91	299	1122	255	73	46	4	2	1	1802
2000-2001	57	1303	333	116	68	7	3a	1	1888

*=Other Institutions. a=Includes NERIST and 2 ITI's.

Source : Statistical Reports of the Government of Arunachal Pradesh.

educational system should be full-proof such that drop out is stopped and people are encouraged for literacy/primary educational programmes. During 1999-2000 the total drop out in the State in primary classes was 50.23 while Girls drop out was 50.81. Drop outs in Assam, Kerala, Manipur, Tripura, Nagaland and all India were less compared to Arunachal Pradesh while second highest literate state-Mizoram had higher drop outs both in primary and elementary classes along with Bihar, Meghalaya, Sikkim and West Bengal. Girls drop-out in West Bengal, Tripura, Sikkim, Meghalaya, Bihar and Assam were more compared to Arunachal Pradesh. These are shown in Table 25.6. To increase literacy rates in this State, the drop-outs should be minimised to have a pleasant environment for education in the State. Placement is perhaps another area where we have to work.

Table 25.5: Enrolment ratio in Arunachal Pradesh (1999-2000) — A Comparison

States	*Classed I-V (6-11 years)*			*Classes VI-VIII (11-14 years)*		
	Boys	*Girls*	*Total*	*Boys*	*Girls*	*Total*
Arunachal Pradesh	126.14	108.35	117.54	74.42	64.63	72.99
Assam	124.25	105.35	114.94	81.02	64.63	72.99
Bihar	94.51	61.46	78.56	41.38	22.04	32.36
Kerala	85.80	84.74	85.28	97.78	93.36	95.61
Manipur	101.87	87.41	94.44	79.62	71.34	75.48
Meghalaya	119.46	111.64	115.43	57.42	62.28	59.83
Mizoram	121.84	107.52	114.62	78.77	76.17	77.47
Nagaland	92.21	87.78	90.03	58.67	61.14	59.85
Sikkim	139.32	138.48	138.91	70.96	76.59	73.69
Tripura	118.28	100.86	109.37	69.96	60.26	65.13
India	104.08	85.18	94.90	67.15	49.66	58.79

Source: Government of India, *Educational Statistics*, 1999-2000, MHRD, New Delhi, 2001, pp. 44,60.

The drop out rates in the State in elementary classes is more which needs to be checked and minimised of achievement of target higher literacy in the State.

Lack of Dialect

The system of formal education, in particular, had been conspicuously absent in the past in Arunachal Pradesh. Excepting the Buddhists, the system of even informal education had been non-existent. It is traced that among the Monpas who were highly concentrated to the North-West and Central part of the West Kameng district, the mythological education to be imparted through Monastery. Except the Khamtis in Lohit District, the Monpas are the only people who can claim to have a script of their dialect (Biswas, 1992). The rest of the non-Buddhist tribes in Arunachal Pradesh do not have their own script. This is an important cause to learn/educate in own language/mother tongue in the State causing low literacy. Recently Mr. Tony Koyu has started a tani-lipi for development of local languages. The effect of this will be seen in future only. However, lack of dialect of its own is also a reason for low literacy in the State.

Table 25.6: Drop-out Rates (1999-2000) — A Comparison

States	*Primary Classes*		*Elementary Classes*	
	Total	*Girls*	*Total*	*Boys*
Arunachal Pradesh	50.23	50.81	64.92	63.38
Assam	33.69	42.20	69.81	71.99
Bihar	57.27	58.64	77.62	80.96
Kerala	(-) 7.05	(-) 5.00	(-) 5.73	(-) 4.06
Manipur	43.30	42.90	43.08	43.25
Meghalaya	57.43	57.22	77.74	77.66
Mizoram	51.64	51.27	65.81	63.36
Nagaland	46.73	46.68	40.27	36.47
Sikkim	58.94	56.35	70.33	67.12
Tripura	49.47	49.25	68.24	68.58
West Bengal	54.07	58.48	70.88	71.99
India	40.25	42.28	54.53	58.00

Source: "Selected Educational Statistics. 1999-2000" (As on 30-9-1999), GOI, MHRD, New Delhi, 2001, pp. 224-31.

Weak Adult Education Programme

Adult education is all pervasive. It is concerned with every phase of human activity and hence it is a lifelong process. Development of an individual in society is a dire necessity and adult education should be in accordance with the needs anu wished of the individual. But this is not observed in Arunachal Pradesh. The necessity of agriculturist and house hold industry is neglected in the process of adult education programme. During 2000-01, Rs. 93.10 lakh was spent for adult education out of total educational expenditure of Rs. 6643.76 lakh.

This is just 1.4 per cent of total expenditure. A large amount is spent on salaries and wages only. During 2001-2002, the Budget amount of adult education is kept at Rs. 94.09 lakhs which is only 1.2 per cent of total budget (AOP, Education). Thus we find that the importance of adult education is decreasing relatively. Adult Education programme, according to AOP, has received the special attention in the State at the instance of National Literacy Mission to cover illiterates in the age group of 15-35 years with thrust on literacy, social awareness and functional literacy. During 1996-97, as many as 1295 Adult Education Centres were functioning in the State. Nearly 31 thousand adult learners enrolled during 1996-97. But achievement of these Adult Education Programmes are not known. We do not have any latest information of achievement. Government is giving higher emphasis on area approach that centre based programme under Adult Education Programme. Accordingly 11 blocks have been taken up during 1994-95 for achieving 100 per cent literacy. We have 56 Number of blocks at present. If 20 per cent of blocks for 100 per cent literacy takes a decade or more, we have no doubt, naturally, for success of these programmes in the State for increasing literacy.

Lack of Women's Literacy

Women's literacy in Arunachal Pradesh is very low and for that our social system is to be blamed. Specially its various restrictions, taboos etc. to be blamed. Maximum of Indian societies had not been given due weightages for women's empowerment earlier. Although men and women are two equal components of the human society and are considered complementary to each other in all aspects of life, nevertheless, the growth of these two components is not at par in many spheres. For example, in literacy, men's literacy is always stressed in our patriarchal societies. And this is the reason that women's literacy is low in most of the societies including Arunachal Pradesh. A comparative female literacy of the State is shown in Table 25.7.

The female literacy in Table 25.7 in Arunachal Pradesh is very low except in Bihar during 1991 and 2001. But growth of women's literacy is very good compared to other States. The female population in the State is mainly scheduled tribes and they are mainly engaged in domestic works beside there is traditional system of child marriage though it is decreasing with the spread of education. In the patriarchal tribal societies the women's education had no meaning earlier and due to this literacy was very low but situation has improved in recent decades. New generation is coming up for education of their female children in the State. Recent policy documents of Government of India on primary education sees women's role in education as mobilisers — mother who must play the role of bringing their children to school. If implemented properly, female literacy will increase further.

Table 25.7: Female Literacy in Arunachal Pradesh — A Comparison

States	*1961*	*1971*	*1981*	*1991*	*2001*
Arunachal Pradesh	1.42	3.71	11.32	29.69	44.24
India	12.90	18.70	24.82	39.29	54.16
Assam	–	–	NA	43.03	56.03
Bihar	6.90	8.72	13.62	22.89	33.57
Kerala	38.90	54.81	65.73	86.17	87.86
Manipur	15.93	19.53	29.06	47.60	59.70
Meghalaya	21.15	24.56	30.08	44.85	60.41
Nagaland	24.04	35.02	50.06	54.75	61.92
Sikkim	4.26	8.90	22.20	46.69	61.46
Tripura	10.19	21.19	32.00	49.65	65.41
Mizoram	34.70	46.71	54.91	78.60	86.13

Sources: (1) RGCC, Occasional paper No. 1 of 1987.
(2) Census of India, Paper-1 of 1993.
(3) Census of India, 2001, Paper 1 & 2.

It is well known that the returns from women's education are exceptionally high. Women's education is instrumental in reducing fertility and infant and child mortality rate's; in improving the nutritional status of children and health care practices and in improving children's school enrolment and performance. All these have significant spill over benefits as well. The lower fertility and infant mortality rates and better health care practice reduce suffering, improve material health and increase female labour force participation rates.

Low Literacy Reduces HRD

Kerala is often being used as an example of high human development despite faltering economic development. In the case of Arunachal Pradesh, despite faltering educational development *vis-à-vis* educational index, human development is better compared to neighbouring States. According to Bhattacharjee (2000:231), the HDI of Assam was 0.21 (1991) compared to 0.28 in Arunachal Pradesh and 0.38 in all-India. In a recent estimate by Antony *et al.* (2001:2977), the HDI of Arunachal Pradesh was 0.623 compared to Assam (0.546), Mizoram (0.839); Meghalaya (0.585), Tripura (0.582), and India (0.640) using maximum income of Indian States in income index. This puzzle can be explained to better economic management and health care facilities in the State compared to neighbouring States. Though there is an improvement in the indices of HRD and standard of living in Arunachal Pradesh, the disparities between the rich and the poor is a matter of concern in the State as per our observation. And this is a cause of low literacy specially among the down trodden people in the State.

Weak Panchayati Raj System

The failure to make the country literate as stipulated in the Indian Constitution and National Educational Policy (1986) prompted various States and Central Government to undertake various strategies to decentralise educational management through the Panchayati Raj System. Recently Assam Government has also decided to decentralise the management system of Primary classes to Panchayats. According to 73rd and 74th Amendments of Indian Constitution, the Panchayats have been conceived for management of education system as a third layer and to be entrusted with the responsibility of implementing universal and compulsory free education. In Arunachal Pradesh, Panchayti Raj Institution is defunct at present and fresh election is expected by end of 2002. This is the main reason for low literacy in the State specially in rural areas and this is due to lack awareness about the benefit of the literacy in villages.

Conclusion

Education helps man to be aware of his rights and duties and it is a panacea for all social evils. It helps man to improve his thought, expression and action, talents and skills. Illiteracy is a malady and it must be eradicated from Arunachal Pradesh. Recently on 9th May, 2002, U.N. General Assembly called for protecting children's right and educating them so that they grew up to be useful citizens. The United Nation stressed for strengthening family values and putting special care on girl's literacy campaign (*Assam Tribune*). The Government of India is supposed to place a *Bill on Right to Education in Parliament.* This will help in eliminating illiteracy from the State. Arunachal Pradesh has to literate about 45 per cent of its people. For that, the following suggestions may be considered for implementation:

(1) To reduce social overhead cost and coverage of all villages under primary education programme, relocation of human settlements is very essential. This cannot be achieved in one day but this perspective has to be constantly kept in mind by everybody associated with development in the State specially for eradication of illiteracy.

(2) There must be basic amenities for schools. There should be proper classroom, blackboards, hostels and housing for the teachers. Road communication and health care facilities are essential as a basic amenities along with power, water supply and information technology.

(3) Adult education programme should cover all the C-D blocks and more fund should be allocated for that.

(4) NGOs should be encouraged for coming forward to eradicate illiteracy.

(5) The expenditures on education is only 3.7 per cent of GSDP (2000-2001) of the State. This is required to be increased to 6 per cent at least.

(6) For girls literacy, they should be encouraged to join schools and for that reason, more girl-hostels are required to be constructed.

(7) Free education for all should be introduced at least up to secondary school both in Government and private schools along with increase in the amount of scholarships for higher education.

(8) Distance education is a new panacea for higher education. Primary education can also be initiated for universalisation of education in the State *vis-à-vis* for removing illiteracy.

(9) The district-wise literacy rates of Arunachal Pradesh is as follows

Papum Pare=70.89; West Kameng=61.67; East Siang=61.22; West Siang=60.31; Dibang Valley=59.45; Lohit=56.05; Changlang=51.98; Upper Subansiri=50.89; Upper Siang=49.80; Lower Subansiri=45.01; Tirap=42.01; Tawang=41.14; East Kameng=40.89.

The literacy rate is lowest in East Kameng district. Therefore following circles whose literacy rate during 2001 is lower than 41 per cent may be taken up as a special programme of removing illiteracy in the State. These are—

Zemithang (24.43%); Lumbla (32.20%); Dudunghar (17.23%); Mukto (27.20%); Thingbu (32.53%); Jamiri (39.20%); Pakke-kessang (31.42%); Richukrong (35.07); Lada (18.04%); Bameng (25.10%); Pipu (18.83%); Khenewa (20.60%); Chayangtajo (32.14%); Sawa (18.55%); Leporiang (31.78%); Mengio (17.79%); Palin (39.31%); Yangte (18.60%); Sangram (24.84%); Nyapin (23.62%); Koloriang (27.48%); Chambang (26.31%); Sarli (16.75%); Parsi Parlo (23.01%); Damin (25.90%); Longding koling (11.25%); Tali (10.23%); Kamporijo (34.74%); Limeking (31.73%); Nacho (25.19%); Siyum (29.37%); Payeng (32.50); Monigong (22.07%); Pidi (27.44%); Tato (37.23%); Rebo-Perging (38.84%); Migging (38.84%); Palling (38.22%); Singa (40.16%); Mipi (39.27%); Anelih (40.76%); Kronli (38.56%); Manchal (7.63); Goiliang (16.33%); Chaglagam (17.68%); Hawai (31.17%); Piyong (40.15%); Khimiyong (36.20%); Diyun (40.69%); Longding (39.75%); Pumao (9.82%); Pangchao (15.30%); Wakka (15.17%) and Laju (25.55%).

(10) It is observed that concentration of teachers are in urban areas or in administrative centres by one or other means. This has to be changed and teachers must go to each and every potential places to eradicate illiteracy. Politics should not influence in transfer and posting of these teachers. More indigenous people should come forward to teach the people. This will ease the unemployment problem too in the State.

(11) Placement is an important part of any education. In the movement of eradicating illiteracy, it should be kept in mind that the employment generation should be part of our educational plans and programme too.

The National Policy on Education (1986) provides a broad policy and a commitment to make primary education free and compulsory up to V standard, besides ensuring higher government and non-government expenditures on education that should constitute 6 per cent of GDP/ GSDP. Arunachal Pradesh spends at present only 3.7 per cent of its GSDP. Thus it should be increased to remove illiteracy. Gender-bias always prevails in our society. Women's empowerment is necessary for socio-economic change and removing illiteracy.

The National Policy on Education visualised education as a dynamic, cumulative, life-long process, providing diversity of learning opportunities to all segments of society. Prime Minister's Special Action Plan (SAP) has stressed the need for expansion and improvement of social infrastructure in the field of education and main facets of this is eradication of illiteracy.

REFERENCES

Antony, Grace Maria; Rao, K. Viswawara and Balakrishna, N. (2001). "Suitability of IIDI for Assessing Health and Nutritional Status" in *Economic and Political Weekly,* Vol. XXXV, No. 31, August, 4-10, 2001.

Bhattacharjee, R.P. (2000). *Economic Development of Arunachal Pradesh,* Himalayan Publisher, Itanagar/Delhi, pp. 28-29.

Biswas, N.B. (1992); Education in Arunachal Pradesh—A Historical Profile", in *Arunachal Review*, Vol. IV, No. 7, July 1991. April, 1992, p. 1.

Bulletin of Statistics, NEFA, Vol. I, (1957), Shillong, p. 116.

Census of India, (1951), Vol. XII, Assam, Manipur and Tripura, Part-III-A, pp. 2-9.

Census of India (2001). Arunachal Pradesh, Series-13. Paper-2 of Census of India, Provisional Population Totals, p. 11.

Department of Education, *Annual Operating Plan,* (2001-2002), Directorate of School Education, Government of Arunachal Pradesh, Naharlogum, p. 4.

DIPR, *Arunachal News – Twenti-fifth Independence Joyanti*, August, 1972, Shillong, pp. 13-15.

Directorate of Economics and Statistics, *Arunachal Pradesh at a Glance,* (2001), Government of Arunachal Pradesh, Itanagar, p. 6.

Directorate of Economics and Statistics, Government of Arunachal Pradesh, *Statistical Pocket Book, 1989*. Shillong p. 3.

Directorate of Information and Public Relation (DIPR), Government of Arunachal Pradesh, *Arunachal News*, Vol. No. 9, August, 1980, No. 4, Shillong, pp.12-13, (According to *Arunachal News,* August, 1972, p. 15, there was 3 schools and 33 students enroled in 1947).

GOI, *Economic Survey,* (2000-2001), Ministry of Finance, Economic Division, p. 195, 1999-2000, p. 171.

GOI, MHRD, *Selected Educational Statistics, (1999-2000)*, New Delhi, pp. 224-31.

Nagappa, T.R.; Rao, H.R.C. (1997). *Towards Total Literacy,* Vikas Publishing House Pvt. Ltd., New Delhi, pp. 1-98.

Osik, N.N. (1990). "Early Education in Arunachal Pradesh", in *Arunachal Review*, Vol. IV, No. 5, (Jan.-July), pp. 18-19.

Rastogi, S. (1991). Education as a catalyst for Tribal Development in Arunachal Pradesh — A changing scenario *RESARUN*, Vol. XVII, Nos. 1 & 2. Directorate of Research, Government of Arunachal Pradesh, Itanagar, p. 16.

Registrar General and Census Commissioner, India, *Recent Literacy Trends in India*, Occasional Paper, No. 1 of 1987, pp. 17, 57-77.

The Assam Tribune, Dated 9th May, 2002.

26

Total Literacy Campaign
A Meghalaya Experience

BILORIS LYNDEM

"The country can't excel with half of its population being illiterate. I am not criticizing anybody. We are all to blame for it and we need to sort it out."

(A.B. Vajpayee, Prime Minister of India)*

Most of us present here cannot be thrilled by the experience of being a literate for the first time because we have learned to read and write in childhood like we did other necessities of life without which, the business of living would have become difficult. We learned to walk, talk, eat harder food and were toilet-trained; similarly, though a little later, we learned to read and write. However, if we only paused a while and reflected, it would become clear how the power of the latter conditions and controls our daily life. The experience of an adult or teenager becoming literate is very different. With literacy, all of a sudden, a new world of possibilities, information and viewpoints became open before the newly literate. This is as much an awe-inspiring as a humbling experience. A newly literate realises how the world was sleeping around her so far, and how subtly she was being a nobody amidst the sea of human being. In fact, literacy is the first and most important skill that a modern human being needs to have in her kit.

India has crossed a long way in the literacy scenario. In the first

* As quoted in *Literacy for All — the Way to a Learning Society* by Sakti Prasad Mishra, in *Learning Society: Compendium of Prize Winning Essays 2000* (New Delhi: Directorate of Adult Education, 2001), p. 109.

Census of the 20th Century only 5 percent of our population was literate and the newest Census reports that this rate has gone up to 65.37 per cent. Meghalaya's case is still more startling; there were only 771 individuals who were literate in 1901 in the two districts, Garo Hills and United Khasi and Jaintia Hills, which now from the Meghalaya state, and now 63.31 per cent of Meghalaya's total population is literate.

The present paper tells the story of Meghalaya's Total Literacy Campaign (TLC). We have tried to say this story full, both the hard facts and the joys of the campaign.

I

Dictionary defines "literacy" as 'ability to read and write.' However, we all know that today 'literacy' has a wider application, with greater emphasis laid on functional literacy. As ability to read and write, literacy implies reading for oneself and reading aloud for others, writing, listening and speaking, and basic numerical skills. On the other hand, functional literacy as enshrined in the National Literacy Mission (NLM) implies much more:

(a) Achieving self-reliance in basic numeracy.
(b) Becoming aware of the causes of one's deprivation and moving towards amelioration of conditions through organisation and participation in the process of development.
(c) Acquiring skills to improve the economic status and general well being.
(d) Imbibing the values of national integration, conservation of environment, women's equality, observance of small family norms, etc.

The skill of literacy should enable the newly literate person to continue his/her learning either on his/her own or through other available avenues. It should be added here that the process of non-literates becoming literate, naturally involves the empowerment of women, which means a definite improvement in the quality of their lives.

II

As this paper unfolds the story of the TLC of Meghalaya, I presume, an introduction to Meghalaya and to the path it tread towards literacy at first, is necessary.

Meghalaya emerged as the 21st state of the Indian Union on 21 January 1972. It has 7 districts: West Garo Hills, East Garo Hills, South Garo Hills, West Khasi Hills, Ri Bhoi, East Khasi Hills and Jaintia Hills. Geographically Meghalaya is a massive plateau of steep hills and deep ravines. Cool, moderate and sultry climate prevails in the different parts of the state, depending on altitude. Heavy rainfall is common throughout the state, Cherrapunjee and Mawsynram being the highest rainfall zones in the World. Though Meghalaya has some of the best roadways in the North East region of India, due to diverse topography, some areas hitherto remain inaccessible except on foot. The state is not connected by any railway until now. May I add here that the physiography of Meghalaya acts as a constraining factor in the promotion of literacy and education in the state.

From the social perspective, Meghalaya may be characterised as a tribal state. It is home of two matrilineal tribes: Khasi-Pnars and Garos. These communities, though categorised tribal, have been in contact with the outside world for more than a century and are witnessing rapid social, economic and educational changes and other societal upheavals, that have taken hundreds of years to happen in other societies, in a very short span of time. More than half of the Khasi-Pnars and the Garos have accepted Christianity as their religion. They are generally a group of warm, simple and cheerful people, who are rooted to their land and proud of their tribal heritage.

Among all peculiarities of the Meghalaya society, the matrilineal social order captures the attention of the observer the most. Matriliny may be defined as that system where the children trace, their lineage by their mother and property rights goes down to posterity by the daughters and not by the sons. In such a system, women generally get a better deal in comparison to women in patrilineal and patriarchal societies. Their status is relatively higher and they are treated with more respect. Still, sexes' response to literacy varies in Meghalaya (Males = 66.14 and Females = 60.41 in 2001), though not as widely as the all-India figures show (Males = 75.85 and Females = 54.16 in 2001). On the International Women's Day this year (March 8), it was reported in *The Telegraph* that among the 8 matrilineal communities of the World, mostly found in South and Southeast Asia, the ones of Meghalaya are fast losing their matrilineal traits. In this context, it may be useful to debate whether the matrilineal system of Meghalaya empowers women at all.

Present day Meghalaya is characterised by increasing gap between the rich and the poor and the urban and rural sections of the population of the state. One of Meghalaya's advantages has been Shillong, its capital town. Though once known as the biggest hill station in India today Shillong is fast developing into a city. It was the favourite spot of the British in the North East; it was the former capital of the undivided state of Assam, even when almost the whole of North East India was known as Assam. Shillong is the first choice educational centre of the tribals of the North East even today. However, there is also that danger of masquerading the real picture of rural Meghalaya by what is seen in Shillong. Development needs to be decentralised in all aspects. Meghalaya is also fast losing its egalitarian tribal heritage of communitarian sharing of the wealth of the village. Hence, it is imperative of the state machinery to make the poor participate in the process of development.

III

It is well known that the Christian missionaries were not only the hearlds of the tidings of the Gospel but also the harbingers of education and literacy to the tribals of the North East India. Selfless and decdicated service from the Presbyterian, Baptist and Catholic missionaries has contributed to the development of education in Meghalaya. Rev. Thomas Jones, a Welsh Calvinistic Methodist, who came to Cherrapunjee in 1841 was the first in this long list of distinguished men and women. Besides proselytisation, they opened schools and hospitals, learned the local languages, gave them the Roman script and produced literature in those languages, which were once utterly foreign to them. They tried to persuade the villagers that education was an important aspect of life. Though it took time, on looking back, one should acknowledge the important message they slowly and surely imparted to generations of Khasi-Pnars and Garos.

Table 26.1, picturing the literacy position of Meghalaya from 1901 to 1941, excluding the age group of 0-4. During this period, the Garo Hills district and the United Khasi and Jaintia district were two districts of the state of Assam. Table 26.1 shows, total male and female literacy per 10,000 male and female population respectively. These figures will surely remind us of the tryst that Meghalaya made with learning ever since.

India's freedom fighters tried to attach supreme importance to education in nation building. Despite the failures of the successive Central and State governments, remarkable progress has been made in the field of literacy and learning in spite of several constraints. In fact, one of the paradoxes of our motherland is that we shall soon have the highest number of degree holders in the world and the highest number of illiterates, too. This is both our problem as well as the success.

Table 26.1: Literacy position of Meghalaya

Districts Name	*1901*			*1911*			*1921*			*1931*			*1941*		
	P	*M*	*F*	*P*	*M*	*F*	*P*	*M*	*F*	*P*	*M*	*F*	*P*	*M*	*F*
Garo Hills	99	171	25	135	239	25	211	348	69	309	505	105	547	823	265
United Khasi & Jaintia Hills	672	964	401	651	957	362	905	1244	578	1094	1473	707	1615	2158	105

Source: Census of India 1961, Volume III, Assam Part A, General Report, Ministry of Home Affairs, New Delhi.

In Meghalaya the post-Independence scenario came as a real boost to education. The Government launched schemes and plans for the development of the hill areas in particular. In fact, Meghalaya has not looked back after that resurgence and has continued to be a learning society. After the passing of the Sixth Schedule of the Indian Constitution in 1949 the Khasi Hills Autonomous District Council was inaugurated in 1952, for the Garos in 1953 and for the Jiantias (Pnars) in 1967. In 1960 the autonomous district councils agreed to the terms and conditions of the Government of Assam in preparation for handing over primary education in the hill areas to their respective councils. This transfer was effected in United Khasi & Jaintia Hills district council in 1962 and thereafter in Garo Hills district council. This was a tremendous boost to primary education and hence literacy

Table 26.2: Literacy Rate of 1981 to 2001

Country/State/District	*Literacy Rates 1981*			*Literacy Rates 1991*			*Literacy Rates 2001*		
	P	*M*	*F*	*P*	*M*	*F*	*P*	*M*	*F*
All-India							65.37	75.85	54.16
Meghalaya	39.95	44.26	35.41	49.10	53.12	44.85	63.31	66.14	60.41
West Garo Hills	25.91	32.04	19.55	38.64	46.10	30.81	51.03	57.51	44.51
East Garo Hills	33.50	39.01	27.66	48.36	54.70	41.70	61.70	67.39	55.74
South Garo Hills	25.04	31.31	19.74	42.88	51.28	34.02	55.82	62.60	48.61
West Khasi Hills	31.97	34.08	29.74	50.52	52.98	47.94	65.64	67.02	64.21
Ri Bhoi	NA	NA	NA	39.92	43.88	35.72	66.07	69.22	62.67
East Khasi Hills	43.73	46.95	40.30	64.57	67.13	61.86	76.98	78.12	75.82
Jaintia Hills	39.95	44.26	35.41	35.32	34.37	36.31	53.00	50.52	55.54

Source: Census of India, 1981-1991 and Provisional district-wise population figures, 2001.

in these districts, particularly in Khasi & Jaintia Hills, where the number of literates had risen from 69,293 in 1951 to 1,45,763 in 1961 and 2,02,487 in 1971. In Garo Hills the transfer was not properly done though the terms and conditions were the same as that in the Khasi Hills. Here the district council set up the Primary Education Board without any proper legislation, due to which the schooling system did not take off properly. In spite of this confusion, in 1951 the number of literates in Garo Hills was 17,710, which rose to 61,334 in 1961.

Decadel variations of literacy rates in the different districts of Meghalaya is furnished in Table 26.2.

IV

Realising that, to deprive a large number of people from education is a very serious aspect of educational and social planning. Thirty years after Independence the Indian policy makers began to think in the line of universalizing primary education for children up to the age of 14 and making elementary education accessible to illiterate adults, who could not study, improve themselves or work according to their competence. Thought the government has not been successful in giving free and compulsory education to children up to the age of 14, policies have been made and repeated in this regard. Similarly, the Adult Education Programme was launched on 2 October 1978 at the National level, though still we have 460 million and more illiterates in the country. The rationale behind the adult education programme was the following:

- illiteracy is a serious hindrance in the progress of an individual's development and the socio-economic growth of the country.
- education need not be always school based and learning process continues in various activities and different situations of life.
- education, work and life cannot be separated and each proves meaningful only when it is coordinated with each others.
- the means by which people participate in the development process are as important as the objectives of development.
- even a poor person can move towards his/her emancipation by means of literacy, expression and work.

The National Adult Education Programme (NAEP) launched in 1978 was the first organised attempt at voluntary mass involvement and it did not achieve the desired results due to lack of public support. In line with the National Policy on Education, 1986, promotion of literacy had been identified as one of the five national Missions and the National Literacy Mission (NLM) was launched on 5th May 1988, which aimed at imparting functional literacy to individuals in the age group of 15-35 years in order to achieve a minimum sustainable level of 75 per cent literacy by the year 2005. Though India still needs to take valiant strides in the literacy front, NLM has gained international acclamation for its literacy achievements; winning the Literacy Prize for 1999. The NLM is now being implemented in 460 of the 520 districts of India and its programmes have been volunteer-based, area-specific, time bound and cost-effective. By 1998 over 150 million non-literates had been accessed and 72 million people made literates, women comprising two-thirds of NLM's target group. According to the Census report, literacy rate has been climbing steadily: 16.7 in 1951, 24.0 in 1961, 29.5 in 1971, 36.2 in 1981, 52.1 in 1991 and 65.37 (provisional) in 2001. NLM is conceived in three stages: (1) acquaintance with reading, writing and arithmetic, and some general knowledge relating to civic and national problems, (2) post-literacy programme which deepens the knowledge and skills gained in the initial state and trains the adults in using literacy gained for solving personal problems and enriching personal life, (3) continuing education, the third stage, came into force from 1 January 1996 and is designed to drive out illiteracy and to prevent neo-literates and semi-literates from regressing into complete illiteracy.

In April 1989 an attempt was made in Kerala's Ernakulam district to convert the adult education programme into a mass movement for the attainment of cent per cent literacy. After a year of effort this district earned the distinction of becoming India's first totally literate district. Some of the visible social impacts of this movement were liberation from liquor addiction, reduction in crimes, change in voting process and decrease in school drop out rates. Modelling on the Ernakulam experiment, the Ministry of Human Resource Development, Government of India decided to take-up huge mass programmes for literacy, which was earlier considered an incorrigible task. This is what is known as the TLC. The TLC is area-based, time-bound, cost-effective, outcome-oriented and volunteer-based programme.

The TLC was a fruit of the realisation that though literacy rate in India was going up due to formal and non-formal education, the problem of illiteracy could not be really arrested since most of the illiterates were outside all modes of education. A TLC district will be declared literate only if 80 per cent of its population become literate. It is presumed that the remaining 20 per cent will soon be swallowed by the tides of literacy. Though TLC concentrates on the age group of 15-35 it also encourages children below 15 to enter school and opportunities are provided to those above 35 to become literate, if they are interested. TLC also strives to set-up continuing education centres for neo-literates so that the flame of literacy may not die. Generally, one such centre is set-up for five or four villages or for a population of 5000. The TLC thrives on both government efforts and mass participation of everyone. Volunteerism is the backbone of the movement. The objective of the programme is to eradicate illiteracy from the country at the earliest by working on a war footing by soliciting active participation from all groups and people of society.

V

The TLC was launched in Meghalaya on 25 July 1995 by the then Union Minister of Human Resource Development, Mr. Madhavrao Scindia at a colourful function held at Nongpoh in Ri-Bhoi district. The three districts chosen were Ri-Bhoi, Jaintia Hills and East Garo Hills. They were chosen on a priority basis since they had a low literacy rate in comparison to other districts of Meghalaya. In fact, the Khliehriat C.D. Block in Jaintia Hills district had the lowest literacy rate in the whole of Meghalaya. As part of the observance of the International Literacy Day on 8 September 1995 the TLC was also formally inaugurated in Jowai by the Governor, Shri M. M. Jacob. Today, six out of the seven districts of Meghalaya are covered under the TLC, the South Garo Hills district being the exception. Some of these districts have completed the campaign while in others the programme is still underway.

According to the 1991 census report, Meghalaya's literacy rate was 49.10 well below the then national average of 52.1, placing the state at 22nd position in the entire country. Even within North East region Meghalaya lagged far behind other states like Mizoram and Nagaland. This was ironic, considering the fact that education came to Meghalaya around 150 years ago with the Christian missionaries and Shillong had been a centre of education and culture since then. Hence, the launching of the TLC in the state was a historical development from the educational point of view and a timely intervention from the part of Government of Meghalaya.

Today Meghalaya is in the process of completing the TLC and Continuing Education Centres (CECs) will be the next in the agenda of the state and a proposal for opening the CECs will soon be presented to the MHRD, Government of India. This is important because it may be relatively easier to make a person literate than to sustain him/her in functional literacy. CECs are meant for this purpose — to keep the momentum of literacy and learning going, to contribute to the creation of a learning society. In the North East, the state of Mizoram — the second most literate state in India — has made the TLC a successful movement and has a well-established system of CECs. The state is marching ahead with the aim of total functional literacy of all its citizens sooner than later. Meghalaya, a state similar to Mizoram in more ways than one, can find in that state a trailblazer in the fight against illiteracy and ignorance. The success of Meghalaya's tryst with the letters is a story that needs to be told because its leap from 49.10 per cent literacy rate of 1991 to 63.31 per cent in 2001 (14.21% increase) was no mean achievement. The National Sample Survey of 1997 had even projected that Meghalaya's literacy rate had surged to 77 per cent, marking a 27 per cent increase. Though this projection was proved wrong in the 2001 census, Meghalaya's march towards total literacy is sure and steady.

Below, I dwell on a brief account of the TLCs in the six districts of Meghalaya where the programme had been set in motion. This has been made possible by the concurrent evaluations of the TLC programmes in these districts.

Ri-Bhoi District

Ri-Bhoi was the first district in Meghalaya to launch the TLC in 1995. The people of the district are known as Bhoi. Though they are Khasis, the dialect they speak "ktien Bhoi", is a variant of Khasi. A concurrent evaluation of the TLC in this district was undertaken by the SRC, NEHU by the end of 1997 with the aim of finding out the effectiveness of the organizational structure of the Zila Saksharta Samiti and people's committees, to check the involvement of the community and to evaluate the literacy skills of the learners as per prescribed norms.

The evaluation found that on an average, the learners in Ri-Bhoi district scored more than 86 per cent marks. The Raitong Circle registered the best performance and the Lailad Circle the worst. The campaign had been especially successful in places like Nongpoh, Bhoirymbong, Tyrso, Umsohlait and Mawhati. In some places illiterate members of minority communities and immigrant labourers joined the campaign enthusiastically and learned the Khasi language to become literate. So the TLC helped in bringing scattered communities together. The TLC has urged the people of the Ri-Bhoi district to think in line with the development and progress. The campaign raised hopes for the underprivileged and the village headmen began to behave in a more responsible manner.

The programme was not without its share of bottlenecks. Inaccessibility of certain areas was a major problem. Moreover, in some cases, resource persons who had registered as volunteers, began to demand pay. Non-adherence to the prescribed norms in preparing TLC handbooks impeded the progress of the learners. Frequent change of the Chairman of the Literacy Society was also a problem in Ri-Bhoi.

According to 2001 census provisional figures, Ri-Bhoi district registered a huge leap in literacy rate from 39.93 (43.88 males and 35.73 females) in 1991 to 66.07 (69.22 males and 62.67 females) in 2001. In 1991 Ri-Bhoi district stood fifth among the seven districts of Meghalaya in literacy rates. In 2001 it stands second. Hence, TLC in Ri-Bhoi has proved to be a successful campaign. The stage is now ripe for launching a post-literacy project in the district so that the learners may not lapse into illiteracy. Intensive training of those who could not reach the NLM norms is required. Implementing post-literacy strategy for the neo-literates will assist them not only in keep up fire of learning but also in learning skills like weaving, wood carving, cane work, carpentry etc. These income-generating skills will enhance the earning capacity of the neo-literates.

Jiantia Hills District

Jiantia Hills was the second district in Meghalaya to launch the TLC in September 1995. In fact, this district deserved the campaign more than any other in Meghalaya, as it had the lowest literacy rate in the state as per the 1991 census report. Though the Jaintias/Pnars are ethnically of the same stock as the Khasis, the Pnar dialect is a variant of Khasi. In 1998 SRC, NEHU conducted a concurrent evaluation of the TLC in this district with the objective of getting to know the effectiveness of the organizational structure of TLC, the involvement of the community and the literacy skills of the new learners.

The evaluation report says that, overall there is a significant improvement in the literacy skills of the learners who were at the initial stage of TLC in 1998. They scored at an average of 89 and 78 marks for the march ahead levels I and II respectively in the four blocks of the district, namely, Amlarem, Khliehriat, Laskein and Thadlaskein. Significantly, the Khliehriat block which had the lowest literacy percentage in the whole of Meghalaya, participated most enthusiastically in the campaign.

On account of socio-economic diversities and geographical variations, the district authorities could not implement the TLC uniformly in the district. So, some remote areas fared badly. Since the TLC is a mass movement, the success of the programme was due to the environment that was created by the district administration. SRC's role as the agency for supplying academic and technical support to the campaign, cannot be denied here.

The evaluation suggested that more thrust needs to be given to numerical abilities, since its helps people in the ordinary businesses of living. Another suggestion was to start the post-literacy phase since more than 77 learners had passed out of the TLC. Unfortunately till today neither the post-literacy project nor the CEC project has been launched in the state. It is a point for everyone, especially policy-makers and government authorities in Meghalaya to think about.

The provisional literacy figures of 2001 Census of India shows the success of TLC in Jaintia district. In 1991, Jaintia Hills stood last in the literacy ladder of the state with only 35.32 per cent literacy rate (34.37% males and 36.31% females). The new Census report shows that Jaintia Hills has overtaken West Garo Hills district (51.03%) with 53.00 per cent literacy (50.52% males and 55.54% females). One thing that needs to be noted here is that Jaintia Hills is the only district in India, which has higher female literacy rate than that of men. It is the first district ever in the history of India to register this phenomenon for the first time in 2001.

The commencing of post-literacy project in Jaintia Hills will be proved important in sustaining the enthusiasm of the people in this district, which has poor literacy rate even now after a successful TLC programme. One of the greatest dangers of slowing down the pace is the waning of ardour among both the learners and the volunteers.

East Garo Hill

In East Garo Hills district, the TLC was launched in 1997. At the time, when the campaign was launched the district stood third in the literacy ladder behind East Khasi Hills district and West Khasi Hills district. Its literacy rate then was 48.36 (54.70 among males and 41.70 among females). Today, after the launching of the campaign, the literacy rate of the district stands at 61.70 (67.39 for males and 55.74 for females). Though there was more than 10 per cent increase in the literacy rate, now the district is behind East Khasi Hills district, Ri-Bhoi district and West Khasi Hills district.

Many reasons have been pointed out regarding the tardy progress of the campaign in this district. The district is still backward in terms of road and other types of communication network. This makes the campaign very difficult in the district. Problems like insurgency, lack of volunteers, the difficult topography of the district and the remoteness of the area — all contribute to the difficulties of the programme. In fact, the TLC has practically died a natural and unceremonious death in the district. The Development of Women and Children in Rural Areas Programme, the Diocesan Board of Education and the Church's Auxiliary for School Action have promised to be the backbone of the literacy programme of the district. Still East Garo Hills is the most literate district of the Garo hills, and has the prospective of becoming a totally literate district with an enthusiastic TLC. The campaign in this district was the one, which promised much cease without a whimper.

East Khasi Hills

East Khasi Hills has been the most literate district in Meghalaya ever since the advent of letters to these hills. This is no wonder since Shillong, the erstwhile capital of the British in the North East, later of the undivided Assam state and now of Meghalaya, is located in this district. Literacy rate in this district now is 76.98 per cent (males 78.12 and females 75.82). In 1991 it was only 64.58 per cent. The TLC was launched in the state in order to reach out to the rural areas outside Shillong and also to those pockets of Shillong, where many people still remain illiterate. The challenging task of formulating and executing the TLC project in this district was done by the District Literacy Society. The project was launched on January l, 1997 with the aim of eradicating illiteracy and making the 1.53 lakhs illiterates of the district in the

9-35 age group, in the span of 18 months. TLC in East Khasi Hills district aimed at achieving the goals through community participation at all levels of the action plan, mass-mobilisation through multimedia like pamphlets, songs, banners, street play, yatra and publicity through the press, radio and television, strong and decentralised organizational set up of the District Literacy Society and involvement of voluntary as well as social work organizations and persons.

In August 1999 the SRC, NEHU conducted a concurrent evaluation of the TLC in the district. The objectives of this evaluation were to describe the geographical as well as socio-economic background of the district, to assess community participation in the TLC, to analyse the literacy skills of the neo-literates and to identify weak pockets of the district where the campaign has not taken root.

The evaluation report observes that there are wide variations in the socio-economic as well as physiographic conditions of the district. Hence, the District Literacy Society could not implement the project uniformly and thus could not reach out to some remote pockets of the district. However, the district organisation has created a good environment for the programme and awareness level among the people has sharply risen. The test of the learners' proficiency has shown that the learners' writing and numeracy skill at Level-I is far better developed than that of the Level-II. Overall, the learning pace and standard has been found satisfactory. The impact of urbanisation is evident on the implementation of the TLC in this district. It may be also mentioned that variations of the extent of implementation is due to weak infrastructure. There are pockets of grossly underdeveloped areas even in this comparatively advanced district with no drinking water, electricity or road connections. Women seemed to have more interested in the campaign in spite of their pre-occupations with the household. While Mawphlang and Mawsynram blocks topped in performance, Mawryngkneng block lagged behind. The functional part of the literacy movement was found to be good since more 80 per cent neo-literates were well-aware of social development, health realities, family planning etc. This means that they have made practical use of their new knowledge.

The evaluation recommended that infrastructural facilities, particularly electrification in remote areas, should be improved and that emphasis on numeracy skills should be greater. It was also suggested that the situation in East Khasi Hills is more than ripe for the launching of post-literacy project and thereafter CECs. Post-literacy programmes, the evaluation team noted, should give greater emphasis on women related matters like maternal and child care, since women have shown greater interest in the programme.

West Garo Hills

In this district, the TLC was launched in the year 2000. The biggest town of the Garo Hills, Tura is situated in this district, but it does not play that role which Shillong plays as the lighthouse of learning and letters in East Khasi Hills district. In fact, this district is the last in the literacy list of Meghalaya state with nearly half of its population still remaining illiterate. The literacy rate of the district according to the 2001 provisional Census report was 51.03 (57.51 for males and 44.51 for females). The Jaintia Hills district was behind West Garo Hills district in 1991, when this district's literacy rate was 38.64 (46.10 for males and 30.81 for females). The difference has been the TLC. While a moving and dynamic TLC has been behind the success of Jaintia Hills, the campaign of West Khasi Hills district observed ups and downs. In fact, after its inception in 2000, the TLC was nearly inactive for about two years. Fortunately the campaign has been revived there towards the end of 2001 and it is now becoming vibrant. Eight blocks of the district has TLC centres totalling 528 catering to 1103 villages, when reports last came in May 2002.

South Garo Hills

Since this is a new district, the TLC is yet to be launched here. The South Garo Hills district has a literacy rate of 55.82 (62.60 for men and 48.61 for women). Presently this district stands fifth in the literacy ladder of Meghalaya, and since nearly 44 per cent of its population is still illiterate, the campaign needs to take root here in order to dispel the darkness of ignorance from among its peoples. In short, South and East Garo Hills district need a revival of the TLC at the earliest.

VI

What lessons do we learn from the TLC in Meghalaya? What roads need we take in the future? What mistakes need we correct? Such questions need to be addressed when we look towards the future in the perspective of such a vital campaign as the TLC.

Literacy as a vital skill is a person's window to the world. The miracle of education, however marginal it is going to be, in a person's life is tremendous. Research studies consistently show that educated parents tend to send their children to school and make sure that they do not drop out. Death rate of infants among educated mothers is consistently lower in comparison. They tend to vaccinate their children on time. They understand the logic of a small family. They are better aware of their social and legal rights. Income generation somehow comes easier to them. They tend to tide over the whirlpool of poverty. We don't need to look for proofs far off: the first human development report of our country, which was made public recently shows that the most literate state (Kerala) of the nation also tops the human development chart.

The TLC in Meghalaya has also borne witness to these facts. The campaign attracted a lot of public attention and people even in the far off villages began to see the need for education and literacy. We must say that the campaign has contributed valiantly to booming literacy rates. Wherever the campaign was alive, it left a mark on literacy figures of the 2001 Census. While there was nearly 10 per cent increase in literacy rate during the decade 1981-91, there was about 13 per cent increase during the period 1991-2001. Increase in school enrolment levels also has been noticed among areas that took the TLC seriously. The success of Jaintia Hills in overtaking both South and West Garo Hills districts in the literacy chart in the 2001 census should be solely credited to the TLC campaign. There have been instances where non-tribal labourers from outside Meghalaya picked up the Khasi language as a lingua franca during the campaign. Functional literacy as a tool to improve one's life situation has come to be accepted in most of the areas where the campaign took root. For instance, elders came to understand the importance of their children's education. Most of them have begun to think seriously about sending the children to school despite all odds.

Despite the many glories of the TLC in Meghalaya, it is doubtful if ever the campaign became a mass movement in this state unlike the original campaign inspiration of Ernakulam district in Kerala. Reasons for this are not hard to find. First of all, volunteers were hard to come by. TLC being a volunteer-based movement, without the driving force of committed people the campaign could never become 'total' and contagious. Many volunteers in Meghalaya dropped out as time passed; many expected remuneration of some kind, though it was clearly spelt out that no remuneration would be permissible. Without payment, many lost enthusiasm—many volunteers just faded into oblivion. Secondly, the soul of the campaign in other parts of the country were some very dedicated NGOs. This aspect too did not come strongly enough in Meghalaya to leave stamp on the general public. Some NGOs did come up, but none of them made it full-time agenda. Imparting of literacy was just one among their many activities. It is also true that charismatic NGOs are few in the state to champion such unrewarding causes, at least monetarily.

All said and done, the campaign did not become a mass movement in the state of Meghalaya. Probably environment building was not done or not done enough. There were also other practical bottlenecks like the frequent transfer of DCs. Without steady and committed leadership, the programme was doomed to fail.

Conclusion

The TLC aimed at raising Indian literacy from 52 per cent in 1991 to 75 per cent in 2001. This has not been achieved. Hence, what we see in Meghalaya is not a case in isolation, but a case in point in many Indian states. However, in comparison with most other regions of the country, the North East is better placed in the literacy scenario. But there is also wide disparity among the North-eastern states. Three North-eastern states—Meghalaya, Assam and Arunachal Pradesh—are still behind the national average of 65.37. Hence, an all-out effort is necessary to make the region totally literate. Literacy is a fundamental human right and the very foundation for a learning society. Eradication of illiteracy is the noble duty of every right thinking citizen. Now is the time to take a pledge to eradicate illiteracy when we have just stepped in to another millennium, where unimaginable progress is taking place on all fronts. It is a gift to humanity when everyone will be able to read, write and know the great feats of human advancement and knowledge in general.

27

Rural Education in the 21st Century North East India

A Case Study of Nongtalang Village, Meghalaya

SHYAMADAS BHATTACHARYYA

The vast multitudes of Indian population, (nearly 80 per cent of the total population of India), live in villages. But in the Colonial system of education devised by the British, there was no room for mass education or rural education. Gandhiji shouted for rural education and evolved his scheme of basic education through the medium of a craft closely related with people's occupation. He also gave a trial of basic education in his Sabarmati Ashram. Rabindranath Tagore set an example of rural education by establishing a school in the village of Santiniketan, which ultimately grew to be the celebrated Viswa Bharati University with its Institution for rural reconstruction at Sree-niketan. But the foreign government liked to shut its eyes to the crying needs of rural education in India. They were happy with their narrow aim of producing English knowing clerks for running their administration. The first Indian Education Commission after Independence (1948-49), headed by Dr. S. Radhakrishnan, therefore, took up the case of rural education and gave it topmost priority. To provide a scientific basis for rural, industry, crafts and agriculture, based on local conditions, it strongly pleaded for a rural University, which would produce trained and specialised manpower from the students of the villages so long neglected. Commissions after commissions followed since then, national education policy was declared with much drum beats. But even after 55 years of Independence, the picture of rural education in India is far from satisfactory.

There is, however, some improvement in states like West Bengal, Kerala, Tamil Nadu, Punjab, Harayana after the introduction of Panchayati Raj, which was also due to individual efforts of patriotic educationists as well as philanthropic organisations dedicated to the cause of rural education.

In North East India, we face different issues, problems and challenges. The author of this paper served the cause of education in an urban centre like Shillong for long 30 years with good liaison with North-Eastern Hill University and then went to build a college in a remote village of War-Jaintia area bordering Bangladesh. His findings, observations and conclusions reflected in this paper are essentially based on his fieldwork at the grassroots level as Principal of Nongtalang College.

Nearly 90 per cent of the total population of tribals live in the villages of the hill states of North East India. Meghalaya is no exception. With the advent of the 21st century we are confronted with a curious paradox in the educational scenario, bringing a short division, hitherto un-noticed, in cities and villages. It is amazing to notice that although 10 per cent of the total population live in urban centres, that have grown up after Independence, nearly 90 per cent of the allotted fund on education is being spent on them. This is because of the fact that those who hold power and authority live in the city. Different pressure groups, political parties, high officials, traders and businessmen — mostly are here. The result is that, all that we see as modern trends and practices in education due to intensive application of science and technology, are in fact the monopoly of urban areas where the rich and affluent class predominate. The electronic media, computers, internet system, cyber space and what not, are being used to meet the aspirations of the urban students where guardians can afford such education. Education for them, is undoubtedly the "best investment", "Invest more and earn more"—is their motto of life.

Our elitist system of education, I emphasise, is not suitable for hill tribal villages. Our education policy is mooted at Delhi with no consideration for the particular local genius of the tribal people. We have uniform system of educational pattern, which does not cater to the psychological basic needs of our tribal brethren. But who cares for the poor and downtrodden tribals living in villages? It is said that a tradition-bound tribal society is slow to change. But I have seen that the attitude of the authorities at the helm of education are far harder to change. They still scaff at the idea of rural education. Their ignorance about the actual situation prevailing in tribal villages is appalling.

The author was invited as a resource person to attend a workshop on reform of examination system. It was organised by Meghalaya Board of School Education, Tura. The Chief-Guest was Director of N.C.E.R.T, from Delhi who gave an illuminating talk on future of education in the 21st century, holding up a rosy picture when the whole system of education would be computerised bringing explosion and expansion of knowledge. When my turn to speak came, I told without hesitation, "Sir, I come from a remote village called Nongtalang which remains dark during the long rainy season of six months. You are speaking about the computerization of education. But at Nongtalang good teachers do not get even blackboards to write on and even if they get, those are not workable. The only teaching aid that we have in such villages is the strong vocal chord that a teacher possesses. On another occasion, an additional D.P.I. whom I took to Nongtalang for college inspection, told me later, "You gave me backache." I quipped "how". He said that due to jerking of the jeep all along the rough and uneven road, to Nongtalang and back, he could not sit comfortably and hence the backache. Even the D.P.I., the highest authority of college education, being annoyed with the frequent approach for ad hoc grant, frowned upon the wretched principal and told him "when are you leaving Nongtalang?" I said, "As soon as you give the grant". He smiled at my answer, "You are an unrelenting person, but look, how can you expect grant for a college in an area where the people are illiterate, where there is no scope for growth of industries and no scope for future development. Moreover, your college is no college at all. It has shabby rooms, broken wet walls and there is also not adequate number of lecturers to teach. First, have a good building, recruit more teachers, fulfil all conditions, and then come for grant.

The D.P.I. was right in his own way. Here lies the crux of the problem. The village is populated by the labour class of Jaintia people who live from hand to mouth. Their means of sustenance are pan leaves and arecanuts, which are seasonal. Most of them work in jungles and hilly slopes. They also work in orange orchards whose owners are rich and live in Jowai or Shillong. The town dwellers come once in a blue moon to taste the niceties of rural life. The poor villagers can hardly spare something for building a fund for the college. But they have aspirations for higher education. That is how the college came.

It may be mentioned here that the foundation of the Nongtalang college took place in 1988 with Chief Minister Purno A. Sangma laying the foundation stone. The poor villagers accumulated what they could from their hard earned income. They themselves donated land through the Durbar Snong and erected an Assam Type building with tin roof to house the college. It is a common knowledge that every institution during its humble beginning requires the dedicated services of some teachers and staff for its running. But the unemployed months with Post-Graduate degrees from Shillong or Jowai were unwilling to go to a remote village and serve the college with the paltry amount of money, the college could afford. In such villages part-timers are also not available as a stop-gap arrangement. The government conditions desire a full-fledged principal with minimum ten years experience of teaching in any affiliated college. But who will go there to face all hardships of hazardous life without being assured of a comfortable salary. The government will not step forward to help a college unless it fulfils its conditions, which means huge financial involvement and the villagers have not the capacity to bear the financial burden for fulfilling the conditions, although they desired that their sons and daughters must go for higher education.

Incidentally, it may be mentioned that Nongtalang is an ideal village for location of a college. The whole Amlarem sub-division covering the entire Southern Jaintia Hills does not possess a single college. The village has 8 (eight) primary schools and one Government High School. It has eight feeder High Schools and one Government Higher Secondary school in the adjoining areas. Moreover, being located in the border area, from the strategic point of view also, it is necessary that the people should have higher education for intelligently dealing with the special problems of trade and defence in border. But the government was unwilling to go for higher education in War-Jaintia area.

However, the North-Eastern Hill University was quick to realise the problem. It granted provisional affiliation and allowed an Examination Centre. Good senses prevailed afterwards in the Education Department also, and at the end of 2000 the college was brought under the Adhoc Grant-in-aid Scheme of the government to the great relief of the old principal, who bade a die with his sick health with full satisfaction yielding place to the new principal and staff members who are now enjoying government pay scales.

But before I conclude my paper, I must say that in general, the standard of education in the Nongtalang village, from Primary to School education, is very low. This is because of the fact that the curriculum is not need based and does not suit local interests and requirements. The medium of instruction at the primary level is Khasi but the mother-tongue of the local children is War-Jaintia, which is a dialect variety of Khasi language. After learning Khasi, which is rendered in English alphabets, they find difficulty in learning English because Khasi phonetics learnt with so much strain comes to clash with English pronunciation with the result that they falter at every stage of learning English. There is also dearth of good English teacher in high school. With poor background of English language they can neither understand what is written in text books, nor can express their thoughts in English. Moreover, most of the students are first generation learners who do not get the help they need from their parents who are illiterates. Under these circumstances, they drop out either at primary level or in the Secondary stage. The cases of drop outs are more pronounced among the boys than among the girls because of discrimination among boys and girls under the matrilineal system binding the War-Jaintia tribals. There is no agency to work for the drop-outs who after few years lapse into illiteracy and swell the number of illiterates. The lack of a proper and special scheme account for the poverty of the villagers who live with their traditional primitive economy, sunk in ignorance and superstition.

This paper, therefore, makes a strong plea for immediate attention to this much neglected area and removal of this great educational imbalance by developing, on a priority basis, human resources of rural areas, through need-based vocational education, which will take care of hill agriculture, environment, forestry, small scale cottage industries, local crafts, horticulture, poultry, pig-rearing, health, hygiene and nutrition, making infrastructure for marketing facilities and trade in border areas. Education must make each tribal village a self-sufficient unit.

28

Literacy Status in Meghalaya
Level Study

BILORIS LYNDEM & PREMALATA DEVI

Introduction

Meghalaya the 21st state of India, emerged as a full-fledged state on 21st January, 1972. The total population of the state is 23,06,069 with 11,67,840 males and 11,38,229 females. The decadal population growth rate between 1991-2001 census has been found to be 29.94 per cent against the all-India growth rate of 21.34 per cent. The density of population in the state is 103 per sq.km. After 30 years of statehood Meghalaya's rank in literacy rate becomes 27th among 35 states and Union territories of India.

Though the present literacy rate of Meghalaya comparatively satisfactory (63.31 in 2001), still it is below the national average (65.38 per cent). Subtracting the segment of population below seven years (4.5 lakh), the illiterate population in Meghalaya comes upto 11.4 lakh, whereas only 11.7 lakh are literate. The decadal growth rate of literacy during 1991-2001 is only +14.21 per cent. Though a substantial increase in literacy rate of Meghalaya is observed during the last decade, its position in terms of literacy rate within the seven states of North-Eastern Region becomes sixth.

The sex ratio of Meghalaya, which is 975 females per 1000 males in 2001 census is much higher than all India figure of 933. The literacy rate of women in Meghalaya is (60.41%) much lower than that of men (66.14%) as per the 2001 census of India. It seems that females are yet to participate fully in all spheres of life. The literacy scene of all seven districts of Meghalaya is as follows: East Khasi Hills shows highest literacy rate, *i.e.* 74.74 per cent, while West Garo Hills shows as low as 50.78 per cent. The literacy rate of Jaintia Hills is 52.79 per cent, 63.67 per cent in Ri-Bhoi, 65.50 per cent in West Khasi Hills, 61.57 per cent in East Garo Hills and 55.21 per cent in South Garo Hills..

The comparative statement of literacy rates between Meghalaya and India indicates that the literacy rate of Meghalaya remain the national average since 1971 (Table 28.1).

Table 28.1: Comparative Statement of Literacy status of Meghalaya and India, 1971-2001

Sl. No.	*Year*	*Literacy rate of Meghalaya*	*India*
1.	1971	29.45	36.45
2.	1981	34.08	43.64*
3.	1991	49.10	52.21**
4.	2001	63.31	65.38

* 1981 Census was not held in Assam.
** Excluding Jammu and Kashmir.
Source: Census of India 1971, 1981, 1991 (Final), 2001 (Provisional).

District Level Literacy Scenario of Meghalaya

The state comprises of seven districts, namely : East Khasi Hills, West Khasi Hills, Ri-Bhoi district, Jaintia Hills, East Garo Hills, West Garo Hills and South Garo Hills district. Among all seven districts of Meghalaya the literacy rate is highest in East Khasi Hills district (74.74%) on the other hand the West Garo Hills district shows the lowest (50.78%) literacy rate in the state.(Map 28.1).

During the last three decades the literacy rate of East Khasi Hills district has increased by 41.41 per cent. While in Ri-Bhoi district it has increased by 39.88 per cent, West Khasi Hills district by 38.29 per cent and Jaintia Hills by 32.88 per cent. On the other hand, among the three Garo Hills districts, East Garo Hills district has recorded increase in literary rate by 31.43 per cent, West Garo Hills district by 29.43 per cent and South Garo Hills district by 25.96 per cent respectively (Table 28.2). The census data of 2001 indicates that male literacy rate in the state as well as in all seven districts of Meghalaya is higher than the female literacy. But it is exceptional in 1991 that Jaintia Hills district had more female literacy (36.31%) than male literacy (34.37%).

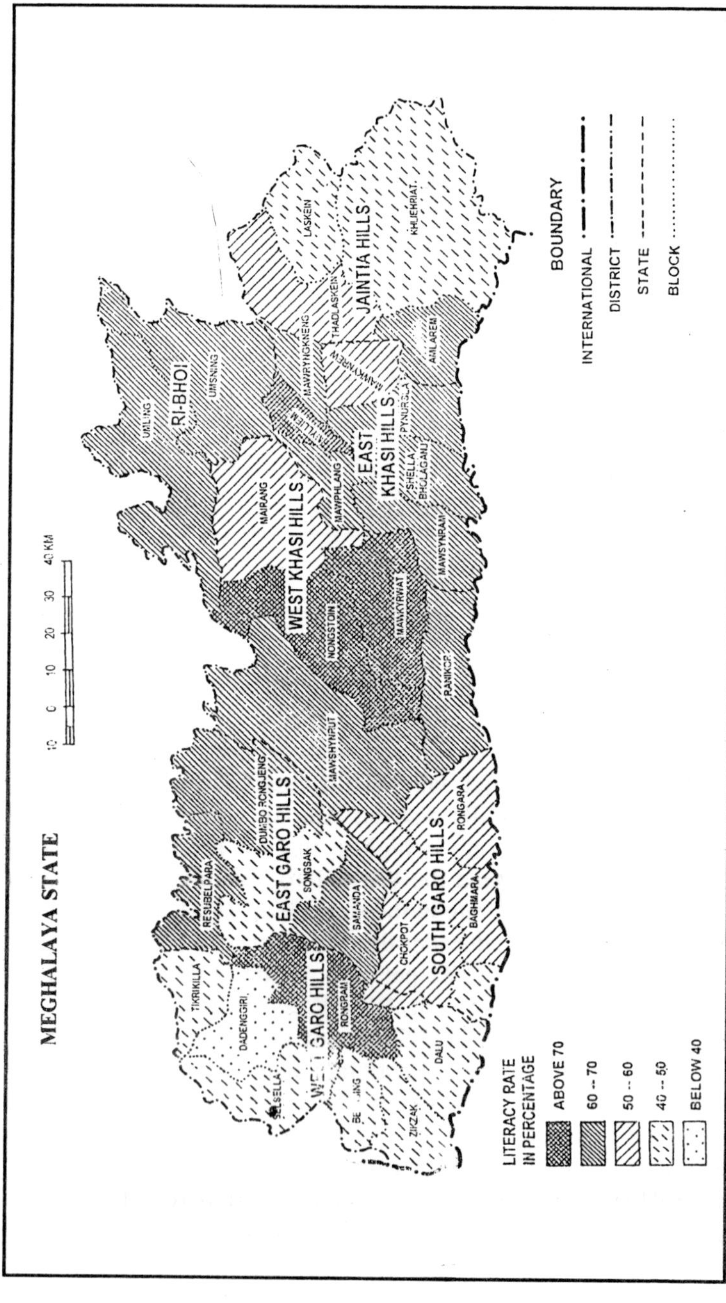

Map 28.1: Literacy Rate of Meghalaya, 2001 (Block-wise)

Table 28.2: Literacy levels and Decadal growth rate of Meghalaya, 1971-2001 (Provisional)

Sl. No.	*Country/State/Districts*	*Year*	*Literacy %*	*Decadal Growth rate*		
				1971-1981	1981-1991	1991-2001
	India	1971	36.45			
		1981	43.67	7.22	8.54	13.17
		1991	52.21			
		2001	65.38			
	Meghalaya	1971	29.45			
		1981	34.08	4.59	15.02	14.21
		1991	49.10			
		2001	63.31			
1.	East Khasi Hills District	1971	33.33			
		1981	43.72	10.39	20.85	10.17
		1991	64.57			
		2001	74.74			
2.	West Khasi Hills District	1971	27.21			
		1981	31.96	4.75	18.56	14.98
		1991	50.52			
		2001	65.50			
3.	Ri-Bhoi District	1971	23.79			
		1981	28.11	4.32	11.81	23.75
		1991	39.92			
		2001	63.37			
4.	Jaintia Hills District	1971	19.91			
		1981	24.50	4.59	10.82	17.47
		1991	35.32			
		2001	52.79			
5.	East Garo Hills District	1971	30.14			
		1981	33.51	3.36	14.86	13.21
		1991	48.36			
		2001	61.78			
6.	West Garo Hills District	1971	21.35			
		1981	25.91	3.56	12.73	12.14
		1991	38.64			
		2001	50.78			
7.	South Garo Hills District	1971	29.25			
		1981	26.82	–2.43	16.06	13.33
		1991	42.88			
		2001	55.21			

Source: Census of India 1971, 1981, 1991 and 2001 (Provisional).

Block Level Literacy Scenario of Meghalaya

The State Meghalaya comprises of 32 Community Development Blocks. Table 28.3 indicates that, out of 32 C.D. Blocks seven C.D. Blocks shows higher female literacy rates. They are Mawphlang (63.31% - 66.61%), Mawryngkneng (58.81% - 67.87%). Mawkynrew (48.39% - 57.89%) of East Khasi Hills district; Thadlaskein (53.47% - 64.00%), Laskein (36.77% - 47.63%) and Amlarem (65.60% - 67.00%) blocks of Jaintia Hills district and Mairang C.D. Block (58.11% - 61.43%) of West Khasi Hills district. These high female literate blocks proves the matriarchal strength in education in the matriarchal state Meghalaya. The block level study also clearly signifies that, out of 32 C.D. Blocks literacy rates of 21 C.D. Blocks are below the state average.

Analysis of Seven Districts with Different Blocks (1991-2001)

East Khasi Hills District

The total literacy rate of East Khasi Hills district has increased from 64.57 per cent (1991) to 74.74 per cent (2001) with male 74.89 per cent and female 74.58 per cent. In the three blocks of this district, Mawphlang, Mawryngkneng and Mawkynrew the literacy level is higher in case of female than male. Mylliem block has the highest literates of 82.18 per cent, where male and female literary rates are 83.11 per cent and 81.23 per cent respectively.

West Khasi Hills District

West Khasi Hills district comprises five Community Development Blocks, where only in one block, Mairang shows higher female literacy rate than males. Out of five blocks the literacy level of two blocks, Nongstoin and Mawkyrwat crossed the National level literacy rate by 5.49 per cent and 5.93 per cent.

Ri-Bhoi District

Ri-Bhoi district is a newly created district of the state with two blocks, i.e. Umsning and Umling. Its literacy rate is 63.67 per cent, it is a plain area where other tribes and non-tribes also inhabitate. The first Total Literacy Campaign (TLC) was launched in this district of the

Table 28.3: Comparative Analysis of Literacy Rate in seven districts with different Blocks, 1991-2001

	State/District/Block	*1991*			*2001*		
		Total	*Males*	*Females*	*Total*	*Males*	*Females*
	India	52.21	64.13	39.29	65.38	75.85	54.46
	Meghalaya	49.10	53.12	44.85	63.31	66.14	60.41
I.	*East Khasi Hills*	64.57	67.13	61.86	74.74	74.89	74.58
1.	Mawphlang	41.00	40.38	41.61	64.98	63.31	66.61
2.	Mylliem	78.88	82.59	75.78	82.18	83.11	81.23
3.	Mawryngkneng	44.71	41.21	48.19	63.36	58.81	67.87
4.	Mawkynrew	36.63	35.33	37.95	53.16	48.39	57.89
5.	Mawsynram	45.90	48.91	42.77	65.44	68.06	62.93
6.	Shella Bholaganj	54.04	55.86	52.24	69.45	70.25	68.63
7.	Pynursla	49.77	50.57	48.96	66.67	66.37	66.96
II.	*West Khasi Hills*	50.52	52.98	47.94	65.50	66.74	64.21
8.	Mawshynrut	53.21	59.06	66.97	61.84	65.73	57.77
9.	Nongstoin	49.32	52.44	46.01	70.87	72.25	69.45
10.	Mairang	48.05	47.07	49.00	59.75	58.11	61.43
11.	Ranikor	*	*	*	63.30	67.64	58.59
12.	Mawkyrwat	52.65	55.66	49.46	71.31	73.11	71.51
III.	*Ri-Bhoi Distɩ ict*	39.92	43.88	35.72	63.67	65.77	61.40
13.	Umling	40.98	43.56	38.29	65.49	71.02	59.60
14.	Umsning	38.35	44.33	31.81	62.44	62.26	62.44
IV.	*Jaintia Hills*	35.32	34.37	36.31	52.79	56.13	55.52
15.	Thadlaskein	42.15	40.96	43.32	58.66	53.47	64.00
16.	Laskein	30.35	25.89	37.74	42.21	36.77	47.63
17.	Amlarem	40.80	41.48	40.09	66.29	65.60	67.00
18.	Khliehriat	28.06	29.30	26.66	48.31	49.49	47.07
V.	*East Garo Hills*	48.36	57.70	41.70	61.57	67.17	55.72
19.	Resubelpara	55.85	61.09	50.33	67.89	74.12	61.48
20.	Dumbo Rongjeng	47.86	54.60	40.83	61.10	65.86	56.06
21.	Songsak	34.85	41.36	28.01	45.70	52.22	38.93
22.	Samanda	46.96	54.61	38.51	64.66	69.65	59.39
VI.	*West Garo Hills*	38.64	46.10	30.81	50.78	57.12	44.41
23.	Betasing	35.39	43.14	27.50	48.93	51.41	46.39
24.	Dalu	36.62	44.36	28.55	49.25	54.85	43.40
25.	Selsella	29.17	36.25	21.82	42.35	48.37	36.26
26.	Dadenggiri	30.41	38.16	22.42	30.71	37.53	23.88
27.	Tikrikilla	*	*	*	46.57	54.20	38.92
28.	Rongram	49.96	66.30	53.04	71.95	80.49	63.82
29.	Zikzak	33.98	42.33	25.14	46.09	53.53	38.34
VII.	*South Garo Hills*	42.88	51.28	34.02	55.21	61.42	48.61
30.	Chokpot	36.83	44.13	29.37	52.64	58.83	46.31
31.	Baghmara	49.36	58.36	49.04	57.05	63.11	56.39
32.	Rongara	39.95	49.34	30.00	55.65	62.12	48.80

*Blocks that were not in existence in 1991.

Source : Census of India 1991 and 2001 (Provisional).

state in 1996, which was inaugurated by the honourable Late Minister Madhav Rao Scindia.

Jaintia Hills District

Jaintia Hills District also shows an important character of high females' literacy rate. Except Khliehriat, the other three blocks Thadlaskein (53.47 Male, 64.00 Female), Laskein (37.66 Male, 47.63 Female) and Amalarem (65.60 Male, 67.00 Female) show higher female literacy than the male.

East Garo Hills

In the East Garo Hills district most critical situation is observed in the Songsak block, where the literacy rate is as low as 45.70 per cent, the female literacy rate is only 38.93 and male is 52.22 per cent as per 2001 census report. It proves that females require more attention in this district for the improvement of their literary.

West Garo Hills

The literacy rate in West Garo Hills is 50.78 per cent (2001). It comprises seven blocks. Out of these, in six blocks the female literacy rate is very low, exceptionally the Rongram block has achieved 63.82 per cent female and 80.49 per cent male literate.

South Garo Hills

It is a new district of Meghalaya, where 55.21 per cent people are literate with 61.42 per cent males and 48.61 per cent females. The district has three blocks, where there is big difference between male and female literacy rate. Comparatively the literacy rate has increased by 12.33 per cent during the last decade.

Male-Female Literacy differences between the Last Decade (1991-2001)

The differences of male and female literacy rate in 1991 and 2001 in percentage is shown in Table 28.4. It is remarkable that out of 32 Community Development Blocks, Dadenggiri Block of West Garo Hills

Table 28.4: Male-Female Literacy Differentials Percentage between 1991 and 2001 of Meghalaya

	Country/State/District/Block	*1991 – 2001 (in Percentage)*	
		Males	*Females*
	India	+11.27	+15.17
	Meghalaya	+13.02	+15.17
I.	*East Khasi Hills District*	+07.76	+12.72
1.	Mawphlang	+22.93	+25.00
2.	Mylliem	+ 0.52	+05.45
3.	Mawryngkneng	+17.60	+19.68
4.	Mawkynrew	+13.06	+19.94
5.	Mawsynram	+19.15	+20.16
6.	Shella Bholaganj	+14.39	+16.39
7.	Punursla	+15.80	+18.00
II.	*West Khasi Hills District*	+13.76	+16.27
8.	Mawshynrut	+06.67	–09.02
9.	Nongstoin	+19.81	+23.44
10.	Mairang	+11.04	+12.43
11.	Ranikor	*67.64 (2001)	*58.59 (2001)
12.	Mawkyrwat	+17.45	+22.05
III.	*Ri-Bhoi District*	+21.89	+25.68
13.	Umling	+27.46	+21.31
14.	Umsning	+17.93	+30.83
IV.	*Jaintia Hills District*	+21.76	+19.21
15.	Thadlaskein	+12.51	+20.68
16.	Laskein	+10.88	+09.89
17.	Amlarem	+24.12	+26.91
18.	Khliehriat	+20.19	+20.41
V.	*East Garo Hills District*	+12.47	+14.02
19.	Resubelpara	+13.03	+11.15
20.	Dumbo Rongjeng	+11.26	+15.23
21.	Songsak	+10.86	+10.92
22.	Samanda	+15.04	+20.88
VI.	*West Garo Hills*	+11.02	+13.06
23.	Betasing	+08.27	+18.89
24.	Dalu	+10.49	+14.85
25.	Selsella	+12.12	+14.44
26.	Dadengiri	– 0.63	+01.46
27.	Tikrikilla	*54.20 (2001)	*38.92 (2001)
28.	Rongram	+14.19	+10.78
29.	Zikzak	+11.02	+13.02
VII.	*South Garo Hills District*	+10.14	+14.59
30.	Chokpot	+14.07	+16.94
31.	Baghmara	+04.75	+07.35
32.	Rongara	+12.78	+18.08

*Blocks that were not in existence in 1991.

District, shows decline in male literacy rate by 0.63 per cent from 1991 to 2001. On the other hand, Mawshynrut C.D. Block of West Khasi Hills district shows the decrease in female literacy rate by 9.2 per cent during the last decade.

Conclusion and Suggestions

The census data of 2001 (Provisional) indicates that male literacy rate in Meghalaya is higher than the female literacy rate. Though the present literacy rate of Meghalaya comparatively satisfactory (63.31% in 2001), still it is below the national average (65.38%). After 30 years of statehood (in 1972), Meghalaya's rank in terms of literacy become 27th among all states and Union territories of India. If we consider the seven states of North-Eastern Region, the position of literacy rate of Meghalaya becomes sixth. The reason behind the low literacy rate in the state may be the lack of awareness of parents towards education and low economic status. It is found that the average family size is more than seven and the children in general help the parents at work and also to take care of the young ones at home. Children are engaged in coal mines, lime stone quarrying cement factory, cutting stones along with their parents. Along with this, they also do a lot of household work like fetching waters, collecting firewood, washing cloths and others and cause low enrolment in school. At this juncture parents are to be made aware that children age between 6 and 14 is to attend the Primary School. The Total Literacy Campaign launched in the different districts of Meghalaya has created a lot of awareness in motivating the parents to demand for education. It is also seen that the village education committee is taking interest in education in the respective habitation. The TLC has also brought a change in the attitude of parents to value education for the children.

29

Literacy in Assam
Dealing with the Needy Groups

D. CH. BHAGABATI

Introduction

It is a constitutional obligation of the 'State' to ensure primary education for all in India. The international community also has admitted the right to education as a basic human right. The UN's Paris Declaration, 1948 clearly sounds, "Everyone has the right to education. Education shall be free at least in the elementary and fundamental stages. Elementary education shall be compulsory" (Mahanty, 1994).

Contrary to all such emphasis our achievement in the concerned field is not yet satisfactory. What the Nation was supposed to achieve in the field of literacy by 1960, unfortunately, majority of the provincial states/union territories still could not. Yes! our literacy rate at the national level has shot up from 18.33 per cent (1951) to 65.38 per cent, which apparently brings a feeling of relief. But the other side of the picture is a concern for bitterness when we find our out-of-school population on a constant increase over the years.

Uneven distribution of educational facilities is characterising the post-Independence moves towards social reconstruction in India. Though the Nation has launched multiple egalitarian schemes for expansion of education, in reality, the disparity in respect of education among the states as well as between the rural and urban habitats still persists. The consequences of such disparity is reflected in concentration of illiterates in the remote rural areas.

Assam, the largest state in the North East also presents wide disparity in her literacy front. Any effort for fulfilment of constitutional obligation of universalisation of primary education in the state must pay utmost attention towards those educationally deprived areas-careful identification of which is to be done first. Attempt has been made in this paper to identify some areas in the state, which are genuine client of topmost priority in effort to ensure education for all.

The Issue

Assam, the most populous state of the North East is showing her literacy rate (64.28%) below the national average (65.38%) as per Preliminary Census Report, 2001. Like other Indian states, Assam also maintains a wide gap between rural and urban areas in her literacy face. In 1991, literacy rate in urban areas in the state was 79.39 per cent against 49.32 per cent among the rural populace; while the state's average literacy rate was 52.89 per cent.

The literacy scenario in the rural areas too, in fact, cannot be generalised. A good number of villages are there, where literacy rates are very closer to that in the urban areas. Contrary to that, numbers of villages in Assam with minimum literates are not too less. On the basis of our first hand experiences with the rural realities of the state the educationally backward villages are categorised here; an analysis of which is presented towards the later part of this paper.

The Magnitude of the Problem

Assam has attained a marked progress during the post-Independence period in the promotion of literacy through expansion of primary level of formal education. Even after that, the achievement is not to the satisfaction of the intelligentsia of the state (Chaudhury, 2000). The bitter fact before all of us is that, in spite of increase in literacy growth, the increase in the absolute number of illiterates could not be stopped till the last decade. However, the latest Census (2001) is showing a marginal negative growth in literacy, which may certainly be termed as the beginning of a healthy trend.

Table 29.1: Literacy rate and total illiterates in Assam

Census Year	*Literacy rate (%)*	*Illiterates (in million)*
1961	32.98	5.8
1971	33.94	6.7
1991	52.89	8.4
2001	64.28	7.9

Table 29.1 that expansion of educational facilities (Primary education) is failing to meet the need of the growing population. Besides, the uneven distribution of facilities are also there, for which, the number of illiterates could not be reduced to a great extent.

The Preliminary Census Report, 2001 reveals that 4.58 per cent of the state's population don't have a primary school within 2 km. from their habitats. Contrary to providing school facilities within the habitats, our expectation on parents to send their children long distance for centralised schooling facilities in fact, proves counter-productive (Dubey : 2001). In addition to all these odds, quite a large number of the existing schools are too poor so far as their material conditions are concerned. We may have an idea about these conditions of the schools from Table 29.2.

Table 29.2: Material Conditions of Primary Schools in Assam

S. No.	*Conditions*	*Percentage of Schools*
1.	Lack of Drinking Water	85
2.	Without urinals/Lavatories	92
3.	Lack of Playground (in usable condition)	92
4.	Single Roomed School	75
5.	Single Teacher's School	21

Source: Sixth All India Education Survey and Preliminary Census Report, 2001.

Further, the housing condition of the schools makes a significant psychological impact on the young mind of the primary school-goers. This dimension of our primary school facilities too presents a disappointing picture. Table 29.3 is highlighting the reality.

Table 29.3: Housing Condition of Primary Schools in Assam

S. No.	*Housing Condition*	*No. of Schools*
1.	Pucca Building	4,102
2.	Partly Pucca	10,464
3.	Kachcha Building	5,568
4.	Thatched Huts	4,695
5.	Tents	352
6.	Open space	709
	Total	28,890

Source: Preliminary Census Report, 2001.

The schools under the categories of Tents and Open space are running, undoubtedly, just for name's sake. Since they lack in minimum required facilities, the quality of education served therein is highly prone to be below standard. A survey conducted by NCERT reveals that "21.5 per cent children in class II in Darrang district, 31.1 per cent in Karbi Anglong do not know even alphabets. 7 per cent of children in Marigaon and 38.4 per cent of children in Karbi Anglong also cannot read a single word" (Barkakoti : 2000).

Identifying the Areas

It is clear that most of the schools in rural areas lack the infrastructural facilities. Moreover, the children who do not get access to a school within a reasonable distance too, do belong to the rural areas. Yet, a good number of villages have attained literacy growth close to urban literacy rate. Such villages are mostly located in easy-accessible areas and predominantly inhabited by the Caste-Hindu families, Neo-Baptised tribals and Muslims of middle class families who inherit a sound tradition of literacy and participation in various intellectual pursuits as well.

From our first-hand experiences with the ground realities of the literacy scenario and related facts, we can classify the most educationally backward villages in the state according to the following categories, *viz.*,

1. Hilly hamlets.
2. Villages in the *char*-areas (Sand Bars).
3. Forest villages.

Hilly Hamlets

Of the total 23 different Scheduled Tribe groups, 14 do well in the hilly areas of the state. Most of them are distributed in the smaller habitats scattered over the hilly-terrains of Karbi Anglong and North Cachar districts as well as in the bordering areas of foot hills of Bhutan and other neighbouring Hill-States. Due to inaccessibility of the location, such habitats are mostly isolated from the national mainstream too. The government functionaries dealing with the developmental interventions seldom reach these people. So is the case in expansion of education too.

Extension of Primary school facilities to the unserved small habitats like the hilly hamlets is certainly difficult task to deal with. But the states like Madhya Pradesh, Rajasthan etc. are marching ahead in dealing with such issues, from which we must have a lesson in tackling the problem in our context. In Madhya Pradesh the programme "Education Guarantee Scheme" (EGS) states that any community with at least 25 children of school going age can demand a primary school from the government within the habitat itself. On the part of the community, it has to provide land for the school as well as to ensure the students attendance in the school (Dubey : 2001).

Villages in Char Areas

The *Char* areas in the state are mostly scattered in the midst of River Brahmaputra. In total 2089 *char* villages are scattered over 14 districts in the Brahmaputra Valley. The district Barpeta comprises 351 such villages, where average literacy rate was found to be only 13.13 per cent against 43.24 per cent of the districts literary rate (1991). Most of the villagers of these habitats are originally immigrants and do belong to a religious minority group. Surface communication to these areas is also very hazardous. Except few ones, most of the families in the *char* areas do belong to lower middle class group. In addition to all the odds, recurrence of floods during the rainy season multiples the difficulties of their life.

Education of the youngsters in these localities is highly prone to negligence under the stresses of their socio-economic life. Scholars also do not rule out the prevalence of a psychological negativism against alphabetic literacy that rooted in the minds of the majority of the *char* dwellers. Since the attainment in the economic front of life of the members of this class has come from their traditional occupations, they do not find education particularly relevant and are unwilling to send their children for education (Singh & Sharma : 1998).

Forest Villages

Forest villages were set-up within the vicinity of reserved forests of the state. Such villages were set-up during the last decade of 19th century and first decade of the 20th century. The very purpose of setting up these villages within the forest land was to utilise the services of the villagers for harvesting the forest resources to fetch the state-exchequer. These villages were governed under the provision of the Assam Forest Regulation Act, 1891. As such, they were kept beyond the purview of Panchayati Raj System. They were destined to be content with what the Forest Department provides (Sharma Thakur : 1998).

As per the provision in force, the Education Department, under the state government, finds nothing to do for expansion of education among the masses in the forest villages. In addition to other interests, providing education to those villagers was the concern of the Forest Department. In a study, conducted by the Tribal Research Institute, Assam, it was found that, out of total 524 forest villages in the state there were only 378 primary schools (Bordoloi : 1998).

The Challenge

The observation of the ground realities of present situation of illiteracy leads us to underline two major responsible causes behind the scene, *viz.*,

1. Non-availability of institutional provision.
2. Non-participation of the concerned groups.

Most of the villages categorised earlier do suffer from non-availability of institutional provision. The genesis of this problem is rooted in the weakness of the government's policy of education. The Government of Assam followed the policy of taking over provincialisation of schools. Such a policy can't satisfactorily benefit the socio-economically backward groups of people. Their awareness towards importance of literacy as well as that to establish a school for their own is very often subdued by their struggle to meet the basic minimum needs for subsistence. Activities of NGOs to motivate the people to have their schools or to provide them with a school are also found to be insignificant in those areas. Sensitisation of these people to attain literacy is certainly a very important task to be performed.

It is also a common scene one can observe that the societies even after having a school of their own for a long period of time do contain a sizeable amount of illiterates. Prevalence of such incidences reaffirms the non-participation of people in the existing facilities. This may be due to either limitation of people's outlook or inefficacy of the schools to retain the children in the school or may be due to both of them. Unattractive schooling provision is the single largest cause behind the enormous wastage rate at the primary school level (Barkataki : 2000). Table 29.2 and Table 29.3 also substantiate the fact.

The problem of illiteracy in Assam is now being more aggravated. Since 1998 the State Government has suspended the process to accord permission to open new public institution of education (school level). People in the backward areas are being seriously affected by such an indiscriminate move. Had there been adequate alternative delivery means, the effects could have been minimised. But, in absence of such infrastructure, government's move is working as a counter force against making the needy groups literate.

Multiplicity of language used in communication also adds another problem in expansion of literacy in the state. Not to speak of non-tribes, we have 23 major tribal groups with their own languages/dialects. Though every child should get his basic education in his own dialect (Phillips : 1975), in our context, still we have to go a long way in this direction. As a consequence, most of the tribal children confront the communication problem right from the day of schooling. This might be one of the reasons of low rate of literacy among the tribals as a whole in the state.

The Task Ahead

Our national aspiration to enter the 21st century with a fully literate society has already shattered down. Once again the Union Government has come forward under the mission of Sarva Siksha Abhiyan (SSA) to provide elementary education of satisfactory quality to all by 2010 as one of its objective (Dubey : 2001). The success of such enthusiastic scheme will naturally depend upon how far it can reach to the unserved groups. Hence the SSA in Assam must not remain blind to the issues and the areas highlighted here. Any effort to ensure primary education for all in the state, should give priority to the following:

1. The permission to open new schools in the needy areas should be accorded without delay.
2. It is to be ensured that every habitat has at least one primary school. Example may be taken from the EGS in Madhya Pradesh.
3. Transparency must be maintained in implementing various literacy schemes.
4. In no case fund allotted for expansion of education be diverted to any other purpose.
5. To ensure the people's participation in intensive propaganda/ sensitisation programme is required to be launched.

6. Steps should be taken to maximum use of tribal languages/ dialects in imparting education in the respective tribal societies.
7. Emphasis should be given on production of reading material in tribal languages/dialects.
8. Special emphasis should be laid upon participation of the female.
9. Material conditions including housing conditions of the school must be developed on the priority basis.
10. NGOs and local voluntary organisations are to be involved to the maximum extent.

Conclusion

In spite of our repeated efforts, the horizon of a fully literate society is going farther and farther. Spreading the light of literacy into the every nook and corner of the state is undoubtedly a difficult challenge to meet. The work-plan chalked out to serve those needy groups will certainly bring the desired result provided the same is implemented with full dedication and honesty. Time will judge all these in the coming day.

REFERENCES

Barkataki, D. (2000). "Status and Experiments in Basic Education in Assam," (Unpublished paper presented in Workshop on Status and Experiments in Basic Education in the North East, OKDISC, Guwahati.

Bordoloi B.N. (ed.) (1998). *Constraints of Tribal Development in North East India*, AIRTSC, Guwahati-22.

Choudhuary, N.K. *et al.* (ed.). *Assam Beyond 2000*, Asom Prakalpa, Guwahati-3.

Dubey, S.N. (2001). *Education Scenario in India-2001*, Author's Press, Delhi-92.

Mohanty, J, (1994). *Education for All*, Deep & Deep Publishers, New Delhi-27.

Phillips, H.M. (1975). *Basic Education : A Word Change*, John Willy & Sons, London.

Sharma, Thakur, G.C. (1998). "Forest-Human Interface and Understanding Common Property Resource Use" *in Forest Resource in Hill Districts of Assam*, AIRTSC, Guwahati.

Singh, A. & Sharma, G.D. (Ed.) (1998). *Higher Education in India : The Social Context*, Konark Publishers, Delhi-92.

30

Role of Education for Economic Development
A Case Study of the Karbis, Assam

R.P. ATHPARIA

Introduction

The term "education" is derived from the Latin word "educare" which means bringing up a child, both physically and mentally. In a broader sense, education is conceived as a group process by which, culture or the knowledge storehouse is transmitted from one generation to another. Olutola (1981) describes education as "a process of socialisation, of change and innovation, of preservation and dissemination of an individual from birth to death (*c.f.* Yash Pal Singh and Anju Agarwal, 2002). Education has a great bearing on societal structure, mode of living, thought and behaviourial patterns and personality structure of the individual.

Since the contribution of education to human progress is vital, there is a great demand for education in todays world. Education is one of the most powerful tools in shaping one's future. Education helps to build up a qualified and creative workforce that can adopt new technologies and advance knowledge in such a way that economic development goes hand in hand with responsible management of the physical and cultural environment.

Economic development is usually defined by the level of national income and its rate of growth. However, no one can deny the significance of intellecutal development for economic development. Intellectual development is the aim and function of education so that we simply reach to the conclusion that education is an instrument of economic development.

There is relation between education, employment and economic development. It is observed that where literacy levels and per capita investment on education are comparatively low, have also low levels of per capita income and high levels of unemployment. As a whole, in India, the low level of literacy is associated with the low per captia investment of education. That is why, we are not succeeding in eradicating unemployment crisis.

Saha and Mathur (2001:307) state that there is significant and positive association between the size of family and the total education score of family. As the family size increases, the level of education also increases. On the other hand, the type of family and total education score of women was not significantly associated. The level of education and occupational structure of women revealed that the occupational pattern did not change even with the education of women.

The authors have found in their study in Khangla village of Jodhpur district of Western Rajasthan, which is 80 kms away from Jodhpur with better communication network, that the socio-cultural factors did not play much important role in the level of education of women. The impact of education on occupational structure was negligible as agriculture was largely practised by the majority of women folk.

Das Gupta and Danda (1984 : vii) have stated that in North East India, some of the tribal groups like Purum (Chota) and the Tangkhul Naga have achieved more than 30 per cent literacy rate (as per 1971 Census). Other tribes that stand out fairly conspicuously in this respect are the Nagas, the Bodo-Kachria, the Lalungs, the Khasis, the Rabhas and the Bhutias, all of whom have more than 20 per cent literacy rate. At the other end of the scale are the Kaman Mishmis, and the Miniyongs had less than 10 per cent literacy rate. The authors have concluded that the later category are either pre-agricultural or non-agricultural in economy and live in isolated villages having very restricted contact with other populations around.

In this paper, an attempt has been made to in explain how the education has brought social change among the Karbis. It is to see the relationship of education with economic development.

The present Chapter is based on the data collected from three Karbi villages, namely, Pankumar, Phonlongpet and Karkok of Diphu Sub-division of Karbi Anglong district, Assam. The growth of population in the said villages is not uniform. In Pankumar village, the growth of population in between the period from 1971 to 1987 was 21.67 per cent. On the other hand, the population growth in Phonlongpet village in the aforesaid period was 59.18 per cent while in Karkok village, the per cent of population growth during the period was 22.92 per cent.

Generally, the Karbis live in homogenous villages. According to 1971 census, the total number of Karbi villages in Karbi Anglong was 1451. The Karbis had a peculiar habitual custom of not settling down at a particular place for a considerable period of time. Permanent habitations were therefore rarely seem. Villages were frequently shifted from place to place within a definite territorial limitation. But now the Karbi villages have become permanent in nature. The surveyed villages as mentioned above are permanent in nature.

Educational Facilities in Karbi Anglong District

According to 1951 census, the literacy rate in the United Mikir and North Cachar Hills district was 5.9 per cent as against 18.2 per cent for the State of Assam. As per 1961 census, the literacy rate of the district was 17.4 per cent as against 27.4 per cent (19.2 per cent for Karbi Anglong and 27.2 per cent for N.C. Hills) where it was 28.3 per cent for Assam. This shows that in education some progress has achieved in Karbi Anglong district in 1971 as compared to 1951 and 1961 censuses.

It can be said that after 1961, efforts have been made by the education department of Karbi Anglong district through introducing various plans and programmes. Earlier, there was only one Inspector of School with Headquarters at Diphu for the two hill districts, *i.e.*, Karbi Anglong (formerly known as Mikir Hills) and North Cachar Hills. After 1961, various posts like Assistant Inspector of Schools, Deputy Inspector of Schools, Sub-Inspectors of Schools and Assistant Sub-Inspector of Schools have been created for educational development in the hill areas of Assam. The Primary education in Karbi Anglong district is under the control of the Karbi Anglong District Council with effect from 1st August, 1961. After that various schemes such as supply of free text books to the students, supply of uniforms to the poor students, provision of attendance scholarship to the regular students and provision of mid-day meals etc. were implemented by the District Council with the financial assistance rendered by the government. Again, the management and control of the Secondary Education have also been entrusted to the District Council from 1970.

Due to the above infrastructure facilities, the literacy rate of Karbi Anglong district has improved during 1951 to 1971.

Table 30.1 shows the number of educational institutions in Karbi Anglong district right from pre-Primary to Higher Secondary level along with total number of teachers and enrolment of students.

Table 30.1: Number of Educational Institutions, Teachers and Enrolment in Karbi Anglong District of Assam in 1989-1990

S. No.	*Type of Institution*	*No. of Institution*	*No. of Teacher*	*Enrolment*	
				1988-89	1989-90
1.	Pre-Primary	10	16	580	602
2.	Primary	1204	2517	61430	70180
3.	Middle School	103	515	13905	15450
4.	High School	86	557	13837	14247
5.	Higher Secondary School	11	200	6309	6318

Source: Das, Girindra Nath, 1990.

The number of Karbi teachers and Karbi students in the various educational institutions during 1988-89, 1989-90 has shown in Table 30.2.

Table 30.2: Number of Teachers and Enrolment of Students in Different Schools of Karbi Anglong District of Assam

S. No.	*Type of Institution*	*No. of Karbi Teachers*	*Percentage*	*Enrolment of Karbi Students*	*Percentage*
1.	Pre-Primary	13	81.25	325	53.98
2.	Primary	1841	73.10	47907	68.26
3.	Middle School	212	41.16	12875	83.33
4.	High School	44	7.91	3871	27.17
5.	Higher Secondary	13	6.50	39	0.61

Source: Das, Girindra Nath, 1990.

Table 30.2 shows that in the year 1990, the enrolment of students in Higher Secondary Schools was very negligible (0.61%). In Middle School, the enrolment was very high, *i.e.*, 83.33 per cent. It was followed by Primary (68.26%) and Pre-Primary (53.95%). At High School level, the enrolment was only 27.17 per cent. It shows that the drop outs of the Karbi students in High School and Higher Secondary Schools comparatively high.

Number of teachers was found to be maximum, *i.e.*, 81.25 per cent in Pre-Primary Schools. It was followed by 73.10 per cent in Primary and 41.16 per cent in middle schools. In Higher Secondary Schools, the number of Karbi teachers was negligible, *i.e.*, 6.50 per cent while it was 7.91 per cent in case of High Schools.

In regard to college education, it may be mentioned that the first college in Karbi Anglong was established at Diphu on 15th July, 1965 with 70 students and seven teachers. Later on, Rangsina college and Thong Nokbe college were started at Donkamokam and Dokmoka in 1983 and 1984 respectively. Table 30.3 shows the number of teachers and enrolment in Diphu and Thong Nokbe colleges during 1988-89 and 1989-90.

Table 30.3: Number of Teachers and Enrolment of Students in Diphu and Thong Nokbe College

S. No.	*Name of the College*	*No. of Teachers*		*Enrolment*	
		1988-89	1989-90	1988-89	1998-90
1.	Diphu College, Diphu	62	62	1473	1361
2.	Thong Nokbe College, Dokmoka	12	13	347	390

Source: Das, Girindra Nath, 1990.

Table 30.3 shows that the enrolment in Diphu College has decreased from 1473 to 1361 (7.60%) during 1988-89 to 1989-90, the other hand, in Thong Nokbe college, the enrolment has increased from 347 to 390 (12.39%) during 1988-89 to 1989-90.

Table 30.4 shows the Karbi teachers and Karbi students in both the colleges during 1988-89 and 1989-90.

Table 30.4: Number of Teachers and Students in Diphu and Thong Nokbe College

S. No.	*Name of the College*	*Teachers*		*Students*	
		1988-89	1989-90	1988-89	1989-90
1.	Diphu College, Diphu	09	10	784	545
2.	Thong Nokbe College Dokmoka	02	04	202	194

Source: Das, Girinda Nath, 1990.

Table 30.4 shows that the Karbi teachers have increased from 09 to 10 in Diphu College and 02 to 04 in Thong Nokbe College, during 1988-89 and 1989-90. The Karbi students have decreased in both the colleges during 1988-89 to 1989-90. In Diphu College, the Karbi students have decreased from 784 to 545 (30.61%) during 1988-89 to 1989-90. In Thong Nokbe College, the enrolment of Karbi students have decreased by 3.96 per cent during 1988-89 and 1989-90.

Besides the above mentioned educational institutions, there are one Hindi Training School, one Industrial Training Institute and one Law college at Diphu. With the aim of reducing the number of illiterates in the age-group of 15-35 years the State Adult Education Programme (SAEP) and centrally sponsored scheme of Rural Educational Literacy Programme (RELP) have been implemented effectively in the hill district of Karbi Anglong. Table 30.5 shows year-wise enrolment and number of Adult Education centres from 1980-81 to 1989-90 in Karbi Anglong district.

Table 30.5: Number of Adult Education and Enrolment

Year	*Duration of each phase*	*No. of A.E. Centres*		*No. of Adult Enrolment*					
		RFLP	*SAEP*	*RFLP*			*SAEP*		
				M	*F*	*Total*	*M*	*F*	*Total*
1	2	3	4	5	6	7	8	9	10
1980-81	10 Months	—	200	—	—	—	2915	1476	4391
1981-82	do	—	300	—	—	—	6454	3974	10428
1982-83	do	—	300	—	—	—	4553	4012	8565
1983-84	do	—	300	—	—	—	4577	3880	8457
1984-85	do		300	—	—	—	4027	4508	8535
1985-86	do	300	300	4247	3914	8161	3646	5030	8676
1986-87	do	300	300	3668	3795	7463	3878	4391	8269
1987-88	do	300	300	3808	4413	8221	4187	4628	8815
1988-89	do	300	300	3996	5072	9068	4232	4415	8647
1989-90	do	300	300	3717	4314	8031	4056	4604	8660

Source: Das, Girinda Nath, 1990.

From Tables 30.1 to 30.5, it appears that the educational facility is better in the urban centres than that of the traditional villages. In the traditional villages the adult education centres have improved the educational level of the villagers. No doubt, urbanisation has accelerated the pace of education in general by generating a sense of utility of education in the matter of service opportunities. A number of Karbi boys are receiving technical education in the Industrial Training Institute, Diphu with a hope of being absorbed in the industrial establishments in the district. In the matter of imparting education to the children, the urban dwellers are better placed than the rural folk. The awareness of the need of education is more among the urban dwellers due to their experience in the urban centres. Moreover, due to their economic solvency and nature of work, the urban dwellers can emancipate their children from the clutch of domestic and agricultural activities. In the rural areas, the children help their parents in agricultural activities and are tied up in some domestic works like rearing the cattle, nursing the younger siblings, when the parents are busy in the agricultural field, even in their early age. When grown up, they are either harnessed in agricultural or they have to earn their livelihood from some other sources. This is the major handicap for the children of average agricultural families to be engaged in or to prolong their studies. Karbi students get free education in the school and stipends are also liberal; but average families cannot avail themselves of these opportunities as found in the above tables.

Dasgupta and Danda (1984 : vi) have stimulated some of the important issues of the hindrances of education of the tribal students of India. These are as follows:

1. Though primary education is within the easy reach in many areas, the secondary schools are not widespread and within the easy reach of most of the villages.
2. A communication gap between the teachers and the students. On the other hand, the text books and the student's mental preparation to receive anything from them is at the primary stage.
3. The economic consideration also sometimes make them disgrunted.
4. A general demand for residential school has to be made in all the tribal areas.
5. The tribal people in the remote areas suffer from a sense of shyness to send their wards to educational institutions.
6. High frequency of drop outs due to lack of awareness about the significance of formal education.

Considering the above facts, it is found that the Karbis in the remote areas have not come out satisfactorily in the educational field. In urban areas like Donkamokam, in spite of the improved educational facilities, the villagers have not taken advantage of them. The shifting nature of hill Karbi villages has posed a serious problem for providing educational facilities (Athparia, 1984 : 19).

Educational Facilities in three Karbi Villages

In the surveyed Karbi villages, namely, Pankumar, Phonglongpet, and Karkok, it is found that there is only one L.P. School in Pankumar village. In Phonglongpet, there is one M.E. School and one L.P. School. The total number of students in High School is 345, out of which, 185 are boys and 160 are girls. The total numbers of Karbi students in High School is 126 and they constitute 36.52 per cent of the total strength. In two M.E. Schools of Phonglongpet and Karkok villages, the total number of students is 199. Out of which, 121 are boys and 78 are girls. Out of 199 students, the Karbi students are found to be 168 and they constitute 84.42 per cent of the total number of students. Out of 168 Karbi students in the M.E. Schools, 57.73 per cent are boys and 42.25 per cent are girls. So far L.P. Schools are concerned, the total number of students in the three L.P. Schools is 369, out of which 194 are boys and 175 are girls. Out of 369 students, the number of Karbi students constitute 82.11 per cent out of the total strength of the L.P. Schools, the boys constitute 51.15 per cent while the girls 48.84 per cent.

It is seen from the above description that the total population of the three villages constitute 1788 persons, out of which 635 persons are literates. The percentage of literacy is 35.45 per cent. The level of literacy of the male and female is found to be 43.81 per cent and 26.67 per cent respectively.

If compared with the Census of 1971, it is found that the percentage of literacy among the Karbis was only 13.18 per cent (males 21.09 per cent and females 4.95 per cent). It now appears that the literacy is favourable in the surveyed Karbi villages.

As regards economy, Bodoloi (1991) found that in Pankumar, the average annual income of each family is Rs. 10,680.27 while in Phonglongpet it is Rs. 8986.56 and in Karkok it is Rs. 18033.33. It is also found that the Karkok village is educationally better than the other two villages. In Karkok, the literacy rate is high (43.98%). Next to

Karkok, the literacy rate is higher is Pankumar, which is 41.00 per cent and the lowest is 26.60 per cent, in Phonglongpet village. The education has changed the economy of the Karkok village. The annual expenditure per family is higher in Karkok, which is Rs. 17,490.55 while it is Rs. 9488.82 in Pankumar and Rs. 7259.16 in Phonglongpet. The per capita income of Karkok is higher than the other two villages. The per capita expenditure is also higher in Karkok, which is Rs. 2552.67. While it is Rs. 1317.41 in Pankumar and Rs. 889.94 in Phonglongpet (Bordoloi, 1991 : 244).

Summary and Conclusion

To sum up, it can be said that the literacy rate among the Karbis has improved in post-Independence period due to the greater awareness of education, availability of educational institutions, importance of education and urge to learn among the younger generation. The younger generation is encouraged and is eager to send their children to the schools. In the district, the Government has established Primary Schools, Middle School, High School, Higher Secondary School and Adult Education Programme like Rural Educational Literacy Programmes. In fact, the enrolment of students in High Schools and Higher Secondary Schools is not satisfactory. Due to this, there is less teachers in High School and Higher Secondary Schools.

The education itself has played an important role in the spreading and progress of formal education among the Karbis. It has brought changes in their attitudes towards the worldview, socio-economic and political changes and also their life style.

The educated section of the people migrates to the urban areas to get the higher education and employment. No doubt, urbanisation has accelerated the pace of education in general by generating a sense of utility of education in the matter of service opportunities. In the matter of imparting education to the children, the urban dwellers are better placed than the rural folks.

Economic growth cannot be achieved with societal growth and that is why we use the term "Socio-economic development" rather than "economic development". Social change and social mobility are two sides of the same coin and both these can be represented by social transformation. Education is viewed as an experience which equips individuals through the process of learning to shoulder the responsibilities of adulthood in society thus, education is a social instrument which functions as a vital agent of socio-economic and socio-cultural changes.

Among the Karbis of the surveyed villages, it is seen that the Karkok village is economically better than the other two villages, namely, Pankumar and Phonlongpet. It is also observed that the literacy in Karkok is much higher than the other two villages. In the economically better village there is a marked tendency of sending more children for formal education. That is why, in Karkok, the literacy rate is higher than the other two villages. The Karbis of these villages in general welcome the programme of formal education. Although in terms of proportion of literates, Pankumar is much behind the other two villages covered for this study, this is largely due to non-availability of educational facility within the village.

Education has changed the attitude of the people in the field of socio-economic and socio-cultural life. It involves a change from the traditional shifting cultivation to settled cultivation. As a whole, education has opened up a new vista of socio-economic changes in the life of the Karkok villagers.

REFERENCES

Athparia, R.P. (1984). Karbi, In : *Tribal Education in India.* Calcutta: Anthropological Survey of India.

Bordoloi, B.N. (1991). *Transfer and Alienation of Tribal Land in Assam.* Guwahati: Western Book Depot.

Das, Girindra Nath (1990). *Statistical of Profile of the Hill Areas of Assam.* Guwahati : Tribal Research Institute, Assam.

Das Gupta, Biman, and Danda, Ajit, K., (1984). *Tribal Education in India.* Calcutta: Anthropological Survey of India.

Singh, Yash Pal and Agarwal, Anju (2002). *Employment News.* New Delhi : 19-25, January.

31

Colleges as Agents of Higher Education in Assam

In Retrospect and Prospects

RAJIB HANDIQUE

The colleges in Assam have been playing a very important role in the higher education system. The proliferation of colleges up to remote and rural areas has made higher education accessible to the masses. The contributions of the colleges both in terms of quality and quantity are significant, though the need of changes in tune with the time is urgently felt. The colleges will have to play as well as realise its role as agents of development and desirable socio-economic changes, relevant to the society.

I

Higher education refers to education in post higher secondary institutions, colleges and universities. Formal arrangements for the education of individuals in the present day societies is conceived in terms of stages arranged in a hierarchy. The education system in Assam as well as in the other states of the country comprises the elementary, secondary, higher secondary and higher education stages. After the approval of the National Policy on Education in 1968 by the Indian Parliament, we are committed to an education structure symbolically referred to as the 10+2+3 structure. This means ten years high school education including five years of primary, three years of upper primary and two years higher secondary and three years of colleges or university education culminating in the Bachelor's degree. The new National Policy on Education, 1986 reaffirms the 10+2+3 structure and most of the Indian states have adopted this structure.

Thus, higher education begins after the 10+2 stage and in Assam the colleges mainly impart the '+3' stage of education, though it must be stated that these colleges have also been imparting education in the '+2' stage, quite erroneously.

Higher education is so called primarily because it constitutes the top most stage of formal education and more importantly because it is concerned with processes in the more advanced phases of human learning. The entrants (students) are about eighteen years of age and therefore they are considered to be mentally mature and capable of performing in the abstract level. They are also considered capable to analyse, synthesise and grasp concepts and ideas of various kinds. Their creative faculties are also developed adequately.

Thus, the First Degree level of education or the post-higher secondary stage of education, which is imparted by the colleges mainly in Assam, constitutes a very important stage of higher education and is linked up directly with the university.

II

The Quantitative Aspect

In Assam, colleges have been playing a pivotal role in the higher education system. The number of colleges has increased several times since Independence and these centres of higher education have proliferated to rural and remote areas, spreading the 'light of higher education'. In the process, access to higher education has become easy for masses and a bachelor's degree has come to be regarded almost as a basic degree. The number of graduates has therefore increased several times since Independence.

There are several important parameters in the growth and development of colleges in Assam, which are noteworthy (Table 31.1 and Table 31.2). The trends as revealed by Tables 31.1 and 31.2 are quite conspicuous and a big margin of error would also not change the trends easily.

It is quite clear that the number of colleges has increased since 1960s and has maintained a steady growth. The demand for higher education is quite obvious, though the demand is at times also engineered by unemployed post-graduates who help in establishing new colleges, where they find employment.

Table 31.1: Growth of Colleges in Assam* during 1940 to 2000

Years	*No. of Colleges*	*Colleges Offering*											
		B.A.	*B.Sc.*	*B.Com.*	*U.B.*	*B.Ed*	*MBBS*	*B.E.*	*M.E.*	*M.C.A.*	*M.A.*	*M.Sc.*	*Others*
Pre-1940	7	6	6	1	1	–	–	–	–	–	2	1	–
1940	11	7	7	1	1	–	2	–	–	–	1	1	1 (B.A.M.S.)
1950	15	13	12	4	–	–	–	1	1	1	1	2	–
1960	72	57	23	15	5	3	1	1	–	1	1	1	–
1970	77	60	20	11	10	2	–	–	–	–	–	–	–
1980	73	64	5	8	3	1	–	–	–	–	–	–	–
1990	74	53	4	4	–	15	–	–	–	–	–	–	–
Total	329	260	77	44	20	21	3	2	1	2	5	5	1

*Database—'Universities Handbook', 29th Edition, Association of Indian Universities, New Delhi, January 2002.

Table 31.2: Establishment of Colleges in Assam and their Location*

Years	*No. of Colleges*	*Category*		
		Urban	*Semi-Urban*	*Rural*
Pre-1940	7	7	–	–
1940	11	11	–	–
1950	15	11	4	–
1960	72	51	14	7
1970	77	38	15	24
1980	73	21	12	40
1990	74	27	10	37

*Database—'*Universities Handbook*', 29th Edition, Association of Indian Universities, New Delhi, January, 2002.

Moreover, with the passage of time, the spread of the growth of colleges proliferated to rural areas. Till 1950s, there were no college in the rural areas. In the 1980s and 1990s, the colleges established in the rural areas outnumbered their urban counterparts.

Though we perceive the growth of a large number of colleges, yet the courses (degrees) offered in the colleges has not undergone any significant change and B.A., B.Sc., and B.Com. continue to be the main degrees (courses) that are offered in the colleges since the pre-Independence days. It is also noteworthy that the number of B.A. course in the colleges of Assam are much more than the B.Sc. or B.Com. courses. The growth of professional colleges is also very limited. These peculiarities have made the very development of colleges in Assam in particular, and higher education in general lopsided. It has also adversely affected the role of colleges as agents of social change and development.

III

A Word on Quality

Several colleges were established under the British Raj in Assam, and these continued to prosper in the post-Independence period. These colonial legacies of higher education served as models to the colleges, which were established in the post-Independence period. Thus, we find that colleges reflect remarkable colonial characteristics.

During the British period, higher education remained an integral element of colonial under-development. Though there were different motives in introducing higher education, it can be generalised that the colonial rulers used this devise to create a set of educated people who can assist the colonial masters to perpetuate their rule in India and insulate the local people against the tide of modern industrial and scientific culture. Lord Macaulay stated in his minute, which he wrote in his capacity as Law member on 2nd February, 1835 replying to the arguments of the *Orientalists*, "We must at present do our best to form a class who may be interpreters between us and the millions we govern, a class of persons Indian in blood and colour but English in taste, in opinions, in morals and in intellect. To that class we may leave it to refine the vernacular dialects of the country, to enrich those dialects with terms of science borrowed from the western nomenclature, and to render them by degrees fit vehicles for conveying knowledge to the great mass of the population....".[1] This came to be known as the *Downward Filtration Theory*, and this concept of education filtering down from the upper classes of society to the masses remained inherent in the Indian education system till date.

As a matter of fact, a number of Indians who served the British were thoroughly de-nationalised, looking with contempt everything that was Indian. But the very education system gradually developed an awakening in the country, which developed a spirit of self-respect and national consciousness. Today, it is recognised that education is not only an important element in improving intellectual standards, but also to provide the right kind of leadership for social and economic improvement and strive to promote equality and social justice by reducing social and cultural differences through the diffusion of education.[2]

But the saddening fact is that, in spite of the tremendous development of education since Independence, we have not been able to eliminate underdevelopment or fanaticism in our country. We have to acknowledge the fact that education is only a constituent sector of the society, and the existing societal milieu will affect the system of education. At the same time it must also be stated with equal emphasis that the education system if effectively developed may help to bring about desirable changes in the society.

However, the absence of any change of direction in higher education resulted in promotion of the existing system (a colonial legacy) and colleges had no option, but to follow the same. Consequently, the number of colleges offering the humanities and social science courses are much higher than colleges offering courses in science and technology. As vouchsafed by many, the educated unemployed are actually educated-unemployable. The desirable change in the levels of knowledge, skill or attitude in the entrants (students) to the colleges does not take place. New courses of studies on management, entrepreneurship, agriculture, mechanics, commerce, accountancy, health and hygiene, child care and development, etc. should be introduced at the college level in Assam to make it more meaningful and useful for the society. Under-graduate education must be made vocational to the largest extent possible.

IV

A Westward Glance

Today's world is regarded by many as a uni-polar world and admittedly the west dominates in terms of power derived through scientific knowledge and technology. In the United States of America (USA), the colleges were developed basically on the provisions as laid down in the first Morrill Act, passed by the US Congress in 1862 and named after its sponsor, Justin Smith Morrill.

Under the provisions of the Act, each state was granted 30,000 acres of federal land for each member of the Congress representing the state. The lands were sold and the resulting funds were used to finance the establishment of one or more schools to teach 'agriculture and mechanic arts'. Though the Act specifically stated that other scientific and classical studies need not be excluded, its intent was clearly to meet the need of a rapidly industrialising nation for trained technicians. Military training was required to be included in the curriculum of all land grant schools, and this provision led to the establishment of the Reserve Officers Training Corps, an educational programme for future army, navy and air force officers.[3]

Some states established new schools with their land grant funds; others turned the money over to existing state or private schools to be used for the establishment of schools of agriculture and mechanics, which came to be known as "A&M" colleges.[4]

The influence of the land-grant colleges on American higher education has been formidable. In recent years almost one-fifth of all colleges seeking degrees in the US were enrolled in land-grant institutions. Pioneering research in physics, medicine, agricultural science, and other fields has been done at land-grant colleges, and as their admission policies were more open than most other institutions of the day, land-grant schools made it possible for women, working-class students, and students from remote areas to obtain under-graduate and professional education at low cost.[5] There were sea-grant colleges also, which were established on similar lines.

The education system helped to develop an entrepreneurial society in the USA, an element totally absent in the society in Assam.

V

On the Future as a Conclusion

In spite of the phenomenal growth of colleges in Assam, there is now a general feeling that the standard of higher education is declining. Stern warning has been voiced by the intellectuals about the future of the colleges in Assam. "........In the future, the number of colleges, there will hardly be any student willing to study in them".[6]

We have to consider why there is heavy demand for higher education. Todaro points out that most people in the less developed countries do not demand education for its intrinsic benefits but simply because it is the only way to get highly paid employment.[7] These derived benefits must be weighed against the costs of education. The demand for higher education is related to the modern sector traditional sector wage differential. If we can reduce such wage differentials we may be able to restrict the demand for higher education to a great extent. The wage differentials can be reduced provided the productivity of the traditional sector can be increased substantially through greater investment in infrastructure and other aspects of development.[8]

Moreover, the demand for education is inversely related to direct private costs of education. The private cost of higher education is exceedingly low. And so long as higher education remains essentially privately free and modern sector jobs are relatively lucrative, the demand for higher education must be excessive. It is, therefore, imperative that educational costs borne privately should be increased, substantially and the rate of educational subsidy at a higher level be reduced. However, the meritorious and deserving students should be given adequate assistance both by subsidy and loan so that they continue their studies without any difficulty. If these three measures are taken, the demand for higher education can be curtailed to a great extent.[9]

The educated people in modern jobs also acquire certain amount of social distinction particularly in developing countries like India. During the British period, the upper class Indian elite, by supporting imperial rule, enjoyed some kind of privilege and affluence. Even after Independence and in spite of a democratic set up, there has been little change in cultural learning and the same alien notions continued in administration for which the employees in the modern sector, with a '*babu culture*' enjoyed privileges of power and position, which were denied to the people in the traditional sector.[10]

Colleges can provide the necessary education to uplift the traditional sector and enhance its productivity and the much sought after prestige in the eyes of the public. For example, colleges might act as agents of begetting knowledge for the people engaged in the traditional sector through liaisoning with the groups/institutions, which can provide the knowledge and inculcate such values in the students, which will attract them towards the traditional sector as well.

We may then perhaps be able to transform the existing trend of higher education, which according to Gandhiji, never taught the student to have any pride in his surroundings. Gandhiji pointed out that the higher a student goes (in the field of education) the farther is he removed or alienated from his surroundings. What Gandhiji states as very unfortunate is the fact that our educated youth suffer intellectually and emotionally an alienation from their motherland, village, community and the nation. In such an environment, education cannot prepare people's mind to receive new ideas and accept new tool, new relationship and new forms of organization.[11] It is in this context that we may think of transforming lot of the existing colleges in Assam into *community colleges*, seats of learning, which will provide the knowledge required for sustenance of the local community based on new curriculum and courses of studies, which may provide the right knowledge, attitude and skill—on agriculture, mechanics, commerce, health and hygine, entrepreneurship, etc.[12]

Recently, the Government of Assam faced a lot of problem, when it tried to reduce the amount of grants provided to the colleges having the *Deficit Grant* status. The Government of Assam may consider granting such colleges a land-grant status, which would help both the government and the colleges to survive with the existing limited resources.

In conclusion, the following words of Dr. Hari Gautam, former Chairman, University Grants Commission (UGC) are pertinently stated:[13]

> The educational system in India is today in a critical state — resistant to change. Though large, our educational system is neither relevant nor effective. India's educational ethos need major reforms in the context of changes that are sweeping our country. Transformation that society is going through warrants a rejuvenation in the way we teach and what we teach. Restructuring of our educational institutions and the contents of the curricula is what is needed to produce the desired outcome. Unplanned institutional proliferation and unabated expansion of students enrolment should be resolutely and effectively curbed. It is, however, more important and pertinent as well to safeguard against mistakes than to unnecessarily expand. Since Independence, though many commissions had submitted their reports and many eminent men have pronounced their plans for rejuvenating the system, but alas there has always been a wide gap between the plan the action. Funds alone cannot help to improve the quality of our education. It urgently needs motivation of all including that of teachers, students, administrators and others.

It is true that the universities determine the curriculum in the colleges and therefore, the change has to begin from the universities. The initiative of the colleges in this regard is also necessary and equally important. We can only hope that with the recent steps taken by the UGC and the National Assessment and Accreditation Council (NAAC) to ensure quality education, and the resulting sense of accountability generated in the mind of the teachers, students, and educational administrators, colleges in particular and the higher education in general will change and develop in tune with desires of the society into useful institutions of higher learning in Assam in the 21st century.

NOTES

1. Saikia, Siddheswar, *History of Education in India*, Gauhati, 1971, p. 15. *Orientalists* referred to that group in the Committee of Public Instruction (under the British Raj in the 19th Century), which advocatd imparting of education in the vernacular medium.
2. Misra, Baidyanath, "Prospects of Restructuring of Higher Education", in the *University News*, Vol. 40, New Delhi, January 14-20, 2002, p.1.

3. *Encyclopaedia Britannica* 2002, Deluxe CD edition, file:<Program Files\Britannica\202\cache\info_000012.html>
4. *Ibid.*
5. *Ibid.*
6. Sharma, Pabitra Kumar, *viswavidyalay anudan ayogor shehotiya niti* (article in Assamese) in the *Amar Asom* (Assamese Daily), Guwahati, 14th June, 2002, p. 3.
7. Todaro, Michael, *Economics for a Developing World*, Longman, 1977 as stated in Misra, Baidyanath, "Prospects of Restructuring of Higher Education", in the *University News*, Vol. 40, New Delhi, January 14-20, 2002, p. 1.
8. Misra, Baidyanath, *op.cit.*, p.2.
9. *Ibid.*
10. *Ibid.*, p.3.
11. *Ibid.*, pp.5-6.
12. *Community Colleges* in India are being established in Tamil Nadu. A Jesuit priest, Fr. Alphonse, is behind this scheme and the UGC has recognised his efforts. He goes around all over the country giving seminars on the 'Community College' concept and has been funded for this. He has written a series of articles in the *University News* journal/magazine in the last 3 years.
13. Gautam, Hari, *Sleeping Grants*, (exerpts from the convocation address at the 18th Convocation of the Dayalbagh Educational Institute, Agra) as published in the *University News*, Vol. 38, New Delhi, February 14, 2000, p.18.

32

Higher Education and Distance Education in North East India

With Special Reference to Nagaland

SUKHENDU MAZUMDAR

Education is the birth right of the citizens of a free country today. Yet there is a gulf of difference noticed between whatever is done in reality and whatever is said. India is a glaring example, where the people of this country has been denied this fundamental right and the poverty stricken people find it a hard nut to crack to arrange for the same. And, to add to this misfortune, India shares 32.3 per cent of the total illiterates of the World today! However the era of 21st century is an era of higher education and distance education and the traditional system of education is facing a stiff competition since the latter one has failed to reach the every nook and corner of the society. In fact, the higher education is in the process of change and the advancement of science and technology has made a great impact on the transformation process. The global issues are to be tackled and forces of democracy are to be strengthened too. Since competition is increasing and the need of the society too has grown in volumes, the universities of today and tomorrow have to be more accountable towards the masses. However developing countries like India, the impact of the internet, telecommunication and either means of communication has not yet been felt to the extent that it should have been. In this regard, the Government of India has taken steps to spread the modern means of communication in the north-eastern states. The IT sector is likely to grow here and the Distance Education too is gradually picking up fast. In Nagaland, with the help of the World Bank, steps have been taken up to launch different faculties of the technical education and IT so that the state of Nagaland can match the rest of the Indian states and particularly the north-eastern states.

The 21st century is rapidly heading towards the commercialisation of the higher education. The field of knowledge is witnessing the contest of private players in the arena and this industry has become quite lucrative. But the public in general expects and obviously deserves output in the real terms. Hence, the institutions of higher education, *i.e.*, the Universities and higher institutions must produce qualitative output of the investment made. Keeping in mind of this challenge, privatisation is set on. So the students have to act likewise and matured customers so that the best can be achieved out of minimum investment in the shape of money and time coupled with intellectual labour. These days, efforts are on to create the guidelines and rules to institute free trade in the field of higher education. Looking at the present trend, it may be said that days are ahead of us when universities will be the part of WTO. But developing countries like ours are likely to suffer as the overseas players may steal the show without considering our national interest and other related development issues. Thus, we find that it will take time to set the ball rolling since accrediting and quality control are to be maintained.

The developing regions of the World will have to accept the reality and must see things in right perspective, so that appropriate efforts can be made and they are not left behind the race. In fact, the entire World has been transformed into a global village through the linkages of communication network. India, though, has not yet made any remarkable headway, the fever is very much on. India has done some good jobs in the field of software development and is developing as a potential market gradually and we can hope to capture a wider market if everything goes in right direction. Though competition is increasing and newer and newer technologies are flooding the system, we hope to survive amidst and go ahead, if the zeal is not lost. However it requires some favourable factors, which would help it grew unhindered. For example, the Political Environment must be accommodating so that issues relating to its development are not disturbed. Sometimes, talents fight shy of these things and fly to the foreign countries and we are deprived of their services. Hence, political climate should remain healthy and should create atmosphere, helping to its rapid growth. In addition to the question of political environment of the country, there are lots more, which too influence the growth of a modern system. To mention a few, the social set-up of the country along with its deep rooted cultural and political and religious values and practices, the ethno-economic scenario etc. are of importance. These factors are of importance since they influence developmental works that are underway. These countries where the political condition is stable and social system is strong enough and economic conditions are sound, the development of higher education will certainly pace up.

The striking feature of north-eastern region is its political climate. The political environment has always been disturbed here, mingled with insurgency issues. This disturbing political scenario has often hampered the progress of developmental projects undertaken from time to time. Expansion of roads, bridges and railway tracks to connect the interior of the north-eastern states has always been hampered and virtually follows a snail-progress. Unless the political environment is sound, investment in such fields does not yield better result. Population too is increasing at faster rate. Such increase in population also may retard the progress if not given a timely check. For example, in Nagaland the population growth has been the highest during last decade. The Naga people are yet to understand the small family norm despite the fact that there is no dearth of government measures. This has certainly slacken the pace of economic growth resulting in all-round effects on the entire economy. However, utmost care should be taken to serve the masses and meet their demand, otherwise it is difficult to make a breakthrough. Here is the role of higher education and the universities, which is very crucial. Because, whatever be the development work, the universities are to act their catalytic role. If universities are involved actively, the pace of work will be smooth and the masses will get the benefits. Truly speaking, we often notice that higher education system has not bothered much about the masses and its gradual expansion and commercialisation has made it as good as a commodity. It is certainly injurious to progress as many may be left out although they deserve and aspire for the same. Hence a problem will always remain whether the same is affordable or not. But the higher education through Distance Education system, may help the people to acquire higher education, since the same is easily accessible within their limited resources. Higher education, truly speaking is not far to seek. Perhaps, for the timing millions of the country and this zone, the umbrella of Distance Education would protect the interest of the students otherwise unable to pursue higher education. Not only to acquire a simple degree but the distance education has reached the maturity of offering the Post-Graduate degrees and even the Ph.D.

degrees. In this regard we can mention the role of the Indira Gandhi National Open University, which has been established as a Central University by an Act of Parliament in 1985 and recognised by all the members of the Association of Indian Universities. Hence, degrees conferred by this university are at par with any other universities of the country. It is heartening to note that the IGNOU has established its Study Centres in almost all the district headquarters of the North East and Regional Centres at the state capitals. So the states like Nagaland or Mizoram can benefit like anything in view of their difficulties and many other problems. The people of the North East also may find it a pleasant surprise to them that organisations like the Assam Rifles (known as the 'friends of the Hill People') have also come forward by opening over twenty study centres in the north east with the Regional Headquarters at Shillong. This will not only cater to the needs of the Jawans or serving Assam Rifles personnel of different ranks but at the same time the civilians populace too can seek the benefits. Thus it is evident that Distance Education would play a pivotal role in the coming days. This is more so for the states of the north east, where the communication link is often disrupted owing to many reasons and also the lack of attitude on the parts of the learners to seek knowledge out of the state boundary. This has become more accessible since the term-end exams can be held at the very study centre close to the learner.

But question may arise regarding the quality of education, which we often happen to ignore. There are many institutions and universities where the academic services rendered are not to the satisfactory level. Obviously the output ranks below the mark. And, the universities and institutions, where the quality education is imparted, the products tend to migrate towards the foreign markets, which is especially observed from the products of the IITs, IIMs, and other reputed institutions. Similarly, our reputed universities and institutions are often utilised by the students of developing countries and also of the underdeveloped countries. Hence, quality education is very important now and the role of private institutions is increasingly felt and the Government is accommodating them too. To ensure the quality, NAAC (National Assessment and Accreditation Council) has been formed, which is assessing and accrediting a number of colleges and universities. The accountability aspect is most important now and the UGC and the NAAC will certainly play an important role irrespective of the name and fame of many of the so-called universities and institutions.

But to enhance the quality aspect, the universities have to come out of the narrow idea of localisation. Unless scholars from different parts of the country and abroad join the system and the products of the same institutions are not encouraged or politically backed for retention in the same parent concern, the environment of higher education will be healthier. Though a majority of scholars do not prefer to move away from the old location, and, thus the bottleneck or stagnation created, it should be cleared and mobility is to be created for better and healthier results. Thus diversity has to be generated facilitating the climate towards the tolerance and multiculturalism and thus stopping the narrow mindedness and sectarian feelings. Here I would like to quote a line uttered by the great patriot of the nation Sri Sardar Patel, "the aim of university is not to produce people who loiter for jobs but to produce responsible citizens". If it is really so and certainly is so, we can indeed produce many more Nobel Laureates. It is obvious that we cannot chain or confine knowledge in a narrow lane of suffocation and must allow it to breathe freely in a free and open air, where we can help the world to progress. It is to be understood by all that the essence of education is to create world brotherhood and fraternity, where the mind and intellect help the heart to accept one and all in the same fold.

Among the North-Eastern states, Mizoram can be singled out as the most advanced one in the race of literacy achievement. In the Census of 2001 (provisional) the rate of literacy recorded has been 88.49 per cent, which is of course higher than that of 1991 census by 6.23 per cent. Mizoram has better rate of literacy than the National average (National average being 65.38%). Kerala, which is on the top of literacy Tables 32.1 and 32.2(a) and 32.2(b) are having 90.92 per cent, which is slightly higher than this remotest part of the north-eastern state.

Nagaland Scenario

Nagaland, which has been subjected to so much of insurgency and disturbance pressure, has made a steady progress in the field of literacy achievement. Even in the field of Higher and Technical Education, the state has made remarkable progress by creating a separate department of higher and technical education, functioning independently with effect from 1st May 1983. However prior to this, it was a constituent of erstwhile Department of Education, which comprised all the wings of Education.

Table 32.1: Literacy Rates in the North-Eastern States by Sex and Overall over Various Census

Category	*Year*	*Arunachal Pradesh*	*Assam*	*Manipur*	*Meghalaya*	*Mizoram*	*Nagaland*	*Tripura*	*All India*
(1)	(2)	(3)	(4)	(5)	(6)	(7)	(8)	(9)	(10)
Total Population	1961#	47.9*	33.0	36.0	–	–	20.4	24.3	28.3*
	1971	11.3	28.7	32.9	29.5	–	27.4	31.0	29.5
	1981	20.8	–	41.4	34.1	59.9	42.6	42.1	36.2$
	1991	41.59	52.89	59.89	49.10	82.27	61.65	60.44	52.21
	2001	54.74	64.28	68.87	63.31	88.49	67.11	73.66	65.38
Male Population	1961#	53.4*	44.3	53.5	–	–	27.2	35.3	40.4*
	1971	17.8	37.2	46.0	34.1	–	35.0	40.2	39.5
	1981	28.9	–	53.3	37.9	64.5	50.1	51.7	46.9$
	1991	51.45	61.87	71.63	53.12	85.61	67.62	70.58	64.13
	2001	64.07	71.93	77.87	66.14	90.69	71.77	81.47	75.85
Female Population	1961#	24.1*	19.6	18.9	–	–	13.0	12.4	15.3*
	1971	0.37	19.3	19.5	24.6	–	18.7	21.2	18.7
	1981	11.3	–	29.1	30.1	54.9	33.9	32.0	24.8$
	1991	29.69	43.03	47.60	44.85	78.60	54.75	49.65	39.29
	2001	44.24	56.03	59.70	60.41	86.13	61.92	65.41	54.16

Note: *Excludes population of that portion of NEFA where all India Census schedule was not canvassed.

$ Excludes Assam and the population of those areas which are illegal occupation of Pakistan and China where Census could not be taken

Excludes population in age group 0-4.

Source: Statistical Abstract (Various Issues), Government of India.

Table 32.2(a): Literacy Rate 1951-2001 (Mizoram)

Year	*Persons*	*Males*	*Females*
(1)	(2)	(3)	(4)
1951	311	462	167
1961	440	534	347
1971	538	605	467
1981	599	645	549
1991	823	856	786
2001	885	907	861

Notes:
1. Literacy Rates calculated per 1000 persons.
2. Literacy rates for 1951, 1961 and 1971 relate to population aged five years and above. The rates for the years 1981 to 2001 relate to the population aged seven years and above.

Table 32.2(b): Literacy Rate in Percentage 1951-2001

Year	*Persons*	*Males*	*Females*
(1)	(2)	(3)	(4)
1951	31.14	46.15	16.70
1961	44.01	53.40	34.69
1971	53.80	60.48	46.7
1981	59.88	64.45	54.91
1991	82.26	85.60	78.60
2001	88.49	90.69	86.13

Note: Literacy percentage for 1951, 1961 and 1971 relate to population aged five years and above. The rates for the years 1981 to 2001 relate to the population aged seven years and above.

The department of higher and technical education has been evolving general policies in liaison with the Ministry of Human Resource Development, Department of Education, Government of India. It is also concerned with perspective planning and policy formulation for collegiate and technical education with necessary co-ordination and guidance from the U.G.C., A.C.C.T.E, N.U. and other universities of the country.

In the year 1959 a college in Mokokchung town was established on 8th September (*viz.* Fazl Ali College), which was the first of its kind in the entire Naga Hills district and was supposed to cater to the needs of the public of Nagaland. However, till then Nagaland was a part of Assam and was known as Naga Hills district of Assam. Perhaps, it was the first venture undertaken on the part of Nagaland to mark the beginning of Higher Education in the state. Later on, many more colleges have been added to the list. The Kohima Science College was established on 15th January 1961. Kohima Science College has been the pioneer of science education in the state and has a respectable position in the north-eastern region.

Over time, the state of Nagaland has witnessed a tremendous growth of higher education and it was vivid from the time, the area got statehood in 1963. Right now, it has eight general colleges, two polytechnics and one professional college for teachers education. Each district has one government college for the people of Nagaland (Table 32.3).

Table 32.3: Government Colleges in Nagaland in 2000-2001

S. No.	*Name of the college*	*Year of establish*	*Government Taking over*	*Number of Teachers*	*No. of Students*	*Streams*
1.	Fazl Ali College, Mokokchung	8.9.59	1.3.62	62	833	Arts/ Science
2.	Kohima Science College, Jotsoma	15.1.61	1.7.64	76	951	Science
3.	Dimapur College	25.7.66	1.2.89	42	825	Arts/ Commerce
4.	Sao Chang College, Tuesang	1.7.73	15.4.83	21	274	Arts
5.	Mt. Tiyi College, Wokha	1.7.74	1.4.87	17	348	Arts
6.	Zunheboto College	16.8.80	1.2.86	18	250	Arts
7.	Phek College	24.7.81	1.2.90	17	138	Arts
8.	Wangkhao College, Mon	7.7.83	1.2.90	23	106	Arts
9.	Nagaland College of Teacher Education, Kohima	=	25.3.75	13	75	B.Ed.
10.	Khelhoshe Polytechnic, Atoizu	=	14.9.72	16	112	Diploma Civil, Mechanical Electrical
11.	Women Polytechnic, Kohima	=	1.6.94	5	33	Modern Office Practice
	Total			310	3995	

But in view of the growing demand of the public for higher education, the government has allowed private colleges too to join the fray. However the growth of Private Colleges was so fast that the government has been more stringent in granting permission to open colleges. In the urban areas of Nagaland, the mushrooming of colleges has really been too much and thus the government has set the criteria to open any new college (see Tables 32.4 and 32.5). To note that the per capita budgeted expenditure has been the highest in the zone and almost three times above the national average.

Table 32.4: Government Colleges in Nagaland in 2000-2001

S. No.	*Name of the College*	*Year of Estd.*	*No. of Teachers*	*No. of Students*	*Streams*
1.	St. Joseph College, Jakhama	1985	32	1471	Arts/Commerce
2.	Oriental College, Kohima	1996	15	197	Arts/Commerce
3.	Modern College, Kohima	1997	16	450	Arts/Commerce
4.	Mountain Christian College, Kohima	1990	14	215	Arts
5.	Kohima College, Kohima	1969	32	1914	Arts
6.	Baptist College, Kohima	1982	24	1048	Arts/Commerce
7.	Alder College, Kohima	1993	24	1036	Arts
8.	Japfu Christian College, Kohima	1997	19	426	Arts
9.	Mount Olive College, Kohima	1992	16	450	Arts
10.	Peren College, Peren	1987	12	48	Arts
11.	Ibaung Thou Memorial College, Jalukie	1995	7	28	Arts
12.	Kilenkaba Memorial College, Dimapur	1994	26	285	Arts/Science
13.	Patkai Christian College, Chumukedima	1975	49	1511	Arts/Science/ Vocational
14.	City College of Arts and Commerce, Dimapur	1992	16	269	Arts/Commerce
15.	Saku Mission College, Dimapur	1994	19	484	Arts
16.	S.D. Jain Girls' College, Dimapur	1993	20	823	Arts/Commerce
17.	Pranabananda Women's College, Dimapur	1991	17	603	Arts

(*Contd.*)

Table 32.4: (*Contd*).

S. No.	*Name of the College*	*Year of Estd.*	*No. of Teachers*	*No. of Students*	*Streams*
18.	Public College of Commerce	1987	10	752	Commerce
19.	Salesian College of Higher Education, Dimapur	1982	9	130	Arts
20.	Salt Christian College, Dimapur	1991	34	1028	Arts/B.Ed.
21.	Tetso College, Dimapur	1994	15	319	Arts
22.	Eastern Christian College, Dimapur	1991	14	415	Arts
23.	People's College, Mokokchung	1986	17	373	Arts
24.	Tuli College, Tuli	1996	7	82	Arts
25.	Loyem Memorial College, Tuesang	1994	12	503	Arts
26.	Yongli College, Longleng	1992	1	113	Arts
27.	Zisaji Presidency College, Kiphire	1997	13	90	Arts
28.	Bailey Baptist College, Wokha	1996	11	90	Arts
29.	Pfutsero College, Pfutsero	1982	8	155	Arts
30.	Kohima Law College, Kohima	1976	4	139	L.L.B.
31.	Mokokchung Law College, Mokokchung	1981	6	70	L.L.B.
32.	City Law College, Dimapur	1994	5	45	L.L.B.
	Total		534	15590	

Stipends/Scholarships : Since inception, the Department of Higher & Technical Education has been implementing various stipends/scholarship schemes for the Naga students studying higher & technical education within and without the state of Nagaland according to the eligibility criteria of each scholarship scheme. The main schemes are:

(a) Post-Matric Central Scholarships.
(b) Technical Stipends.
(c) Merit Scholarships
(d) Research Fellowships.

Table 32.5: Number of Beneficiaries and Financial Involvement in Different Scholarship Schemes in Nagaland

(Amount in Lakh

Scholarship Schemes	*1998-99*		*1999-2000*		*2000-2001*		*2001-2002*	
	No. of Students	*Amount*	*No. of Students*	*Amount*	*No. of Students*	*Amount*	*No. of Students*	*Amount*
P.M.C.S.	32424	873.90	25923	778.92	24058	797.60	21862	750.90
Technical Stipends	633	33.00	552	20.05	481	34.87	494	20.09
Merit Scholarship	612	15.00	945	25.66	1181	58.97	1642	84.95
Research Fellowship	51	6.00	64	8.45	66	6.76	82	8.55

Source : Directorate of Higher & Technical Education, Nagaland.

Table 32.6: Budget Expenditure (Revenue Account) on Education

State	*Per Capita Budgeted Expenditure*		*Percentage of Budgeted Expenditure on Education to Total Budget (Revenue)*	
	1991-92	1995-96	1991-92	1995-96
(1)	(2)	(3)	(4)	(5)
Arunachal Pradesh	512.50	735.37	14.63	15.24
Assam	217.41	411.53	24.33	27.37
Manipur	433.93	723.06	26.49	30.00
Meghalaya	436.81	667.12	20.36	22.68
Mizoram	670.75	919.85	15.43	17.03
Nagaland	605.55	830.58	16.25	15.18
Tripura	453.83	619.14	22.13	21.88
All India	243.92	340.69	13.33	21.48

Source: Selected Educational Statistics, 1992-93 & 1996-97, Ministry of Human Resource Development, Government of India.

But in a state like Nagaland, we find that entry of scholars in the academic field is being tightened in a routine manner to make room for the local candidates. However the same is more or less being witnessed in other parts of the zone also. Hence, a time is not far when the outside scholars may not be available making it difficult for these areas to achieve academic excellence. Keeping the future and the trend of globalisation in mind, knowledge should be given an open air to breathe and the doors for the scholars should remain open to enrich the academic environment of these states and their people.

Conclusion

In comparison to mainstream education the advantage of distance education is clear since the latter can be shifted from the classroom to anywhere and from fixed time to anytime, convenient to the learners. It also encompasses life-long activity of education instead of one-time activity and here the teacher obviously plays the role of facilitator rather than a so called instructor. Thus the transferring of knowledge takes the shape of technology-centric rather than lecture-centric delivery. Hence, a large segment of society can be covered through this viable method of imparting higher education. But again, the quality control is an important issue and many have expressed their apprehensions too. Quality and standard of any education system are inseparable and of course is the central focus of any education system. So, for the distance education and the open education system too, the assessment and accreditation should be applied. Moreover, the voluminous growth of this method of learning in open and distance education institutions with their varied programmes and student enrolment need the tight rope of NAAC to maintain the quality aspect. If the quality is assured, accreditation policy applied, students may have the option to choose the institutions in this era of competition. Also the decision of funding policies will be easier for the UGC, the Government and the Distance Education Council. Thus, upgrading the educational quality is the need of the hour and society, without which the very purpose of Higher Education and Distance Education will be meaningless.

33

Working of Educational System in Nagaland

HEMANT RAI

The root of education in Nagaland may be discovered in the effort of the Christian Missionaries who took herculian task to reach the semi-civilized Nagas at the cost of their lives. Though their primary aim was to spread the teaching of christianity among the animist Nagas, the task could not be fulfilled until the Nagas were educated. Hence they set up some primary Mission's schools, which became instrumental in spreading education in Nagaland. Over the years, the number of schools and teachers began to multiply. Independent India set up a number of schools in the villages and upgraded the Primary Schools to the level of High Schools and Higher Secondary Schools. Later on, various colleges appeared with Central University of their own. The Department of Education took the responsibility both at lower and higher level to manage educational system in Nagaland. The financial aid provided by the Central Government enable every Naga youths to obtain education at their door. Thus the dazelling light of education enchanted both the guardians and students to take the benefit of circumstance and follow new civilization by obtaining certificates and degrees from schools and colleges. With this, major clusters of old social, economic and physical commitments eroded and people became available for new pattern of socialisation and behaviour.

It is interesting to note that standard of education is falling down at greater speed in Nagaland today. Like other countries, in Nagaland also education is passing through a system of struggle between capitalist, monopolist and dynamic younger intellectual and educated classes. The schools and colleges lack quality teaching because of the appointments of the teachers below the prescribed norms and qualifications. Nepotism and favouritism has taken deep root in Nagaland. The authorities of education department are reluctant to their duties. Students want certificates and degrees, not knowledge, and that also without labour. They hardly prepare for examinations. Copying on mass scale has become the order of the day in educational institutions from lower to higher level. The educational administrations do not display either rationality or genuine commitment. Due to poor quality of teaching, character of students hardly develop. According to Kiremwati, the popular Naga educationist "in Nagaland neither the educational authorities nor the teachers are aware of such significance of education and examination". But according to my understanding standard of education has fallen down in Nagaland due to growth of materialist approach among the Nagas where knowledge, is not preferred is materialistic achievement.

A Brief Historical Account of Education in Nagaland

It was the seal of the Christian Missionaries, which founded a proper system of education in Nagaland with the marked objective to convert the animist Nagas into christianity and enable them to read the Bible. In the words of P.T. Philip "whenever missionaries went in Nagaland, they started schools at the stations and nearby villages."[1] It was Mr. & Mrs. Clark, who took real pain to work with the Nagas and gave sound foundation of religious education in Nagaland. They opened several Primary and Middle Schools in Kohima and Mokokchung areas. Impure (nearby to Mokokchung) became the main centre of education. While giving foundation of education in Nagaland the object was "the proclamation of the Gospel to the people of village."[2] The school of Impure was designated as Impure Mission Training School in 1919. Impure became the centre of education and also the centre to produce trained teachers who were deployed to other parts of Nagaland. The mission schools despite imparting knowledge of christianity also taught arithmetic, writing, spelling, physiology, hygience, geography and history.

By the end of the nineteenth century the education which was provided by the missionaries lacked secular character. The government was still reluctant to take interest in education. This was all because government found itself unable to take over the management and non-commitment to secular education.[3] However impure, the main educational centre during the British period, "changed the entire course of our (Naga's) culturals and customs. It enlightened the dark crage of Naga hills and brought the rays of modern life........and removed the grimness of social environment"[4]. By 1940s the government although reluctantly, began to take interest in setting up more schools in Nagaland. Now education in Nagaland is under the control of Board and Government, with "the short-sighted objectives and the organisational dichotomy, which generated instability; and the system failed to lay a firm foundation of basic education."[5] The school working under management and control of the government followed the curriculum including arithmetic, geography, English, geometry etc. The number of the students began to multiply. After independence of India, the basic intention of the government was not to provide the strong educational policy but to open more schools in the villages and to take over the mission schools to please the Nagas and divert their attention from freedom movement to Indian nationalism.

Account of Schools and Colleges in Nagaland

Today there are altogether 327 high schools and 43 colleges in Nagaland, which are operating all over the state admitting thousands of students. Table 33.1 mentioned below gives a full account of the existing colleges and high schools in Nagaland.[6]

Table 33.1: Number of Recognised High Schools

Place	*Private Management*	*Religious Management*	*Government*	*Total*
Dimapur	46	17	10	73
Kohima	34	24	19	77
Mokokchung	17	5	16	38
Mon	5	3	9	17
Pekh	4	10	19	33
Tuensang	8	6	21	35
Wokha	7	7	9	23
Zunheboto	15	1	11	27
Total	136	73	114	323

Source: *Result Gazette of 2002*, Nagaland Board of School Education, Kohima.

Table 33.1 clearly indicates that number of schools under private management is greater than those under religious and government management. There are 136 schools under the private management while the government managed only 114 high schools. Religious bodies managed 73 high schools, which are also under private management. These are non-secular by their nature. The table also shows that the maximum number of high schools under the private and religious management are at Kohima. Perhaps, it is because Kohima is the capital of state and highly developed city. The maximum number of high schools running under religious and private management's yield better result and that is why they attract maximum number of guardians and students. On the other hand, the management of government schools in this regard is weak and teaching quality is not attractive, that is why the products are not good.

The people of Nagaland witnessed the first degree college in 1959 at Mokokchung, namely, Fazl Ali college and first science college in 1961 at Kohima. When the number of the students increase all over the state due to establishment of maximum number of schools from primary to higher secondary level, the need was felt to establish more colleges. By 1970 the number of private and government colleges increased. The Government of Nagaland set up atleast one government college in each district headquarter. Table 33.2 given below shows the number of colleges.

Table 33.2: Number of Colleges under Private and Government Management

S. No.	*Types of Colleges*	*Number of Colleges*
1.	Government Colleges	8
2.	Private Colleges	24
3.	Agricultural Colleges	1
4.	Law Colleges	4
5.	Theological Colleges	8

Source: *Statistical Hand Book of Nagaland*, 1997, published by Directorate of Economics and Statistics, Government of Nagaland (Kohima).

Table 33.2 clearly shows that number of private colleges in Nagaland is several times greater than that of the government colleges. The government managed 8 recognised degree colleges. There are four higher professional college managed by private bodies, where law graduates are produced. There are 8 theological colleges managed by religious bodies. These colleges produce every year graduates in theology. Though the teaching cost in government colleges is less than the private colleges, the most of Naga students prefer private college.

Besides this, a number of higher secondary schools are also coming up in Nagaland under government and private management. The government has upgrade various high schools to the level of higher secondary. There is no village today, that has no primary school. Education in Nagaland has reached to the door of the people.

Before 1974 the Naga students had to go to Guwahati, Shillong or other parts of the country for post-graduation, because the state had no university of its own. There was NEHU Campus at Kohima, which used to impart university education in few subjects like English, education, history and commerce. The Government of India set up the Central University in 1994 at Kohima opening new department at Lumami and Medziphema. The university is directly controlled by Ministry of Human Resource Development and UGC, and the colleges are affiliated to the Nagaland University. Moreover the department of higher and technical education of Nagaland managed and look after the government colleges in respect of appointment of teachers, their salary, promotion, service rules and college buildings. The schools from primary to higher secondary is managed by director of school education and examination of high schools and higher secondary are managed by Nagaland Board of School Education. A good amount is paid to students of both private and government schools in form of stipend and scholarship by the government.

A Critical Evaluation of Educational System Working in Nagaland

Besides a number of schools and colleges in Nagaland, where thousands of teachers have been employed, the educational system is not well organised. The state has numerous schools, colleges, industrial training institutes, law colleges, technical institute like polytechnic, agricultural and adult education centres. Despite various facilities provided to the educational institutions, teachers and students, the standard of teaching is not satisfactory. There are several reasons for deterioration of education in Nagaland. This is evident from physical observation of the working of educational institutions in Nagaland. Prof. T. Chuba the then Education Minister expressing his views in the Assembly of State in this regard, in 1988 said, that "If we look into the schools, these are not running well. The old system, which still continues, is very archaic and does not suit the situation."[7] Prof. Kiremwati, the ex-Pro-Vice-Chancellor of the Nagaland University also said "The persistent political turmoil, the economic scenario, educated unemployment and frustration, dominant unproductive citizens, and the social and cultural compulsion have made every serious Naga thinker to ask within himself, whether education so far imparted was right and relevant."[8] In respect on deterioration of education in Nagaland Rev. Nuh said that "The educational institutions in Nagaland are not able to produce twenty per cent of socially productive citizens.... because of the philosophy of secularism and materialism in educational concept of life."[9] Rev. Nuh is correct in his observation. Modern education in Nagaland has made educated Nagas materialistic in approach, depriving them of moral standard. The teachers are appointed without paying much need to norm of appointment. Educational administrators hardly do their general duties. Teachers are not committed to the profession. Syllabus, prescribed are not up-to-date and the students adopt mass copying during examination. In the words of Kiremwati, "Education does not aim at passing of written examination only, but it involves development of entire personality and life of the student.....the immeasurable qualities of life such as health, character, hard work, honesty and such others develop through proper education and stand above certificates and degrees obtained through examination. Education is not an end in itself, but a means to produce useful citizens, who in turn make or unmake a nation."[10] The student are more interested in obtaining certificates and degrees, not the quality. The parents also do not bother for quality teaching but for degree for their children. The physical condition of primary and middle schools in villages are vunerable. The institutions have neither building nor furniture. Syllabus prescribed are not up to the standard. Observing the situation of primary schools in the villages the visiting team of Naga Student Federation has rightly remarked that "If proper education is not imparted to the children during this stage, it will be like house without good foundation. In Nagaland primary schooling is the most neglected."[11]

NOTES

1. P.T. Philip, *The Growth of Baptist Church in Nagaland*, Christian Literary Centre, Guwahati, pp. 187-88.
2. *BMM*, July, 1884, p. 259.
3. P.T. Philip, *The Growth of Baptist Church in Nagaland*, *op. cit.*, p. 188.
4. Cited in *Ibid*, p. 188.

5. Kiremwati Ao, *Education and the Nagas*, (Mokokchung Ao Baptist Church), Kohima, 1995, p. 18.
6. Proceeding of the Nagaland Legislative Assembly, Sixth Session, February, 1966 (Assembly Secretariat, Kohima, 1966), p. 5.
7. The Proceeding of Nagaland Legislative Assembly, March 1988, p. 336.
8. Kiremwati Ao, *Education and Nagas* (Mokokchung Ao Baptist Church) Kohima, 1995, p. 43.
9. V.K. Nuh, *Education from Christian Point of View*, Nagaland Page, August 1999, Dimapur, p. 5.
10. Kiremwati Ao, *Education and Nagas*, op. cit. pp. 34, 35.
11. N.S.N. Lotha, NSF Educational Tours Finding, *Nagaland Post*, Wednesday April 12, 2000, p. 5.

34

Role of Media and Prospect of Distance Education in North East India

A. HENIA

Introduction

Distance Education is an effective alternative to the formal education. It has immense significance for the emerging learning society in general and educationally underdeveloped society in particular. It has its message both for life-long education as well as for universalisation of education. It is a useful medium for promoting diversified education for those, who have dropped out of it at some stage or other. In other words, the distance education is an organised provision for learning opportunity on part-time basis, outside the time-table of the normal system of education and more or less according to learners perception and at his own convenient time. It is, therefore, democratic as well as socialistic in nature. Distance education has been described in different ways, like correspondence education, open education, open learning etc. It is characterised by relaxed or no rigid entry qualifications, learning according to one's own convenience, flexibility in the choice of course and use of most modern and appropriate educational and communication technology. Distance education has made quite headway during the last two decades.

It is a system of non-formal education in its own right. It has own philosophy, its own goals and its methodology. If the normal system has served the society fruitfully, so does the system of distance education hope to do. It does not complete with the formal system, but supplementary to it. It caters to those sections of society which either being located in far-flung remote areas and because of economic compulsions cannot take advantage of formal system. No system of distance education however well planned and well organised, will succeed in the absence of adequate student support service. There services include study centre providing for guidance and counselling services and libraries. A network of public libraries is a pre-condition for the success of any Distance Education Programme. Distance education, broadly defined, as the system of education in which, education is imparted to student from a distance. It contains two basic elements:

(a) The physical separation of teacher and learner, and
(b) The changed role of teacher, who may meet the students only for selected tasks such as counselling, giving tutorials or solving students' problems. The system is heavily dependent upon the printed material or instructional materials, supplemented partly by the electronic media, radio, television and computer, in addition to limited face to face contact sessions. In fact, distance education means the process of teaching and learning which is not confined within the four walls of the classroom any more. With its horizontal mobility, distance education transcends the barriers of time, space, sex, creed, community and religion, thus breaking the myth of elitism in conventional higher education. Distance education can be successfully used for relating to groups who, for geographical, economic or social reasons are unable or unwilling to make use of traditional (classroom-based) provision of education. Keegan's latest definition of distance education (1986) has synthesised all the various views held with regard to the definition of the term, distance education.

Distance Education is a form of education characterized by

1. The quasi-permanent separation of teachers and a learner throughout the length of the learning process. This distinguishes it from conventional face to face education.
2. The influence of an educational organization both in the planning and preparation of learning materials and in the provision of student support service, it distinguishes itself from private study and teaching programmes.

3. The use of technical media-print, studio, video and computer, to unite teacher and learner can carry the content of the course.
4. The provision of two-way communication that the student may even initiate the dialogue, this distinguishes it from other uses of technology in education.
5. The quasi-permanent absence of the learning group throughout the length of the learning process so that people are usually taught as individuals and not in socialisation purposes.

The major objectives of the Distance Education Programme are as follows:

1. To provide an alternative method of education to enable a large number of persons to acquire knowledge and improve the professional competence.
2. To impart education at the individuals convenience and to help the individuals utilise their leisure time for education purposes.
3. To provide a second chance at education for them, who have had to discontinue their formal education or could not join regular colleges/universities owing to pecuniary or other circumstances.
4. To provide a means for continuing and life-long education for enriching the lives of the people.
5. To supplement the conventional university system and to reduce the pressure on it.
6. To strengthen and diversify the degree, certificate and diploma course related to the needs of employment and necessary for building the economy of the country on the basis of its natural and human resources.
7. To provide an innovative system of university education, which is both flexible and open in terms of method and pace of learning, combination of course, eligibility of enrolment, age of entry, conduct of examination and operation of the programmes with a view to promoting, learning and encouraging excellence in new fields of knowledge.

Role of Media in Distance Education—Prospect in the North-Eastern Region

Media plays a vital role in creating people's awareness about national policies and programmes by providing information and education besides healthy entertainment. It helps people to be active partners in the nation-building endeavour. The use of audio-video material including print materials can certainly enrich distance education. A multi-media approach is required in the preparation and presentation of self-instructional material. To be relevant, acceptable and long-lasting, alternative to the system of formal education, it has to be well designed, effective education to the students through an effective communication network. Media can help adapt education to complex individual needs, wishes and conditions. The teacher, the pillar of the present educational system is missing in distance education, making the use of audio-visual aids very relevant. The audio-visual aids can play a major role in making distance education, to begin with, a possible reality, for a large number of both illiterate and literate masses in the far-flung interior places of the region. It can improve the quality of education at a lower cost and help the youths to a great extent. Media also helps create a more dynamic learning environment in distance education. The greats individualised and independent instruction in distance education to overcome the barriers of space and time, in a decentralised learning environment makes use of audio-visual aids imperative. The major objective of any media can be to help maximum learners to learn effectively, in other words to comprehend and gather knowledge. This hints at mass communication approach. Distance education can employ both small media and advanced technologies.

Media for Distance Education

(A) *Convention*: Print materials-structures lectures, pamphlets, handbooks, manuals and books.

(B) *Modern (Involving use of Communication Technologies)*

   (i) *Teacher made and self-operated*: Slide, synchronized slides and types, slide commentary workbooks, transparencies, audio cassettes, and telephone teaching, teleconferencing etc.

   (ii) *Academic and Technical Expert made*: Radio broadcasts, motion pictures, televised broadcasts, video cassettes, electronic books, and self-structured programmed materials aided by computers, if possible.

In North East India, distance education opportunities are available at the IGNOU- North-Eastern Regional Centre, Shillong, which provides varied programmes in distance education. Further, the regional centre at Shillong set up a good number of study centres in different states of the region. In addition to that some Universities of the region also conducts distance education programme according to U.G.C. guidelines and directions. In recent years, the region noticed increase in the number of student enrolments in the distance education system; which indicates the progress of such education and acceptance by the people at large for it. In this context great emphasis is to be laid on the role of media towards the promotion of distance education, as it fully depends on it for its achievement and success. Therefore, better media system is needed in the region. Society now realised that distance education as an alternative system, provides educational opportunity to the masses for improvement in literacy rate in the region and universalisation of education. It, at the same time contributes towards the betterment of socio-economic and industrial development of the region. Hence, the role of media in distance education.

Suggestion for Improvement of Role of Media in Distance Education in North-Eastern Region

1. The Regional centres and all study centres, spread over all North East Indian states must have access to all the media facilities as per its requirement for conducting educational programmes.
2. To create physical infrastructure in the form of building, better library-cum-study centre, studio for the production of software, etc., it is necessary that capital grants should be allotted by the U.G.C. as well as by the State Government Council.
3. Teams of first rate media persons and academic experts for technology based communication media to locate and evaluate suitable material and give scholarly treatment for depth and breadth of knowledge and to produce a harmonious picture.

Conclusion

Distance education is gaining ground as an alternative system of education in North East India. It helps the people on various fronts. Besides, media can further enhance educational development and literacy growth too. Thus media systems are needed for the success of such education in the region.

REFERENCES

Aooper R. London (1974). *New Media in the Open University: An International Perspective.*

Bates, Anthony (1974). *Broadcasting and Multi-media Teaching*, The Open University, Oppens.

Daniel, John and *et al.*, (1982). *Learning at a Distance: A World Perspective Edmontion*, Athabasea Autlon.

35

Open School System in Promoting Literacy in the 21st Century North East India

RAMA BASU

Socio-cultural reconstruction in the North East India should be discussed in the context of the ethnic identity of the people of the land. The strongest impact on culture and identification is believed to come from formal school education.

The National Policy on Education 1986 (as updated in 1992) and the Programme of Action reaffirms the national commitment to universalisation of elementary education. In this context, the Government of India's concept paper on "Education Reform : Issues of Priority (1997)" should be referred. The education is to be linked with the socio-economic needs of the society as an effective instrument of social change.

This paper attempts to emphasise the policy of education to improve the quality of life of the people in rural areas of North East India. The rural education should be considered in respect of education for diverse cultural and ethnic groups, medium of education, education for the drop out students and the infrastructure itself.

Education, which has come to mean formal examination-oriented learning is not of much help to the poor underprivileged rural people in India. The rural people treats their children as a source of income. So there is a heavy reduction in enrolment at higher stages, though student population is composed of 70 per cent at the primary level. The retention rate is only 30 per cent in the high school level. For the large drop out students, Open School is the most suitable system of education rather than formal school education.

To cope with the right to culture and education as guaranteed by the Indian Constitution, the Open School System is a challenge aiming at spread of education among everybody. The Open School is not alternative to the formal school but supplementary to it.

The Open School System is most suitable for—

- rural youths, who depend mostly upon manual work for their livelihood and have virtually no time to take formal education,
- part-time workers,
- self-employed persons,
- child labours,
- physically disabled persons,
- prisoners,
- homeless child,
- wives of deceased soldiers, and
- those who have failed in the formal school examination.

It is to be noted that most of the drop out cases are either after passing Class-IV or Class-VIII. They can attempt to pass the school leaving examination through Open School System. The infrastructure should be made with a liberal outlook and with flexibility in respect of age, sex and curriculum of study. In this connection I may mention the Open School System in West Bengal, *e.g.*, Rabindra Mukta Vidyalaya with its 50 study centres.

For running of the Open School properly, the following matters must be given the priority:

- Syllabus,
- Language,
- Mode of instruction,
- Examination procedure, and
- Finance.

While framing the syllabus it should be taken into consideration that it will be specially beneficial to those drop out students who have to leave the formal classroom under pressure of circumstances. Students must read a compulsory language, either English or State Language with four or five optional subjects, which include History, Geography, Political Science, Economics, Life Science, Home Science,

Mathematics, Book Keeping etc., most of which humanity oriented subjects. In case of states in North East India, students will learn history, culture, economics in the context of north east and in the national perspective as well.

Language or medium of instruction is most important thing for the students in the North East India, where diverse language and culture exists. The language of the reading material may be State language or more than one language within the states.

There will be a good number of study centres throughout the states. The study centre will supply books, which will be written in a very easy language so that students will understand it without the help of instructor. Instructors will be available in the holidays or week end so that working students may get the advantage of it. If possible, the study centres may use video and audio system to enhance student's understanding with the subject.

Examination procedure should be easy and flexible and to be conducted by the study centres. The students will answer objective type of question or short type questions along with essay type question. There will be regular tutor marked assignments and after completion of the course, students will appear formal examination. The course curriculum and the examination should follow the norms of HSLC examination, because, if a student wants to continue study in the higher stage, this accredited study will be beneficial. Not only that those who will take vocational training will get the benefit of basic education from the Open School.

The State Government with the help of the Central Government, will come forward for management and finance, with commitment to provide effective education for establishment of real democracy. If we take the open system of education as a three-tier system the lower level is the Open School and the willing and able students will rise upto Open University. Non-Government organisation may come forward but under the direct administration and supervision of the Government, specially in financial matters.

The integrated open education scheme should give emphasis on the following aspects:

- bridging the gap between the world of knowledge and the world of work.
- inculcating the value of respect for manual work and dignity of labour.

- conceptualising course content and pedagogy with local and regional needs, so as to develop an appropriate indigenous technology for development and change.
- developing skill of creativity, logic, communication, management and information technology.

We may conclude thus, poor growth in education has an adverse effect on the political participation of the people of the region and a menace to sustainable development process in all respect, which may be wiped out by improving human resources development. Education under State-run Open School System must help developing self-respect and confidence for those under-privileged sections.

36

Training and Development

A Distance Education Perspective with Reference to North East India

A.S. GUHA

North East India — A Profile

North East India is understood as a specific unit or region in the geopolitical context of India. The expression is common reference to the states of Arunachal Pradesh, Assam, Manipur, Meghalaya, Mizoram, Nagaland and Tripura. It is precariously linked to the rest of India through a narrow corridor about 20-40 kms width. The region is a confluence of more than 350 tribes and 200 languages/dialects. It is a melting point of indigenous tribal peoples of Austro-Asiatic/Tibeto-Burman/Tai/Kuki-chin origin and immigrants from Nepal or the then East Bengal (now Bangladesh). In the overall context of racial demography there is a sharp polarity between tribal and non-tribal cultures in the region. Each specific state in the region is contiguously placed. The region is also anthropologically complex as each society has its unique set of traditions, values and compositeness. Matriliny for example distinguishes one tribe from another. The political system is characterized by tradition and modernity : traditional institutions and the modern systems of governance or bureaucracy. This often results in ideological conflicts. The current trends in almost the entire region is a strong urge towards emancipation, which has resulted in either secessionist movements or agitations by student organisations, which are very powerful. There is thus in the region a constant dialectic between regionalism/sub-nationalism and nationalism. The currents of ethnicity are a stark reality.

The physiographic divisions of the region consists of mountainous terrain as in Arunachal Pradesh, plateaus, hills and alluvial plains. The climatic conditions range from extreme winter to severe heat.

Distance Education provisions are not reaching the remote and disadvantaged sections of the society because of major communication bottlenecks and the geo-political contexts of the region marked as it is with underground movements guerilla tactics and internecine feuds amongst the different tribes or communities in the region.

Against a background the need is:

- Proper dissemination and streamlining of information
- Vigorous publicity with the help of both the print and electronic media
- Interactive radio counselling
- Setting up special study centres in rural areas with the help of voluntary organisations
- Establishing mobile libraries/study centres
- Identifying new courses suited to indigenous needs in the local languages/vocalisation of courses
- To effectually use distance education philosophies for integration of societies in the midst of pluralistic cultures

North East India is normally described as a backward region of the country. Yet this 'backwardness' is not always specified : but the geographical insularity of the region has most certainly a distinct bearing on the economic conditions of the people. To think of the region as one whole and single entity is also a fallacy as there are innumerable tribes and communities in the region speaking languages or dialects and professing different religions. Community based institutions are a potent force among the tribal societies and they could be harnessing factors in the means to development. There is great potential for agricultural production but there are many factors, which hamper agricultural growth. These may be summarized as under:

- traditional agricultural practices of the people
- lack of scientific training among farmers
- lack of know-how, skills, and expertise to increase production
- lack of training facilities in land and water management
- inadequate innovations in farming
- poor credit financing to farmers

Land is a bone of contention in the region and the economic life of the people is directly linked with the possession of land. Ownership of land is not only a means of economic livelihood but also very sensitively, a question of identity. Clinging to the roots of identity has for the people a historical, social and cultural basis. Thus it is not surprising that the issue of land has led to conflicts and tensions, between the indigenous people and 'outsiders'. In fact this has also created tension between one tribe and another tribe. Societal tensions have led to economic hardships and an alienation from the 'mainstream'.

Yet, it is the community based organisation such as Headman's Council, youth club, a women's organisation, a church related organisation to which the people will listen to and look up to with deference. Let us now look at the charts underlink certain basic statistics of the region, with state-wise break-up. The conclusions are,

1. The population of women is very high
2. The percentage of urban population is low excepting that of Assam
3. It is basically a tribal dominated region
4. Literacy rate is high, as high as 82.27% in Mizoram and female literacy excepting that of Arunachal Pradesh is fairly high
5. Industrial position is very weak excepting that of Assam
6. There is a great deal of drug abuse and, AIDS cases are preponderant in Manipur
7. The number of school drop outs from classes one to ten is very high maintaining a figure of 50+% at least. The factors of drug abuse and drop outs undoubtedly have a cause-effect relationship.

Training and Education

Training exacerbates the process of development by which a person can develop skills and is able to transform the information that he or she acquires into knowledge, which is work based ("Learning to Do"). Education can cut across the barriers of formal qualification and even illiteracy. In fact a technology based system of education will be a source of appeal to illiterates and neo-literates. The target groups for training are not far to seek. They could be:

- Village elders/headmen
- Social workers
- Youth and community leaders
- Church workers
- NGO functionaries

Training to train them, should be our motto, where training will be used as a means for self-reliance and auto didacticism. Training can then in turn specifically be used by distance education methodologies in areas such as agriculture, horticulture, farming, credit financing, generating self-employment and for self-help groups. The help and collaboration of organisations such as the Nehru Yuva Kendra, the state institutes for rural development, the government departments at the block levels and non-government organisations working in the field of training matters.

The Disadvantaged

In the context of an open university displaying concern for the 'disadvantaged' sections of the society, North East India offers laboratory conditions to promote education for the disadvantaged. However the course material must also be adapted in as many languages as possible. The training programmes described above can be of very short-term duration in the form of capsules ranging from one to three months. The translation of print material into audio-visuals will perhaps be the mainstay in imparting training, once again in the local language.

To stem the frustrations of disgruntled youth in the region career counselling bureaus may also be set up with information disseminated by both the print and electronic media. The career prospects by way of the opportunities provided by an Open University should also be used as vigorous tool to provide such information and advice. Also, thinking in terms of entrepreneurial development schemes *vis-a-vis* distance education methods can be effective for the unemployed youth. Mother and Child Care, Health care, Environment and Cleanliness, Population education, Sex education are other such areas, which need to be addressed. The relatively high rate of literacy in the region is an advantage to begin with, which needs to be utilised to the full. Partnerships and alliances with like minded organisations and people is indeed a must; as community leadership is a great and significant workforce in this region.

Conclusion

Distance Education which is essentially media based can be used for:

(a) Literacy campaigns.
(b) Extension work/training.

Learning processes will train the potential learner,

- To know,
- To do,
- To be, and
- To live together.

The last mentioned will invest the meaning of education with the spirit of continuity, concern and integration. This is a must in the socio-political contexts of North East India given the present crises.

REFERENCES

Delors Commission(1996). *Learning the Treasure Within*; UNESCO, Paris.
Nongkynrih, A.K. (1999). *Building North East India*, Shillong.
Nongkynrih, A.K. (1999). *Basic Understanding on N.E. India*, Shillong.
Sources of Annexure : North-Eastern Council, Basic Statistics of North- Eastern Region (1995) North East India : Problems and Possibilities (1997), *North-East Sun Magazine* (New Delhi, 1999).

37

Commerce Education in the New Millennium
Need for Professionalisation

G.P. PRASAIN & KH. DHIRAN MEETEI

Introduction

The importance of commerce education has increased due to the expansion of trade and commerce, banking and financial institutions, introduction of various rules and regulations in commercial activities, taxation laws and the fast changing technological developments, new inventions, contemporary innovations in products, processes, designs, methods and services, widening and burgeoning markets, volume of operations, the emerging trends to take over bids both hostile and friendly, merger, de-mergers, amalgamations, acquisitions, restructuring of operations, economic and social necessity for revival of viable sick units, the need for continuous growth by expansion, privatisation, diversification or modernization of undertakings, increasing complex economic, social and environmental legislation's etc. In the increasing competitive business situation prevailing nationally and internationally, all the business enterprise must not only try to survive, consolidate and growth within the legal framework of the law of the land, but also should genuinely strive to serve the varying and conflicting requirements of various groups such as share holders, debenture holders, depositors, employers, creditors, customers, government, local bodies, consumer associations, environmental and religious groups, political parties and the general public.

At present in all the Universities, Commerce education comprises the courses in Business Economics. Quantitative Technique, Enterpreneurship Development, Accounting Information System,

Financial Management, Management Information System, Accountancy and Auditing, Commercial Law, Cost and Management Accountancy, Money and Banking, Income Tax and other Commercial Taxes, Labour Laws, International Financial Management, Security Analysis and Portfolio Management, Project Management, Human Resource Management, Marketing Management, Industrial Economy, etc. There is, however, no uniformity amongst the different universities with regard to both core and specialised courses. Although specialisation at each stage is aimed at certain broad principles should be followed to make the commerce education more useful for business firms, banks, industrial units, public corporations, multinational companies, professionals, consultancies etc.

Now-a-days, it is true that commerce education to a certain extent, is away from realities of industrial environment and the student coming out of the portals of educational institution do not make a separate mark. The knowledge imparted by educational institutions has remained the knowledge of books and papers, knowledge for the sake of knowledge. It is agreed by researchers and teachers that commerce education today lacks dynamism. The course contents do not give any professional approach and its contents, method, to impart education and skill are all traditional. The framers of education policy and the course curriculums has ignored the professional and social need of the country.

Demerits of Commerce Education

The present system of commerce education suffers from the following demerits:

(a) Commerce education provides narrow, traditional, conceptual education and its lacks practical orientation as well as unable to solve the industrial and social problems.

(b) There is lack of job orientation, which is provided by industry, financial institutions and others occupational areas.

(c) Commerce education is not fully success in fulfilling the need of the growing economy and ignores the changing role of functional areas in economic organisation.

(d) Commerce education at present is not suited to some extent for the growing complexity of the organisation. The systems approach to organisation is demanding specialist and professionals in all areas. Commerce students possess conceptual knowledge of various areas but they lack professional skill.

(e) In India, commerce education is based on the theoretical areas of technology, organisational system and some areas of the executive functions. Graduates of commerce must have the ability of interpersonal skill but it is not fully found in the present curriculum.

(f) The other demerits are lack of uniformity in curriculum, indiscriminate admission, no linkage with professional institutions, apathy of Government and U.G.C. towards commerce education, and absence of practical approach.

So, realising the above demerits, the educationists become interested in development of commerce education and are giving serious thoughts and taking necessary steps to re-draft the structure, system and curriculum of commerce education from under-graduate level to the post-graduate level.

Professionalisation and Social Relevance of Commerce Education

Recently the requirement of professionals in industry, financial institutions, multinational corporations, social welfare organisation, government offices etc. has increased, but commerce graduates have failed to meet such requirement. So, to make the system socially workable and for professionalisation, there is an urgent need to reorient the commerce education and restructure the curriculum. To make commerce education socially relevant and professional, all the universities in India should try to train their graduate to suit the regional requirements with uniform curriculum. Universities also should try to study the need of the region around them. They can enjoy the privilege to contribute in the socio-economic transformation, social welfare, commerce, trade and industry of the country. Universities should also try to re-frame the course materials from under-graduate level up to post-graduate level according to the needs assessed by them.

Commerce education requires various streams of specialisation from under-graduate level, such streams of specialisation should be framed for both professional course and advanced studies. The commerce education in universities should keep good co-operation with the professional institutes of the country. Such institutes are Indian Institute of Cost and Works Accountants, Indian Institute of Chartered

Accountants, Indian Management Association, Indian Institute of Company Secretaryship, Institute of Chartered Financial Analysis etc. The Universities should help their commerce departments and college in developing interaction with the industrial units of the country to get the practical and professional training and knowledge.

The curriculum has to be re-frame to fulfil the challenges of latest development in commerce and management. Students should be provided knowledge with new developments such as accounting standards at national and international level, mechanical devices, computers etc., which is used to the present competitive world. The course should contain the practical training as its part.

The methods of imparting commerce education should be changed and students should be given opportunity of playing their part, live cases must be brought to the classroom as well as professionals, industrialists and executives should be invited to discuss the practical problems. Modern technologies and appliances should be used in the class to make students interested in the subject and to be more analytical and practical. Emphasis must be provided for practical training in the area of specialisation both at under-graduate and post-graduate levels. If such steps are taken up, commerce graduate will be more demanded by professionals. Each commerce department should open practical training of the specialisation within a given period. Both theoretical and practical courses should be given the same weightage.

The education system should consider the social changes, which are taking place. The system of commerce education should be a concrete, result-oriented and needed by the society. The quality of commerce education should be developed to make it more productive and useful to the present society. Such system can be achieved if effort is made by the universities, UGC, State and Central governments. The teachers should be trained, facilities to be created in the institutions and universities, and required funds should be given for smooth running of the institutions.

For commerce education, establishment of all-India body with regional offices is required on the basis as used by All India Council for Technical Education, to make the assessment of social demand of professionals, to guide implementation of same curriculum and also help in developing and designing of courses for regional requirements. If such steps are taken up, commerce education can be covered under professionalisation and a linkage with other professional bodies can be developed. It will also help universities and institutions in developing interaction with financial institutions, business establishments, industry, commerce and government departments as well as social organisations. Modern information technology should be included as a compulsory subject of the commerce education.

Commerce Education *vs.* Management Course

Commerce education in our universities is facing challenges from management institutes. In the recent years, management course in the universities like MBA is coming to occupy the centre of the stage. Now whether, commerce education will retain its own identity or will be merged in the stream of management education is a point of endless debate. The impact of management courses on the commerce syllabus of our universities has been notable and commerce courses have to be more improved, modernized to meet the needs of the students and requirements of trade and commerce. Modernization and improvement in the commerce education is the burning point for revival of commerce education.

Commerce education is a distinct discipline and survived for a long time in all universities even facing challenge from management education. Trade and industry requires a lot of trained personnel, skilled in the field of accounting, banking, tax procedures, inventory contract, market analysis, financial management, etc. Commerce graduates and post-graduates are skilled manpower for these field. All those persons who obtain MBA degree can outright become managers. They may start somewhat as junior manager and then advance to higher levels of management on the basis of their performances. Commerce graduate in large number is required to render useful service to management. If a manager wants to formulate business policy, then commerce graduates are required to process the data and analyse and refine the same for managerial decision-making. In commercial bank, there may be one or two managers but there will be various staffs who supports in the field of banking and accounting.

An organisation cannot employ MBAs at all levels, and such organisation demands graduates and post-graduate in commerce for its various departments, for handling different works. For meeting such demand, it is required to improve the quality of commerce graduate. It depends upon curriculum and teaching method of commerce education. Commerce education is not for only Cost Accounting, Management Accounting, Taxation etc. but also impart knowledge of Management Information System, Quantitative Techniques as well as written and oral communication. From this point of view, commerce curriculum may be upgraded and formulated from time to time.

If MBA programme has to be more project-oriented, it applies with added emphasis to teaching of commerce course also. To challenge against management course, colleges and universities in India should make commerce teaching more work-oriented through projects, field works and practical training facilities. Real world business experiences should be forecasted with classroom teaching to commerce students.

Uniform Syllabus for Commerce Education in India

A paper entitled "Universities and Charted Accountants — Role and Utility" was presented by the Secretary of University and Higher Secondary Boards Liaison Committee on 19th December, 1998 in the Open General Session of the seminar organised by the Association of Indian Universities at Indore. Most of the vice-chancellors of those universities, where commerce is taught as a subject at under-graduate level and who were present at the seminar express the desire for a common syllabi for B.Com. students in the country. The vice-chancellors of these universities also felt that, the Institute of Chartered Accountants in India is the most competent and appropriate body to do justice in deciding about the syllabus to be prescribed at the under-graduate level, in the commerce education in the country.

The Universities and Higher Secondary Board Liaison Committee accepted the challenge and decided to design model syllabi for B.Com. students of various Indian Universities. For finalising the syllabus for B.Com. course, the Institute seeks the support and cooperation of Universities in the country. In such case, the paper includes the syllabus of various subjects, which must be taught to B.Com. students of various Indian Universities during three-year tenures of University Education. These subjects have been selected after taking into account the various avenues available for commerce students after passing B.Com. Examination as well as the curriculum for different professional course generally opted by the commerce students and also the changes which are expected to come in the field of Accounting Education in the coming years.

The University and Higher Secondary Boards Liaison Committee has been taking special initiative for holding joint seminars with various Indian Universities on the theme of "Commerce Education in the New Millennium". The Committee has brought the background material for conducting various seminars with universities and with special emphasis on the following areas:

1. Framework for making Accounting Standards,
2. Financial aspects of Corporate Governance,
3. Information Technology and Business,
4. Financial Instruments in the Capital Market,
5. Winning Communication Skill,
6. Management Constancy Service, and
7. E-commerce.

Conclusion

Therefore, the commerce education in the new millennium should *inter alia*, concentrate on the aforesaid areas in view of their increasing importance and relevance in the changing scenario.

Basic education in commerce is imparted at the +2 and graduation level. Graduates have different options—(1) to join for employment in business concern as junior executives, (2) to pursue post-graduation in the university, (3) to join for MBA course in Business School, (4) to join for a professional course like Chartered Accountancy/Cost Accountancy/Company Secretaries. Therefore, a commerce graduate should have the knowledge and training to opt for any of the above routes and the syllabus should be suitably framed.

The core subjects in commerce education at graduate level should include advanced accounting, auditing, economics, commercial laws, business organisation and management, fundamentals of electronic data processing and communication skill. Optional subjects could be corporate laws, direct and indirect taxes, cost accounting, financial management, industrial relations, marketing and export management, banking and insurance etc. It should be possible to evolve a syllabus for B.Com, harmonizing the university level education with that of Business Schools and Accounting and Professional Institutions.

REFERENCES

Singh, C.D., *Graduate Education in Commerce*. Deep and Deep Publications, New Delhi.

Tofflor, Alvin, (1974). *The Psychology of the Future in learning from Tomorrow*. • Edited by Alvin Tafflor (New York : Randon House).

University level seminar on Commerce Education. University and Higher Secondary Boards Liaison Committees, ICA, 1999-2000.

38

Status and Scope of Management Education in the North East

KASTURI BORKOTOKI BARUAH

Introduction

Education plays an important role in the social fabric of a region. The past decade of social and economic changes brought about by the change in the economic policy in 1991 and subsequent globalisation and competition threw all of the world into a global village. Its impact on business and society at large could be explicable by the various shifts in trends in the educational interests. Management education came to be looked upon with new awe as management graduates absorbed the plum jobs by demanding and receiving whopping amounts as salaries. The idea that hardcore professionals could be created through two-year management diplomas gained new ground, resulting in the mushrooming of management Institutes all over India. Even today after the recent IT boom, management continues to be the most sought after stream of education.

At this point it is important to note that the jobs of today and more importantly, the future hold demand for highly specialised jobs along with a high degree of creativity and innovativeness. Another fact, which is noteworthy, is that after trends of privatisation and mergers and consequently retrenchment and Voluntary Retrenchment Schemes, the Indian concept of associating a job to security has slowly declined.

Background

"Tracing back to the advent of management education in the North-

East India, it was in 1979 that the department of Business Administration was set-up in Guwahati to start a full time MBA programme. It was after 1991 that few more business schools came up. Management Education is expected to provide a nesting fabric of direction and purpose to the education system of a region as a whole and is expected to be application oriented.

Present Status

The Management Institutes of this area have had to grow and survive amidst several social and political problems. Some of the problems have been highlighted below:

Regional Problems

Firstly, the North East is more like the "Far East" to the main business hubs of Indian trade and industry. Poor presence of the private sector industries and lack of entrepreneurs have had a negative impact on the industry. The predominant industries here remain to be only tea, oil and plywood. Most of the other industries have gone sick over the years. Lack of infrastructure is one of the main stumbling blocks to industrialisation. Perhaps the most killing effect has been the ongoing insurgency for the past two decades and more. No Multinational Corporation wishes to risk investing its financial resources in the North-East for fear of extortion and held up projects.

Then another factor is the fund crisis faced constantly by the state government. The whole region looks upto Central government grants and subsidies in order to maintain and sustain whatever industries it has. This has been a limiting factor as far as harnessing of available resources is concerned which again acts as another hurdle in setting up viable industries. This could be one of the main explicable reasons for the lack of entrepreneurial effort in this region.

The above mentioned factors have had a negative impact on Management Graduates. The very idea of graduating with a management diploma in a place where the corporate sector has the least role to play works against them, when they want to apply for jobs outside the state.

Again, they can hardly hope to find employment within the North-Eastern states as there are very few places to apply for Managerial jobs. So, the scenario represents a vicious circle of low education, growth and productivity. The ideal role of a management institute as an integrator between various organisations (both corporate and non-corporate) and itself has not been really developed or exploited.

The Placement Scenario

It has been observed that most of the management graduates of this region get absorbed in marketing jobs initially. One of the major reasons for this is that Corporate Offices do not physically set up offices in this region. Most of them do the work through Clearing and Forwarding Agents and so, they do not recruit MBA's and even if they do, the scales of remuneration are not commensurate with the general market rates of MBA's. As such, it is not very comfortable to run a placement cell in the business schools of this region once again due to the simple fact that the corporate sector is not visibly present in this part of the country. Moreover, even if some of the companies agree to give a break to the graduates of this region, the costs incurred in bringing these officials to and fro for just a placement interview seem to be colossal. The students from the Human Resources background or finance background find that it is not easy for them to get an initial break in any organisation. So, most of the institutes of this region give dual specialisation, where it is found that most of the students take marketing as a common specialisation. The placement scenario seems to be the major hurdle in Management Education as an institute's success is measured by the number of students placed and the organisations they are placed in.

Perception of MBA

Management Graduates as such seem to have a different attitude to career, which have a definitive impact on their expectations from a job.

Firstly, it is seen that a job is not the only objective of the management graduates. Rather, their objective is to choose a career, which offers them greater opportunities, and freedom to innovate and excel. They are found to be more hardworking than their counterparts in the other streams of education as the social perceptions of management being synonymous with a job puts them in a socially vulnerable position. This also consequently puts more pressure on them to try and live up to the expectations of their projected image. Mostly, they are seen to experience dissonance with the fact that their expectations regarding salary and position from a job do not match with what they are mostly offered in the market. After completion of a management course, they are mostly absorbed in marketing jobs or so-called marketing jobs which are more sales oriented. Those wishing to take a break in other fields have to wait for a few years to get a job of their choice.

Faculties of the Future

Faculty members of the Business Schools of this region have a heavy responsibility on their shoulders. It is not an easy job, to firstly recruit quality faculty. Most business schools have their academic programme divided among core and guest faculty where the latter are mostly from the practical field and corporate area. This diligent mix is again difficult to maintain in this region, the reason again being poor presence of corporates in this area. Even amongst the few business schools present, there is very rare interaction among faculty with similar and complementary interests, which hampers quality research. Moreover, faculty exposure to frequent and meaningful training is rare, as only one of the management schools is seen to regularly refresh the faculty through faculty development programmes. It can be said that most of the faculty are in the evolving stage and are themselves going through the learning stage.[1]

Infrastructures

A management school differs from other educational institutes on the fact that it is nowhere without proper infrastructure and this is another factor where the north-eastern institutes are lagging behind. The All India Council of Technical Education (AICTE) under which a Management School has to affiliate its diploma, has, as one of its mandatory clauses that premises and other supportive infrastructure pertaining to specific standards given by it has to be adhered to and are supposed to be part and parcel of a successful institute. Most of the business schools are struggling on this behalf. Those under an university have a tough time convincing the university authorities that management education as such needs a different nurturing than other departments and then those, which are running privately, have to constantly work on these aspects to better their status. One of the premier institutes has recently got land granted from the government for their campus and hopes to build its own premises in the near future.

Remedies and Scope

Having pointed out the status of management education and associated problems it would be noteworthy to comment here that in spite of the above hurdles, management education has struggled to place itself amongst the premium sector and what has been achieved cannot be put to nought. In spite of the bleak scenario, a majority of the students have been able to find work in some of the good organisations outside and within Assam, of course, mostly after an initial brief struggle. A lot of potential lies within this education area and if exploited in the right direction a lot of fruitful results will come about. The problems discussed in the above discussion can be hopefully tackled by the following remedial steps:

Firstly, it will be noteworthy to state that redressal of the problems will call for a complete attitudinal change in the society. There has to be a shift in the way in which society views the prospects in the North-East. Each issue has been tackled one by one and suggestions have been offered for each one of them:

Lack of privatisation and industry

What we have: We have the resources and we have the manpower, but we are waiting for a third party to do it for us. If the jobs are not there, we have to create them for us. Entrepreneurship as a career option should be emphasised by the management schools. In fact this has better prospect in the future, because a local student will have better idea about the possible ways to exploit the indigenous resources. After the initial financial problems, if a break-even could be brought in, then it would be much more rewarding than a job.[2]

What has been done: A bright spot is that entrepreneurahip has already been introduced into the curriculum of one or two of the Management Schools in the North East and the results have already been witnessed. A few students of Assam Institute of Management Guwahati, who passed out in 2001 have set up the trend by setting up their own enterprises. Hopefully this trend will gain momentum in the coming years as it has utmost scope for this side of the country.

Placement

Placement as we have examined has been one of the tough jobs for these institutes. A lot of expenses go into making a placement brochure every year and the efficacy of the brochure is highly questionable. The institutes of this region can combine and make a centralized placement plan, which will involve participation from the faculties of the institute as well as the students by contributing to one pooled fund for placement. This will have many benefits:

- The best of the students will get a chance to face the best of the companies and *vice versa.*
- Time management will be better.
- There will be healthy competition and ample ground for learning and growing for students as well as faculties of the institute.
- There will be more exposure through each others' contacts.
- And most importantly, financial problem of bringing recruiters from other parts of the states will be over. So a lot of scope lies here if exploited fully by the concerned institutes. All that is required is effective networking amongst the institutes.

Faculty

The faculty of this region is perhaps the most hardworking. Here also inter-institute networking will play a major role as it is important for the faculty to start interacting amongst the institutes. Short-term training programmes should be conducted between these institutes on a regular basis. On top of that there should be outstation programmes at least once in a year or otherwise there should be some exposure to training programmes from experienced faculty from premier institutes of the country. In fact this would be a better, as more people would be able to avail the opportunity at the same cost. Of course, it is again important to make it combined effort from all the North-Eastern institutes to make it financially viable.

Financial Problem

What we have?: The financial crisis so often a hurdle in management institute's developmental work, has to be tackled from a different angle.

Most of the institutes are dependent on somebody for majority of their funds be it the state government or University Funds. This has to be totally refreshed as generation of own funds is very very important for these institutes. A healthy option will be more and more reliance on training programmes and project related work which, if done successfully can generate surplus revenue.

What has been done?: Some effort has been seen here also as faculties of two of the major institutes have been seen to be actively and gradually involved in the working of projects for the last two to three years. Moreover, one of the main institutes have been conducting Management Development Programmes for the past few years for industries like Airlines, Insurance, Health, Oil etc. So this field has considerable and maximum scope for both revenue earnings as well as faculty development.

Attitude Change

A major haul in attitude is required for the redressal of the whole problem. The North-east has ample natural resources, which have not been rightfully exploited. The main scope lies in making the area seem more investor friendly and this can only be done through effective marketing. The whole region has to be marketed by presenting it as a promising land, which it really is. Only management professionals can undertake and understand the mammoth responsibility of turning the scales in favour of development of this region.

Tourism itself has immense potential to be successfully brought up as a revenue earning industry. What is lacking is the marketing and proper management of the system.

Another noteworthy change has to be brought about in the attitude of the people by making them more acceptable to ideas of entrepreneurship. The persistent problems of unemployment can be hopefully reduced if people change their outlook of relying on an employer and thinking of self-employment. Management professionals play a mammoth role in trying to bring about this attitude change from the grassroots level.

Financial crunch is the ultimate hurdle for a management school. The only way the institutes of the North East can hope to pacify this problem is by combining and forming a corpus fund where each of the institutes contributes on a regular basis. The only way this will be possible will be through effective networking amongst the institutes in the North-east also as well as some premier institutes outside.

Conclusion

Quality assurance in management education affects not only the probable performance of the economy, but also the very health of the society. Management schools have to orient themselves as social sector institutions since management studies incorporate a vast area of subjects under its profile. Knowledge resource has to be effectively built around the natural resources of a region for its effective growth.

Management Education needs to apply a marketing perspective to its conceptualisation, design and implementation. Opportunities, as we can see are tremendous. A change in orientation and customer-centred approach is required. The answer lies in trying to convert the environmental threats into opportunities. Thus Management Education will emerges as the harbinger of the academic and social development in the North-Eastern Region and serve the quality requirements of the students, business communities and society as a whole.

NOTES

1. Business School Societal Interface – Opportunities and Challenges in North East India. Theme paper presented by Dr. N.N. Sharma, Assistant Professor, Assam Institute of Management, in the workshop organized by Association of Indian Management Schools (AIMS), 2002.
2. Career Opportunities for Management Graduates of North East, paper presented by Dr. Sriparna B. Baruah, Faculty, Indian Institute of Entrepreneurship, Guwahati, 2002.

Index